THE GUNPOWDER AGE

THE GUNPOWDER AGE

China, Military Innovation, and the Rise of
the West in World History

TONIO ANDRADE

PRINCETON UNIVERSITY PRESS
PRINCETON AND OXFORD

FOR SYLVIA

who understands both sides
with love

Contents

THE GUNPOWDER AGE

Introduction

THE MILITARY PATTERN OF THE CHINESE PAST

"China is a sleeping lion. When it wakes, the world will tremble."[1] These words, attributed to Napoleon, are quoted often these days, usually followed by the observation that the lion is now awake.[2] China's leaders promise that their country's rise will be "peaceful, pleasant, and civilized," but there is much trembling.[3] Napoleon's prophecy seems to be coming true.

Yet he made his prediction in 1816. Why did the lion take so long to wake? And why was it sleeping in the first place? China was once the wealthiest, most technologically advanced, most powerful country in the world. How did it lose its lead to the upstart countries of Western Europe? Or, to put it another way, how did the once marginal states of Europe surge to global power and predominance after 1500?

These are key questions of world history, and in recent years they've generated a flurry of answers, and much debate.[4] Nearly all of this literature focuses on economics.[5] So today we know a great deal more about Chinese and European wage levels, fertility rates, and agricultural productivity than we used to, but we still know relatively little about what Napoleon was really talking about: war. He made his famous prediction in response to a question from his Irish surgeon, who wondered whether it was a good idea for the British to attack China. No, Napoleon replied, because the Chinese, once roused, "would get artificers, and ship-builders, from France, and America, and even from London; they would build a fleet, and in the course of time, defeat you."[6] Eventually the British did attack China, and China did acquire artificers and advisors. Its subsequent path to modernization was longer than Napoleon would have expected, but throughout the journey reformers were always focused on military matters. They still are.

This book examines the Great Divergence between China and the West by concentrating on warfare. It suggests that there is a military pattern to the Chinese past that can help us make sense of China's periods of strength, decline, and resurgence. But it doesn't focus on China alone. It's aim is to bring Asian and European military history into conversation, asking not just how China diverged from the West but also how the West diverged from East Asia.[7] Europe's is not the normalizing trajectory; each case illuminates the other.[8]

The unifying theme is gunpowder warfare. Historians have long studied gunpowder's revolutionary effects, but they've paid most attention to the West. Indeed, you've probably heard the saying, false but often repeated, that the Chinese invented gunpowder but didn't use it for war. This meme is still widely circulated, appearing in scholarly works, and even in China itself.[9] But in fact the Chinese and their neighbors explored gunpowder's many uses, military and civilian, for centuries before the technology passed to the West. These Asian origins are often glossed over, and most studies of gunpowder warfare focus on the early modern period (ca. 1500–1800).[10] This was, historians have argued, when the first gunpowder empires were born and when the "gunpowder revolution" and the "military revolution" helped transform Europe's feudal structures, laying the groundwork for Western global dominance.[11]

But the gunpowder age actually lasted a millennium, from the first use of gunpowder in warfare in the late 900s to its replacement by smokeless powder around 1900. Examining its full sweep can help us answer—or at least clarify—the question of the rise of the West and the "stagnation" of China.

One of the most enduring explanations for Europe's dynamism and China's supposed torpor is the "competitive state system" paradigm. Antagonism between European states, so the theory goes, exerted a selective pressure on European societies, driving them to improve their political, economic, and military structures. China, on the other hand, had a unified imperium, which impeded experimentation and led to stasis. This idea is as old as social science itself, going back to Montesquieu and animating the works of Karl Marx and Max Weber.[12] Today it's nearly ubiquitous, found among authors as different as Jared Diamond, Immanuel Wallerstein, David Landes, and Geoffrey Parker.[13] China experts, too, rely on the model, suggesting that China, being a unified state, lacked the dynamism of a more competitive Europe, although some believe that lack of competition also conferred economic benefits.[14]

Of course, as any student of Chinese history knows, China's past is filled with war and interstate competition. Indeed, the very term "China" presupposes a unity that was absent for much of history.[15] The most famous period of division is the Warring States Period (475–221 BCE), which many scholars have explicitly compared to Europe's early modern era, arguing that both periods saw similar military and political developments.[16] For instance, the great Geoffrey Parker begins his book *The Military Revolution* with a discussion of the Chinese Warring States Period, arguing that in both that period and Europe's early modern period, constant warfare drove state centralization and innovation in military tactics, technology, organization, and logistics.[17]

Yet there were many other periods of warfare and interstate competition in China's long history, and scholars have tended to neglect those times and exaggerate China's imperial unity. The hypothesis of this book is that such periods are vital to understanding world history.

Consider the Late Imperial Age (1368–1911), a period during which China was supposedly unified and, according to many authors, stagnant. It's true that both the Ming (1368–1644) and Qing (1644–1911) dynasties oversaw periods of great unity. Yet there were also periods of intense warfare, particularly around the dynastic transitions (1368 and 1644). This is no shock, but nonspecialists may be surprised to learn how long those transitions were, and how warlike. The transition from the Yuan dynasty (1279–1368) to the Ming dynasty lasted nearly a century, from around 1350, when statelets emerged and began fighting, through the bloody interstate wars of the famous "field of rivals" (1352–1368), through the violent campaigns of consolidation by the first Ming emperor (r. 1368–1398), through the bitter succession war that erupted after his death, through the reign of his bellicose son, the famous Yongle Emperor (r. 1402–1424), who launched huge expeditions into Vietnam and Mongolia, and, finally, through a period of intermittent warfare that ended only in 1449. In total the warfare around the Ming dynastic transition lasted a century, from around 1350 to around 1450. The wars were frequent, intense, and of a scale far exceeding anything in Western Europe at the time, with armies of hundreds of thousands clashing throughout East Asia, armed with guns, bombs, grenades, and rockets.

The next dynastic transition was of similar length and intensity. Interdynastic warfare erupted in the 1610s and continued until 1683, when the last holdouts of the Ming dynasty finally fell to the Manchu Qing dynasty. Afterward, warfare continued into the early eighteenth century, when the famous Kangxi Emperor (r. 1661–1722) carried out campaigns of consolidation in Northern and Central Asia. In fact, this is a conservative periodization: intense warfare actually began around 1550 and included the Korean War of 1592 to 1598, the most destructive Sino-Japanese conflict before World War II. Scholar Sun Laichen has called the period 1550 to 1683 the most warlike in East Asia's history, pointing out that warfare extended well beyond China itself, engulfing all of Eastern Eurasia, including Southeast Asia.[18]

It's no surprise that dynastic transitions saw intense warfare, but the length of these periods is significant. They lasted generations. Of course not all this warfare was of the type that is considered to have contributed to European dynamism, that is, sustained interstate conflicts. Some scholars have argued that China engaged in too much of the wrong sort of warfare, focusing on defense against nomads and rebels rather than on external conquest, a preoccupation that supposedly sapped China of European-style dynamism.[19]

Yet these periods of warfare did indeed stimulate rapid and deep-seated military innovation. Napoleon well understood that a country, when challenged militarily, responds with innovation. Historians call this the "challenge-response dynamic."[20] During the intense wars of the Yuan-Ming transition, from 1350 to 1450, there were a lot of challenges and a lot of responses, and China's infantry forces became increasingly focused on firearms, which were used far more frequently and effectively than in Europe at the same time. In the early Ming period, policies prescribed that 10 percent of soldiers should be armed with guns; by the last third of the 1400s, the figure rose to 30 percent, a rate not seen in Europe until the mid-1500s.[21] Historians have labeled the Ming dynasty the world's first "Gunpowder Empire."[22]

It seems, however, that around 1450 the military pattern of the Chinese past diverged from that of Europe. For a guide to the chronology underlying this book, see Appendix 1: Timeline, p. 311. From 1450 until 1550, China engaged in fewer and less intense wars, and military innovation slowed. This happened to be a period when military innovation was speeding up in Europe, fueled by increasingly violent and large-scale warfare. By the 1480s, all types of European guns had become better, so much so that when Portuguese mariners brought them to China in the early 1500s, Chinese acknowledged their superiority and began copying them. We might call this period, from 1450 to 1550, the first divergence, or the little divergence.[23]

It didn't last. Starting in the 1550s, warfare increased throughout East Asia, and military innovation accelerated. Chinese, Japanese, and Koreans mastered the manufacture of European cannons and muskets, improving them and deploying them with advanced tactics, such as the famous musketry volley technique, which, as we'll see, was probably first used not in Europe or Japan or the Ottoman Empire, as scholars have suggested, but in China.[24] During this period of rapid innovation—1550 to 1700—East Asians maintained military parity with Western nations. Whenever trained military forces from East Asia met those of Europe, the former won decisively. There has been little study of such conflicts, but they suggest that the military balance was relatively even during the Age of Parity (1550–1700). Europeans did have advantages in deep-water naval warfare and fortress architecture, but East Asians fielded dynamic and effective forces, defeating European troops not just by superior numbers but also by means of excellent guns, effective logistics, strong leadership, and better (or at least equivalent) drill and cohesion. Nor was this parity limited to East Asia; it may have obtained through much of Asia.[25]

The Age of Parity, however, gave way to a Great Military Divergence, which became manifest during the Opium War of 1839 to 1842, when British forces consistently outfought the Qing. Why did China fall so far behind?

Partly, of course, the answer lies with Britain's industrialization, a process unprecedented in human history, but as we'll see, Britain's military advantage cannot be reduced to steamships and mass production alone. We must also recognize that the Qing dynasty had become

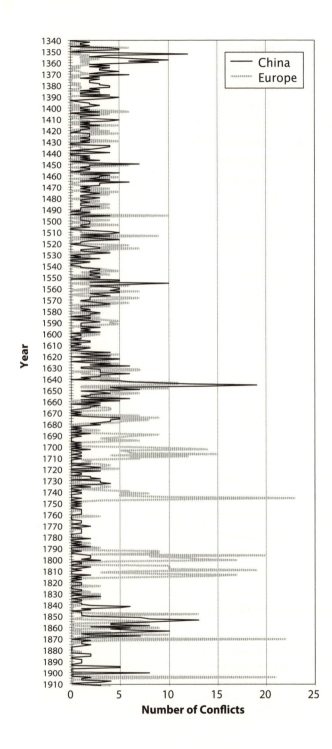

militarily stagnant. Why? A lack of practice. By the mid-eighteenth century, the Qing had succeeded in doing something that had eluded previous dynasties of China: it subdued the Mongols and Turks of Central and Northern Asia.[26] Since it had also cowed the Russians, the Qing no longer had to fear invasion from the north. Its sea borders were also secure, so China faced no serious external threats for several generations, from around 1760 until 1839. There were internal threats—rebellions and revolts—some of which were quite significant, but compared to earlier periods in China's history, this period was extraordinarily free of warfare. China's armies atrophied, and military innovation slowed.

The Great Qing Peace can be seen visually in Graph I.1, which charts the frequency of warfare in China and Western Europe between 1340 and 1911. Tabulating wars is a very difficult business, of course, and one must be cautious, but when corroborated with other sources, qualitative and quantitative, charts like this can help us make some significant observations.[27] (For more information on this and other datasets used in this book, see Appendix 2.)

The first thing to note is how similar Chinese and European patterns of warfare are for the period from 1350 through 1700. Although China's patterns show peaks around the dynastic transitions at 1368 and 1644, the entire period from 1350 to 1700 is nonetheless marked by frequent wars on both sides of Eurasia, with a relative lull in China between 1450 and 1550.

During the eighteenth and early nineteenth centuries, however, the patterns diverge markedly: Europe saw repeated bouts of intense warfare while China saw warfare fall to the lowest sustained levels in the series. This relative lull in warfare—which we can call the Great Qing Peace—stretched from the mid-eighteenth century to 1839, and it happens that Korea and Japan, too, saw few wars during this period. Experts in Qing history will rightly point out that this period saw significant armed conflicts, with particularly destructive ones during the

GRAPH I.1 Warfare by year in Western Europe and China.

The solid line represents China, the dotted line Europe. For more information on this graph, its dataset, and other corroborating data, as well as for caveats about their use, see Appendix 2. Data from Zhong guo jun shi shi bian xie zu, *Zhong guo li dai*, vol. 2; and Dupuy, *Encyclopedia of Military History*.

years on either side of 1800. Yet external wars were largely nonexistent, and records suggest that even armed rebellions were relatively less common during the Great Qing Peace than most other periods in China's history post-1200.

In contrast, although Europe saw longer periods of peace in the eighteenth century than in the seventeenth century, Europe's eighteenth-century warfare was becoming increasingly intense, culminating in the Revolutionary and Napoleonic Wars that convulsed the subcontinent at the turn of the nineteenth century. So it's no surprise that during the Great Qing Peace, military innovation slowed in China even as it accelerated in Europe, with the development of powerful new artillery, firearms, organizational structures, and tactics.

The period of the Great Military Divergence—from the mid-eighteenth through the early nineteenth century—also happens to be the period when Westerners acquired the image of China as stagnant, monolithic, and mired in its ways.[28] Charles Dickens had this to say after touring a Chinese ship: "thousands of years have passed away since the first Chinese junk was constructed on this model, and the last Chinese junk that was ever launched was none the better for that waste and desert of time."[29] Immobile and ancient, China seemed to present the negative image of a dynamic, modernizing West. Today, some scholars still express this notion nearly as contentiously as Dickens did a century and a half ago. Example: "There was no cumulative innovation [in China] after the precocious Tang and Sung dynasties [618–1279 CE]."[30]

As we'll see there was plenty of cumulative innovation in China after 1279, but the point is not to discard the stagnation idea entirely, just to deploy it more precisely. From a military perspective, it works only for two periods: mildly for 1450 to 1550, and significantly for 1760 to 1839.

More importantly, we must be careful about how we explain these periods of military stagnation. Scholars of a traditionalist bent tend to blame deep-seated cultural and institutional characteristics. China, they argue, was stymied by conservatism, closed-mindedness, civilizational arrogance, and Confucianism.[31] Perhaps we should expect views like this from conservative scholars, many of whom believe that "multiculturalism is an effort to destroy the uniqueness of Western nations," but similar perspectives are widely prevalent in works on military history.[32] For example, the author of a recent and otherwise excellent book on gunpowder writes, "The denizens of the Chinese court looked on gunpowder technology as a low, noisy, dirty business. The fact that guns were useful did not matter, usefulness lacking the overriding value that it held for occidentals."[33] Another author, an expert in renaissance military history, has written that "China's ruling bureaucrats . . . remained essentially aloof; the mechanics of warfare were beneath their interest."[34] Even scholars writing from a global historical perspective express such views. The book *Warfare in World History* tells us that "China preferred not to experiment too much with the new technologies for fear of disrupting the Confucian order of society and state," and the book *World History of Warfare* contains similar language.[35] We find the same perspectives expressed in other genres as well, including journalism.[36]

Yet as we'll see, imperial China's leaders and bureaucrats were fascinated by gunpowder and gunpowder weapons and worked hard to invent, adapt, and innovate. Among them were the most prominent Confucian scholars of their day. These men studied gunpowder weapons, tested them, experimented with their manufacture, developed tactics and strategies for deploying them, and wrote about all of this in detail. When foreigners had effective technologies—Vietnamese, Portuguese, Dutch, British—they studied and adopted them, often at considerable expense in time and treasure.

It's just that some periods in Chinese history called for less military innovation, particularly the Great Qing Peace of 1760 to 1839. During this time, Confucian scholars understandably tended to focus on nonmilitary matters. When war came to China again in 1839 (and the wars of the mid-nineteenth century were among the most destructive in Chinese history) Confucian scholars were once again at the forefront of military innovation. Their efforts were also more fruitful than was once believed.

It's not my intention to reduce the puzzle of China's nineteenth-century weakness to the frequency of warfare. War is just one variable among many: ethnic tensions, unwieldy political structures, factionalism, the fact that China had unusually powerful enemies, and so on. Nor should we discard the many other models China experts have proposed to explain the puzzle of China's apparent stagnation: Mark Elvin's famous model of agricultural stagnation; Kent Deng's sophisticated model of structural equilibrium; the classical idea that China lacked an activist bourgeoisie (an idea held by the great historian of Chinese science, Joseph Needham); R. Bin Wong and Jean-Laurent Rosenthal's brilliant model of geopolitical competition, capital, and wage labor; and many others.[37]

By the same token, we should not discount all of the cultural explanations that traditionalist scholars are fond of, particularly when it comes to science. Although many scholars currently downplay the significance of experimental science in the Great Economic Divergence (they are found on both sides of the revisionism debate), the evidence has convinced me that science played a key role in the Great Military Divergence.[38] Traditionalists are thus right to focus on science, and we shouldn't dismiss the other cultural and social elements they highlight: legal systems, fiscal structures, financial systems, municipal governance, educational institutions, and so forth. We need more comparative work on these questions, and specialists in East Asian history are conducting fascinating research along these lines.

Nonetheless, levels of geopolitical instability—warring states periods, if you will—help explain military aspects of the rise of the West and the decline of China in world history. Europe's state system may have been unusually stable and long-lasting, but patterns of military competition had significant effects in China as well.

Indeed, one of the fascinating points that emerges out of a global warring states perspective is that modernization—the systematic adoption of more advanced technologies and techniques—is not something that arrived suddenly in Asia in the 1800s. As other scholars have suggested, it's a long, deep process. The first gunpowder weapons evolved in a process of mutual interadoption during a period of warfare in East Asia from 900 to 1300. They spread beyond East Asia—probably carried by warring Mongols and their allies—and took root in Europe by 1320 or so, where they evolved quickly, only to be reexported in turn. The Ming adopted Portuguese cannons in the early 1500s, Japanese and Portuguese arquebuses in the mid-1500s, and advanced Western artillery in the 1600s. One scholar argues that China's adoption of such artillery was China's first "self-strengthening movement."[39] And it was effective.

Chinese artillery technology became in some ways superior to European artillery.[40] Guns helped the forces of China defeat Europe's two great seventeenth-century imperial powers: the Dutch and the Russians.[41] Nor were the Chinese alone—from Marrakesh to Edo, states adopted and innovated, passing techniques and technologies back and forth.

This perspective on deep modernization illuminates China's attempts to modernize in the modern age. China's nineteenth-century self-strengthening has generally been viewed as a failure, but in fact China and Japan were, in the second half of the nineteenth century, the most successful modernizing powers of Asia. It's easy to think of Asian modernization as a matter of "catching up," as though the Asians were closing a static gap. But in fact, Europeans themselves were modernizing. All were trying to catch up with Britain, and then, as the pace of change increased, each state struggled to stay abreast of rivals. Even Great Britain, the most technologically advanced of the nineteenth-century powers, was undergoing revolutionary change.

To be sure, the European powers had a head start, but China and Japan caught up quickly in military capacity, and Japan's greater success, manifested in its defeat of China in the Sino-Japanese War of 1894–1895, was due not so much to its superior ability to understand steam power or build guns and battleships (Chinese made steam engines first and built better battleships into the 1880s) but to China's political dysfunction. The Chinese had an old, creaky state; the Japanese had a new, effective one. Ten years after defeating China, Japan defeated another rusty state: Czarist Russia. Among the ships in the Japanese fleet were Chinese-made vessels Japan had captured a decade before.

China's modern weakness—apparent not just in its loss to Japan in 1895 but in the debilitating and nearly constant warfare that afflicted it from 1850 to 1949—may best be viewed not as a symptom of a failure to modernize but rather as the most recent variation on an ancient theme: the tumult of dynastic transition, which is invariably accompanied by frequent and intense warfare, rebels from within, invaders from without. Dynastic transitions are also associated with military, technological, and political innovation.

In any case, the dynamics of military modernization shouldn't be reduced to Westernization. The process marked global history for all of the gunpowder age, and not just on the far western and eastern sides of Eurasia. The lands in between played a key role as well, although not one that will be examined in this book. Our purpose here is to outline a binary framework, in the hope that it will be of use in developing a truly global military history.

Our story begins in one of the most fascinating periods of Chinese history: the divided and dynamic Song dynasty.

PART I

Chinese Beginnings

CHAPTER 1

The Crucible

THE SONG WARRING STATES PERIOD

In 1280, an explosion rocked the city of Yangzhou. "The noise," wrote one resident, "was like a volcano erupting, a tsunami crashing. The entire population was terrified."[1] The shock wave—or, as people called it, the "bomb wind"—hurled ceiling beams three miles and rattled roof tiles thirty miles away. At first, residents thought it must be an attack—war had seized their world for generations—but they soon realized it was an accident. Yangzhou's arsenal had recently dismissed its experienced gunpowder makers, and the new ones had been careless when grinding sulfur. A spark escaped and landed on some fire lances, which began spewing flames and jetting about "like frightened snakes." This was amusing to watch, until the fire reached the bombs. The entire complex exploded. A hundred guards were killed, completely obliterated. The crater was more than ten feet deep.[2]

At the time of the blast, gunpowder was almost unknown in the Europe. The first Western description had been written by the scholar Roger Bacon (1214–1292) a bit more than a decade before, and it would take another fifty years before the substance was used in Western warfare in any significant way.[3] Yet by 1280, the inhabitants of what is today China had been living in the gunpowder age for centuries.

Most people, even professional military historians, know little or nothing about this early history of gunpowder warfare. We tend to associate gunpowder with Europe, and it's true that Europeans began to excel in cannon and handgun technology by 1480 or so. Yet 1480 is six hundred years removed from the invention of gunpowder and at least five hundred years removed from the first gunpowder weapons. What happened during the first half millennium of the gunpowder age?

The story of gunpowder's development into a deadly technology is a vital part of global history. It's also fascinating and bizarre. Early gunpowder weapons are not like the weapons we think we know—cannons and muskets and mortars and grenades. They were odd, ungainly, even preposterous. Consider the fire bird, a bundle of gunpowder attached to a bird. Deployment was simple, if imprecise. You lit the powder, released the bird, and shooed it toward the enemy, hoping it would alight on a wooden structure (Figure 1.1). The fire ox was a similar idea. It was a terrifying spectacle, hooves thundering, smoke and sparks jetting out.

There were "flying rats," fire-spewing devices that leapt around unpredictably. (Once, in a demonstration, a recreational version of one nearly went up the empress's leg.)[4] There were rolling logs propelled by gunpowder rockets with fuses timed to release flying rats upon contact with the enemy. There were "fire bricks" that could be thrown onto a foe's ship and that released "flying swallows" that sprayed fire and set sails on fire. There were gunpowder gourds that shot flames and poison gas forty feet into the air or toward enemy soldiers. The names of other devices give a sense of the variety: "flying incendiary club for subjugating demons," "caltrop fire ball," "ten-thousand fire flying sand magic bomb," "big bees nest," "burning heaven fierce fire unstoppable bomb."

Many of these weapons represented paths not taken, and when you page through the great military compendium from 1044 called the *Wu jing zong yao*, it's as though you're looking at a stratum of fossils from an earlier geological era: the types show commonalities with modern forms, but most are extinct.[5] So it was with gunpowder weapons. The early experiments eventually coalesced into a smaller number of dominant types: most notably bombs and guns.

The process took two hundred and fifty years, from about 1000 CE, when the first gunpowder battles occurred, to around 1250, by which point gunpowder logs and firebirds had given way to primitive guns. The documentary record of this evolution is surprisingly clear. China has the deepest and most continuous historiography of any civilization on earth, and its sources allow us to trace the emergence of many

火 禽

FIGURE 1.1 "Fire bird" 火禽, 1044 CE.

This image of an early biological gunpowder delivery device is from the famous military treatise *Wu jing zong yao* 武经总要 of 1044. The gunpowder was not explosive but conflagrative. The intention was for the bird to land on an enemy structure and set it on fire. From the *Si ku quan shu zhen ben chu ji* 四庫全書珍本初集 (Shanghai: Shang wu yin shu guan, 1935). Courtesy of the National Library of China 國家圖書館, Beijing.

weapons and date them to within fifty years or a couple decades, remarkably accurate for the medieval period.[6] We have records of sieges and battles, data about requisitions and production, descriptions of the deployment of new weapons, sometimes by spellbound participants who were shocked to experience "iron fire bombs" and "heaven-shaking-thunder bombs."

There is no comparable record of experimentation in any other historiographical tradition. Guns appear suddenly in Europe a couple of generations after they appear in China, and there is no evidence of the bizarre experiments and early steps that are documented in China (although Europeans did experiment with fire birds—and fire cats—later on). It seems to be the same with other parts of the world, such as India and the Islamic world.

Scholars have suggested that the Chinese were slow to explore the possibilities of gunpowder, that it took Europeans to truly grasp the implications of the new technology.[7] Even Sinologists believed this.[8] But were the Chinese slow to adopt gunpowder? As we'll see there were tremendous technical barriers, but the larger point is that if we look at the evolution of gunpowder weapons in a global context, we find that Chinese developments were actually rapid. Certainly the speed can be compared to the evolution of guns in the West in the 1300s and 1400s.

Consider that in the hundred years from 1127 to 1279, the second part of the Song dynasty, known as the Southern Song, human beings went from primitive gunpowder weapons like gunpowder arrows to a whole array of more sophisticated weapons, including fire lances, proto guns, and, by the end of the period, true guns. Add the previous Northern Song period, from 960 to 1127, when we start with no gunpowder weapons at all, and the three-century period of the Song saw the most momentous developments in military technology in human history until the twentieth century. The evolution was actually tremendously fast. In a sense, modern warfare began in Song China.

Many other things we associate with modernity also began in the Song.

The Song Dynasty, 960–1279 CE

The Song dynasty has long been considered among the most magnificent periods of Chinese history. It was, according to Song specialist Dieter Kuhn, "the most advanced civilization on earth," showing "the most pronounced features of enlightened modern capitalism."[9] This may be an exaggeration, but there's no doubt that technologically, economically, scientifically, and culturally the Song was a time of efflorescence.

Historians of China have shown that more people lived in urban centers during the Song period than at any other time until the late eighteenth century, and the urbanization rate of the Song was at least 10 percent, a level European societies didn't reach until around 1800.[10] The largest cities in Europe at the time had populations of around a hundred thousand—Seville had a population of 150,000; Paris of 110,000; Venice of 70,000; London of 40,000.[11] The Song capital of Kaifeng had more than a million.[12] When the Southern Song reestablished their capital in Hangzhou, that city, too, boomed, home to well more than a million (some estimates reach two and a half million), making it the largest city in the world.[13] Marco Polo was flabbergasted by it, as was the famous Moroccan explorer Ibn Battuta, who traveled all over the known world and said Hangzhou was "the biggest city I had ever seen on the face of the earth."[14]

China's flourishing cities were linked by the world's most advanced transport network, which created, on the Great China Plain, "the world's most populous trading area."[15] This system served as the infrastructure for what historians call a Song "economic revolution"—some scholars even call it an "industrial revolution."[16] At the heart of this economic miracle was an advanced monetary system. Banknotes had been developed by merchants during the preceding Tang dynasty, and the Song government made the practice official, printing millions in intricate color patterns with anticounterfeiting techniques.

Song citizens could spend their cash on a dizzying array of goods and services. It has been estimated that the Song's production of iron around 1100 was roughly the same as what the entire continent of Europe produced six hundred years later.[17] This iron was produced by the most advanced techniques in the world, using coal and the coke or "refined coal" that became a hallmark of European industrial iron production, centuries later. Massive Song iron works employed thousands of employees, who operated bellows machines that provided a constant flow of oxygen and were far more sophisticated than contemporaneous European devices.[18]

In textile production, too, Song developments were far ahead of those of medieval and even early modern Europe. Complex spinning and weaving machines used ingenious mechanical mechanisms. A Chinese inventor described how "it takes a spinner many days to spin a hundred catties, but with water power it may be done with supernatural speed."[19] It wasn't until the eighteenth century that Europeans matched such devices.[20] The fame of Song manufacturing spread far and wide. As a Persian scholar wrote, around 1115, "The people of China are the most skilfull of men in handicrafts. No other nation approaches them in this. The people of Rum (the Eastern Roman Empire) are highly proficient (in technology) too, but they do not reach the standards of the Chinese. The latter say that all men are blind in craftsmanship, except the men of Rum, who however are one-eyed, that is, they know only half the business."[21]

Song silks and porcelains and handicrafts were prized throughout the world, and Song mariners shipped them in huge vessels across the China Seas, through the Strait of Malacca, and across the Indian Ocean to India and the Middle East. The scope of this trade was enormous: the government at times drew 20 percent of its total revenues from taxes and tolls on maritime trade. As one Song emperor noted, "The profits from maritime commerce are very great. If properly managed they can be millions. Is it not better than taxing the people?"[22] Song vessels had watertight bulkheads, staterooms, lifeboats, and sophisticated rudder and anchor systems.

They navigated by means of the magnetic compass, one of the many inventions and discoveries of the Song period. Aside from the three that the philosopher Francis Bacon (1561–1626) famously described as constitutive of modernity—gunpowder, the compass, and printing—there were also significant advances in anatomy, the discovery of tree dating, rain and snow gauges, rotary cutting discs, the knowledge of magnetic declination, thermoremanent magnetization, magnetism in medicine, relief maps, all kinds of mathematical innovations and discoveries (including effective algebraic notation and the "Pascal" triangle of binomial coefficients), steam sterilization, pasteurization (of wine), artificial induction of pearls in oysters, effective underwater salvage techniques, all kinds of silk processing devices, including reeling machines, multiple-spindle twisting frames, and others, smallpox inoculation, the discovery of urinary steroids, the use of the toothbrush and toothpaste, a method for the precipitation of copper from iron, the chain drive, the understanding of the camera obscura phenomenon, and new types of clock mechanisms.[23]

Song-era military technology was also advanced. Aside from gunpowder weapons, the inventors of the Song and neighboring states developed long-range catapults of increased accuracy, new types of rapid-fire crossbow cartridges, huge and powerful artillery crossbows, double-acting force pump flamethrowers, and new techniques for forging swords, lances, and armor.[24]

The people of the Song may even have become anatomically modern before people elsewhere in the world. Song-era jaws—at least of high-status individuals—exhibit what physical anthropologists have called the "modern overbite." For all of human prehistory and most of human history, people's top and bottom incisors met tooth to tooth, making it possible to clamp food tightly. When humans started cutting their food into small pieces, however, their jaws began developing differently, with the top incisors hanging out over the lower ones. This happened in Europe during the eighteenth century, when the fork and knife began to be used regularly at the table. But, as anthropologist Charles Loring Brace noted, "modern practices of dining etiquette date at least from the Song Dynasty. . . . Consequently, chopsticks, like the fork in the West, should serve as a symbol denoting the change in eating habits that leads to the development of the overbite."[25]

In so many ways, then, the Song was advanced, especially by the standards of medieval Europe, but there's a paradox. Despite being the most developed country in the world, the Song did not manage to achieve hegemony in East Asia. Previous dynasties—such as the Han (206 BCE–220 CE) and the Tang (618–907)—had achieved positions of unquestioned preeminence, and successors to the Song like the Ming (1368–1644) and the Qing (1644–1911) also managed to unify "All under Heaven" and overawe their neighbors. But the Song state was often militarily outclassed, losing more wars than it won, forced to accept humiliating peace treaties.

This paradox has puzzled scholars, who have considered it a "curious anomaly [that] haunts the three centuries of the Song."[26] To explain it, historians tended to emphasize Song culture, particularly Confucianism. Under the influence of Confucianism, the Song emphasized words over war, or, as the Chinese put it, *wen* (文) over *wu* (武).[27] In the Song period, the argument goes, *wen* (words, culture, civilization) was overvalued by Confucians, who devalued the military in the belief that the ethical conduct of the monarch and the virtue of his ministers would naturally order the human world, and that resort to force was considered barbaric and uncivilized. If the Song had devoted due attention to war, it would have become the undisputed power of all of East Asia.[28]

Yet recent work on Song history shows that the Song didn't neglect war nearly as much as this argument would suggest.[29] As Yuan-kang Wang writes, "considerations of the balance of power—not cultural aversion to warfare—dominated the decisions to use force."[30] Similarly, historian Don Wyatt writes that in the Song period, "Chinese . . . became intent on maintaining the territorial integrity of China by any means necessary" and "had just as much recourse to the prosecution of war as they did to the pursuit of negotiation."[31] Scholars are increasingly finding strong strains of militarism in the Song.[32] The Song oversaw massive programs of military production, and the weapons they developed were the most advanced in the world. Even the official *Song History*, a 496-volume monument compiled by their successors (and conquerors), notes that "their tools of war were exceedingly effective, never before seen in recent times."[33] It goes on to note that "their troops weren't always effective," but "their weapons and armor were very good."[34]

So how do we resolve the puzzle of the Song's inability to prevail? The answer has less to do with the weakness of the Song than with the strength of its enemies. Over its 319 years, the Song faced four primary foes. The most famous (and deadly) was the Mongol Empire, which didn't just overpower the Song: its conquests stretched from Kiev to Baghdad, Kabul to Kaifeng. Before the Mongols, the Song faced other implacable enemies from Central and Northern Asia: the Tanguts of the Xi Xia dynasty, the Khitans of the Liao dynasty, and the Jurchens of the Jin dynasty (see Maps 1.1 and 1.2).

These weren't just unsophisticated nomads. They ruled some of the most effective states in the world.[35] As Paul Jakov Smith writes, "The rapid evolution of Inner Asian statecraft in the tenth to thirteenth centuries allowed states on the northern frontier to support formidable armies that offset agrarian China's advantages in wealth and numbers,

MAP 1.1 East Asia during the Northern Song period, 960–1127.

thereby blocking [the] Song from assuming a position of supremacy at the center of a China-dominated world order and relegating it to a position of equal participant in a multistate East Asian system."[36] The Song just happened to rule China during a time of exceptional power for Central Asian states. Song weakness was not absolute but relative.

In Europe, the competition of states within a state system has been taken to be, in a sense, salutary: it created selective pressures for the development of sophisticated techniques, administrative structures, and technologies. Why, then, shouldn't we see the Song's inability to prevail over neighbors not as a sign of weakness but as a source of dynamism?[37]

MAP 1.2 East Asia during the early Southern Song period, 1127–1227.

The Song Warring States Period

When we talk about technological and other advances in Song China we're in fact being inaccurate. Song innovations didn't come in isolation. Liao, Jin, Xi Xia, and Mongol developments were also important, as each state stimulated and challenged the others. The Song and their neighbors were in constant rivalry, but also in constant communication. Their inhabitants moved across borders, seeking opportunity or fleeing scarcity. Officials defected with alarming regularity. Trade flowed despite attempts at prohibition. And although the non-Song states were founded by non-Chinese peoples, they were deeply influenced by Chinese culture and institutions. The Liao and the Jin states, for example, which controlled northern China in succession, first the Liao (916–1125) and then the Jin (1115–1234), were essentially Sinitic states ruled by a stratum of inner Asians. In fact, the Liao leaders felt that their state was the direct successor of the Tang dynasty, as "Chinese" as the Song State; Jin leaders made similar claims.[38] The Xi Xia, which ruled the western lands, was less Sinitic, but it, too, was deeply influenced by Chinese culture and institutions.[39]

In all these states, most of the officials, scholars, merchants, artisans, and farmers were Chinese, and Chinese was the lingua franca throughout East Asia. Chinese books produced in one state were read in the others. Military treatises crossed borders despite attempts to prohibit their export, and they were much sought-after as spoils of war, with entire libraries and archives weighing down victors' caravans of plunder.[40] Liao, Jin, and Xi Xia war makers didn't just read Chinese military classics in the original; they also sponsored translations into Khitan, Jurchen, and Tangut.[41] But the stimulus went both ways. Experts in Song military history have written that "the military leaders of the Khitan, the Jurchen, and the Tanguts, who admired Chinese civilization, even as they studied the essence of Chinese military science . . . also positively stimulated the advance of the Song Dynasty's military science, thereby causing the second great wave in history of advance and florescence for Chinese military science."[42] (The first wave was the ancient period, the time of Sun Zi.)

This mutual stimulation was facilitated by another key feature of the Song competitive state system: its stability. The European state system of 1500 to 1945 is said to have been conducive to dynamism partly because the states were balanced against each other. To be sure, the number of states decreased markedly from the late medieval period to the modern period, but certain units endured, and this stability within competition drove innovation. The Song-era warring states were also militarily balanced, and although the Song was at times weaker than its neighbors, it proved too strong to destroy. When ousted from its northern capital in 1127, it reconstituted itself in the south, and the Song dynasty is therefore divided into two periods, the Northern Song (960–1127) and the Southern Song (1127–1279). The other states proved less durable. The Xi Xia, the Liao, and the Jin were swept away by each other or by the Mongols, who emerged in the early 1200s.[43]

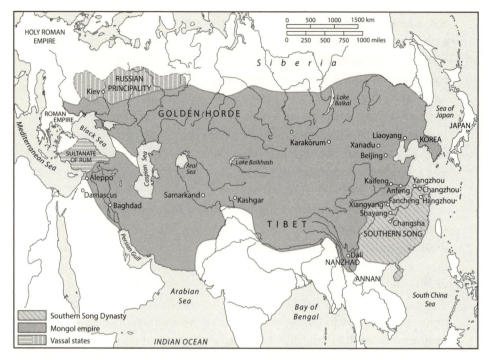

MAP 1.3 The Mongol Empire and the Southern Song, 1246–1259.

And the Mongols, who conquered much of the known world, needed nearly fifty years to defeat the Song (see Map 1.3).

This kind of stability, this sustained rivalry between long-lived states, is vital to the warring states dynamic. A balance between chaos and stability creates a productive equilibrium, and the Song Warring States Period was unusually stable and long-lived for China. The original Warring States Period (475–221 BCE) was of course famously long and sustained, with seven major states contending over two centuries or more depending upon when we date the onset of "system formation."[44] That period thus saw many military and administrative innovations, and the structures that were so formed were then carried on by first the Qin (221–206 BCE) and then the Han (206 BCE–220 CE) dynasties, becoming the fundamental institutions of imperial China. After the Han fell, China entered a brief period of competitive stability known as the Three Kingdoms Period (220–280 CE), but the ensuing period, from 280 CE or so to 581 CE, saw a wild profusion of states rising into and falling out of existence, competing, to be sure, but with a decided lack of stability. The period is so untidy that most textbooks discuss it only cursorily or leave it out altogether. "No set of boundaries lasted very long,"[45] writes one historian: "the political history of these three-and-a-half centuries is one of the most complex in Chinese history."[46] Only with the centralization brought about by the Sui dynasty (581–618 CE) and carried forth in the glorious Tang dynasty (618–907 CE) did the chaos end, but after the collapse of the Tang, China devolved once again into manifold states, a situation that lasted until the Song established their rule in 960.[47]

The Song Warring States Period thus presents a picture of strained stability comparable to the original Warring States Period, albeit with fewer states. For most of the Song period, there were generally three principal rivals coexisting in an uneasy balance of power, and we can divide the Song Warring States System into three separate phases. In Phase I, which lasted from the late 900s to 1125, the Song faced the Tangut Xi Xia state to the northwest and the Khitan Liao dynasty to the northeast (Map 1.1). In 1125, the Liao were conquered by the newly arisen Jin, who replaced the Liao in the north and then drove southward into Song territory, forcing the Song to regroup as the smaller but still powerful Southern Song state. This inaugurated Phase II, which lasted from 1125 until 1234, and during which the Southern Song faced off against the Jin and the Jin faced off against the Xi Xia in a new tripartite pattern (Map 1.2), which prevailed until the rise of Genghis Khan in the early 1200s. Genghis Khan destroyed the Xi Xia state in 1227, and his successors destroyed the Jin state in 1234. After 1234, there was a two-way struggle between the Song and the Mongols (Map 1.3). This struggle, Phase III in the Song Warring States System, ended in 1279, when the Mongols finally defeated the Song.

Within each of these three phases, borders shifted, cities were captured, treaties were signed, and tribute was paid, but geopolitical structures were generally stable. The Song Warring States Period was thus comparable to the original Warring States Period in that it was a long-term state system, and it was also similar in terms of geopolitical fragmentation to the European warring states period of 1450 to 1945, albeit with fewer (and much larger) units.[48] It was one of the most stable periods of non-unity in Chinese history.

Did this geopolitical competition drive the cultural, economic, and scientific florescence for which the Song period is famous? We can't reduce Song-period dynamism to geopolitical competition, just as we shouldn't do so for early modern Europe. Many transformations swept the Song and their neighbors: agricultural, commercial, fiscal, techno-logical. War was only one variable in a complex and dynamic period.

Still, there's no doubt that geopolitical tensions fomented tremen-dous military innovation, particularly when it came to gunpowder weapons.[49] Mention in historical sources of gunpowder weapons' use in battle continually increases during the course of the Song, particu-larly during the second half of the Song period. As historian Su Pinx-iao writes, "In the Southern Song period, and particularly in the later Southern Song period, gunpowder weapons become an increasingly widespread and frequently-mentioned aspect of military equipment and preparation [in the historical sources], and on the battlefield as well they played an increasingly important role."[50] The second half of the Song dynasty, from around 1120 or so to the Song collapse in 1279, was a time of rapid development in gunpowder warfare.[51]

As we'll see, these developments followed what Geoffrey Parker has called the "challenge and response" dynamic, which is brought about by sustained military rivalry.[52] States that survive a bout of warfare learn a bit, alter their technological and organizational structures, and then apply the lessons the next time they fight. This dynamic was pres-ent in Europe from the late medieval period until 1945, and historians have suggested that China's unity was one of the reasons it lost its lead to Europe. The Song Warring States Period shows precisely the same sort of challenge-response dynamic.

But to appreciate the rapid military developments, we must first understand early gunpowder itself.

CHAPTER 2

Early Gunpowder Warfare

Today, equipped with the tools of two and a half centuries of modern chemistry, we understand why when you mix nitrates, sulfur, and charcoal in the correct proportions and apply activation energy in the form of heat you get a terrific conflagration, but our forebears didn't know about elements or atoms or molecules. It wasn't until late in the eighteenth century that humans discovered the existence of oxygen and nitrogen, which make up nitrates, and only in the course of the following century did they grasp how the reaction works, to wit, that the nitrates' abundant oxygen allows the charcoal to combust rapidly, with the sulfur boosting the reaction by facilitating the oxygen's reaction with the charcoal.

When you consider the infinite ways that substances can be combined, and that alchemists' ingredients were impure, then you have some grasp of how a substance like gunpowder was unlikely to be discovered by chance. That's not to say the alchemists who discovered gunpowder were trying to create a volatile powder. In fact, their goal was to make medicines. They were conducting experiments to reduce compounds to their base components and understand their properties.

The term "experiment" is not a stretch. These were deliberate investigations. As the great historian of science Joseph Needham wrote, "The theoretical structure of medieval Chinese alchemy was both complex and sophisticated. An elaborate doctrine of categories, foreshadowing the study of chemical affinity, had grown up by the Tang [dynasty], reminiscent in some ways of the sympathies and antipathies of the Alexandrian proto-chemists; but more developed and less animistic. [The development of gunpowder] arose in the course of century-long systematic exploration of the chemical and pharmaceutical properties of a great variety of substances."[1]

The discovery of gunpowder seems to have occurred as the alchemists sought to isolate stable and pure compounds: to precipitate arsenic, for example (arsenic was used in many medicinal compounds), or to "subdue sulfur" (make it into a more stable product such as potassium sulfate).[2] Occasionally the alchemists would stumble onto an especially volatile reaction, as when one master apparently destroyed his house in purple flames.[3] But what's intriguing about early gunpowder recipes is how rare the flames were.

It turns out to be quite difficult to combine the active ingredients of gunpowder—a nitrate, sulfur, and charcoal—in the correct proportions, to mix them properly, and to form them into granules of the proper size and humidity to create a compound with enough reactivity to be considered gunpowder. When alchemists finally did develop the first effective formulas, probably sometime in the ninth century, they called the discovery fire medicine (火藥). The term is still used in modern Chinese to refer to gunpowder, a reminder of its heritage: a side result in the quest for drugs.

Various formulas were recorded, but the earliest extant recipes for military use are found in the famous military classic the *Wu jing zong yao*, from 1044.[4] Each of the formulas had varying proportions of the main reactants and an array of miscellaneous ingredients, such as white lead, yellow wax, pine resin, and arsenic.[5]

How well did those recipes work? A team of Chinese scholars used them to make batches of gunpowder, and although it's extraordinarily difficult to reconstruct past practices from written records, what they learned is significant. First, they found that the mixtures did in fact work well, producing recognizable (and dangerous) gunpowder conflagrations. From this they concluded that previous generations of scholars were correct to suspect that although these 1044 formulas are among the earliest military gunpowder recipes, they represent the fruit of considerable prior experimentation.[6]

Second, and more intriguingly, they found that the gunpowder mixtures were surprisingly difficult to set alight. When you light a modern firecracker, which is likely to contain gunpowder, the fuse sparks to life. But the Chinese team found that they couldn't use flame to set their replica mixtures alight at all. They had to use a red-hot iron rod.

Third, and most important, they found that these mixtures worked effectively only in the open air. When placed in sealed containers or in tubes, they burned slowly and incompletely. Gunpowder is so volatile because its nitrates supply oxygen, allowing rapid combustion, but these early recipes had low concentrations of nitrates relative to later formulas. The fact that these early gunpowder compounds required externally supplied oxygen to deflagrate effectively is an important finding.

Since early gunpowder formulas were unreactive and difficult to ignite, they wouldn't have seemed suitable for guns or flamethrowers or bombs. This fact, not Confucian scholars' supposed reluctance to take advantage of new technologies, explains why the Chinese didn't immediately start making guns and bombs. Gunpowder appeared at first to be useful primarily as an incendiary. This also explains why so many of the miscellaneous ingredients in these first formulas were other incendiaries, like oil, pitch, and resin. As the authors of the study write, "Early Song gunpowder was at a very early and primitive state. . . . It's not possible that at that time and before that time one could have made explosive gunpowder weapons and tube-shaped gunpowder weapons."[7] It was only after another century of experimentation that the nitrate proportions went up, the extraneous elements were reduced, and gunpowder suitable for bombs and guns began to seem a possibility. In the meantime, there arose a mad profusion of early gunpowder weapons.

The Northern Song and the Birth of Gunpowder Weapons

Perhaps the earliest evidence for a gunpowder weapon's use in war predates the Song period. In 904, at the end of the Tang dynasty, a famous commander named Yang Xingmi was attacking a city, and one of his officers ordered troops to "shoot off a machine to let fly fire and burn the Longsha Gate."[8] Scholars have suggested that this passage may refer to the use of gunpowder arrows, and, indeed, a later source offers corroboration, explaining that "by let fly fire (飛火) is meant things like firebombs and fire arrows," that is, incendiary gunpowder bombs and gunpowder arrows.[9] The evidence isn't conclusive, but it's plausible, and there's no doubt that fire arrows were among the very first gunpowder weapons ever used. This is no surprise, because incendiary arrows had a long history in China.[10] If it's true that early gunpowder produced an effective flame only when exposed to oxygen, then arrows were a perfect application, because the rush through air brought oxygen to the reaction.

Gunpowder may have been used in war during the Tang dynasty, but it was during the Song Warring States Period that gunpowder weapons became widespread. During the Northern Song period (960–1127), the development and manufacture of gunpowder weapons became a deliberate government policy, a matter of research and development.

For example, the Song government encouraged experimentation with gunpowder arrows, rewarding innovators. In 970—very early in gunpowder history—a certain Feng Jisheng (馮繼升) was sent by the head of a weapons manufacturing bureau to demonstrate for the emperor a new type of gunpowder arrow. The experiment succeeded and the inventor was rewarded handsomely.[11] Thirty years later, another military man, Tang Fu (唐福), appeared before the emperor and demonstrated gunpowder arrows, gunpowder pots (a type of fire-spewing proto-bomb), and gunpowder caltrops of his own invention. He, too, received a rich reward.[12] A particularly intriguing case occured in 1002 CE, when a man named Shi Pu (石普), who was affiliated with a local militia, audaciously showed imperial officials his own invention of fireballs and gunpowder arrows. The officials were impressed, and Shi Pu was summoned to demonstrate his designs to the imperial court. Impressed, the emperor issued a decree that Shi Pu's inventions be disseminated widely. Indeed, the court went even assembled a team to print the plans and instructions and promulgate them throughout the realm.[13] This sort of dissemination of military technology was not limited to Shi Pu. The military manual *Wu jing zong yao*, whose recipes we've already discussed, was created by direct decree of the Song court.[14] As the official *Song History* noted, the court's policy of rewarding military inventors "brought about a great number of cases of people presenting technology and techniques (器械法式)."[15]

The Song made the manufacture of gunpowder weapons a part of its official armament policy. In the Northern Song capital of Kaifeng there was a military production complex with thousands of employees, and one source lists all the types of artisans working there circa 1023.[16] Alongside large-scale carpenters, small-scale carpenters, and tanners worked gunpowder makers (*huo yao zuo* 火藥作). We know little about these gunpowder artisans, but the fact that they worked at this massive facility suggests that gunpowder production had been centralized by this early date, having reached, in the words of historian Wang Zhao-chun, "a stage of large-scale factory-style assembly line production, capable of manufacturing large batches."[17] Most gunpowder seems to have been used for fire arrows. Song sources note that in 1083, for example, the imperial court sent 100,000 gunpowder arrows to one garrison and 250,000 to another.[18]

Yet the Song wasn't alone in its use of gunpowder. Records about the Liao dynasty and the Xi Xia dynasty are much sparser, but it's intriguing that in 1076 the Song court decreed that private subjects were thenceforth prohibited from trading saltpeter and sulfur across the border to inhabitants of the Liao dynasty. This indicates the existence of a cross-border trade in the ingredients of gunpowder that was significant enough to draw the attention of the imperial court.[19]

Eleventh-century experiments and adaptations were significant, but it was during the following century that the gunpowder age began in earnest. Phase II of the Song Warring States Period saw a series of wars between the Song and the Jin, whose military strength was stronger than the Liao or the Xi Xia. The Jin took experimentation with gunpowder weapons (and all manner of other weapons) very seriously. During the Song-Jin Wars, the first true explosive gunpowder weapons appeared, as did a proto-gun known as the fire lance.

The Song-Jin Wars: The Gunpowder Age Begins in Earnest

The ascendancy of the Jin state circa 1115 was so sudden that it shocked contemporaries and still perplexes historians today.[20] For the 150 years preceding its rise, East Asia had been balanced between the Liao, the Song, and the Xi Xia, but in the early 1100s a group of Jurchen tribes in the forestlands of northern Manchuria rose up against the Liao. A leader called Aguda united them, forged a powerful military, and declared himself emperor of the Jin dynasty in 1115.

What happened next seems to have surprised everyone, including Jin leaders themselves. The Jin defeated the Liao in engagement after engagement, their victories coming "faster than they could make plans for."[21] They captured the Liao Eastern Capital in 1116, the Liao Supreme Capital in 1120, and the Liao Central Capital in 1122. (The Liao liked capitals and had five, in accordance with their nomadic heritage.) Song leaders decided to make an alliance with the Jin, seeing an opportunity to strike a blow against the Liao and reclaim territory lost in earlier wars, but the Song couldn't keep its end of the deal. Song armies were supposed to capture the Liao Southern Capital (near present-day Beijing), but they were instead defeated by Liao forces. The Jin got impatient and captured the Liao Southern Capital themselves.[22] Not long thereafter they captured the Western Capital and with that the Liao were driven away.[23]

The Jin rulers saw no reason to stop expanding and directed their horses southward into Song territories.[24] Given how poorly Song armies had performed against the dying Liao, Jin leaders expected their conquest to proceed quickly, but they were mistaken. When Jin forces attacked the Song capital of Kaifeng in 1126, they met stout resistance. The city's defenses had been overhauled, and it boasted immense walls, a deep and wide moat, and advanced fortification structures, including bastions and barbicans.[25] Song defenders also had powerful gunpowder weapons. Aside from standard gunpowder arms like gunpowder arrows and gunpowder fire bombs, they also possessed a terrifying new weapon called a thunderclap bomb (霹靂炮). As an eyewitness wrote, "At night the thunderclap bombs were used, hitting the lines of the enemy well, and throwing them into great confusion. Many fled, screaming in fright."[26]

The Jin decided to withdraw from Kaifeng, not because of the thundering bombs but because it was expedient and because the Song were willing to pay a ransom of silk and treasure.[27] Yet Song bombs had apparently made an impression. It seems that the Jin studied gunpowder weapons from captured Song troops and artisans. According to historian Wang Zhaochun, when the Jin returned several months later to besiege Kaifeng again, "the [Jin] abilities were already far superior than before."[28]

In this next battle for Kaifeng (1126–1127), both sides—the Jin and the Song—used gunpowder bombs extensively.[29] The sources for this battle are particularly detailed. As Wang Zhaochun writes, this battle and another Song-Jin battle of that same year "are, in the sources of ancient China, the very earliest truly detailed descriptions of the use of gunpowder weapons in warfare."[30] The records show that the Jin used gunpowder arrows and huge catapults hurling gunpowder bombs. The Song countered with gunpowder arrows, gunpowder bombs, thunderbolt bombs, and a weapon called the "molten metal bomb" (金汁炮).[31] Ultimately, the Jin prevailed. When they attacked the city's Xuanhua Gate, their "fire bombs fell like rain, and their arrows were so numerous as to be uncountable."[32] The Song defenders turned to a mystic martial artist who promised to turn back the Jin assault if they'd just open the gate and let him out. The mystic failed and the Jin captured the city, taking enormous trains of booty, among which were twenty thousand fire arrows.[33]

The Song fled southward, eventually establishing a new capital in today's Hangzhou. The Jin chased them, and in the intense fighting that ensued, a new weapon made its first definitive appearance: the fire lance, ancestor of the gun.

The fire lance, as its name implies, is a long staff at the end of which is affixed a tube filled with gunpowder. The gunpowder is lit and then, ideally, spews forth. At first, as we'll see, it wasn't a particularly powerful or versatile weapon, but as the decades passed and as gunpowder increased in power, the fire lance's tubes grew longer and stronger, and people began adding pellets to the gunpowder, until it eventually became a gun.

Some scholars have suggested that the fire lance made its first appearance even before the Song period, basing their case on a famous silk painting dated to circa 950. In the painting, a demon points what seems to be a fire lance at the Buddha, trying to disturb his meditation.[34] Given what we know about the effectiveness of eleventh-century gunpowder formulas, this early date seems unlikely, and most Chinese scholars dismiss it, although there are very brief mentions of fire lances in a Song text from 1000 and in the *Wu jing zong yao* of 1044.[35] In any case, the first detailed descriptions of the fire lance's use come from accounts of an otherwise unimportant battle of 1132:

the Jin siege of the Song city of De'an (modern-day Anlu City 安陆市, Hubei Province).

What is exciting about the Siege of De'an is that contemporary sources mention an innovator by name: a resourceful leader named Chen Gui (陳規, 1072–1141). He was serving as prefect of the city when it was attacked by a force of ten thousand troops. An account of the siege provides rich descriptions of medieval siege tactics: how the enemy systematically encircled the city walls, establishing some seventy stockades around them, with tall towers from which watchmen peered into the city and communicated enemy movements by means of fires at night and bright flags during the day.[36] It also outlines how the besiegers recruited carpenters and smiths and leatherworkers from nearby areas and had them construct mobile assault towers called sky bridges. They could be wheeled to the walls, and they were so tall that enemy soldiers could rush out the front right onto the ramparts. How could Chen Gui defend against them, when the enemy held the city "so thoroughly surrounded that air and water couldn't pass from inside to outside"?[37]

He prepared carefully. He ordered the construction of defensive structures on top of the walls to hide his troops' activities and protect them against enemy arrows and catapult rocks.[38] He set up catapults, carefully placing them so they could reach the enemy's lines outside the walls and stationing men on the walls to report on the effectiveness of each shot so that the catapults could be re-aimed. He readied ammunition for them—stone balls of twenty-five to thirty kilograms—and used wooden structures to protect his artillerists. He selected the bravest soldiers and divided them into fourteen platoons of twenty-five men and sent them out onto the walls and barbicans. He set up mutual aid teams for reinforcements and for the inspection of walls and defenses.

De'an was surrounded by moats, which the enemy needed to fill in order to bring their sky bridges into position. This meant they had to prevent Chen Gui's archers and artillerists from killing their laborers. So they pummelled Chen Gui's wooden defense structures with catapults, but "as they destroyed the defenses bit by bit, [Chen Gui's defenders] repaired them bit by bit, and [the enemy] never managed to strike a single person either on the walls or within the city."[39] In the meantime, Chen Gui's catapults were doing their job. "Fortunately," the account goes, "when the enemy moved forward and placed siege machines, he did so in such a way that they were lined up one by one exactly as [we had] foreseen."[40] Spotters on the walls helped Chen Gui's catapulters to refine their aim, blasting artillerists, workers, and soldiers to bits.

These setbacks troubled the enemy, who had already ravaged the countryside for food stores and were growing hungry. Many wore rags. They resorted to forcing women and children and elderly people to gather wood and straw and stones and old bricks to fill the moats, and when these unfortunate people were killed by fire arrows or catapult stones, their corpses were thrown into the moats, although sometimes hunger drove enemy soldiers to first "cut off the flesh and eat it."[41] Chen Gui's archers also shot gunpowder arrows at the stuff in the moat, trying to set the straw and wood alight. This succeeded beyond expectations. The fire burned for three days and nights.

The enemy was forced to start over. This time they fireproofed their moat-filling materials with a layer of bricks and mud. Eventually they decided that the moats had been filled in enough. The sky bridges began rolling toward the walls, escorted by soldiers with lances, protected by archers and artillerists. Chen Gui's defenders used long beams to keep the sky bridges from getting any closer than ten or so feet (three meters) from the walls. This was too far for the stormers to cross, but it was just close enough for Chen Gui to unleash his secret weapon: fire lances.

Chen Gui had prepared them in advance: "Using fire-bomb powder [literally fire bomb medicine] long bamboo fire lances were made ready, more than twenty of them, as well as good numbers of striking spears and hook-blade staves (鉤鎌), all of which would be deployed, with two people holding one together, and which were made ready in such a way that when the sky bridges approached the wall, [the defenders could] emerge from above and below their defense structures and deploy them."[42] As planned, when the sky bridges approached, the fire lancers came out from the wooden defense structures and attacked, accompanied by other specially prepared soldiers.

What role did the fire lances—these proto-guns—play in this engagement? Historians have suggested that they were used to burn the siege towers.[43] This is certainly what the official *Song History* implies, which, as usual, is concise to a fault: "Taking advantage of the fact that the sky bridges got stuck in the moat, Chen Gui and sixty men holding fire lances came out of the western gate and burned the sky bridges, using fire oxen to help in this, and in an instant it was all over. Heng [the enemy commander] struck camp and left."[44]

Yet a close reading of a more detailed firsthand account suggests a different interpretation. After using the beams of wood to hold off the sky bridges, Chen Gui directed his fire lancers to attack the enemy personnel who were trying to maneuver them into place: "As the sky bridges became stuck fast, more than ten feet from the walls and unable to get any closer, [the defenders] were ready. From below and above the defensive structures they emerged and attacked with fire lances, striking lances, and hooked sickles, each in turn. The people [i.e., the porters] at the base of the sky bridges were repulsed. Pulling their bamboo ropes, they [the porters] ended up drawing the sky bridge back in an anxious and urgent rush, going about fifty paces before stopping."[45] The enemy tried to move the sky bridges back into position again, but now the most favorable spots were obstructed by the beams, so they were forced to pull them to less expedient places. As they did so, the sky bridges became mired in the moat, which had not been entirely filled in. Ropes snapped. The sky bridges became completely immobile. At this point, Song soldiers emerged from the walls and attacked the sky bridge soldiers, while Song defenders on the walls threw bricks and shot arrows, as Song catapults hurled bombs and rocks. The enemy was driven back with great loss of life. At this point Chen Gui's defenders used "fire oxen," incendiary bundles of grass and firewood, throwing them at the base of the sky bridges (sometimes fire oxen contained gunpowder as well, but it's not clear whether they did in this case). The sky bridges burned fiercely, driving the remaining enemy personnel away.

So in contrast to what historians have suggested, the fire lances were not used to burn the sky bridges. Rather, they were used as infantry weapons, to drive away the porters who were pulling them and the troops who were within them. The burning of the sky bridges was accomplished later, by piling incendiaries at their base.

This is significant because it suggests that gunpowder weapons were making a transition. As Peter Lorge has noted, the description of Chen Gui's manufacture of fire lances uses an atypical word for gunpowder: "fire bomb medicine" (火炮藥) rather than simply "fire medicine" (火藥). This implies that there were new formulations being used, and they may have had more nitrate and fewer extraneous ingredients. "Fire bomb medicine" seems to have been more volatile than previous recipies.

It's also notable that the description of Chen Gui's attack notes a sequence of deployment: fire lances were in the vanguard, followed by striking lances and then sickle swords. This implies that the fire lances had the longest range, because each of the following weapons is a closer-quarter weapon. This suggests in turn that the fire lances were shooting flames. How far and for what duration is impossible to determine, but it seems clear: gunpowder was increasing in power, and humanity was on its way to the true gun.

That early fire lances were being used as antipersonnel weapons and not just antistructure incendiaries is supported by evidence from other battles around this time. For example, they were mounted on carts for antipersonnel use in land battles. In 1163, a Song commander named Wei Sheng prepared several hundred "at-your-desire-war-carts" (如意戰車), each of which contained fire lances, whose barrels protruded through protective coverings on the sides. The carts were used to defend mobile catapults that hurled firebombs. The Song court was impressed with the innovation and ordered that the carts be copied by other divisions of the army.[46] Historians have made much of the use of armored mobile firearm platforms among the Hussites in the early 1400s, the Muscovites in the late 1400s, and the Chinese in the mid-1500s.[47] The armored fire lance carts of the Song period were their forerunners.[48]

The Song-Jin conflicts also spurred naval innovation. In 1129, a decree established that all Song warships must be equipped with trebuchets for hurling gunpowder bombs, and we have accounts of subsequent water battles in which gunpowder weapons were decisive. For example, in 1159, a Song fleet of 120 ships caught a Jin sea fleet at anchor near a place called Shijiu Island (石臼島, which lay offshore the Shandong peninsula). The Song commander "ordered that gunpowder arrows be shot from all sides, and wherever they struck, flames and smoke rose up in swirls, setting fire to several hundred vessels."[49] According to the official Jin history, the Jin commander, realizing that his position was hopeless, jumped overboard and drowned.[50] The Song siezed weapons, supplies, intelligence documents, and official seals, and then burned what they couldn't carry: "The flames and smoke lasted more than four days and four nights."[51]

Another naval battle occurred not at sea but on the Yangtze River. In 1161 Jin troops arrived in force on its banks, preparing to cross into the heart of Song territory, banners held high. The Song fleet hid behind a tall island, while Song scouts watched from the peak. Sun Zi, the great classical master of strategy, writes that when an enemy is crossing a river you should wait until he's halfway across before attacking. When the Jin troops reached the halfway point, the Song scouts raised a flag, at which the hidden fleet glided forth, but these were no ordinary river craft. Many were paddle wheel vessels, powered by men running on treadmills, a Song specialty.[52] They launched thunderclap bombs. According to a Song commander, the Jin "men and horses were all drowned, and they were utterly defeated."[53]

In the early 1200s, a new threshold was reached: the maturation of explosive bombs. As we've seen, there is evidence of explosive weapons in the mid-1100s, and other evidence suggests that gunpowder firecrackers were used by the third decade of the 1100s.[54] But in the 1200s gunpowder bombs became truly devastating weapons.

Consider the Jin siege of the Song-held city of Xiangyang in 1206–1207, as detailed in an account of a minor military official named Zhao Wannian 趙萬年 (b. 1168).[55] Most gunpowder weapons mentioned in this account are incendiaries, with the usual entries about conflagratory attacks by fire arrow (火箭) and fire bomb (火炮).[56] Song defenders used such weapons to burn Jin trebuchets, while Jin troops shot gunpowder arrows to destroy the city's moored vessels.[57] But Zhao Wannian also makes clear that bombs played a key role in the Song defense.

The first time Song defenders hurled "thunderclap bombs," they caused Jin troops and horsemen to run away in panic.[58] The second time, thunderclap bombs drove back a major Jin cavalry attack: "We beat our drums and yelled from atop the city wall, and simultaneously fired our thunderclap missiles out from the city walls. The enemy cavalry was terrified and ran away."[59] But the third firing was most decisive. The Jin had retreated to a riverside encampment, and on a dark rainy night thirty Song boats were loaded with gunpowder arrows, thunderclap bombs, and troops: a thousand crossbowmen to shoot the arrows, five hundred infantry, and, interestingly, a hundred drummers. A witness described events from the perspective of the Jin troops: "As the . . . troops were sleeping in their fortified encampment, a sudden drumming broke out, and crossbows let fly. Thunderclap bombs were hurled inside, and they [the enemy] were shocked into panic. They couldn't saddle their horses or gather their things. They just trampled each other in their haste, and two or three thousand troops were killed or wounded, along with eight or nine hundred horses."[60] The Jin abandoned their camp.

These thunderclap bombs played a key role in the Song victory, but were they true explosives? The term "thunderclap bomb" had appeared previously, most notably in the famous *Wu jing zong yao* of 1044, but in that text it refers to a pseudo-explosive: a large section of bamboo surrounded by incendiary gunpowder, whose explosion was caused not by gunpowder gasses but by the expansion of heated air inside the bamboo. Historians have suggested that the thunderclap bombs used in Xiangyang in 1206–1207 were true gunpowder bombs, and this seems likely.[61] Indeed, soon thereafter an incontrovertibly explosive gunpowder weapon appeared in the records: the devastating iron bomb.

Legend has it that the idea for the iron bomb came from a fox hunter named Iron Li.[62] Around 1189—so the story goes—this Iron Li developed a new method for trapping foxes by taking a strong ceramic bottle with a small mouth, stuffing it with gunpowder, and inserting a fuse. He would find a watering hole or other place frequented by foxes, place some nets at strategic egress points, and then hide the bottle, wait until foxes got near, and light the fuse. The bomb exploded with a tremendous report, and the panicked foxes ran right into his traps, where Iron Li calmly dispatched them with an ax. Although it's impossible to say whether this story is true, tradition holds that Iron Li's ceramic bomb inspired the Jin to develop an iron version.

The first evidence we have of the iron bomb's use in battle comes fourteen years after the Siege of Xiangyang, when the Jin besieged the Song city of Qizhou in 1221 (Qizhou is in modern-day Hubei Province). It may be the first siege in human history in which bombs proved decisive. Song military commander Zhao Yurong (趙與褣) wrote a sad and erudite account of the siege, which is rich in details of gunpowder warfare: iron bombs, improved fire lances, leather bombs, paper bombs, fire birds in action, and, of course, gunpowder arrows.[63]

Qizhou was an imposing walled city near the Yangtze River, and when news arrived that a twenty-five-thousand-man Jin force was advancing on it, Zhao Yurong and the other commanders resolved to hold out even though their forces were outnumbered nearly eight to one. As in all sieges, the details are important—Yurong's account has descriptions of trenches dug, fortifications established and destroyed, sorties and countersorties—but what stands out repeatedly is the attackers' deadly use of the iron bomb.

The Song defenders had bombs of their own. Yurong lists in the city's inventory some three thousand thunderclap bombs and twenty thousand "great leather bombs" (皮大炮), along with thousands of gunpowder arrows and gunpowder crossbow bolts. These thunderbolt bombs and great leather bombs were almost certainly explosive gunpowder bombs, but they weren't nearly as powerful as the Jin iron bombs. "The barbaric enemy," wrote Yurong, "attacked the Northwest Tower with an unceasing flow of catapult projectiles from thirteen catapults. Each catapult shot was followed by an iron fire bomb [catapult shot], whose sound was like thunder. That day, the city soldiers in facing the catapult shots showed great courage as they maneuvered [our own] catapults, hindered by injuries from the iron fire bombs. Their heads, their eyes, their cheeks were exploded to bits, and only one half [of the face] was left."[64]

The Jin artillerists were remarkably accurate and seemed to be able to target the leadership's quarters: "The enemy fired off catapult stones . . . nonstop day and night, and the magistrate's headquarters [帳] at the eastern gate, as well as my own quarters . . . , were hit by the most iron fire bombs, to the point that they struck even on top of [my] sleeping quarters and [I] nearly perished! Some said there was a traitor. If not, how would they have known the way to strike right at both of these places?"[65] Yurong was able to examine the bombs, and he wrote, "In shape they are like gourds, but with a small mouth. They are made with pig iron, about two inches thick, and they cause the city's walls to shake."[66]

Iron bombs blew apart houses, battered down towers, blasted defenders from walls, and then, after nearly four weeks of siege, began pounding all four town gates. The assault was unremitting. It was also successful. The Jin scaled the walls and hunted down soldiers, officers, and officials of all levels. Most people were slaughtered, but Zhao Yurong managed to clamber over a battlement and flee across the river, although his family perished. Later he returned to the scene and searched the ruins, but "the bones and skeletons were so mixed up that there was no way to tell who was who."[67]

The Jin commander who had perpetrated the massacre was no more fortunate. Shortly after returning home, he was tried for treason and he and two sons were executed. Awaiting execution, he supposedly reflected on the bad karma he and his father and grandfather—all generals—had accumulated: "The sages are right. A family should not have three generations of generals in a row."[68]

Perhaps karma had finally caught up with the entire Jin dynasty, because it was soon destroyed by the Mongols.

CHAPTER 3

The Mongol Wars and the Evolution of the Gun, 1211–1279

The rise of the Mongols was a key event in the evolution of gunpowder technology. Their wars drove military developments in East Asia and spread gunpowder technology westward. You'd think this statement would be uncontroversial. After all, the Mongols created the world's largest empire, connecting East Asia to South Asia, Western Asia, the Middle East, and Eastern Europe. Mongol commanders excelled at incorporating foreign experts into their forces, and Chinese artisans of all kinds followed Mongol armies far from home. Yet oddly, experts disagree about the extent to which—or even whether—Mongols used gunpowder weapons in their warfare, and some deny them a role in the dissemination of the technology.[1]

How can there be disagreement about such a fundamental question? One reason is that most historians have a poor understanding about what early gunpowder weapons were like and what they were used for—they expect to find gunpowder weapons blasting down stone walls, as cannons would eventually come to do in the West.[2] As we've seen, that's not how gunpowder weapons worked in this period. Even the iron bombs of the Jin—the most powerful gunpowder weapons yet invented—were used not to batter walls but to kill people or, at most, to help destroy wooden structures. Moreover, at the time of the Mongol Wars, the most common gunpowder weapon was still the gunpowder arrow, used primarily as an incendiary. There's no shortage of accounts referring to blazing arrows and fiery orbs hurled by Mongol catapults, but historians have argued that these were not gunpowder weapons on the grounds that gunpowder weapons would have attracted much more attention.[3]

Another problem is that the Mongols left few historical documents to posterity. Even the records left by the Mongols' regime in China—the Yuan dynasty—are fragmentary, and China is a place that takes its history seriously. The official *History of the Yuan Dynasty*, compiled by scholars in China after the fall of the Yuan in 1368, is sloppy and patchy compared to other official histories in the Chinese canon, and Sinologists have noted that Yuan documents are particularly reticent about military details.[4] Scholars must piece together Mongols' history from the sources of their beleaguered enemies, whose records tended not to survive burning cities. So although we can paint a fairly clear picture of the development of firearms technology during the Song-Jin Wars, our understanding of the more intense and catalytic Mongol Wars is less complete.

Even so, there seems to be little doubt that the Mongols were proficient in gunpowder weapons. No one fighting in the Chinese context—and the Mongols met their most determined resistance in the Chinese realm—could remain unconvinced about the power of gunpowder, which by the early 1200s had come to play an essential role in warfare.

Indeed, the Mongols had a chance to learn about gunpowder weapons from the masters of their use, the Jin dynasty.

The Mongol-Jin Wars

Genghis Khan launched his first concerted invasion of the Jin in 1211, and it wasn't long before the Mongols were deploying gunpowder weapons themselves, for example in 1232, when they besieged the Jin capital of Kaifeng.[5] By this point they understood that sieges required careful preparation, and they built a hundred kilometers of stockades around the city, stout and elaborate ones, equipped with watchtowers, trenches, and guardhouses, forcing Chinese captives—men, women, and children—to haul supplies and fill in moats. Then they began launching gunpowder bombs.[6] Jin scholar Liu Qi (劉祁) recalled in a mournful memoir, how "the attack against the city walls grew increasingly intense, and bombs rained down as [the enemy] advanced."[7]

The Jin responded in kind. "From within the walls," Liu Qi writes, "the defenders responded with a gunpowder bomb called the heaven-shaking-thunder bomb (震天雷). Whenever the [Mongol] troops encountered one, several men at a time would be turned into ashes."[8] The official *Jin History* contains a clear description of the weapon: "The heaven-shaking-thunder bomb is an iron vessel filled with gunpowder. When lighted with fire and shot off, it goes off like a crash of thunder that can be heard for a hundred li [thirty miles], burning an expanse of land more than half a mu [所爇圍半畝之上, a mu is a sixth of an acre], and the fire can even penetrate iron armor."[9] Three centuries later, a Ming official named He Mengchun (何孟春, 1474–1536) found an old cache of them in the Xi'an area: "When I went on official business to Shaanxi Province, I saw on top of Xi'an's city walls an old stockpile of iron bombs. They were called 'heaven-shaking-thunder' bombs, and they were like an enclosed rice bowl with a hole at the top, just big enough to put your finger in. The troops said they hadn't been used for a very long time."[10] Possibly he saw the bombs in action, because he wrote, "When the powder goes off, the bomb rips open, and the iron pieces fly in all directions. That is how it is able to kill people and horses from far away."[11]

Heaven-shaking-thunder bombs seem to have first appeared in 1231 (the year before the Mongol Siege of Kaifeng) when a Jin general had used them to destroy a Mongol warship.[12] But it was during the Siege of Kaifeng of 1232 that they saw their most intense use. The Mongols tried to protect themselves by constructing elaborate screens of thick leather, which they used to cover workers who were undermining the city walls. In this way the workers managed to get right up to the walls, where they began excavating protective niches. Jin defenders found this exceedingly worrisome, so according to the official *Jin History* they "took iron cords and attached them to heaven-shaking-thunder bombs. The bombs were lowered down the walls, and when they reached the place where the miners were working, the [bombs were set off] and the excavators and their leather screens were together blown up, obliterated without a trace."[13]

The Jin defenders also deployed other gunpowder weapons, including a new and improved version of the fire lance, called the flying fire lance. This version seems to have been more effective than the one used by Chen Gui a century before. The official *Jin History* contains an unusually detailed description:

> To make the lance, use chi-huang paper, sixteen layers of it for the tube, and make it a bit longer than two feet. Stuff it with willow charcoal, iron fragments, magnet ends, sulfur, white arsenic [probably an error that should mean saltpeter], and other ingredients, and put a fuse to the end. Each troop has hanging on him a little iron pot to keep fire [probably hot coals], and when it's time to do battle, the flames shoot out the front of the lance more than ten feet, and when the gunpowder is depleted, the tube isn't destroyed.[14]

When wielded and set alight, it was fearsome weapon: "no one dared go near."[15] Apparently Mongol soldiers, although disdainful of most Jin weapons, greatly feared the flying fire lance and the heaven-shaking-thunder bomb.[16]

Kaifeng held out for a year, during which hundreds of thousands died of starvation, but ultimately it capitulated. The Jin emperor fled. Many hoped the Jin might reconstitute the dynasty elsewhere, and here and there Jin troops still scored successes, as when a Jin commander led four hundred fifty fire lance troops against a Mongol encampment: "They couldn't stand up against this and were completely routed, and three thousand five hundred were drowned."[17] But these isolated victories couldn't break Mongol momentum, especially after the Jin emperor committed suicide in 1234. Although some Jin troops—many of them Chinese—continued to resist (one loyalist gathered all the metal that could be found in the city he was defending, even gold and silver, and made explosive shells to lob against the Mongols),[18] the Jin were finished. The Mongols had conquered two of the three great states of the Song Warring States Period, the Xi Xia and the Jin. Now they turned to the Song.

The Song-Mongol Wars

It's striking that the Song, this supposedly weak dynasty, held the Mongols off for forty-five years. As an eminent Sinologist wrote more than sixty years ago, "unquestionably in the Chinese the Mongols encountered more stubborn opposition and better defense than any of their other opponents in Europe and Asia."[19]

Gunpowder weapons were central to the fighting. In 1237, for example, a Mongol army attacked the Song city of Anfeng, "using gunpowder bombs [*huo pao*] to burn the [defensive] towers."[20] (Anfeng 安豐 is modern-day Shouxian 壽縣, in Anhui Province.)[21] "Several hundred men hurled one bomb, and if it hit the tower it would immediately smash it to pieces."[22] The Song defending commander, Du Gao (杜杲), fought back resourcefully, rebuilding towers, equipping his archers with special small arrows to shoot through the eye slits of Mongol's thick armor (normal arrows were too thick), and, most important, deploying powerful gunpowder weapons, such as a bomb called the "Elipao," named after a famous local pear.[23] He prevailed. The Mongols withdrew, suffering heavy casualties.[24]

Gunpowder technology evolved quickly, and although sources are sketchy, scattered references to arsenals show that gunpowder weapons were considered central to the war effort. For example, in 1257, a Song official named Li Zengbo was ordered to inspect border cities' arsenals. He believed that a city should have several hundred thousand iron bombshells, and a good production facility should produce at least a couple thousand a month.[25] But his tour was disheartening. He wrote that in one arsenal he found "no more than 85 iron bomb-shells, large and small, 95 fire-arrows, and 105 fire-lances. This is not sufficient for a mere hundred men, let alone a thousand, to use against an attack by the . . . barbarians. The government supposedly wants to make preparations for the defense of its fortified cities, and to furnish them with military supplies against the enemy (yet this is all they give us). What chilling indifference!"[26]

Fortunately, the Mongol advance paused after the great khan died in 1259. When it resumed in 1268, fighting was extremely intense, and gunpowder weapons played significant roles. Blocking the Mongols' advance were the twin fortress cities of Xiangyang and Fancheng, which guarded the passage southward to the Yangze River. The Mongol investment of these cities was one of the longest sieges of world history, lasting from 1268 to 1273. The details are too numerous to examine here, but two episodes are salient, each of which involved a pair of heroes.

The first was a bold relief mission carried out by the so-called Two Zhangs. For the first three years of the siege, the Song had been able to receive food, clothing, and reinforcements by water, but in late 1271 the Mongols had tightened their blockade, and the inhabitants had become desperate. Two men surnamed Zhang determined to run the blockade and take supplies to the cities. With a hundred paddle wheel boats they traveled toward the twin cities, moving by night when possible, red lanterns helping them recognize each other in the darkness.[27] But a commander on the Mongol side learned about their plans and prepared a trap. As they approached the cities they found his "vessels spread out, filling the entire surface of the river, and there was no gap for them to enter."[28] Thick iron chains stretched across the water.

According to the official *Song History*, the two Zhangs had armed their boats with "fire-lances, fire-bombs, glowing charcoal, huge axes, and powerful crossbows."[29] Their flotilla opened fire, and, according to a source recorded from the Mongol side, "bomb-shells were hurled with great noise and loud reports."[30] Wang Zhaochun suggests that the fire bombs used on the two Zhangs' boats were not hurled by catapults but were shot off like rockets, using the fiery coals the vessels carried.[31] This would be exciting, but unfortunately the evidence is inconclusive.[32] Historian Stephen Haw suggests that the vessels carried guns, which is also possible, but again the evidence is inconclusive.[33]

In any case, the fight was brutal and long. The Zhangs' soldiers had been told that "this voyage promises only death," and many indeed died as they tried to cut through chains, pull up stakes, hurl bombs.[34] A source from the Mongol side notes that "on their ships they were up to the ankles in blood."[35] But around dawn, the Zhangs' vessels made it to the city walls. The citizens "leapt up a hundred times in joy."[36] When the men from the boats were mustered on shore, one Zhang was missing. His fate remains a mystery. The official *Yuan History* says one Zhang was captured alive. The official *Song History* has a more interesting story. A few days after the battle, it says, "a corpse came floating upstream, covered in armor and gripping a bow-and-arrow. . . . It was Zhang Shun, his body pierced by four lances and six arrows. The expression of anger [on his face] was so vigorous it was as though he were still alive. The troops were surprised and thought it miraculous, and they made a grave and prepared the body for burial, erected a temple, and made sacrifices."[37] Other sources suggest that Zhang Shun was indeed killed in battle.[38] He was later immortalized in the famous novel *The Water Margin* (水滸傳).

Alas, the supplies didn't save Xiangyang, because the Mongols had a pair of heroes of their own. Two Muslim artillery specialists—one from Persia and one from Syria—helped construct counterweight trebuchets whose advanced design allowed larger missiles to be hurled farther. They came to be known in China as "Muslim catapults" or "Xiangyang catapults," and they were devastating.[39] As one account notes, "when the machinery went off the noise shook heaven and earth; every thing that [the missile] hit was broken and destroyed."[40] Xiangyang's tall drum tower, for example, was destroyed in one thundering crash.[41] Did these trebuchets hurl explosive shells? There's no conclusive evidence, but it would be surprising if they didn't, since, as we've seen, bombs hurled by catapults had been a core component of siege warfare for a century or more. In any case, Xiangyang surrendered in 1273.

The Mongols moved south. A famous Mongol general named Bayan led the campaign, commanding an army of two hundred thousand, most of whom were Chinese. It was probably the largest army the Mongols had commanded, and gunpowder weapons were key arms.[42] In the 1274 Siege of Shayang, for example, Bayan, having failed to storm the walls, waited for the wind to blow from the north and then ordered his artillerists to attack with molten metal bombs (金汁炮).[43] With each strike, "the buildings were burned up and the smoke and flames rose up to heaven."[44] What kind of bomb was this? The sources on the Battle of Shayang don't provide details, but earlier references suggest that it was a type of gunpowder bomb. A reference to it appears in an account of a battle of 1129, when Song general Li Yanxian (李彥仙) was defending a strategic pass against Jin troops. At one point, the Jin attacked the walls day and night with all manner of siege carts, fire carts, sky bridges, and so on, and General Li "resisted at each occasion, and also used molten metal bombs. Wherever the gunpowder touched, everything would disintegrate without a trace."[45] The molten metal bomb was a probably a catapult projectile that contained gunpowder and molten metal, a frightening combination. It didn't work for General Li in 1129: he lost the battle and either committed suicide or was killed, depending on which account you believe, but it did work for Bayan in 1274. He captured Shayang and massacred the inhabitants.

Gunpowder bombs were also present at a more famous Mongol massacre, the Siege of Changzhou of 1275, the last major battle of the Mongol-Song Wars.[46] Bayan arrived there with his army and informed the inhabitants that "if you . . . resist us . . . we shall drain your carcasses of blood and use them for pillows."[47] His warnings were ignored. His troops bombarded the town day and night with fire bombs and then stormed the walls and began slaughtering people.[48] Perhaps a quarter million were killed. Did his troops get new pillows? Sources don't say, but it seems that a huge earthen mound filled with dead bodies lasted for centuries. Bones from the massacre were still being discovered into the twentieth century.[49]

The Song held out for another four years, often with mortal bravery, sometimes even blowing themselves up to avoid capture, as when, in 1276, a Song garrison managed to hold the city of Jingjiang (靖江) in Guangxi Province against a much larger Mongol force for three months before the enemy stormed the walls. Two hundred fifty defenders held a redoubt until it was hopeless and then, instead of surrendering, set off a huge iron bomb. According to the official *Song History*, "the noise was like a tremendous thunderclap, shaking the walls and ground, and the smoke filled up the heavens outside. Many of troops [outside] were startled to death. When the fire was extinguished they went in to see. There were just ashes, not a trace left."[50]

Bombs like this one were the most significant gunpowder weapons in the Song-Mongol Wars, but in retrospect the most important development was the birth of the gun.

The Gun

What is a gun? The efficiency of a projectile-propelling firearm is directly related to how much of the expanding gas from the gunpowder reaction can get past the projectile. The technical term is "windage," and less windage means more energy imparted to the projectile.[51] A true gun therefore has a bullet that fits the barrel. During the Jin-Song Wars, fire lances were loaded with bits of shrapnel, such as ceramics and iron. Since they didn't occlude the barrel, Joseph Needham calls them "coviatives": they were simply swept along in the discharge.[52] Although they could do damage, their accuracy, range, and power were relatively low.

In the late 1100s and the 1200s, the fire lance proliferated into a baffling array of weapons that spewed sparks and flames and ceramics and anything else people thought to put in them. This Cambrian Explosion of forms is similar to that found in the early gunpowder period itself—the fire birds, rolling rocket logs, and so on—and a famous military manual known as the *Book of the Fire Dragon* (火龍經), compiled in the Ming period but partially written in the late 1200s, describes and illustrates many of these weapons, which historians have called, as a general category, "eruptors."[53]

These eruptors had fantastic names. The "filling-the-sky erupting tube" spewed out poisonous gas and fragments of porcelain.[54] The "orifice-penetrating flying sand magic mist tube" (鑽穴飛砂神霧筒) spewed forth sand and poisonous chemicals, apparently into orifices.[55] The "phalanx-charging fire gourd" shot out lead pellets and laid waste to enemy battle formations.[56] We find these and other weapons jumbled together in the *Book of the Fire Dragon*, which makes it difficult to determine when they emerged and how they were used. But unfortunately, we must use whatever sources we can find, because starting in the Song-Mongol Wars, our documentary record becomes sparse, and it remains so through the Mongol period that followed, whose leaders, as I've noted, left unusually poor documentation relative to other Chinese dynasties.[57]

It is clear that fire lances became common during the Mongol-Song Wars. In 1257, a production report for an arsenal in Jiankang Prefecture refers to the manufacture of 333 "fire-emitting tubes" (突火筒),[58] and two years later the *Song History* refers to the production of something quite similar, a "fire-emitting lance" (突火槍), which emitted more than just fire: "It is made from a large bamboo tube, and inside is stuffed a pellet wad (子窠). Once the fire goes off it completely spews the rear pellet wad forth, and the sound is like a bomb that can be heard for five hundred or more paces."[59] Some consider this "pellet wad" to be the first true bullet in recorded history, because although the pellets themselves probably did not occlude the barrel, the wad did.[60]

Yet a truly effective gun must be made of something stronger than bamboo. Traditionally, historians have argued that metal guns emerged after the Mongols defeated the Song and founded the Yuan dynasty in 1279. Researcher Liu Xu, for instance, writes, "It was the Yuan who completed the transition from the bamboo- (or wood- or paper-) bar-reled firearm to the metal-barreled firearm, and the first firearms in history appeared in China in the very earliest part of the Yuan."[61] Simi-larly, other scholars, including Joseph Needham, have suggested a date of around 1280.

Archaeological evidence tends to corroborate this view. Take, for instance, the Xanadu gun, so named because it was found in the ruins of Xanadu (上都), the Mongol summer palace in Inner Mongolia. It is at present the oldest extant gun whose dating is unequivocal, cor-responding to 1298.[62] Like all early guns, it is small: just over six ki-lograms, thirty-five centimeters long. Archaeological context and the straightforward inscription leave little room for controversy about the dating, but it was certainly not the first of its kind. The inscription includes a serial number and other manufacturing information that to-gether indicate that gun manufacture had already been codified and systematized by the time of its fabrication. Moreover, the gun has axial holes at the back that scholars have suggested served to affix it to a mount, allowing it to be elevated or lowered easily for aiming pur-poses. This, too, suggests that this gun was the product of considerable prior experimentation.[63]

The Xanadu gun is the earliest dated gun, but undated finds may predate it.[64] One famous candidate is a piece discovered in 1970 in the province of Heilongjiang, in northeastern China. Historians be-lieve, based on contextual evidence, that it is from around 1288.[65] One careful analysis argues persuasively that it was likely used by Yuan forces to quash a rebellion by a Mongol prince named Nayan (乃顔, d. 1287).[66] Like the Xanadu gun, it is small and light, three and a half kilograms, thirty-four centimeters, a bore of approximately two and a half centimeters.[67]

Yet archaeologists in China have found evidence that may force us to move back the date of the first metal firearms. In 1980, a 108-kilogram bronze gun was discovered in a cellar in Gansu Province.[68] There is no inscription, but contextual evidence suggests that it may be from the late Xi Xia period, from after 1214 but before the end of the Xi Xia in 1227 (Gansu was part of Xi Xia territory).[69] What's intriguing is that it was discovered with an iron ball and a tenth of a kilogram of gunpowder in it. The ball, about nine centimeters in diameter, is a bit smaller than the muzzle diameter of the gun (twelve centimeters), which indicates that it may have been a coviative rather than a true bullet-type projectile.[70] In 1997, a bronze firearm of similar structure but much smaller size (just a kilogram and a half) was unearthed not far away, and the context of its discovery seems to suggest a similar date of origin.[71] Both weapons seem more primitive than the Xanadu gun and other early Yuan guns, rougher in appearance, with uneven casting.[72] Future archaeological discoveries will develop our understanding with greater certitude, but for now, it does seem possible that the earliest metal proto-guns were created in the late Xi Xia state, in the early 1200s.

Although historians debate the precise date of the gun's origin, at present the disputes are in terms of decades.[73] It seems likely that the gun was born during the 1200s and that the Mongols and their enemies aimed guns at each other. After defeating the Song dynasty in 1279 and founding the Yuan dynasty, the Mongols and their Chinese troops invaded Japan, Vietnam, Burma, and Java, wars that stimulated further innovation, although, alas, records are few and say little about gunpowder weapons.

Equally important, although the Yuan brought relative peace within the borders of the Middle Kingdom itself, it was not a lasting peace. As the Yuan dynasty dissolved during the early 1350s, guns played a central role in the bloody wars that followed. The most successful gunpowder lord was a poor monk named Zhu Yuanzhang, whose gunmen succeeded in establishing one of the most impressive dynasties in China's history, the great Ming, which scholars now call the world's first gunpowder empire.[74]

CHAPTER 4

Great Martiality

THE GUNPOWDER EMPEROR

When the strange-looking former Buddhist monk Zhu Yuanzhang founded the Ming dynasty, he declared his reign to be the era of Hongwu, or "Great Martiality." Rarely has there been a more suitable appellation for a reign. He'd defeated his rivals in bitter and bloody wars and driven the Mongols out of China. But the fighting didn't stop once he was emperor. From the dragon throne he directed wars in all directions: north against the Mongols, still a great power; west against a Sinified state based in Sichuan, whose military was tremendously powerful; southwest against the state of Yunnan, whose army of a million soldiers was one of the largest in the world. His successors launched huge expeditions into Vietnam and Mongolia.

The extraordinary success of the Ming dynasty was based on the effective use of guns, and historians in China now celebrate the early Ming as a period of technological brilliance, when Chinese arms—guns in particular—were unparalleled.[1] By 1380, Ming policies stipulated that gunners should comprise 10 percent of soldiers.[2] Since the total number of soldiers at that period was likely between 1.3 and 1.8 million, the number of gun specialists must have been on the order of 130,000 to 180,000, meaning that there were more gunners in early Ming China than knights, soldiers, and pages in France, England, and Burgundy combined.[3] Under Hongwu's successors, the percentage of gunners climbed higher. By the 1430s and 1440s, it reached 20 percent.[4] By 1466, it had risen to 30 percent.[5] In Europe, on the other hand, it wasn't until the mid-1500s that gunners made up 30 percent of infantry units.

Supplying all these men with guns, ammunition, and powder was a massive undertaking, and Hongwu created specialized manufacturing bureaus. His Bureau of Armaments (軍器局) was required to produce, every three years, three thousand bowl-mouth bronze guns, three thousand handheld bronze guns, and three thousand signal cannons, as well as huge amounts of ammunition and accoutrements such as ramrods.[6] His Military Armory Bureau (兵仗局) was responsible for an even wider array of weapons: in addition to bowl mouth cannons and hand-grip guns, it was responsible for producing guns known as "great generals," "secondary generals," "tertiary generals," and "gate seizing generals," as well as "miraculous [fire] lances," "miraculous guns," and "horse-beheading guns," among many other weapons.[7] Of course, we can't be sure that the bureaus produced all they were supposed to, but they were also just the pinnacle of a larger and more distributed system of production, in which enormous numbers of weapons were manufactured at the local level. The Hongwu Emperor oversaw a massive arms industry, the largest and most advanced in the world. Wang Zhaochun is not exaggerating when he writes that "in the Ming Hongwu period, the technology and capacity of gun manufacture was of a highly advanced level, the foremost in the world at the time."[8]

Yet Ming guns were quite different from the classic guns of our imagination, which is to say those of the sixteenth and seventeenth centuries. They were smaller, lighter, and shorter, and they were used in quite different ways. Since Ming guns were similar to those that began appearing outside of China in the 1300s and 1400s, the study of early Ming warfare opens a window on global military history, raising new questions and resolving mysteries that European sources and historiographies cannot address.

The best place to start is with the Hongwu Emperor himself. We could begin his story with the death of his parents in a famine-induced epidemic, or with his flight to a monastery, or with his itinerant begging as a monk, or with his joining a group of rebel Buddhists who called themselves the Red Turbans, but since our subject is guns, we'll begin with a blue-eyed Daoist wanderer who may never have existed.

The only person who actually met this wanderer (or supposedly did) is an equally mysterious character named Jiao Yu (焦玉), who is said to have compiled the philosopher's teachings about guns into the *Book of the Fire Dragon,* a mysterious and controversial tome.[9]

This Jiao Yu says, in his preface to the *Book of the Fire Dragon,* that as a youth he pored over the civil and military classics but was dissatisfied and therefore sought wisdom on the open road. While traversing the Tiantai Mountains he came across a man humming and dancing under a pine tree, black robes fluttering in the wind. Yu bowed in greeting, at which the stranger introduced himself: the Philosopher Who Knows When to Stop. The two men sat together on a boulder, and by the end of their conversation Jiao Yu was convinced he'd found a true sage. The two wandered together until one day Knows When to Stop fixed his blue eyes on Jiao Yu and said he had a secret book that would save the realm and bring peace to the people. He told Jiao Yu to take it to the Huai Valley, where he would find a man who would rise up and establish a new dynasty. Three days later, Knows When to Stop vanished into the mist.

Jiao Yu went to the Huai River Valley, met the young Zhu Yuanzhang, and, recognizing him as the great leader his master had prophesied, demonstrated weapons from the book. The weapons "were found to behave like flying dragons, able to penetrate layers of armor," and the future emperor was delighted.[10] "With these types of fire-weapons," he said, "I shall be able to conquer the whole empire as easily as turning the palms of my hands."[11] And so it was. He vanquished his enemies, established a new dynasty, and instituted special bureaus for the manufacture of powder and guns. "Such," Jiao Yu's preface notes, "was the attention our first sage-emperor paid to military matters."[12]

The story is delightful, but it isn't true. Although Western historians have tended to accept Jiao Yu as a historical figure, Sinophone historians have convincingly demonstrated that there was probably no such person and that the book's famous preface, in which Jiao Yu recounts his meeting with the blue-eyed mystic, was actually composed well after the early Ming period.[13]

Still, the story does illustrate a truth: firearms gave Zhu Yuanzhang an edge in the warlike world of the 1350s.

Ming Firearms in Battle

Consider, for instance, the most famous battle of the early Ming period, the Battle of Poyang Lake of 1363. It was one of the largest naval battles in world history, involving hundreds of vessels and around 500,000 combatants.[14] It also marks the first definitive appearance in historical sources of guns in water warfare.[15]

Poyang Lake was of strategic significance because it connected the Yangze River with other river basins (see Map 4.1). In the early 1360s, Zhu Yuanzhang held key garrisons on the lake, which he administered from his capital in Nanjing, 350 miles downriver. Upstream was the state of Han, controlled by a man named Chen Youliang, who was determined to wrest control of the lake, secure a hold on the lower Yangze, and then advance on Nanjing.

Some sources say that Chen Youliang's invasion force consisted of six hundred thousand men. This is exaggerated, but historians do accept a figure of three hundred thousand, still larger by an order of magnitude than any force a contemporary European state could raise. Chen's men were transported by hundreds of vessels, many of which were "tower ships," floating fortresses three decks high with iron-sided towers for archers and crossbowmen. They were designed not for ship-to-ship combat but for rowing up to riverside cities and depositing soldiers on walls. Chen had managed to take cities in this way before, and his intent was to capture the city of Nanchang, which guarded a key southern approach to Lake Poyang.[16]

Chen hadn't led an expedition himself in years but took personal command, attacking Nanchang in June 1363. The city's commander was Zhu Yuanzhang's nephew Zhu Wenzheng. The walls of Nanchang had been moved back from the shore, so Chen Youliang couldn't just land troops on the ramparts with his tower ships. He landed men on shore and personally led an assault against one of the town's gates. A huge breach was created, but the Ming defenders counterattacked with firearms. The sources are, alas, very terse about the types of weapons used, saying only that the Ming "used guns (火銃) to attack and drive the enemy back."[17] Whatever they were, the guns did the trick. Chen Youliang, unable to capture the town, surrounded it to starve the defenders into submission. Fortunately for them, a small fishing boat

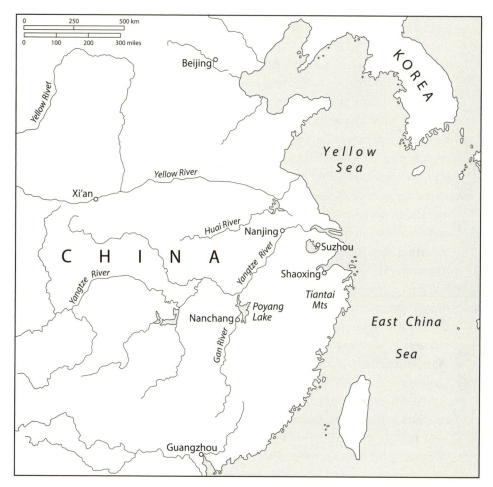

MAP 4.1 Eastern China, with Yangtze River and Poyang Lake.

managed to get through enemy lines, evade patrols, and reach Nanjing to alert Zhu Yuanzhang.

Zhu Yuanzhang immediately prepared a fleet. On 29 August it faced Chen Youliang's much larger fleet on Poyang Lake. The Ming were outnumbered three to two, and Chen's ships towered over theirs, so it's understandable that Zhu Yuanzhang's victory has become so famous.

Yet the way that we imagine this battle is more likely to reflect our own preconceptions than the realities of Ming-era technology. Consider, for example, how the battle was portrayed in a recent historical drama *Zhu Yuanzhang*, which aired on China's Central Television Network in 2006.[18] The scene opens on a misty lake. As the Ming soldiers watch, Chen Youliang's huge ships materialize out of the vapor, a thousand of them, and advance steadily under full sail. When they draw near, a commander yells, "Cannon teams, fire your cannons" (炮隊, 開炮), and the ships begin firing broadsides at each other. Decks explode into splinters. Bodies fly into the air. Chen Youliang's large ships prevail, forcing the Ming to flee while Chen's archers shoot the Ming soldiers who have fallen into the water and Chen's men laugh.

It's a dramatic scene, but the reality was different. For one thing, the drama portrays Chen Youliang's forces as having superior firearms and winning the first engagement, with one of the Ming commanders reporting that "the enemy's cannons were larger than ours, with much larger muzzle bores!" In fact, there is no evidence that Chen Youliang's firearms were superior. There's not even any evidence that Chen Youliang's forces employed gunpowder weapons in this battle at all, although it's quite likely that they did. But there is a more fundamental problem with the scene: the cannons are anachronistic. They look like Western cannons from the 1600s: large guns, on carriages, with long barrels.

The most important difference between such cannons and real Ming cannons is the size. Cannons like those portrayed in the drama would have weighed at least five hundred kilograms, yet most early Ming guns weighed two or three kilograms, and the ones considered at the time "large" weighed only seventy-five or so kilograms.[19] In addition, the cannons in the drama, with their long barrels, have small muzzle bores relative to their length. In reality, early Ming guns were short, with relatively large bores.

So what kind of guns would have been found on Zhu Yuanzhang's ships? Among the early Ming guns excavated in China is a type called the "Great Bowl-Mouth Tube" (大碗口筒), a short, small, wide-mouthed gun. One extant exemplar has an inscription saying that it was produced for a naval defense unit in 1372, nine years after the Battle of Poyang Lake.[20] It weighs just 15.75 kilograms and is short: 36.5 centimeters in length. Its muzzle opening is 11 centimeters in diameter, nearly a third as large as the length of the gun.[21] Other specimens of this type of gun range from about 8.35 to 26.5 kilograms. Thus, although they were not handheld firearms—they were usually mounted on ships or gates—they were nonetheless far smaller than the massive cannons we associate with naval warfare of the sixteenth and seventeenth centuries.[22]

They were also used quite differently. Ming military sources suggest that such guns usually shot stone or iron balls, although it's possible that they were sometimes loaded with pebbles or metal pellets. With their wide mouths and short barrels, accuracy would have been low, and so they were most effective at close range, within fifty paces or so. Most importantly, whereas the naval cannons of the 1600s were designed to blast holes in hulls, these large-mouthed Ming guns were probably used primarily against men. This is a general truth about early Ming guns: they were designed not for bombarding ships or walls but for killing people. This, as we'll see, is an important difference from European weapons.

Perhaps the most important way that the television scene is incorrect is that it depicts just one type of gun, whereas early Ming warfare featured an enormous variety of gunpowder weapons. According to one Ming source, Zhu Yuanzhang's forces on Lake Poyang were armed with "fire bombs, fire guns, fire arrows, fire seeds [probably grenades], large and small fire lances, large and small 'commander' fire-tubes, large and small iron bombs, rockets," and, most odd of all, a weapon called the "No Alternative." This ungainly weapon was "made from a circular reed mat about five inches around and seven feet long that was pasted over with red paper and bound together with silk and hemp—stuffed inside it was gunpowder twisted in with bullets and all kinds of [subsidiary] gunpowder weapons."[23] The No Alternative was hung from a pole on the foremast, and when an enemy ship came into close range, the fuse was lit, the weapon fell onto the enemy ship, and all the things inside shot out "and burned everything to bits, with no hope of salvation."[24]

How were such weapons actually used in the battle? Extant sources describe how Zhu Yuanzhang surveyed the enemy fleet and then said to his generals, "The enemy's great ships are connected together head to tail, which isn't good for advancing or withdrawing. We can destroy them."[25] He divided his fleet into a number of squadrons (twenty or eleven, depending on the source) and ordered them to "prepare fire weapons and bows and crossbows [to be used] in sequence."[26] Then he commanded them to "get close to the enemy's ships and first set off gunpowder weapons (發火器), then bows and crossbows, and finally attack their ships with short range weapons."[27]

This sequence—first firearms, then traditional missile weapons, and then close-range weapons—has been viewed by historians as an early tactical adaptation to gunnery. As Wang Zhaochun writes, "The Decisive Battle of Poyang Lake is the first war in Chinese history in which guns [火銃] (which is to say the earliest shipboard guns) were used in water warfare. This battle employed three methods: first, using, at a long distance, cannons [炮] to attack the enemy fleet and smash and burn the enemy's vessels, destroying and decreasing their combat effectiveness and mobility; second, using bows and crossbows to kill enemy soldiers, further decreasing the enemy ships' combat effectiveness; and, finally, to use short-range units to board the enemy ships and engage in close-quarter combat, wiping out the enemy soldiers in a final action."[28] Wang explicitly contrasts these tactics with those of the Song period, calling Zhu Yuanzhang's tactics the inauguration of a new era (階段) of naval warfare.

In fact, however, it seems that the battle was actually much more like Song battles than Wang would have us believe. To be sure, sources make clear that Ming troops indeed proceeded as ordered, shooting and hurling off the gunpowder weapons that had been readied for deployment. But how precisely were these gunpowder weapons used in the firefight? Wang Zhaochun refers to naval artillery (艦炮) smashing ships, but it is very unlikely there were broadsides à la *Pirates of the Caribbean.* Moreover, given the variety of weapons that the Ming vessels were armed with, how did they coordinate with each other? Fire lances have much shorter ranges than bowl-muzzle guns, for example, and the No Alternative was useful only when an enemy ship was right up against one's own. It seems clear from Zhu Yuanzhang's orders that at least some of the gunpowder weapons had a range greater than that of bows and arrows, since he ordered his men to set off "firearms" first. Yet this term "firearms" (火器) is frustratingly nonspecific. It could refer not just to the new guns but also to old-fashioned fire bombs hurled by catapults. It might even refer to rockets.

Indeed, it seems that old-fashioned fire bombs may have played a key role in this battle. After the first clash of the day proved undecisive, the official *Ming History* says that a commander named Yu Tonghai "took advantage of favorable winds and shot off fire *pao* (發火炮)."[29] When you fire cannons and guns, you must of course take into account prevailing winds, but that's just a matter of compensation when aiming. In this case, the phrase "took advantage of favorable winds" suggests that the Ming were using incendiary gunpowder weapons, and indeed the passage continues to note that the attack succeeded, "burning twenty or more enemy vessels and killing or drowning many enemy troops."[30] It was precisely during this period that the term *pao* began to change its meaning, coming to signify a gun rather than a bomb.[31] In this case, the phrase "shot off fire *pao*" probably refers not to cannons but to firebombs like those that the Song and their enemies lobbed at each other, and they were probably launched by old-fashioned shipborne catapults.[32]

This shouldn't surprise us. It's a pattern in the history of technology that new inventions don't completely displace old ones. During the early Ming, older gunpowder weapons remained in use alongside guns. Military manuals discuss an enormous range of such weapons: fire lances that shot out poison gasses or caltrops; gunpowder arrows and crossbow bolts; exploding rockets; and bombs and grenades that would make Lucifer himself proud, such as arrow and shrapnel bombs, "watermelon" bombs (which shot out hooks and caltrops), "one mother and fourteen children" bombs, and so on.[33]

In fact, in the Battle of Poyang Lake, the gun attacks didn't defeat Chen Youliang. The most decisive attack employed the oldest combustion weapon of all: fire, although that fire was fortified by gunpowder.

The first day of battle had left Zhu Yuanzhang's commanders disheartened. Despite their victories, Chen Youliang was still in a better position. Some Ming commanders even advised leaving Poyang Lake to Chen Youliang and regrouping elsewhere. Zhu said they must fight, but when the battle resumed two days later, many remained diffident. The enemy ships "seemed like mountains."[34] Zhu had ten of his commanders beheaded for failing to press the attack.

An underling suggested a new tactic: "If our men would obey orders, the [enemy's] large vessels wouldn't stand up to our smaller ones. Nonetheless, I believe that without employing a fire attack we cannot prevail."[35] The *Ming Veritable Records* describes what happened next:

"[Zhu Yuanzhang] ordered that seven boats be prepared, loaded with reeds and prepared with gunpowder. Man-shaped bundles of straw were dressed up in armor and helmets and posed, each one holding lances as though fighting the enemy. He ordered that men unafraid of death be found to man them and that fast warships follow behind to press the enemy vessels."[36]

The fireboats floated into Chen Youliang's ships, and although the wind was mild at first, Ming forces managed to get the fires stoked. When the wind picked up the fire spread. "Several hundred of their fortress ships were entirely burned. Smoke and flames rose up to the skies, making the water red. Half of them were killed."[37] Some of Chen Youliang's top commanders were burned to death, including his younger brothers. Ming troops pushed their advantage, boarded the ships, and began hacking away at the enemy, capturing two thousand heads.

This fire attack, not the earlier gun attack, was the turning point in the Battle of Poyang Lake, and as the fighting continued, Chen Youliang's commanders began defecting to Zhu. Eventually Chen Youliang himself was killed, pierced through the eye by an arrow. In early October, the remainder of his forces surrendered, and Zhu Yuanzhang became the most powerful hegemon in the "contest of rivals."

The Battle of Poyang Lake is seen in China as a landmark in the history of gunpowder weapons, and indeed guns played a role, but they were not decisive. Moreover, they were deployed quite differently than once thought. This was also true of many other battles in the violent wars of the fourteenth century, including one particularly instructive battle: the 1366 Siege of Suzhou, a city held by Zhu Yuanzhang's other main rival, the wealthy and wily Zhang Shicheng (張士誠, 1321–1367). Zhu Yuanzhang's gunpowder weapons played a key role, but, again, the details do not support our standard image of gun warfare.

The Siege of Suzhou, 1366

When we think about siege warfare in the gunpowder age, we are wont to imagine rows of cannons bombarding walls, and historians have suggested that this image is justified in the case of the Siege of Suzhou in 1366. One Ming specialist writes that "flaming arrows and rockets were used for incendiary purposes, while cannon of a more standard cast battered the walls."[38] Another historian, one of the West's top experts on China's military history, writes, "Zhu's army completely enclosed the city [of Suzhou] in a circumvallation, and pounded it with artillery. Ten months of firing resulted in that rare occurrence in Chinese city fortifications, a wall breach."[39]

Yet if we look carefully at the historical sources, we see that guns played a minor role—if any—in getting through Suzhou's walls. To be sure, guns were present during the siege, and they were significant, but just as the cannons on Poyang Lake weren't used to destroy ships, so the guns at Suzhou weren't used to breach walls. Just as at Poyang, guns were aimed at human beings. Suzhou's fortifications were targeted not by guns but by weapons of a more traditional sort: trebuchets hurling stones and bombs.

To understand the Siege of Suzhou, we must keep in mind two things: walls were thick and guns were small. Historians have suggested that Suzhou had "weak fortifications."[40] This is a misconception. Various sources suggest that the commanders who invested Suzhou saw its fortifications as formidable. As one contemporary wrote, "Suzhou's walls were strong and its troops were excellent. It had been attacked many times and not fallen."[41] The city's walls had been rebuilt in 1352, and records indicate that its seventeen kilometers of walls were over seven meters high, eleven meters thick at the base, and five meters thick at the top.[42] Moreover, the walls were made of tamped earth and faced with brick, which made them highly resistant to artillery, the force of whose projectiles was absorbed by the earthen core.[43] The walls were also battered, meaning that they sloped markedly from bottom to top.[44] This, too, would have protected them against projectiles fired horizontally, whose force would be deflected rather than imparted directly to the wall.

These three characteristics—the thickness, the earth fill, and the slope—were not unusual for a Chinese city, and they made Suzhou's walls highly resistant to artillery. Historians have suggested that the wall breach at Suzhou was the rarest of occurrences in Chinese sieges.[45] It's true that wall breaches were extremely uncommon in Chinese military history up through the mid-seventeenth century, but the breach at Suzhou in 1366 wasn't even a proper wall breach. The breakthrough occurred at a gate, and it seems that it wasn't caused by guns.

Zhu Yuanzhang's famous commander Xu Da (徐達, 1332–1385), who directed the siege, recognized that it would be nearly impossible to break through Suzhou's walls, so he prepared for a long blockade, sealing the city off by surrounding it with fortifications. A man named Yu Ben (俞本), who lived through the early Ming period, described the blockade: "[Xu] Da ordered all his divisions to set up camps outside the four sides of the walls. They prepared long moats, which connected all around. They also set up structures called 'enemy towers' to help them take the city, they four zhang [thirteen meters] high. From them one could peer into the city and watch the men and women walking about, and one could see details and count the people."[46] Other sources note that the towers were three stories high, as tall as the famous pagodas within Suzhou itself.[47]

These "enemy towers" were also heavily armed. "On each story," the *Ming Veritable Records* notes, "were placed bows and crossbows and guns."[48] Here the word I translate as "guns" is *huo chong* (火銃), which would become a standard term for firearms during the Ming period. Other sources about the Siege of Suzhou employ an older term: "fire tubes" (*huo tong* 火筒).[49]

How many guns were present at the Siege of Suzhou? Yu Ben notes that each of the forty-eight Ming divisions (*wei* 衛) that invested the city was equipped with fifty or more large and small "general tubes" (大小將軍筒), twenty-four hundred guns in all.[50] When Edward Dreyer writes about the "standard cannon" that he believes battered Suzhou's walls and eventually created a breach, these "general tubes" are presumably the guns he has in mind. Later in the Ming period, the term "great general cannon" did indeed refer to large pieces, weighing hundreds of kilograms, and in the late Ming period (post-1550 or so) some weigh a thousand kilograms or more. But during the early Ming period (i.e., before 1500), "general guns" were much smaller and were usually used as mobile field guns.[51]

Indeed, of the extant early Ming guns—that is, from the 1350s through the mid-1400s—nearly all are less than eighty kilograms in weight, and the great majority weigh a couple kilograms or less. Guns considered "large" weighed only seventy-five kilograms.[52] The only exception is a trio of guns from 1377, which were a meter long, with a muzzle diameter of twenty-one centimeters, and which had two handles on either side, shaped for easy grip for human transport.[53] The existence of these guns shows—if any proof were needed—that Zhu Yuanzhang's arsenals were capable of making larger guns. But what is notable is that these are the only relatively large guns preserved from the early Ming period (pre-1500), and no other examples are known either from archaeological or textual evidence.[54] These guns were an anomaly: during the fourteenth and fifteenth centuries Chinese guns remained small and light.[55]

Given that even industrial age artillery had trouble overcoming traditional Chinese walls, it seems certain that the small guns of the early Ming period could have had little effect on Suzhou's walls. So what were the twenty-four hundred guns used for? We lack for the Siege of Suzhou any day-to-day account such as those we've seen for Song-era sieges, but we can gain a sense of how sieges were conducted by examining other accounts from the same period. Eight years before the Siege of Suzhou, Zhu Yuanzhang's forces besieged Shaoxing (紹興), which was held by one of Zhang Shicheng's generals. An insider's account has survived, perhaps because Zhu's forces failed to capture the city.[56]

The account suggests that guns were aimed at people, not fortifications. For example, on one occasion the defenders "used . . . fire tubes to attack the enemy's advance guard" (以炮石火筒擊其前鋒).[57] On another occasion, a defending commander sallied against the attackers: "the fire tubes went off all at once, and the [attackers'] great army could not stand against them and had to withdraw."[58] But perhaps the most intriguing passage in this account describes how one of Zhu Yuanzhang's commanders, Marshall Cai, was struck by a bullet while he sat, bedecked in armor, and directed his men in their attack. The author of the account writes, "Our troops used fire tubes to shoot and fell him, and the great army quickly lifted him and carried him back to his fortifications."[59] This indicates not only that guns were used against humans, but also that they were considered accurate enough to aim at individual targets from a distance. In any case, they weren't used against walls. German Sinologist Herbert Franke wrote a detailed study of the Siege of Shaoxing, and he noted that guns "could not cause much damage to walls or gates" and that "their use was limited to man-to-man fighting."[60]

Evidence from the Siege of Suzhou, eight years later, is much sparser, but it, too, suggests that guns were used against people not walls. In fact, scholars claim that a gun killed Zhang Shicheng's younger brother Zhang Shixin, one of the highest ranked officials in the Zhang political organization. Shixin was directing operations from up on top of Suzhou's walls, where he'd established a command post with a tent. He made a tempting target. One day, as he was sitting in a silver chair, being served a meal by attendants, "a flying pao suddenly broke his head open and he died."[61] He hadn't even tasted his food.

It's a famous incident, immortalized in a poem called "The Bronze General," which describes how Zhang Shicheng established his regime, how his younger brother, Zhang Shixin, held the reins of power and caused chaos, and how the bronze general (the gun) acted on behalf of heaven to destroy Shixin and help end the Zhang regime, bringing peace to the world:

> The bronze general—
> No eyes, but the sighting is accurate
> No ears, but the hearing is supernatural.
> [Zhang Shicheng] came south to start a government . . .
> Strong troops, rich land
> four countries joined . . .
> But the younger brother
> occupies the position of prime minister (國鈞)
> and holds the reins of power. . . .
> [When] waterborne troops, ten thousand crossbows
> overwhelm and shake the marshes . . .
> the gods are worried, the ghosts are scared
> ten thousand people cry.
> The bronze general
> acts on behalf of heaven.
> A sudden thunderclap
> an attack
> and smashed to pieces [are]
> a thousand metal bodies.
> The demon tendrils are hacked,
> and the roots of evil yanked out.
> For three days the raging flames
> burn the jade-colored clouds

but finally [Zhang Shicheng]

is taken west

hands tied

to be a guest of [Zhu Yuanzhang].[62]

As this poem suggests, the death of Zhang Shixin was a central event in this siege, and Chinese historians have made a great deal of it, from the famous Ming scholar Qian Qianyi to the world's greatest expert on the history of Chinese guns, Wang Zhaochun, who cites the incident as evidence that guns were becoming increasingly important in warfare.[63]

But was Zhang Shixin really killed by a gun? The most authoritative source, the *Ming Veritable Records*, says he was killed by a "flying pao" (飛炮), which sounds more like a projectile hurled by catapult than a bullet. This interpretation is corroborated by Yu Ben, who says that Shixin was "struck in the cheek by a stone pao and died" (頰中石炮而死).[64] Another good source says that "a war catapult smashed to pieces his head and he died" (忽戰礮碎其首而死).[65] And a third says that he was "hit by a catapult stone and died" (中礮死).[66] The notion that Shixin was killed by a bronze general gun may well have begun with the poem itself, although the famous scholar Qian Qianyi, writing in the mid-1600s, says Shixin was killed by a "Longjing cannon" (龍井炮).[67] There's no way to know for sure, but the bulk of the evidence does suggest a catapult bomb.

And this raises an important point: the Siege of Suzhou involved hundreds of catapults. According to Yu Ben, each of the forty-eight divisions investing the city set up five Xiangyang Catapults and five or more catapults of a type called "Seven-Component Catapults" (七梢炮).[68] Xiangyang catapults were based on the designs brought by the Mongol's Islamic engineers and were enormously powerful. "Seven-Component Catapults" seem to have been a non-counterweighted, less powerful type.[69]

In any case, catapults—not guns—were Zhu Yuanzhang's structure-destroying machines at Suzhou. "Everything they struck," the *Ming History* notes, "immediately burst into pieces."[70] Of course, this sentence refers not to the walls themselves but to the wooden structures on and within them, the targets at which the catapults were aimed. Even the Xiangyang-style catapults could cause little damage to Suzhou's thick earthencore walls. Yu Ben says that there were four hundred eighty or so catapults at Suzhou, and they operated incessantly: "the noise of the guns and the paos went day and night and didn't stop."[71] Although we can't be sure, it's likely that they hurled not just stones but also bombs. In any case, the various accounts of the siege agree that the catapults were powerful: "within the walls there was fear and shock."[72]

Yet the besieged built catapults of their own. A man named Xiong Tianrui (熊天瑞) "taught those within the city to make an imposing catapult [pao] to attack the troops outside, and many were hit and wounded. Within the city, all the wood and stone was used up, to the point that they tore down temples and people's dwellings to use as catapult tools."[73] In response, the attackers constructed covered wooden structures within which men could hide. In this way, they advanced toward the walls, "and arrows and stones couldn't hurt them."[74]

Eventually the attackers made a breach. But if neither guns nor catapults had much effect on Suzhou's walls, how did they do it?

By attacking the gates. It was very rare in Chinese history for a siege to be decided by the breaching of walls, which were simply too impregnable. Armies either stormed walls, starved a city into submission, or aimed their efforts at the gates. Gates were also good targets from a psychological standpoint because they were symbols of the city's power and authority. But we Westerners, to whom the word "gate" calls up an image of a castle drawbridge, must adjust our perspective. The gates of Chinese towns were much more imposing than standard Western city gates.

In fact, the first thing you would see as you approached a Chinese city were the curved and ornate roofs of the wooden gate towers, which loomed above the gates and could rise to a height of eighty to a hundred feet (twenty-five to thirty meters). Since Chinese cities had few other multistory structures, gate towers were often their most prominent structures. They also had civic and spiritual significance, housing offices and serving as sites for ceremonies and public announcements.[75] But the gate you saw from the outside of the wall was just one part of a complex structure. Once you made it through you found yourself in a sort of courtyard, with tall walls all around. You had to pass through another thick gateway before entering the city proper. Many gates complexes were also guarded by outworks, structures that prevented easy access to even the outer gate. Suzhou had six gate complexes, five of which had both a land entrance and a water entrance, for boats and barges. Some were defended by outworks that had been built in 1352.

One of the first thing attackers would do when investing a city was to try to destroy gate towers with catapults and firebombs, attacking the physical structure, but also making an assault on the symbolic authority of the gate. The towers, being made of wood, were quite vulnerable. But the gates below them were much more troublesome for an attacker, who had to get past the outwork, get through the outer gate, pass through the kill zone of the gate courtyard, and then get through the inner gate.

Suzhou's gates held for ten months, but by mid-autumn of 1367 the defenders were weakening. The city's grain had been eaten "and even one mouse cost up to a hundred pieces of copper cash, and when the mice were gone, they even boiled the leather from the bottom of their old shoes and ate that."[76] Zhu Yuanzhang's commander, general Xu Da, felt it was a good time to force an entrance. While he attacked the Feng Gate, his subordinate Chang Yuchun focused on the Chang Gate, which was protected by new outworks. (Suzhou was unusual in that its gates had single-character names, a sign of its ancient heritage.) Both attacks succeeded:

> Da led his troops to burst through the Feng Gate. Meanwhile, Chang Yuchun broke through the new outworks at the Chang Gate, led his troops across the bridge, and advanced to a place beneath the walls [at the Chang Gate] where the fortifications were weaker. The head of the imperial council [on Zhang Shicheng's side], Tang Jie, climbed up on the walls and offered a stiff defense, while Shicheng himself set up his troops within the gates, ordering the counsellors Xie Jie and Zhou Ren to set up stockades and mend the external walls. Tang Jie couldn't endure and surrendered his troops. Zhou Ren, Xu Yi, Pan Yuanzhao . . . and others all surrendered. In the late afternoon, Shicheng's troops were routed, and all the [Ming] generals swarmed like ants up the fortifications, and the walls were taken.[77]

Here it seems like there was indeed some breaching of walls, but this occurred at the gate structure itself, and it quite possibly took place through the gate itself. Moreover, there is no record of cannons or catapults being used to effect this breach. It was probably done by traditional manual mining or battering, since the accounts focus on troops and men, not on machines of any kind. In any case, Zhu Yuanzhang's forces made it into the double-gate security area, where defenders fought to keep them from passing through but finally succumbed.

Having secured the gate complex, Zhu Yuanzhang's troops poured into the city. For a time, Shicheng held out with twenty thousand troops, but ultimately he withdrew to his palace, where his wives and concubines burned themselves to death. He tried to hang himself but was captured and taken back to Nanjing, as "a guest."[78]

Both the Siege of Suzhou and the Battle of Poyang Lake show that early Ming guns were different from the classic guns of our imagination. They were smaller, and they were used not to destroy ships and walls but to kill people. Catapults were the missile weapon of choice for destroying structures, hurling stones or bombs, both explosive and conflagrative.

Chinese guns remained small through the 1400s and well into the 1500s.[79] Some historians believe that a collection of guns known as the Zhou cannons, which weighed between fifty and two hundred fifty kilograms, were cast by Zhang Shicheng in the 1350s or 1360s, but recent work establishes beyond a doubt that they were actually made in the 1670s, and all extant pieces that actually were from Zhang Shicheng's time were small.[80]

China thus did not develop wall-destroying gunpowder artillery. Its guns remained small and were used for antipersonnel purposes. In contrast, European guns became very large indeed. Historians have lauded this European genius for artillery, suggesting that large guns inaugurated the "age of gunpowder empires" and underlay European military power starting in the late medieval period.[81] Why did Chinese guns stay small while Europeans became large? To answer that question we must look at the early history of guns in Europe.

PART II

Europe Gets the Gun

CHAPTER 5

The Medieval Gun

Scholars today overwhelmingly concur that the gun was invented in China.[1] Yet it is a curious fact that early evidence of guns seems to be scarce or absent in the lands between China and Europe. In Iran and Central Asia, firm evidence of firearms emerges only in the late fourteenth century. In India the first clear references do not occur until around 1442. In the Middle East and other western Islamic areas, the earliest reliable references are from the 1360s or 1370s, although some evidence suggests that guns were present in Andalusia as early as the 1330s.[2] Russian chronicles seem not to have reliable mentions of firearms until 1382. As Thomas Allsen notes—and there is no better authority on medieval technology transfer across Eurasia—"in the Latin West the first uncontestable evidence of firearms is from 1326, surprisingly somewhat earlier than in the lands that lie between China . . . and western Europe."[3]

We know that guns were born in China because China's records have, and Europe's records lack, evidence of precursors. The fire lance, ancestor of the gun, emerged in China in the tenth or eleventh century, and, as we've seen, it appears over and over again in sources from the following centuries. We have traced the stages of its development, its barrel made first of bamboo or paper, then of metal, its lethality increasingly based on projectiles rather than sparks and flames, until it eventually evolved into a primitive gun.

There are no records of any such developments in Europe.[4] The gun appears fully formed around 1326. As Joseph Needham writes, "all the long preparations and tentative experiments were made in China, and everything came to Islam and the West fully fledged, whether it was the fire-lance or the explosive bomb, the rocket or the metal-barrel hand-gun and bombard."[5] Similarly, whereas formulas for gunpowder varied widely in China, with differing proportions of the three ingredients—saltpeter, sulfur, and charcoal—the range of variation in European recipes is far lower.[6] This variation is evidence of experimentation in China, where gunpowder was at first used as an incendiary and only later became an explosive and a propellant. In contrast, formulas in Europe diverged only very slightly from the ideal proportions for use as an explosive and a propellant, suggesting that gunpowder was introduced as a mature technology.

The fact that gunpowder arrived in Europe already formulated for military use is reflected in the fact that in most European languages the mixture is generally referred to as *gun*powder. Whereas the Chinese referred to it as the "fire-drug" and explored a variety of different uses, both military and nonmilitary, Europeans immediately began using it almost exclusively for its explosive and propellant qualities in warfare. The Chinese origins of gunpowder technology was also reflected in odd traces and vestiges, as for example, in the fact that an Andalusian botanist referred to saltpeter as "Chinese snow," while in Persia it was called "Chinese salt."[7] As an expert in European medieval history writes, "gunpowder came [to Europe], not as an ancient mystery, but as a well-developed modern technology, in a manner very much like twentieth-century 'technology-transfer' projects."[8]

The fact that guns spread within fifty years from China to Europe may seem mysterious. Previous Chinese inventions—such as the compass, printing, and paper—took centuries to travel across the steppes and seas and take root in Europe. Why did guns spread so quickly? Oddly, scholars have found no clear route of transmission. Most agree that the Mongols were the most likely vector, or, to be more precise, the many people employed or protected by the Mongols: soldiers, artisans, merchants. But it is probably the fact that gunpowder had a clear military application that best explains the speed of its diffusion.

We will probably never know precisely when or how guns arrived in Europe, but what is clear is that it had happened by the 1320s, which is when the first unambiguous references to guns appear in European

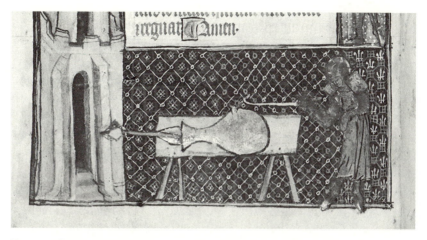

FIGURE 5.1 Early representation of a gun in Europe, ca. 1326.

From Walter de Milemete, *De Nobilitatibus, sapientii et prudentiis regum* [Concerning the majesty, wisdom, and prudence of kings], preserved at Christ Church College, Oxford, manuscript 92, fol. 70v. With thanks to the Governing Body of Christ Church, Oxford.

sources.[9] The most famous is an illustration found in an illuminated manuscript of 1326–1327: Walter de Milemete's *De Nobilitatibus, sapientii et prudentiis regum* (Concerning the Majesty, Wisdom, and Prudence of Kings) (see Figure 5.1).[10] It shows what is unmistakably a gun with a large arrow emerging from it. A man has lowered a long stick to the touchhole to light it off. Another illustration of the same year is quite similar, showing a darker gun of the same shape being set off by a group of knights. The two may in fact have been drawn by the same artist, because the works that they appear in are both by Walter de Milemete.[11]

Around the time the Milemete manuscripts were produced, guns were referenced in a decree by the government of Florence (February 1326), which tasked officials to make metal guns for defense.[12] A record from the following year from the Turin area notes that a certain sum was paid "for the making of a certain instrument or device made by Friar Marcello for the projection of pellets of lead."[13] A few years later, guns seem to have been deployed by two German knights at the Siege of Cividale (Friuli) (1331).[14]

There is some evidence suggesting that guns were unknown before the 1320s, because in 1321 a well-traveled Venetian gave a comprehensive list of weapons to be used in a new crusade in the Holy Lands, and the list does not include gunpowder weapons.[15] Of course absence of evidence is not evidence of absence, and it's always possible that new sources will be uncovered, but for now scholars accept the mid-1320s as the date when guns first came into use in Europe.

They spread quickly. In 1341 the town of Lille had a "tonnoire master" (a tonnoire was an arrow-hurling gun).[16] In 1344, the town of Ehrenfel in Germany had a firearms master (*Fürschutzen*), as did Mainz (*Feueurschütze*).[17] In 1345, Toulouse had two iron cannons. In 1346, Aix-la-Chapelle possessed wrought iron cannons that shot arrows (*busa ferrea ad sagittandum tonitrum*). Around 1348, the town of Deventer possessed three *dunrebussen*, or cannons,[18] while Frankfurt had cannons that shot arrows (*büszenpyle*).[19]

Those who could make guns were highly prized, although it was a risky occupation. This was made clear to a man named Peter de Bruges on a late summer day in 1346. The consuls of the town of Tournai had asked him to make them a gun and were gathered just outside town to watch him test it. Peter loaded it with a large arrow tipped with a one-kilogram piece of lead and then aimed it at the town wall, presumably for safety. The gun went off with "a terrible and tremendous noise," but when the smoke cleared, the arrow wasn't in or near the wall. Did it fly over, into the town? People searched the streets but found no trace. Finally they discovered that the arrow had soared over the town, fallen into a monastery plaza on the other side, and struck a man right in the head, killing him.[20] When Peter heard the news, he ran, afraid he'd be prosecuted for murder. But the consuls decided it wasn't his fault, just a sad accident.[21]

Because of their noise and ability to spew death, guns quickly acquired a reputation as infernal instruments. Around 1344, Petrarch wrote, "I wonder that thou hast not also brazen globes, which are cast forth by the force of flame with a horrible sound of thunder. Was not the wrath of an immortal god thundering from heaven sufficient, that the small being man—oh cruelty joined to pride—must even thunder on earth? Human rage has endeavored to imitate the thunder which cannot be imitated . . . and that which is wont to be sent from the clouds is now thrown from an infernal instrument."[22] Petrarch compared guns to the plague, virulent and all-too-common. Writing in 1344, he noted, "This plague was only recently so rare as to be looked on as a miracle;

now . . . it has become as common as any other kind of weapon."[23] Although he judged the invention to be hubristic, others saw them as frankly demonic. The Englishman John Mirfield spoke of "that devilish instrument of war colloquially termed gunne."[24] Francesco di Giorgio Martini thought that the discovery of guns and gunpowder was to be attributed "not to human but to devilish agency."[25]

What were these early European guns like? The guns depicted in the Milemete manuscript of 1326–1327 look like vases turned on the side, bulbous with a narrow neck. Other early references suggest that this shape was common. A record from 1338 notes that the city of Rouen had an "pot that shot iron arrows with fire" (*pot de fer à traire garros à feu*), which was equipped with saltpeter and sulfur "to make powder to shoot the aforementioned arrows."[26] In those days, the word "pot" in both England and France was used to refer to metal urn- or flask-shaped objects. In fact, pot makers, or, as they were called in England, "potters," who worked primarily in copper and bronze, were among the most prominent early gun makers.[27]

Yet it's hard to get a clear sense of what early European guns were like because there are so few extant ones, especially when compared to China, in which many early guns are still extant. This may partly be attributed to the fact that Chinese guns nearly always have dates inscribed on them while European ones do not, but it also seems that early European guns simply haven't been preserved, probably because there weren't as many of them as there were Chinese guns. There were around a hundred thousand gunners in late fourteenth-century Ming armies, at least an order of magnitude more than in Western Europe at the same period. Whereas we have dozens of Chinese guns that we are certain are from the 1300s, only one surviving European gun can be firmly dated to that century, and it has been dated to 1399, which is quite late—by then guns had undergone considerable development.[28]

There is one extant European gun that most experts believe was produced well before the end of the fourteenth century: the Loshult gun, named after the Swedish parish where a farmer dug it up in 1861.[29] It is small, just nine kilograms in weight, and short, at thirty centimeters. It is thus remarkably close in size and weight to the earliest Chinese guns, such as the Xanadu gun of 1298 (about six kilograms and thirty-five centimeters).[30] Yet whereas the Yuan guns are tubular, the Loshult gun

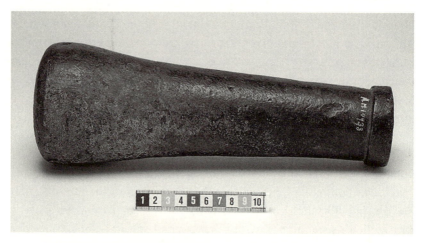

FIGURE 5.2 The Loshult gun, fourteenth century.

This gun is one of the few fourteenth-century guns preserved in Europe. It is small, just nine kilograms in weight, and short, just thirty centimeters long. It is in the collection of the Swedish Historical Museum, Stockholm, SHM 2891. Courtesy of Statens Historiska Museum, Stockholm.

is similar in shape to the guns in the Milemete manuscript illustration (see Figure 5.2).

The Loshult gun has been the subject of considerable debate. One question is whether it shot arrows like the Milemete guns. To find out, enterprising scholars built a replica and fired it on a Danish artillery range, using powder mixed from medieval recipes (but with modern ingredients). They found it could shoot both arrows and other projectiles—lead balls, grapeshot, pieces of flint—and it performed surprisingly well. The arrows and lead balls were able to penetrate iron sheets that were the thickness of late medieval plate armor much more effectively than arrows from medieval-style longbows.[31] It was also more accurate than expected, able to hit a stationary target at two hundred meters. Yet scholars believe it was most likely used at close range, because there are deep ruts and scratches in the barrel, indicating that it was used to fire shrapnel—inaccurate but lethal.[32]

Not all early European guns looked like the Loshult gun, squat and vaselike. Others looked like the Chinese fire lance: a metal tube with a socket in the back for the placement of a wooden stock, used to hold and aim. For instance, the Tannenberg gun, dated to 1399, was of this

Figure 5.3 European tiller gun, early 1400s.

This illustration depicts a firearm that was quite similar to Chinese guns of the same period, with a clear lineage to the Chinese fire lance. Konrad Kyeser of Eichstadt, manuscript from ca. 1400, Georg-August-Universität Göttingen, Niedersächsische Staats- und Universitätsbibliothek Göttingen, Ms. Philos. 64, fol. 104v. Courtesy of Niedersächsische Staats- und Universitätsbibliothek Göttingen.

type, and its wooden staff was discovered with it but decayed once exposed to air.[33] Similar stock guns may be referred to in the earliest European records of guns in battle. When King Edward III of England launched the famous sieges of Crécy and Calais in 1346, some of his soldiers were equipped with guns that had tillers (or "telars"), which may have been stocks of this type, although they may instead have served as supports.[34] Manuscript illustrations show stock guns in action. One famous example, from around 1400, shows a soldier in armor aiming one while touching a red-hot iron rod to its touchhole (see Figure 5.3). In China, too, guns in this period were fired by means of an iron rod with a red-hot tip. Sometimes stock guns were mounted on carriages, many per carriage, and fired at advancing enemies, just as Chinese fire lances were.[35] But what is most striking about early European guns is how small they were.

Little Guns

Whereas later European pieces grew far larger than anything found in China, early European guns would not have been out of place in the Chinese context. The Loshult gun weighs only nine kilograms. The gun with which Peter de Bruges inadvertently killed a man was also quite small, shooting a lead-tipped arrow of only one kilogram. Most stock guns were designed to be operated by one gunner, and some allowed one person to operate two guns.[36]

To be sure, we lack extant examples of early guns, and it is possible that large guns simply haven't survived, but an innovative nineteenth-century scholar named Henry Brackenbury found a way to use textual evidence to estimate the sizes of early European guns. He reasoned that since the cost of a gun was directly related to the amount of metal used to make it, one could deduce gun sizes from price data. He pored over early sources recording the costs of forging and casting guns—and there were many such sources. For example, one French receipt from 1342 notes that twenty-five livres were paid for the manufacture of five bronze cannons and five iron ones. Using comparative price and wage data, Brackenbury figured that this sum would have sufficed to purchase five wrought iron cannons of eleven kilograms each and five of bronze weighing ten kilograms each.[37]

His exhaustive survey led him to conclude that until the middle of the 1300s guns averaged around twenty-five pounds (eleven kilograms) and none exceeded about a hundred and twenty pounds or so (fifty-four kilograms). They increased slightly in size over the next couple decades, but not by much. His research led him to conclude that early European guns were "but feeble weapons in comparison with the great warlike engines of the period [i.e., catapults], which still were employed for the more serious operations."[38] Other scholars have confirmed his work and extended it, and he has modern admirers.[39] One of today's foremost historians of early artillery writes that Brackenbury "is one of the few authors who uses the documentary evidence in a systematic and thorough manner and one which later writers have singularly failed to follow."[40]

Because they were so small, early European guns were useless against fortifications. Peter de Bruges knew this, which is why when he tested his gun he pointed it at the town wall, and the town councilors who watched the test clearly weren't worried about their masonry. As Brackenbury wrote, early European guns "had little or no effect against the walls of cities or castles; they were quite incapable of making, or even assisting to make, a breach."[41]

So how were these guns used? For Ming China we have many descriptions of guns used on the battlefield: against Chinese rebels, Shan elephants, and Mongol horsemen. But Western military historians have found few such descriptions.[42]

One of the earliest cases in which scholars believe guns were used is the Battle of Crécy of 1346. Crécy is among the most famous battles of the medieval age, and it's frequently held up as a triumph for English longbowmen. Yet guns also played a role. The English king, outnumbered by the French, had chosen a hilltop spot near a windmill to make his stand. He arranged his supply carts into a makeshift fortress and had his men dig ruts and trenches to trip up the enemy. Then, as rain fell, he watched the arrival of the French from the windmill and positioned his troops. How precisely they were placed is the subject of much controversy, but the Florentine chronicler Giovanni Villani, whose accounts are considered quite accurate, writes "The English king arranged his archers, of whom he had many, on the carts, and some below and with guns [bombarde] that threw out small iron pellets [pallottole] with fire, to frighten the French horsemen and cause them to desert."[43] Note that although the term "bombard" later came to refer to large guns, in those days it just referred to guns of any kind.[44]

The English guns were probably intended to protect the archers from knights, because the longbowmen's arrows were too light to penetrate the knights' thick armor. Although early guns were less accurate than longbows, and much slower to load, they were very powerful. As we've seen, the replica of the Loshult gun easily shot through thick iron plate. So the English archers probably stood above, with a clear view of the action, ready to shoot long-range at knights' horses and other targets, while the gunners stood below, with less visibility because they needed less range. They would fire when the knights got near enough, hoping not just to kill some armored men but also to frighten their horses.

Were their guns loaded with individual pellets, one to a gun, or were they loaded with many pellets each, the grapeshot approach? A series of English records contains information about the kinds of guns and shot that the English king ordered for his expedition to France. Some records specify large ready-formed pellets, while others specify large unformed pieces of lead, which could be molded into the desired form on site, depending on the requirements of circumstance.[45] The grapeshot approach would be more effective at short range, and the fact that Villani says that the guns ejected "small pellets with fire" is an intriguing clue. It might mean simply that fire was used to project the pellets, but it's also possible that it means that the fire was spewed for a good distance along with the pellets, which is what happens when pellets are coviatives—that is, if they don't occlude the barrel but are ejected as part of the spray of fire. In this case, these guns might have been more akin to Chinese fire lances.

It's impossible to tell, of course, but what is clear is that the guns were effective. The French led the attack not with their knights but with Genoese crossbowmen, thousands strong. The crossbow was a fearsome weapon, but the crossbowmen had left their shields in the French baggage carts. As they advanced over the wet ground, yelling, with drums and horns blowing, the English waited. Only when the Genoese had raised their crossbows and begun to shoot did the English archers let fly, their arrows filling the sky so that it "looked like a cloud in the air."[46] The guns, too, began to shoot, "and the blows of the guns caused such fear and tumult that it seemed as if God was thundering, and there was great slaughter of people and bashing [sfondamento] of horses."[47] The arrows and guns caused damage and panic, but the poor Genoese perhaps suffered even more from their own allies. Chronicles say that when they began to withdraw, French knights trampled right over them, wounding many, either because they wanted to force them back into battle or because they were overly eager to get to the English.[48]

The English and their allies took advantage of the confusion to press the attack, possibly with guns. According to an anonymous chronicle, "when the men-at-arms [*cavalieri*] of England saw that so many French-men had been injured, they mounted their horses . . . and, along with many Welshmen, who were like wild men, and others as well, along with many guns [*bombarde*], they vigorously attacked the French camp, firing all the guns at once, at which the French began to flee."[49] Were the guns really mobile enough to press an attack like this? It's possible, since early guns were small, but the only thing we can be sure about concerning the further course of the battle at Crécy—or indeed any part of the Battle of Crécy—is that it was extremely confusing and that the English won overwhelmingly.[50] Moreover, guns were far from the most important factor in English success.[51] Longbowmen deserve the primary credit.

Indeed, Western historians have consistently argued that firearms were not of much use on the battlefields of Europe in the late medieval period, which is to say before 1500 or so. Although historians of Europe believe that large guns became significant by the 1380s or so, they have considered handheld guns secondary and inferior, at least until the 1500s. So much is this the case that some have even wondered whether early European guns were used on the battlefield at all.[52] There's no doubt that they were, as data from Crécy show, but even so, Western historians have suggested that they didn't play important roles.[53] Why? Many historians believe that it's because of technology: "The technology was not yet there to make the gun an effective battlefield weapon. It was not until the late fourteenth and fifteenth centuries that guns began to appear regularly in battle."[54]

Yet the Chinese were able to make their small guns work on the battlefield, which is why 10 percent of early Ming soldiers were firearm units. Was Chinese small-gun technology better than European small-gun technology? It's possible. But it's more likely that Chinese forces were simply better at deploying guns than European forces. As we'll see, the Chinese had a strong and vibrant practice of infantry drill, including the use of the volley fire technique, in which ranks of gunners took turns firing and kept up a constant hail of bullets, making up for the slow rate of fire of early guns. Europeans seem not to have developed volley fire for firearms until much later. At Crécy, for example, as the anonymous chronicle I cited suggests, "with many guns they vigorously attacked the French camp, firing all the guns at once."[55]

We'll address drill in subsequent chapters, but for now what is intriguing is that early guns seem to have been put to a variety of different uses, sometimes shooting single bullets, sometimes shooting shrapnel, and, most intriguing of all, sometimes shooting fire, like the Chinese fire lance.

Consider, for example, data from a battle of 1356, when the French attacked the English-held castle Breteuil. They were hurling stones at it from catapults and had also built a belfry, that is, a siege tower on wheels. It must have been huge, because the chronicler Froissart says that each of its three stories could hold two hundred men. To counter the belfry, the English prepared "cannons throwing fire and large quarrels" (*kanons jettans feu et grans gros quariaus*), with which they planned to "destroy everything."[56] At first the English held these weapons in abeyance, fighting hand-to-hand from the walls. But when the French got the upper hand the English "began to shoot their cannons and throw fire onto and into the belfry, and with this fire they shot thick quarrels, and large ones, which wounded and killed large numbers, and made them [the French] so anxious [*les ensonnyèrent*] that they did not know what to do. The fire, which was Greek, took hold on the roof of the belfry, persuading those within to come out of it fast, or otherwise they would have been lost, turned to ash."[57] At another battle of the same year there is a similar use of cannons "to shoot quarrels and Greek fire," in this case to set fire to the roofs of towers on a castle.[58]

This "Greek fire" was not the classic Greek fire of Byzantium, a petroleum-based liquid projected from siphons.[59] Europeans had a tendency to apply the label "Greek fire" to all kinds of incendiaries, and in this case what was used was almost certainly an adulterated gunpowder mixture similar to early Chinese gunpowder recipes, in which the active ingredients of saltpeter, sulfur, and charcoal were mixed with other combustibles.[60] For example, a recipe for "Greek fire" from circa 1450 reads as follows: "One calls 'Greek fire' a certain confection and brew [*bouillement*] of willow charcoal [*charbon de saux*], saltpeter, eau-de-vie, sulfur, pitch, and incense with a soft wool thread from Ethiopia."[61] This compound may have acted somewhat like early Chinese conflagrative gunpowder mixtures, although the idea of brewing all these things together is quite foreign to standard gunpowder manufacture procedures. Whether the gunners of the mid-1300s were using this recipe or another is impossible to determine, but it seems likely that some kind of gunpowder-like mixture was used.[62]

In any case, it seems that medieval European gunners sometimes used their guns as the Chinese used fire lances, loading them with a gunpowder mixture and then, instead of hammering in a wooden plug to increase the projectile quality of the shot, leaving the plug out, stuffing the barrel full of quarrels and gunpowder, and firing the weapon as a fire-spewer, the quarrels shooting out as coviatives rather than bullets proper. This is precisely the way that fire lances had been used in China. Indeed, the parallels between the Siege of Breteuil in 1356 and Chinese sieges from the same period are clear: "guns" were used as antipersonnel weapons and as incendiaries. On both sides of Eurasia, the line between the fire lance and the gun was probably quite fluid, as guns were adapted and used in different ways for different circumstances. Indeed, in both China and Europe the fire lance continued in use for centuries alongside the gun.[63]

But what is intriguing is that by the end of the 1300s, Europeans—and the Ottomans, too—were beginning to develop guns that were quite different from those of China. Previously, in both Europe and China, guns had been used primarily as antipersonnel devices and perhaps secondarily to attack and set fire to wooden structures. Yet in the last quarter of the 1300s, European guns became huge and were increasingly used to blast down fortifications, whereas guns stayed small in China. Why? The answer may have to do with the fact that Europeans and Chinese built very different types of walls.

CHAPTER 6

Big Guns

WHY WESTERN EUROPE AND NOT CHINA
DEVELOPED GUNPOWDER ARTILLERY

The story of artillery is inextricably linked with a polity that no longer exists: the Burgundian state. In its day it was one of the most powerful states of Europe, and that power was based on big guns. The first Duke of Burgundy, Philip the Bold (1363–1404), built what became the most effective artillery army in Europe.[1] He and his heirs amassed arsenals of guns of all types and sizes. The dukes of Burgundy also "supported 'research and development' of all aspects of gunpowder weaponry technology."[2] Thanks to their improving guns, the dukes' territories expanded constantly, and the map of Europe might look very different today if it hadn't been for the disastrous leadership (and sonlessness) of the final Duke of Burgundy, Charles the Bold (1467–1477), whose sobriquet should perhaps be "Charles the Foolish."

When Philip the Bold, founder of this Burgundian dynasty, began his reign in 1363, Burgundy was a minor power. By his death it had become one of the major states of Western Europe, a worthy rival to France (see Map 6.1). Among Philip the Bold's wise moves was his attention to guns. He established manufacturing centers and ended up employing more cannon masters than any European ruler had ever done before.[3] He wasn't the first to build huge guns. They first appeared around 1375, when, sources indicate, a dozen or so smiths in the French city of Caen labored for six weeks to forge a bombard weighing two thousand

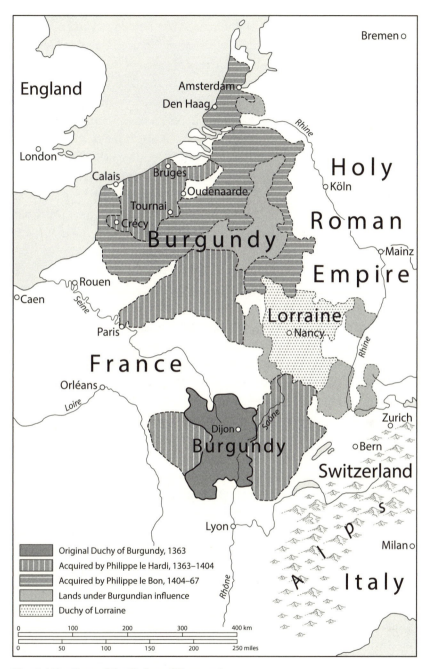

England

Bremen

Amsterdam
Den Haag

Holy

London

Roman

Calais
Bruges
Oudenaarde
Tournai
Crécy

Burgundy

Köln

Empire

Rouen

Mainz

Caen

Lorraine
Nancy

Paris

France

Orléans

Dijon
Burgundy

Zurich

Bern

Switzerland

Lyon

Milan

Italy

Original Duchy of Burgundy, 1363
Acquired by Philippe le Hardi, 1363–1404
Acquired by Philippe le Bon, 1404–67
Lands under Burgundian influence
Duchy of Lorraine

0	100	200	300	400 km

0	50	100	150	200	250 miles

MAP 6.1 Territory of the Dukes of Burgundy.

pounds (about nine hundred kilograms).[4] But he appears to have been the first to prove their value in battle, when he used them to help the French capture the English-held fortress of Odruik, in 1377.

Odruik was located not far from Calais and was, in the words of the famous medieval chronicler Jean de Froissart, "a pretty castle, and strong."[5] Its stout walls might have held off an enemy armed with earlier European guns, which fired projectiles of just three or four pounds, but Philip's projectiles were much larger. "Among them," Froissart writes, "were up to seven [guns that shot] projectiles of two hundred pounds (ninety kilograms)."[6] In fact, some versions of the Froissart text say that there were "up to 140" of these cannons,[7] and a record from the English side supports a number of that magnitude, saying that there were "109 large cannons."[8]

However many guns he had, they did the trick. After his forces surrounded the castle they fired off five or six preliminary shots, "to scare those within," as Froissart writes.[9] Some of these shots went right through Odruik's walls. "When those within the castle saw the powerful artillery that the Duke had, they began to have doubts, but they still, to the point of madness, put forth the appearance that they would defend and hold it."[10] In response, the Burgundians began gathering wood and lumber and straw to fill the moats, preparing for a long siege. It turned out that such preparations were needless. The cannons made short work of the walls.[11] Odruik surrendered.

In the past, sieges in Europe were similar to sieges in China. Guns were used merely for antipersonnel purposes, or to burn wooden structures. But the Siege of Odruik of 1377 marked a new era. Europe's guns had gotten big enough to destroy walls.

Europeans raced to build larger and larger artillery. The year Philip the Bold captured Odruik (1377), his smiths constructed a gun that could throw balls of 450 pounds (200 kilograms).[12] By 1382, an "incredibly huge bombard" was leveled at the town of Oudenaarde.[13] Its muzzle was about sixty inches (53 pouces) around, or twenty inches in diameter (fifty centimeters).[14] "One could hear it for five leagues in the daytime, and ten leagues at night, and it made such a huge noise that . . . it seemed as though all the demons of hell were present."[15]

These huge guns represented an enormous investment in treasure and time, and they were so prized that they were given names. Dulle

Griet (known in English as Mad Meg) was a wrought-iron monster forged in 1431 that weighed more than twelve thousand kilograms and could fire projectiles of three hundred kilograms.[16] The name Griet was a popular one for cannons in the Low Countries, because Dulle Griet was a famous figure in Dutch and Flemish folklore: ill-tempered, loud, and sharp-tongued.[17] Other powerful cannons had similar names. Lazy Mette (Faule Mette) was cast in 1411 and could shoot stone balls weighing more than four hundred kilograms, although she didn't very often, whence her name.[18] A bombard of 1404 was inscribed "I am named Katrin. Beware of what I hold. I punish injustice."[19] Some were named after legends, such as a pair of bombards from 1463 named Jason and Medea. Others were named after cities (Paris, Londres), or after those who commissioned them. For example, Pope Pius II (1405–1464) named guns after himself and his mother. This tradition of naming powerful guns got ever more delightful as time went on. The "Brutal Butcher," a broadsheet noted, "will dance across moats, through ring walls, inner walls, and bastions, through churches, houses, cellars, kitchens. He will move through halls, living rooms, bedrooms."[20]

These behemoths transformed European warfare. At the beginning of the 1300s, the Frenchman Pierre DuBois had written that a "castle can hardly be taken within a year, and even if it does fall, it means more expenses for the king's purse and for his subjects than the conquest is worth."[21] A century later, European walls were falling with alarming regularity.

The arrival of the age of artillery was heralded by English king Henry V's campaign in France in the early 1400s. In 1415 his huge guns battered the walls of Harfleur. Mighty Caen's walls were breached in September 1417 and then taken by storm. Then followed Bayeux, Tilly, Villers Bocage, Argentan, Alençon, Falaise, Saint Lô, Carentan, Valognes, Cherbourg, Coutances, Avrances, Domfront, Saint Saveur-le-Vicomte, and prosperous Rouen. Then Arques (Arques-la-Bataille), Lillebourne, Vernon, Mantes, Neufchâtel, Dieppe, Gournay, Eu, Fécamp, Tancarville, Honfleur, Gisors, Ivry, La Roche-Guyon, Pontoise, Meulan, Poissy, Saint-Germain, and Château Gaillard. Arques, Lillebourne, Vernon, Mantes, Neufchatel, Dieppe, Gournay, Eu, Fecamp, Tancarville, Honfleur, and Rouen.[22] Not all these walls were destroyed by guns— many citizens found it expedient to surrender before the first shots were fired, and privation and starvation played their usual roles—but Henry's campaign made clear that the balance had swung in favor of the offence.[23]

The English weren't the only ones to blast their way through France. The Burgundians battered the walls of Vellexon in 1409.[24] In 1411 they took the town of Ham with just three shots from their bombard Griette: one missed, the other two were devastating.[25] Other victories followed: Allibaudières, Montereau, Sens, Melun, Saint-Riquier, Abbeville, Guise, Terraisse, Anglure, Coursent, Mussy-l'Eveque, Fortepice, Avallon, Saint-Valery-sur-Somme, Haplincourt.[26] Again, not all were conquered through artillery fire; sometimes its mere threat sufficed.

Eventually the hapless French began to achieve their own successes, thanks partly to Joan of Arc. Our image of the famous virgin is of a warrior in shiny armor wielding a bare sword, but in fact she was also an excellent artillerist. Her first great triumph was at the Siege of Orléans (1429), one of the most important gunpowder battles in European history. Kelly DeVries writes, "There had never been an engagement in the world's history to that time that had involved more gunpowder weapons on both sides than the siege of Orleans."[27] DeVries is clearly not taking into account Chinese battles, many of which involved far more guns than were present at Orléans, but there's no doubt that this siege was a key artillery battle, and Joan of Arc herself played a key role in developing artillery tactics. As one participant in the battle noted, "she acted so wisely and clearly in waging war, as if she was a captain who had the experience of twenty or thirty years; and especially in the setting up of artillery, for in that she held herself magnificently."[28]

After Joan helped defeat the English, she and other French leaders used cannons to turn the tide of the Hundred Years' War, but it was after her death, with the reforms of the French king Charles V (1422–1461), that France developed the most effective artillery organization in Europe. Thanks in part to that organization, France won the Hundred Years' War, and afterward artillery undergirded France's devastating incursions into Italy in the 1490s.[29]

But Western Europeans weren't the only ones building wall-smashing artillery. Perhaps the most famous large guns in world history were made in the Ottoman Empire and aimed at the walls of Constantinople, helping the Ottomans to capture it in 1453. The defenses of that ancient city were much more impressive than those surrounding the towns and castles the English and Burgundians and French were conquering. As a Greek historian writes, "the walls of Constantinople have been the most famous and complicated system of defence in the civilized world; it secured the city for fifteen centuries from every presumptive conqueror."[30] If we replace the phrase "in the civilized world" with "in the Western world," the historian is correct. The defenses of Constantinople were considered nearly impregnable.

Not, however, to Sultan Mehmed II (1432–1481). Young, smart, and determined, he prepared carefully, gathering materials—saltpeter, sulfur, copper, iron—and wooing cannon makers to his side with large salaries and creative autonomy. The most famous was a Hungarian named Urban, a disgruntled employee of the Byzantine emperor.[31] Angry that he'd been denied a raise, he crossed the border and gained an audience with Mehmet II. The sultan asked if Urban could make a gun powerful enough to damage the walls of Constantinople. Urban supposedly replied that "the shot from my cannon could reduce them, and even the walls of Babylon itself."[32] Mehmet hired him, paying a handsome salary. As one chronicler noted, "Had the emperor [of Byzantium] granted him one fourth of this sum, he would not have escaped from Constantinople."[33]

For three months Urban worked, amassing forty tons of tin and copper, designing molds, melting, casting.[34] At the end, wrote a contemporary, "a terrible and unprecedented monster was constructed."[35] Sources indicate that the gun was between twenty and thirty feet long (six to nine meters).[36] It required hundreds of pounds of powder to fire one of its specially formed stone balls, each of which weighed between twelve hundred and eighteen hundred pounds (between five-hundred and fifty and eight hundred kilograms).[37] A surviving cannonball from the monster was measured by some scholars in the early 2000s and found to be thirty-nine inches in diameter (ninety-nine centimeters).[38]

The gun was, a Byzantine contemporary wrote, "something . . . frightful to see; one would not accept or admit its existence if one heard about it."[39] As they prepared to fire a test shot, inhabitants of the capital were warned to seek cover: the noise might strike people dumb or cause pregnant women to miscarry.[40] It was fired near Mehmet's palace's great gate. The ground shook, the roar was heard four miles away, and the projectile flew a mile, leaving a crater six feet deep.[41] To transport the gun required sixty oxen pulling thirty wagons, led by two hundred handlers. Fifty carpenters and two hundred laborers preceded them, building bridges and leveling terrain.[42]

Finally it was wrested into a battery and aimed at the walls of Constantinople. It wasn't the only bombard pointing at the city. Mehmet had dozens of huge pieces. As one witness wrote, some of the guns shot stone balls that reached the knees, others reached the waist.[43] Another eyewitness wrote that "they had fifty large guns and five hundred smaller ones."[44] And yet another suggests that the other large guns weren't much smaller than the monster.[45] Many threw five-hundred-pound balls, others eight-hundred-pounders.

The guns opened fire on the weakest sections of Constantinople's walls, bombarding them for fifty-five days. As a Greek contemporary, Kritoboulos, wrote, "The stone, borne with tremendous force and velocity, hit the wall, which it immediately shook and knocked down, and was itself broken into many fragments and scattered, hurling the pieces everywhere and killing those who happened by be near by. Sometimes it demolished a whole section, and sometimes a half-section, and sometimes a larger or smaller section of a tower or turret or battlement. And there was no part of the wall strong enough or resistant enough or thick enough to be able to withstand it, or to wholly resist such force and such a blow of the stone cannon-ball."[46]

The monster itself wasn't particularly effective. To aim it one had to pile up beams of wood underneath it, piece by piece, and then it had to be secured in its place with rope "so that it would not slip from its spot and miss its target by the force of the explosion."[47] After a shot it had to be cooled with hot oil and could be fired only once every three hours. Some accounts even say it cracked early in the siege and was never properly repaired.[48]

But Mehmet's other guns were effective, including smaller artillery pieces, which were beginning to replace huge bombards in Europe and the Ottoman Empire.[49] (These smaller artillery were still much larger than contemporaneous guns in China.) The defenders repaired breaches and fought off stormers with their own very good guns, which "fired . . . five or ten bullets at a time, each about the size of a . . . walnut, and having a great power of penetration. If one of these hit an armed man it would go right through his shield and his body and go on to hit anyone else who happened to be in his way, and even a third, until the force of the powder diminished; so one shot might hit two or three men."[50] But the defenders were outnumbered. In a final assault, the sultan's forces stormed the breaches. The Ottomans plundered, pillaged, raped, and slaughtered: "blood flowed in the city like rainwater in the gutters after a sudden storm."[51]

The fall of the ancient city is considered a key event in military history, a symbol of the triumph of artillery. The famous historian Michael Howard wrote that "the demolition of the walls of Constantinople by Turkish artillery symbolized . . . the end of a long era in the history of western man."[52] More recently, a scholar has written that "the capture of Constantinople by Mahomet II in 1453 was probably the first event of supreme importance whose result was determined by the power of artillery."[53] This idea goes back to the Enlightenment-era English historian Edward Gibbon, who wrote that "this thundering artillery was pointed against the walls and towers which had been erected only to resist the less potent engines of antiquity."[54] And how did Gibbon think the Turks got so modern? It was Europeans' own fault: defectors leaked techniques and technologies, a "treachery of apostates."[55]

This view is flawed, of course. The Turks weren't backward. Their military was state of the art, on a par with or superior to anything Western Europeans were capable of.[56] Equally important, the idea that technology destroyed Constantinople is overstated. For one thing, the Byzantines also had state-of-the-art guns. Moreover, economic and fiscal factors also played a role. The Byzantines were vastly outspent. The cannon maker Urban wasn't the only one who felt he was poorly paid and found better opportunities on the other side of the walls. And we must credit Mehmet himself, a taciturn but canny leader who took a deep interest in the conquest. Contemporaries even note that he "devised machines of all sorts."[57] At one point, for instance, his gunners were trying to target some enemy vessels but found their aim blocked by walls. According to a chronicler, Mehmed proposed constructing "a different sort of gun with a slightly changed design that could fire the stone to a great height, so that when it came down it would hit the ships amidships and sink them. He said that they must first aim it and level it, getting the measures by mathematical calculation, and then fire."[58] The gun worked beautifully. The Byzantines were not just outspent. They were outled.

Still, there's no doubt that artillery transformed siegecraft. When modern guns met ancient walls, the walls lost. As Gibbons wrote, "in the general warfare of the age the advantage was on *their* side who were most commonly the assailants; for a while the proportion of the attack and defence was suspended."[59] Scores of historians have followed Gibbon, and the idea that artillery changed the balance between offence and defense has become an accepted theory in military history. Eventually, the balance was restored, as Europeans learned to construct new types of fortifications, but what is curious is that none of this happened in China.

In China, the birthplace of gunpowder, the gun remained small, and ancient walls stood until torn down in the twentieth and twenty-first centuries. Whereas Westerners were making guns that weighed many tons, Chinese guns from the 1300s and 1400s were much lighter: guns considered large weighed less than eighty kilograms, and most guns weighed two kilograms or less.[60] As we've seen, Chinese records make clear that although guns were ubiquitous at sieges, they were not used to blast down walls. Rather, they were aimed at people and, sometimes, wooden gates and towers. It's not that the Chinese were incapable of making large guns. Their metallurgy was sophisticated, and they did construct large guns in the 1370s. They just never pursued the practice.[61]

Why? Historians have suggested that Chinese gun makers didn't need to destroy walls because China was a unified empire: "Since China was under a single sovereignty, gunpowder weapons were only needed on ships and for defence of fortified places against barbarian harassment. For both these purposes, smaller and more mobile guns alone made sense."[62] But of course as we've seen, walls stood in the way of many Chinese armies, and China was often not unified.

A better answer has to do with the culture of fortification. The Chinese built different types of walls than Europeans, walls that were much less vulnerable to bombardment.

European and Chinese Walls

Toward the middle of the twentieth century, a European expert in fortification reflected on how astoundingly large China's walls were: "in China . . . the principal towns are surrounded to the present day by

walls so substantial, lofty, and formidable that the medieval fortifications of Europe are puny in comparison."[63]

Is it possible that China's massive walls were one of the key reasons guns developed differently in China than in Europe? Chinese walls
were so thick, were constructed so artfully, and were so prevalent that
early guns—even the huge bombards of Europe—would have had tremendous difficulty attacking them. In fact, in the late 1400s and 1500s,
when Europeans began rebuilding their walls to resist cannon fire, they
adopted principles of construction that were quite similar to traditional
Chinese principles, yet traditional Chinese fortification techniques predate guns or even catapults.

Walls were culturally significant in traditional China, symbolizing
political authority, kingship. When the scholar Wu Zixu (d. 484 BCE)
was asked how one goes about building a state, he is said to have replied, "Putting the ruler in a secured, supreme place and the people
in reasonable order is the priority in the *dao* of ruling a state. . . . The
way to attain this *dao*, to seek hegemony, and to extend your dominion
from those near to those afar, must be firstly to erect city walls, set up
a system of defense, replenish the stocks, and manage the arsenals."[64] A
city wasn't a proper city unless it was surrounded by a wall. The most
commonly used character for "city" means "wall," and the character
for "state" or "polity" also depicts walls.[65] As urban historian Yinong
Xu writes, "Constructing city walls was interpreted as equivalent to
establishing the state."[66]

This emphasis on great walls was present even in prehistoric times,
when the ancestors of the Chinese surrounded their settlements with
massive fortifications. The capital of a Neolithic polity from the Long-
shan period (3000–2000 BCE), known as Chengziya (ca. 2500 BCE), was
enclosed by a long wall eight to ten meters wide.[67] By the Shang period
(1600–1046 BCE), Chinese city walls were even more massive. The walls
of the Shang city of Zhengzhou have been the object of considerable archaeological research, which has established that they stood ten meters
high and had a width of more than twenty meters at the base and five
meters at the top.[68] For the following millennia, the Chinese continued
building huge walls. By the Ming period, nearly all prefectural and provincial capitals were fortified with walls between ten and twenty meters
wide at the base and five to ten more meters wide at top (see Figure 6.1).

European walls were much thinner. Romans were the great wall builders of European antiquity, and although Roman walls often reached 10 meters in height—about the height of many Chinese walls—they were only 1.5 to 2.5 meters wide.[69] Among the most impressive Roman walls were those of Rome itself. Its Servian Walls could reach 3.6 meters thickness at the base, and during the reign of Emperor Aurelian, they were rebuilt and eventually attained a thickness of around 4 meters and a height of 6 meters.[70] Walls in the far reaches of the empire could also reach 4 meters thick, such as the Diocletian-era walls known as the Saxon Shore Forts, which were 4.3 meters.[71] This is far thinner than Chinese walls of the same period, which were often 20 meters wide at their base.[72]

The most impressive walls of the Western world were those of Constantinople, which had an outer wall two meters thick and an inner wall four meters thick, separated by a no-man's land of about fifteen meters across.[73] These defenses have been justly lauded. As we've seen, one author has written that Constantinople had "the most famous and complicated system of defence in the civilized world."[74] Another has called Constantinople's "the most formidable development of fortification systems in the ancient world."[75] But Constantinople's outer wall was a tenth the width of a major Chinese city wall, and even the much stouter inner wall was merely a quarter or a third as thick.

In fact, for much of the Middle Ages, most towns in Europe had no walls at all. Some scholars have argued that in the German lands around 1200, there were only twelve towns with proper walls, and nine were left over from Roman times.[76] French and English towns were also usually free of walls, unless, again, they happened to have Roman walls. That's not to say they were defenseless. Many European towns surrounded themselves with ditches, stockades, or low earthen ramparts. This was the case with many German towns in the 1100s and 1200s.[77] These earthen ramparts could sometimes be quite thick, but they tended to be low and rudimentary. An earthen fortification in twelfth-century Hereford, England, for example, was probably about fifteen meters wide at the base but just three meters high and seems to have been protected from erosion only by a layer of gravel. No wonder that it was replaced by a stone wall in the 1200s.[78]

Hereford was not alone. In the 1200s and 1300s, new walls rose throughout Europe.[79] They sometimes matched but rarely exceeded the thickness, height, and length of Roman walls. Late medieval French walls were almost always 2 meters or less in thickness. England's tended to be even thinner, with those of Southampton only 0.76 meters thick and those of Shrewsbury 1.37 meters thick.[80] Other English towns had walls of French thickness: those of Bristol ranging between 1.5 and 2.5 meters, those of Bath 1.9 meters, those of Newcastle 2.1 meters.[81]

It is telling that Western historians and archaeologists often use the phrase "very thick" to refer to walls that would be considered very thin in the Chinese context, as, for example, when Kelly DeVries and Kay Smith write about the Southern French keep at Najac, begun in 1253: "Its walls were also *very thick*, measuring 2.2 meters in width."[82] Or when they write that most French walls in the late medieval period were "*very wide*, most measuring nearly two meters in thickness."[83] To be sure, DeVries and Smith are making comparisons within the European context, but it still bears noting that these "very wide" walls were less than a tenth the thickness of average Chinese walls.[84] In fact, the *marketplace* of the Chinese city of Chang'an boasted walls thicker than the walls of European capitals, and that marketplace stood within the walls of Chang'an itself, which were far, far thicker.[85]

It is of course much easier to blast your way through a two-meter wall than a fifteen-meter wall, but it wasn't just the thinness of European walls that made them vulnerable to artillery. It was also the way they were built. European walls were made of stone, often with a filling of gravel or rubble, with limestone mortar often used as a bonding agent, a practice dating to Roman times. Chinese walls, however, had an earthen core. Earthwork absorbs the energy of an artillery shot. It might become riddled with holes during an attack, but those holes tended not penetrate deeply, and they wouldn't shatter the wall.

One must not imagine that Chinese walls were filled with loose earth, though. The Chinese were able to create sturdy, hard walls by using an ancient earth tamping method. Laborers first built a framework of wooden planks the desired height and width of the walls. Then they poured in a layer of earth and tamped down until it was highly compact. Then they added another layer and repeated the process, and

Figure 6.1 Walls of Xi'an.

These walls in their current form were built during the early Ming dynasty, based on ancient walls, and refurbished during the Qing dynasty. Photo by Maros Mraz, 2007. Multi-license with GFDL and Creative Commons CC-BY-SA-2.5, http://commons.wikimedia.org/wiki/File:Xi%27an_-_City_wall_-_014.jpg, accessed 2 December 2014.

so on.[86] When the wall reached its desired height, workers removed the planks and used them to make the next section of the wall. This tamped-earth method created walls that were surprisingly durable. Some ancient walls have survived four thousand years of rain and wind. To protect them from erosion, workers sometimes encased the earthwork in brick or stone, a practice that became more prevalent starting in the Song period (960–1279).[87] The walls of Ming cities were built this way, and so was the Great Wall, rebuilt during the Ming: a tamped earthen core (the earth sometimes interspersed with stone and rubble) encased in stone and brick.

But the tamped-earth method wasn't the only thing that made Chinese walls resistant to artillery: Chinese walls were also sloped. Whereas a vertical wall that is struck by a projectile perpendicularly receives the full force of impact, a sloped wall deflects the projectile and absorbs less energy.

What is intriguing is that when Europeans began adapting their fortifications to resist artillery, they made them more like Chinese walls. In the course of the 1400s, Europeans began building walls of sloped earthwork. The practice seems to have begun in France and the southern Netherlands, where artillery warfare was particularly intense. To protect their brittle walls, defenders built earthen outworks called *boulevards* in French and *bolwercqen* in Flemish, whence the English word "bulwark." They were made with wooden planks on the outside and earth on the inside, and they were sloped to lessen the force of horizontal fire. As boulevards' utility became recognized, they were made permanent and faced in stone.[88]

The boulevard began as an ad hoc measure to protect existing walls, but Europeans soon began building wholly new types of fortifications. These new walls were quite similar to traditional Chinese walls: filled with earth, encased in stone, and much thicker. They were designed to resist artillery, and they worked. Artillery, which once breached walls regularly, was countered, and sieges became drawn-out affairs. Gone were the days in which garrisons surrendered after a cannonball or two pierced the wall.

A Florentine diplomat wrote, in the early 1490s, that "the French claim their artillery is capable of creating a breach in a wall of eight feet in thickness."[89] Of course, as the diplomat conceded, "the French are braggarts by nature."[90] But let's take the French at their word and suppose that European siege artillery circa 1490 was capable of creating breaches in walls of up to two and a half meters—very thick in the European context. Would that siege artillery have proven useful against Chinese walls? What if they had been aimed at the walls of Suzhou, which, at eleven meters, were fairly typical of China but more than four times thicker than the Frenchmen's hypothetical walls? How would those French guns have fared? Probably not very well.

More important, would Europeans have bothered to develop wall-smashing artillery—either the huge bombards of the early 1400s or the lighter but more powerful guns of the late 1400s—if they had faced walls like those of China? Large guns were enormously expensive to make, to transport, and even to fire—the largest required more than fifty kilograms of powder or more for a single shot.[91] Later (i.e., smaller) siege artillery required less powder, but the expense was still significant.

Scholars have estimated that a shot from a sixteenth-century cannon cost the equivalent of a month's wages for an infantry soldier.[92]

The kings and dukes of Europe paid these exorbitant sums because it was worth it. They knew that their artillery trains had a good chance of breaching an enemy town's walls or, even better, intimidating its garrison into surrender. In China artillery would not have repaid the heavy investments. To be sure, the Chinese used catapults and perhaps guns to destroy wooden structures on walls, but the massive tamped-earth walls of China acted as a deterrent to the development of gunpowder artillery. Even Mehmed's monster would barely have dented Suzhou's walls.

Yet walls can't explain everything about the military divergence. European guns didn't just get bigger. They also got more effective. By 1490, European guns achieved a form so successful that it would hardly change for the next three centuries. Why did the classic gun emerge in Europe and not China? It's a central question of global military history.

CHAPTER 7

The Development of the Classic Gun in Europe

When did China fall behind Western Europe, and why? This question and its many variants form one of the central preoccupations of world historians. Did the Great Divergence occur late in history—around 1800—as many global historians argue? Or do the roots of divergence run deep, as more traditional historians believe? The debate has been vehement, but researchers on both sides have tended to focus overwhelmingly on economics, devoting little attention to military matters. To be sure, traditionalists are fond of asserting that the West must have led the world in military technology and techniques after 1500 because it was able to create so many colonies, often defeating Asian powers. Revisionists have argued back by suggesting that traditionalists overstate the extent of Europeans' dominance. Yet neither side offers arguments compelling enough to win the debate because so far there has been little evidence to draw on. We need a truly comparative military history, or what you might call global military history.

Let's start with one indisputable fact: In the 1510s and 1520s, the Chinese encountered European guns and immediately recognized that they were superior to their own. This suggests that some kind of military divergence occurred before 1500.

In fact, we can date the divergence even more precisely. Around 1480 European cannons achieved their classic form: longer, lighter, more efficient, and more accurate than earlier cannons. Cannon designs remained relatively constant over the following three centuries, so that classic cannons from the 1480s are remarkably similar to cannons from the 1750s. This is certainly not the case for any cannons from the 1450s.

Why did the classic cannon emerge in Europe—and not elsewhere—in the late 1400s? Walls played a role. As we've seen, Chinese walls just happened to be highly resistant to guns, whereas Europe's walls were vulnerable. But although this accounts for the development in Europe of large guns, it doesn't explain why the form of guns changed, and the related question of why guns of all sizes become more powerful and accurate in Western Europe than in China.

In fact, guns in China were developing along a similar trend to those of Europe, growing longer relative to muzzle bore. But the development slowed in China about a generation before the development in Europe of the classic cannon. Why? The reason probably has less to do with to do any putative cultural ingenuity on the part of Europeans than with the frequency of warfare. After 1449, China entered a period of relative peace, while Europe entered a period of sustained, intense, existential warfare. By existential warfare I mean conflict that threatened the very existence of the states involved. Chinese guns had evolved quickly between the late 1200s, when the first true guns seem to have emerged, and the early 1400s, a period during which China was wracked by existential warfare. The century from 1350 or so to 1449 was especially turbulent, as the Ming strove to establish and consolidate their empire, and during this time the evolution of guns, toward longer barrels, seems to have been proceeding along quite similar lines in China and the West. In the middle of the 1400s, this evolution stopped in China and accelerated in Europe, precisely when warfare decreased in China increased in Europe.

The Classic Gun

Two cannons from 1488 exemplify the change in European guncraft. These guns, preserved in a plaza in Neuchâtel, Switzerland, are svelte compared to their predecessors. Whereas older guns were squat, these are long and thin, tapering toward the muzzle (see Figure 7.1). They have been firmly dated to 1488, yet as artillery expert Kay Smith has written, "If you compare the cannon from Neuchâtel with a 17th or

FIGURE 7.1 The classic cannon: the Neuchâtel guns, 1488.

These two guns, preserved in Neuchâtel, Switzerland, are exemplars of the so-called classic ordnance synthesis, which emerged in Western Europe in the late 1400s. One is 224 centimeters long, with a bore of 6.2 centimeters. The other is slightly longer, 252 centimeters, with the same bore size. Earlier cannons of this length were much thicker and had a much wider bore. Image courtesy of Kay Smith.

18th-century cannon the differences are hard to see."[1] Smith argues that this new design became the norm for the next three and a half centuries, with only the most minor of modifications.[2] Other scholars have reached similar conclusions.[3]

Why did guns evolve to this form? After all, the long barrels were quite a departure from earlier guns. Whereas Mehmet II's monster bombard had a length about eight times the width of its muzzle, fairly typical for artillery of its time, the Neuchâtel guns have a length-to-bore ratio of forty-to-one.[4] They are thus four times longer relative to their muzzle bore than old-style bombards. The longer barrels gave the gunpowder more time to impart energy to the projectile, accelerating it within the barrel for four times the distance of earlier models. Accuracy also improved because the longer barrel was better able to focus the projectile on its path. Of course any smoothbore gun is inaccurate compared to rifled guns that impart a spin, but the increased barrel length was an improvement over earlier models.

Adding to their power was the fact that these guns shot not stone but iron cannonballs. Although the Chinese were using iron ammunition consistently by 1370 or so, in Europe the transition from stone had occurred gradually through the 1400s.[5] The use of iron increased the power of guns immensely because it is much denser than stone. For instance, marble—a stone of choice for cannonballs—has a density of 2.7 grams per cubic centimeter, whereas iron has a density of 7.9 grams per cubic centimeter. Whereas a marble cannonball of ten centimeters in diameter weighs 1.4 kilograms, an iron cannonball of the same dimensions weighs 4.1 kilograms. Yet an iron ball, three times denser than a marble ball of equal size, was capable of achieving far more than just three times as much kinetic energy when traveling at a given velocity. The kinetic energy of a projectile is half its mass times the square of its velocity ($E_k = \frac{1}{2}mv^2$, where E_k is kinetic energy, m is mass, and v is velocity). Thus, an iron ball could be ten or twenty or thirty times more destructive at the same velocity than a marble ball of the same dimensions, depending on that velocity. The new guns, by accelerating denser projectiles to higher velocities, were far more powerful than older designs.

Equally important, the new guns were much lighter than the old ones. Whereas traditional bombards had thick barrels, the new guns were thin-walled, particularly at the front. This made transport easier. But it also proved valuable when it came to the dissipation of heat. Artillerists had resorted to all manner of expedients to cool their massive bombards, pouring vinegar or hot oil down the barrel, and even so the guns were slow to cool—the largest were able to fire only two or three shots per day.[6] The new guns cooled quickly and could fire several shots per hour.[7]

They also conferred advantages in loading. Earlier guns were often loaded with the help of a wooden plug, which was hammered in after the powder was loaded into the powder chamber. (Sometimes the plug was made of a softer material, like straw or fabric.) The projectile was then placed on top of the plug. The new guns didn't require wooden plugs because they allowed a tighter fit between projectile and barrel. Orders for wooden plugs, which used to accompany orders for cannonballs in the accounting records, decreased markedly in the late 1400s, disappearing by 1500 or so, except in the case of mortars.[8] This, too, allowed for faster reloading and probably also correlated with an increase in accuracy.

Historian Bert S. Hall has labeled the development of the long style of gun the "modern ordnance synthesis."[9] Other scholars don't use this term, preferring instead to call it the "classic" gun.[10] They agree, however, that by 1480 or so cannons had attained a form that remained stable over the next three and a half centuries. Handguns followed a similar trend.

Why did Europeans develop the classic gun and not the Chinese? Data show that until the mid-1400s, Chinese guns had length-to-bore ratios very similar to those of European guns of the same period, an average of seventeen to one (see Table 7.1).[11] Even more intriguingly, evidence suggests that Chinese gun design was following a similar trend of development. Some historians in China have noted that between the beginning of the Hongwu reign (1368) and the end of the Yongle reign (1424), there was a marked increase in barrel lengths.[12] If we look closely at the data, we find that the trend is even longer, as can be seen in Graph 7.1.

European guns continued further along the path of a high length to bore ratio, and when the Portuguese brought their cannons (similar in barrel length and ratio to the Neuchâtel guns) to China in the 1510s, the Chinese were highly impressed, recognizing the many advantages that the longer barrel length and thinner walls conferred.

Explanations for the First Divergence

So why did Europeans develop the classic gun in the late 1400s, while the Chinese didn't? Historians of Europe have argued that new types of gunpowder played a role. Gunpowder is a tricky substance. Even though it brings to the combustion reaction its own oxygen, it still requires space between its granules to ignite. Traditionally European artisans ground the three ingredients—saltpeter, sulfur, and charcoal—into a powder. To load a preclassic cannon, one poured the powder into a special powder chamber, which was of a narrower bore than the gun's main barrel. But you couldn't fill up the entire powder chamber with powder. You had to leave space so the powder could ignite. Then you'd hammer a wooden wedge into the top of the powder chamber and insert the projectile into the barrel proper. When the powder was set off, the space within the chamber allowed the powder to burn. Once pressures had reached a high enough level, the plug and cannonball were ejected.

But European powder makers learned in the course of the 1400s that if you used gunpowder that had been formed into granules, or "corns," you could achieve different types of reaction, depending on the size of the granules. Small guns, which were less likely to burst, could handle a fast reaction. Large guns, in contrast, had a tendency

TABLE 7.1 Ratio of length to bore, Chinese guns, 1332–1444.

Year	Length (cm)	Bore (cm)	Length-to-bore Ratio	Year	Length (cm)	Bore (cm)	Length-to-bore Ratio
1332	35.3	10.5	3.4	1377	27.0	2.3	11.7
1352	43.4	3.0	14.5	1377	38.5	1.9	20.3
1368	45.0	2.0	22.5	1377	31.5	10.0	3.2
1368	21.2	1.5	14.1	1377	100.0	21.0	4.8
1368	40.0	2.0	20.0	1378	43.8	2.0	21.9
1368	74.0	7.0	10.6	1378	43.5	2.0	21.8
1372	43.0	2.0	21.5	1378	31.0	4.0	7.8
1372	44.2	2.2	20.1	1378	36.4	11.9	3.1
1372	37.0	13.4	2.8	1378	36.0	12.0	3.0
1372	36.5	11.0	3.3	1378	52.0	10.8	4.8
1372	37.0	12.2	3.0	1379	44.2	2.1	21.0
1375	63.0	11.0	5.7	1379	44.5	2.0	22.3
1375	61.0	11.0	5.5	1379	29.5	2.5	11.8
1377	43.5	2.0	21.8	1400	40.3	2.2	18.3
1377	44.0	2.0	22.0	1409	34.5	1.7	20.3
1377	43.0	2.0	21.5	1409	35.0	1.5	23.3
1377	32.3	2.1	15.4	1409	35.5	1.5	23.7
1377	44.0	2.0	22.0	1409	35.2	1.5	23.5
1377	43.7	2.3	19.0	1409	55.0	7.3	7.5
1377	42.7	2.3	18.6	1412	36.0	1.4	25.7
1377	44.0	3.3	13.3	1412	36.0	1.5	24.0
1377	44.0	2.2	20.5	1413	35.7	1.4	25.5
1377	42.0	2.1	20.0	1413	35.7	1.5	23.8
1377	31.0	2.0	15.5	1413	36.0	1.5	24.0
1377	44.0	2.1	21.0	1415	44.0	5.2	8.5
1377	31.2	2.0	15.6	1415	43.6	5.3	8.2
1377	42.0	2.2	19.1	1415	44.0	5.2	8.5
1377	36.0	1.9	18.9	1421	35.7	1.5	23.8

TABLE 7.1 (*Continued*)

Year	Length (cm)	Bore (cm)	Length-to-bore Ratio	Year	Length (cm)	Bore (cm)	Length-to-bore Ratio
1421	35.8	1.5	23.9	1425	35.9	1.4	25.6
1421	36.0	1.7	21.2	1435	34.5	1.5	23.0
1421	35.0	1.5	23.3	1435	35.9	1.5	23.9
1425	36.0	1.5	24.0	1435	36.0	1.3	27.7
1425	35.8	1.4	25.6	1443	38.0	1.5	25.3
1425	35.8	1.7	21.1	1444	35.8	1.2	29.8
1425	35.9	1.4	25.6	Average			17.3

Source: Data from Li Bin, "Ming Qing," 17–19, 23–24, 28, 34–37, 52, 63–97.

Note: Chinese guns through the mid-1400s or so had similar length-to-bore ratios as those of Europe around the same period, an average of 17.3. To be sure, comparisons are tricky, since guns intended for different uses had different ratios. Data from Li Bin, "Ming Qing," 17–19, 23–24, 28, 34–37, 52, 63–97. Data consolidated from other, less comprehensive works (including Wang Rong, "Yuan dai"; Yuan, "Shan dong"; LX, 107, 117; Hu, "Ming dai tie pao"; Liu Shanyi, "Shan dong"; Yin, "He zhang"; Chen Lie, "He bei"; Shi Wanlin, "Gan su"; Shi, "Zhen jiang"; Liu Hongcai, "Ding bian") yield similar results. For those data, see Andrade, "Late Medieval."

to crack. A slower reaction kept the pressures inside the chamber from mounting too quickly: the projectile was accelerated down the barrel evenly and continually until it exited the muzzle. Thus, whereas small guns could use fine powder or small grains, larger guns used larger grains.

Powder corning allowed big guns to have longer, thinner walls, because the controlled reaction kept pressures down. But the powder smiths were probably not trying to achieve this result. They were more worried about humidity. Gunpowder spoilage was a particular problem for Europeans because they found it difficult to obtain pure saltpeter, which is to say saltpeter supplies consisting of potassium nitrate (KNO_3) rather than sodium nitrate (NaO_3) or calcium nitrate ($CaNO_3$), which absorb water vapor much more readily. Since European gunpowder mixtures had high levels of the inferior forms, powder smiths formed their product into corns to expose less surface area to the air. This might not have happened, so the argument goes, if Europeans had

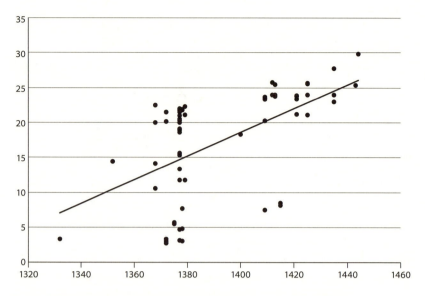

GRAPH 7.1 Trends in the development of Chinese guns, 1300–1450.

The vertical axis is the ratio of length to muzzle bore, and the trend is clear: through 1440 or so, Chinese guns were growing longer relative to muzzle bore, or toward the ratio that characterized the so-called modern ordnance synthesis achieved in Europe in the late 1400s. Data are from Table 7.1 and Li Bin, "Ming Qing." Data consolidated from other, less comprehensive works show nearly identical trend lines. For these data, see Andrade, "Late Medieval."

had better saltpeter. Conversely, Asians supposedly had an easier time obtaining and manufacturing proper saltpeter and so corning wasn't so necessary, at least from the perspective of spoilage.[13]

It's an intriguing hypothesis, but there are problems with it. First, recent evidence strongly suggests that powder corning was present in China by 1370. Chinese archaeologists have examined a trove of early Ming land mines and concluded that they contained corned powder, an innovation that strengthened the explosive power of the mines, providing the spacing that gunpowder granules require for rapid combustion.[14] There is even evidence suggesting that corned powder may have been used in East Asia as early as the 1200s.[15] Although corning may have been a necessary condition for longer guns, it was probably not a sufficient condition. Second, recent work suggests that the development of corning in Europe was considerably less straightforward than once believed, and the timing of the emergence of the classic gun doesn't necessarily coincide with the spread of corning techniques.[16]

If corned powder doesn't explain the emergence of the classic gun, then what does? Some scholars have pointed to changes in manufacturing techniques. Kay Smith suspects that the key development occurred when Europeans learned to cast their cannons muzzle side up:

> The surviving pieces of ordnance from earlier in the 15th century are big pieces with large bore sizes. They do not look like the long thin gun. . . . Essentially they are parallel-sided tubes with flat ends. The explanation is, probably, that they were cast muzzle down in the traditional bell-founding method whereas the long thin guns were cast muzzle up. . . . Perhaps this marks the real ' revolution' in artillery. Once the technique of casting muzzle up with the attendant advantages, and it is not clear what those are at present, had been mastered by cannon founders, the way was open for the development of the 'classic' form of artillery.[17]

It's impossible to know at this stage whether this is right, and Smith displays a reassuring humility, admitting that it's not even clear what advantages this technique conferred. We know it must have been better because it was widely adopted, but why was it better? It's a reminder of how little we know.[18]

So far, our explanations have been Europe-focused, but what about explanations that take into account the Chinese experience? Maybe Europeans just had the advantage of being late adopters. As Peter Lorge writes, "Free from preconceived notions . . . [Europeans] set off with renewed creativity. Progress in China continued slowly."[19] This is an intriguing idea, although it doesn't account for the fact that in the 1300s and early 1400s guns developed in parallel in China and in Europe, whereas after 1450 development slowed in China and accelerated in Europe.

Another Asianist offers a fascinating explanation. Kenneth Chase argues that China lagged in the development of guns because guns were not useful against its most fearsome enemies: inner Asian nomads. To fight against horse-borne nomads, logistics were the challenge, because enemies could flee and draw out supply chains. They could sally and retreat, lure and engage at their will. Guns, no matter how good, simply weren't so effective in such a context. Europeans, in contrast, fought large infantry field armies and sieges, types of warfare that suited guns. As a result, Chase argues, guns evolved more rapidly in Europe than in China.[20] The Chase hypothesis is a compelling one, but there are reasons to doubt it.

For one, Chinese themselves considered guns to be highly useful against nomads. The Ming used them to smash Mongol power in the late 1300s and early 1400s, and to defend against a Mongol invasion in 1449. Guns remained in high demand in China, whose northern borders were studded with gun emplacements. Numerous sources make clear that Chinese war makers found guns very effective against nomads throughout the fifteenth and sixteenth centuries, or precisely when European guns were improving so rapidly.[21] The famous scholar and military leader Weng Wanda, for example, felt that only with firearms could one fight against the swiftly moving Mongols, and he designed special guns both for the Great Wall defenses and for the troops who ventured into the steppes, guns that appear to have played key roles in fighting against the Mongols.[22] More important, the Chase hypothesis downplays the tremendous variety of warfare within China itself. Nomads may have been the primary enemies in the north, but southern China was often beset by warfare that was similar to that of Europe: huge infantry armies clashing with each other and attacking cities. The Chase hypothesis should certainly not be discarded, but it probably represents only part of the explanation.

There are also, of course, a slew of explanations focusing on China's supposedly stifling culture: China lost the lead because it was too autocratic.[23] China's decline resulted from isolationism.[24] China suffered from Confucianism and a deeply seated cultural conservatism.[25] Sinologists today generally reject such cultural explanations, because so much evidence shows that China was not nearly so autocratic or isolated or conservative as has been portrayed.[26]

But perhaps the answer to the puzzle is straightforward, with no need for explanations involving powder corning or nomads or late adoption or isolationism or autocracy or conservatism. What if the Ming stopped improving their guns because they didn't need better guns?

Guns evolved quickly in the pre- and early Ming period, a time of constant and existential warfare, as Zhu Yuanzhang and his rivals fought incessantly for survival and preeminence. This competitive environment led to rapid innovation. After the Ming dynasty was founded in 1368, the warfare continued, and so did the innovation. Ming armies marched west into Sichuan, north into Mongolia, and southwest into Yunnan. These were massive wars against states whose militaries possessed, especially in the case of Sichuan, state-of-the-art weaponry. When Zhu Yuanzhang died, the Ming dynasty was rocked by an intense civil war, in which tremendous armies shot guns at each other in China's heartland. The usurper Yongle won and immediately began planning other massive expeditions, most notably a massive war in what is today northern Vietnam and five great campaigns into Mongolia, expeditions that involved hundreds of thousands of troops, many armed with guns. All of this warfare stimulated innovation in firearm manufacture, tactics, and administration.

But after the Yongle Emperor died in 1424, the frequency and intensity of Chinese warfare decreased dramatically. From his death until the mid-1500s, there was only one dynasty-shaking military event: the Tumu Episode of 1449, when firearms played an important role in preserving the capital from a Mongol onslaught. Thereafter, as the Mongol threat lessened, warfare became less frequent, less intense, and, most important, less existential. In general, wars between 1449 and the 1540s were closer to police actions against minor enemies. The Ming were overwhelmingly dominant. There were far fewer existential challenges and there was thus less impetus for further innovation.

Europe, in contrast, saw no respite from the nearly constant warfare that had marked the 1300s and early 1400s. The learned monk Honoré de Bovet had written in 1389 that the West, or, as he put it, "Holy Christendom," was "so tormented by wars and divisions, robberies and dissensions, that one can scarcely name a petty province, be it duchy or county, which enjoys peace."[27] When de Bovet was writing, China was no different. Its wars were if anything more frequent, larger, and more destructive than those of Europe, but whereas China settled into a Ming Peace from 1449, Europe's wars grew larger and more intense.

England was engaged in the Wars of the Roses from 1455 to 1485, and also frequently battled France and Scotland; Spain's naval armada fought with the rising English Royal Navy over control of the seas; France underwent countless campaigns to expand its territory, such as invasions of Normandy and campaigns into Italy as well as never-ending battles with England; Germany was driven into chaos by multiple revolts in Austria, Hungary, and the Netherlands, as well as the Hussite Wars in Bohemia; Italy had to defend against multiple invasions from Spain and France; the Portuguese attacked Morocco; the Spanish captured Granada; and, in general, in the words of one scholar, "wars erupted around the Mediterranean and southwest Asian spheres as if volcanoes had suddenly thrust up around their rims. . . . [a] terrible tapestry of conflict weaving throughout the Mediterranean and Hispano-Maghrib arenas."[28] As historian Frank Tallett writes, "between 1480 and 1700, England was involved in 29 wars, France in 34, Spain in 36, and the Empire in 25. In the century after 1610 Sweden and the Austrian Habsburgs were at war for two years in every three, Spain for three years in every four."[29] Wars were, he notes, not just frequent but long and intense.

Thus, while Chinese fought less, Europeans fought more. Perhaps this fact, more than anything else, explains why European guns kept improving. Europe was at the beginning of a long warring states period, one that would last until 1945.

Historians suggest that all this fighting had tremendous effects. Gunpowder warfare, they argue, sparked the changes that underlay European modernity, or at least its early modernity: the end of feudalism, the rise of centralized states, colonial dominance overseas. But how much did the gun really bring about these changes? And why hadn't the gun caused similar developments in China?

CHAPTER 8

The Gunpowder Age in Europe

The idea that the gun transformed Europe goes back at least to Francis Bacon (1561–1626) and was taken up by many thinkers over the following centuries.[1] Adam Smith (1723–1790) developed the idea in his 1776 work *Wealth of Nations*, describing a "great revolution in the art of war, to which a mere accident, the invention of gun-powder, seems to have given occasion."[2] Guns themselves were expensive, Smith argued, and so were fortresses to defend against them, so the revolution in the art of war favored wealthy states.[3] Modern war, he wrote, altered the balance between the civilized and the barbarous, allowing rich, developed nations with standing armies to dominate other peoples that once threatened them. "The invention of fire-arms," he writes, "an invention which at first sight appears to be so pernicious, is certainly favourable both to the permanency and to the extension of civilization."[4]

Historians today eschew dichotomies between "civilization" and "barbarousness," but they still believe in a direct link between gunpowder and modernity. The gun, they say, destroyed European feudalism, or, to use the pithy phrase of Smith's most famous follower, Karl Marx, "gunpowder blew up the knightly class."[5] The process is often referred to as the "gunpowder revolution."

The idea is that under the feudal system, knights and lords and free towns resisted central power, keeping central states weak. Guns upended the balance because larger, wealthier, and better-organized political structures were better able to afford gunpowder warfare. Therefore, the weak, the poor, the badly organized structures died away. A feedback cycle ensued: the more control a state managed to achieve, the more revenue it could raise, the more guns it could buy, the more fortresses it could build. Thus, gunpowder warfare selected for effective, centralized states. It's a widely held notion, nearly ubiquitous.[6] Even historians who are cautious about periodization and grand statements tend to accept it.[7]

But why didn't similar revolutionary effects occur in China, where gunpowder was invented and where, as we've seen, guns played a key role in warfare by the mid-1300s? Historians' attempts to answer this question have tended to focus on deep-seated differences in culture and institutional structures, or on Chinese styles of warfare (China supposedly privileged defense while Europeans privileged offence).[8] Such explanations are inadequate, failing to account for the rich data about Chinese warfare that are now becoming known. Someone who knows these rich data is Peter Lorge, who suggests that the explanation is perhaps more straightforward: Europe needed to become more like China before it could fully use guns, which is to say that it first needed centralized states with permanent standing armies.[9]

Lorge is speaking delicately, but one could put it more boldly: China was in certain ways more advanced than Europe, meaning that it was further along on the developmental path that scholars like Victor Lieberman have determined was a long-term underlying trend throughout Eurasia: toward fewer but increasingly centralized political units.[10] The great Islamicist Patricia Crone once wrote that "to a historian specializing in the non-European world there is something puzzling about the excitement with which European historians hail the arrival of cities, trade, regular taxation, standing armies, legal codes, bureaucracies, absolutist kings and other commonplace appurtenances of civilized societies, as if they were unique and self evident stepping stones to modernity: to the non-European historian they simply indicate that Europe had finally joined the club."[11] Thus, we might rather look at Europe as an aberration, a bit slow on the uptake. Perhaps guns hastened the end of Europe's decentralized system, but feudalism was probably doomed in any case.

Intriguingly, there are a few hints that the gun may indeed have brought China toward more direct, centralized rule: not in core areas of China, where centralization was firmly established, but in colonial peripheries, where decentralized, quasi-feudal structures still prevailed.

Before the Ming period, the central government ruled over peripheral minority peoples by appointing local chieftains. It seems, however, that this chieftain (土司) system ended during the Ming and early Qing periods (1300s–1600s), morphing into a structure of direct rule. Why did it change then, after so many centuries? Historian Zhang Wen argues that guns gave the central government a decisive edge over local powers, allowing it to assume direct control over aboriginal areas that had for centuries—millennia in some cases—been governed indirectly.[12] There is a clear parallel here with the gunpowder revolution model for Europe.

So it is possible that guns did weaken feudal structures in China, where such structures existed, yet the transformative effects of guns have nonetheless been overstated for Europe. Defeudalization would likely have occurred without guns. Some European historians have argued this point without reference to China, such as the great Renaissance historian J. R. Hale, who argued that the centralization "began before cannon were effective or readily transportable and can be explained without reference to gunpowder weapons."[13] Others have argued similarly, and China adds weight to the case.[14]

So much for centralization. But what about the other point made by those who posit a European "revolution in the art of war," to wit that Europeans, through their gunpowder revolution, gained a military advantage over peoples elsewhere in the world?

The Military Revolution

The most influential proponent of this view is historian Geoffrey Parker, author of the celebrated book *The Military Revolution*.[15] For Parker, the crucial period was the 1500s and 1600s. He argues that Europe's continual interstate competition resulted not just in state centralization and consolidation, but also in the rapid development of arms and military practices that gave Europeans a significant military edge vis-à-vis the people of the rest of the world.

Parker's argument is nuanced, but, roughly put, it suggests that the trigger in these changes was improvements in gun technology. In the late 1400s and early 1500s, Europeans developed powerful mobile field artillery, which made it much easier to besiege towns and castles.

Medieval walls tumbled down, and in response engineers designed walls that were much more resistant to artillery: the thick earth-filled bastions that were so similar to traditional Chinese walls. To meet this challenge, military leaders fielded larger armies to surround the new walls. Those armies stayed in the field longer as well, because sieges lasted so long. Building fortresses and putting together larger armies to besiege them cost an enormous amount of money, so political leaders developed new ways to raise revenue, through more pervasive taxation and fiscal and financial innovation. States that couldn't compete expired. Successful states perdured. The challenge-response dynamic that led from mobile artillery to more centralized states also led to other military innovations: soldiers trained and drilled more effectively; ships became floating cannon platforms; new tactics emerged at sea and land.

Although some people have declared the military revolution model passé, books and articles continue to invoke, extend, and critique it.[16] Parker's book *The Military Revolution* is cited as much today as when it was first published in 1988, and students all over the world discuss it in class.

Why is the military revolution model so fruitful? For one thing it seems, at base, to work. Scholars may quibble about the word "revolution" and prefer instead "evolution" or "punctuated equilibrium."[17] But it's clear that momentous changes happened in warfare in the 1500s and 1600s, that those changes were brought about by Europe's ongoing geopolitical fragmentation, and that they were linked to other key developments, to wit, the centralization of European states and the expansion of European power abroad.

Even more important, the military revolution model is flexible. Parker himself adapted the theory from one of his mentors, Michael Roberts, arguing that the formative period was earlier than Roberts had suggested.[18] Medieval historian Clifford Rogers has since argued that the key period was even earlier, identifying three separate revolutions: an infantry revolution in the 1300s, an artillery revolution in the 1400s, and a fortress revolution in the early 1500s.[19] Historian Jeremy Black has argued that the true revolution happened in the late 1600s, when bayonets replaced pikes and armies truly became gun armies.[20] Fernando Gonzalez de León says that "the authentic military revolution" was inaugurated during the Spanish wars against Granada in the 1480s and 1490s.[21] Olaf van Nimwegen believes that there was a "tactical revolution" around 1600 and an "organizational revolution" in the 1660s.[22] Historians have applied the model beyond Europe: to the Northern African Islamic states, the Ottoman Empire, India, Japan, Korea.[23] And global historians, such as Sun Laichen and myself, have suggested that the military revolution might best be seen as a global process that started in China.[24]

This speaks to the model's flexibility, but in all the debate, few scholars have actually tested Parker's claim that the military revolution underlay European colonialism. To what extent did Europe's military innovations between 1450 and 1700 actually provide Europeans an edge in warfare? The case seems clear for the New World, whose populations lacked the guns, germs, and steel that proved so invaluable in European conquest. But what about the Old World, and particularly Asia, where guns and steel were invented, and where the germs were as virulent as those of Europe?

Certainly, many Europeans of the time felt that their military power was more than a match for that of China. The Portuguese merchant Vasco Calvo, for example, believed that just two or three thousand Portuguese would be enough to sieze China's Guangdong and Fujian Provinces, whose combined population was fifteen times that of Portugal, and use the territory as a base from which to conquer all of China.[25]

Intriguingly, the military advantages he attributed to Portugal are precisely those that today's military historians believe gave Europeans an edge in warfare over peoples in the rest of the world: better artillery, superior soldiers, powerful ships, and deadly forts.

A Plan to Conquer China, 1536

Vasco Calvo wrote in straightened circumstances, "constantly on the watch lest some Chinaman should come."[26] He was in prison in Guangzhou and had been for more than a decade, during which time he appears to have learned Chinese quite well.[27] He also somehow gained access to Chinese books, including an unidentified atlas that provided detailed information about geography and defense. He believed that if he could smuggle his plan out of prison, the detailed knowledge it contained would allow the Portuguese to make the most of their military

MAP 8.1 The Ming dynasty ca. 1517.

advantage. He was not the only European who proposed plans to conquer China in the 1500s, but his instructions are the most detailed and informed.[28]

The first step of his plan relied on the superiority of Portuguese cannon ships, which he believed could easily capture Chinese positions on the Pearl River, culminating in the capture of the trade metropolis of Guangzhou: "a galleon that entered this city would make it surrender, because it would place the city under its power, and not a man would appear when the artillery fired."[29] If just one galleon could achieve this, imagine what a small flotilla could do: "With six ships . . . all can be accomplished."[30]

This may sound ridiculous, but in the early 1500s ships bristling with guns had enabled the Portuguese to dominate the Indian Ocean, defeating powerful enemies and capturing key ports, including the city of Goa, which they conquered in one day (after an earlier setback). The same powerful ships helped the Portuguese conquer Malacca in 1511, one of the most important ports in the world.

The secret to Portugal's naval success lay in shipborne artillery. Asian vessels carried guns—the Hongwu Emperor had used gunboats to defeat enemies in China and Vietnam, and his son Yongle had sent gun-bearing ships to India and the Middle East nearly a century before the Portuguese arrived in India. But Portuguese ships were far better armed.[31] A description of Vasco Da Gama's ships notes that "each of the caravels carried thirty [armed] men, and four heavy guns below, and above six falconets [a midsized gun], and ten swivel-guns placed on the quarter deck and in the bows, and two of the falconets fired astern; the ships [ships are larger vessels than caravels] carried six guns below on the deck, and two smaller ones on the poop, and eight falconets above and several swivel-guns, and before the mast two smaller pieces which fired forwards; the ships of burden [the largest ships of all] were much more equipped with artillery."[32]

Why shouldn't such ships work in China as well as they had worked in Africa, the Middle East, India, and Southeast Asia? As Calvo wrote, "the whole world, Sir, would not be enough to capture one of our ships, how much more two, if they showed them their teeth."[33] With gunships, the Portuguese would blast away at Chinese defenses along the Pearl River, and there was no reason to worry about a significant challenge, because the Chinese, he believed, had no significant artillery to counter with. A fellow prisoner of Calvo's corroborated this view in a smuggled letter of his own: "Before the Portuguese came, they had no bombards, only some made after the manner of the pots of Monte Mór, a vain affair."[34] Calvo wrote that the Chinese could be "severely punished with artillery; for speaking of it now they put their finger in their mouth, amazed at such a powerful thing."[35]

Once artillery had cleared the river of boats and forts, the Portuguese would be free to land troops and set up bases, starting with a fortress near the river armed with great bombards. Under the protection of this improvised stronghold, the Portuguese would then build a "strong fortress, with towers or bastions."[36]

The Portuguese had long been famous for powerful fortresses filled with artillery, which sprouted up throughout the Portuguese Empire, from Brazil to Africa to India to Southeast Asia. In the early 1500s, the Portuguese conquistador Duarte Pacheco Pereira bragged that "in fortresses surrounded by walls . . . Europe excels Asia and Africa."[37] And, indeed, Portuguese forts proved enormously difficult to dislodge, much to the chagrin of local leaders. As a source from Malabar, India, lamented, the Portuguese forts of southern India "could never be taken."[38]

It's not clear what kind of fortress Calvo had in mind, but historians have shown that by the early 1500s Europeans were building extraordinarily effective fortifications, whose angled bastions and geometrical defenses allowed an interpenetrating crossfire that was nearly impossible for stormers to penetrate.[39] Geoffrey Parker has famously referred to this type of fortress as an "engine of European expansion" because it allowed small garrisons of soldiers to hold out against far larger numbers of besiegers.[40] As he writes, "the invention and diffusion of the 'Italian style' of fortification represented an important step in the West's continuing—perhaps unique—ability to make the most of its smaller resources in order, first, to hold its own and, later, to expand to global dominance."[41] Early Portuguese fortresses in Asia lacked angled bastions, but around the time that Calvo was writing, the Italian-style artillery fortress was beginning to spread to the Portugese empire. These new fortresses, with their angled bastions, were even harder to dislodge than the earlier forts.

In any case, Calvo believed that once the Portuguese had built a proper fortress "with towers or bastions" near Guangzhou, they would control the river, allowing them to methodically approach the city's walls with a breastwork, "which would go on approaching the gate of the city, so that the city would be entirely dominated—because all is ground flat as the palm of one's hand."[42] Guangzhou would probably surrender. If not, one would aim three cannons (*camellos*) at the city's gates and batter them down. Then the Portuguese should immediately build another fortification inside Guangzhou. There was a hill there, covered in temples, from which stone could be gathered and used to construct a four-story artillery fortress that could command the entire city and its environs. He believed that just a hundred men would be needed as a garrison, and "the city will then become so strong that not a bird will be able to descend that will have an opportunity of escaping."[43]

With Guangzhou under Portuguese control, other Chinese cities would throw off the mandarins' yoke and come over to the Portuguese, who could then expand quickly, building artillery fortresses in the other settlements. "This," he writes, "is the reason why artillery must be brought from India, so that it will be possible to do great things against any people whatsoever."[44]

Wasn't Calvo worried that Portuguese troops might be overcome by Chinese soldiers? No, he wrote, "so weak a people are they, and they have no kind of defense."[45] The Chinese might try to place troops on the rivers or shores to hold the Portuguese back, but, he argued, they would be poorly armed relative to the Portuguese, and "any force would be able to capture them."[46] As for the three thousand soldiers guarding Guangzhou itself, "there is not a Malabar that could not fight with forty of these men and kill them all, because they are just like women. They have no stomach; simply outcries."[47]

Thus, according to Calvo, Portugal's superior soldiers, better guns, stronger ships, and powerful fortresses would allow it to defeat China easily. To be sure, he admitted, a dozen years before he penned his plan, the Portuguese *had* in fact fought against the forces of China, and they had lost. Calvo himself had been captured. But Calvo assured his readers that this defeat had been a fluke, due to bad leaders, who failed to take advantage of Portugal's overwhelming military superiority.

Was he right about that Sino-Portuguese conflict? Did the Portuguese really have military superiority vis-à-vis the Ming forces they fought? It's worth looking into, because scholars still debate this question today.

CHAPTER 9

Cannibals with Cannons

THE SINO-PORTUGUESE CLASHES OF 1521–1522

The Sino-Portuguese War was the first major military conflict between Chinese and European forces in history. One might expect it to have been studied closely.[1] One would be wrong.[2] The lack of data has not stopped scholars from using the war to make opposing points about European military capacity. Some argue that the Chinese victory demonstrates that European superiority has been badly exaggerated, and that the Chinese had the military wherewithal to create global empires if only they had wanted to.[3] Others say that the Chinese managed to win only because they had an overwhelming numerical advantage and that European firepower was "vastly superior."[4]

As we'll see, the truth lies between these two extremes, but what is most interesting is that the Sino-Portuguese conflict allows us to glimpse the challenge-response dynamic in action. The "war" was in fact two separate sets of engagements, a year apart. During the first set, in 1521, Portuguese firepower was far more effective than that of the Chinese. During the second set, in 1522, Chinese artillery was more than a match for the Portuguese, causing serious damage and playing a key role in the Chinese victory. If there was a gun gap in 1522, it was much smaller than the year before.

In fact, even before the conflict Chinese officials had recognized the effectiveness of Portuguese guns and begun adopting them. The Sino-Portuguese conflict sped up this process. The main Chinese commander was a scholar and official named Wang Hong (汪鋐, 1466–1536). Having witnessed the power of Portuguese artillery, he became a partisan of reform, and thanks in part to his advocacy thousands of Portuguese-style guns were installed on the Great Wall by the mid-1500s. Although his enemies nearly succeeded in having him written out of history, today Chinese celebrate him as an anti-imperial hero and the first successful partisan of "learning from the west."[5] But he wasn't the only one. During this period many Chinese (and Japanese and Koreans) paid close attention to the new arms arriving from Western Europe, and their adoptions were not slavish. They innovated, adapted, modified, and improved.

Indeed, the Sino-Portuguese Conflict marks the threshold of a new era of rapid military modernization in East Asia, an era we might call the Age of Parity. Throughout this period—1522 through the early 1700s—if Europe had a military lead, it was slight and easily closed.

The First Sino-Portuguese Conflict, 1521

Like so many Sino-European clashes in ensuing centuries, the Sino-Portuguese conflict took place in southern China, near the bustling port city of Guangzhou. Ambassadors of Portugal had arrived in Guangzhou in 1517, hoping to meet the emperor and open formal relations.[6] Portugal wasn't listed on the Ming's register of foreign countries, so it took a couple years of diplomacy before the embassy was able to proceed to the imperial court. When it arrived in 1520 it ran into more trouble. Some Confucian officials complained that the ambassadors were ill-behaved, and one official even beat a member of the embassy for failing to kneel in his presence.[7] Yet the Portuguese managed to make influential friends, probably by means of bribes.[8] They may even have found favor with the emperor himself, who, some sources suggest, enjoyed learning the ambassadors' language.[9]

Unfortunately, while the ambassadors were passing bribes, their compatriots in Guangzhou were eating babies, or that's what Ming sources would have you believe. One account describes how the children were cooked: "Their method is to use a huge cauldron to heat up water until it boils, and then an iron cage with a small child in it is placed on top, and the child is steamed until sweat comes out. When the sweat is gone, [the child] is taken out, and iron scrubbers are used to remove the bitter flesh. The child is still living at this point. Then they kill it, excise the stomach, take out the intestines, and steam and eat it."[10] Allegations of Portuguese cannibalism appear in many Ming sources, even the official *Ming History*.[11] In reality, of course, the Portuguese were far more partial to fish than to human flesh. The stories of cannibalism probably arose from the fact that they were acquiring children as slaves and servants.[12]

They were misbehaving in other ways, too. Reports accused them of blocking other nations from trading in Guangzhou, of knocking hats off Ming officials, of firing guns so that "the sound of their cannons pervaded the land."[13] Even more worrisome were reports that they were "building houses and setting up stockades, relying on their guns to protect themselves."[14] When the emperor died suddenly, the Portuguese fell out of favor, and their main patron in the imperial court was executed. The ambassadors were sent back to Guangzhou. When they arrived things had gotten quite bad indeed.

In the spring of 1521, a fleet of Portuguese ships had sailed up the Pearl River to trade in Guangzhou. City officials told them to leave. The Portuguese refused. When some Portuguese went ashore to trade, they were promptly arrested. One of them was our own Vasco Calvo, who would later author the plan to conquer China. His brother Diogo Calvo captained the largest vessel, and once Vasco was captured, Diogo naturally became even less willing to leave, demanding the return of the prisoners.

In response, a Chinese fleet assembled itself. Commanding it was Wang Hong.[15] Born in 1466, Wang Hong had passed the top imperial examinations in 1502, and since 1514 had been stationed in Guangdong, tasked with maritime defense.[16] Before 1521, his main foes were pirates, whom he fended off with mixed results.[17] His fight against the Portuguese proved more challenging but ultimately more glorious.

Although the precise details of the first skirmishes are not clear, it seems that Wang Hong started by attacking in a straightforward way, ship to ship. According to an account in a Guangdong gazette from the Ming period, the Portuguese "fired their guns several times and defeated our troops."[18] Portuguese sources corroborate this, saying that "God saw fit to deal with them [the Chinese] in such a way that they departed from the encounter much damaged by our artillery, with the death of many of their people."[19]

Wang Hong had numerical superiority, but the Portuguese guns kept his vessels away. Each time he tried to close, the Portuguese fired. As Portuguese chronicles note, the Chinese "tried to encircle our vessels, but the place was so narrow that it aided our five vessels far more than it helped their far more numerous ones, primarily because of the better artillery that we had."[20] Despite a significant numerical advantage, Wang Hong had no effective way to attack the Portuguese. Some Chinese sources even suggest that he tried recruiting divers to bore holes in Portuguese hulls of the Portuguese vessels, a tactic that would have been ineffective and isn't mentioned in Portuguese accounts.[21]

All of this supports the military edge argument, and, indeed, like many Chinese from the period, Wang Hong himself acknowledged the superiority of Portuguese artillery. "I daresay," he wrote later, "that the ferociousness of the Portuguese depends on these guns alone. Since ancient times, no weapons have ever surpassed these powerful and violent ones."[22]

Nonetheless, by encircling the Portuguese, Wang Hong had gained the upper hand. The Portuguese were unable to resupply and suffered hunger and illness. Wang Hong might well have gained their surrender if his men hadn't made a mistake. Having focused on keeping the enemy in, they failed to keep the enemy out. Some Portuguese ships slipped through with reinforcements. The most powerful was commanded by a "very Catholic" man named Duarte Coelho. He and the other captains resolved to break through the cordon. They made their move just before dawn on 8 September 1521.

Wang Hong was ready. As a Chinese source notes, he'd worked out a plan: "All of it was carefully thought through. The barbarian vessels are all large and difficult to maneuver, and when desiring to act must rely upon wind and sails. At that time the southern wind was extremely intense. His Excellency [Wang Hong] daubed together some shabby bandit boats, loaded them up with all kinds of dried firewood and tinderlike materials, and poured into them grease and fat."[23]

The wind was favorable, and Portuguese chronicles record that "there was in this attack a resemblance to hell itself, with fire and smoke, because collision was not the sort of thing our side wanted to do, because they had no other desire than to find a clear route for their passage, which they did not dare to make, so fiercely had they already been burned in this attack."[24]

Here Chinese and Portuguese sources diverge. The Chinese account quoted above goes on to say that Wang Hong "ordered the many [troops] to board, to the sound of drums and war cries, and it was a great victory and there were no survivors."[25]

Portuguese sources, however, record a different outcome: divine intervention. The day of the battle, 8 September, happened to be the festival of the birth of the Virgin Mary. The devout Duarte Coelho ordered everyone to pray, and according to the most famous Portuguese chronicle, the virgin answered the prayers. "Our Lady, who aids those who call on her in such times of need, responded by sending a thunderstorm, which for us was wind at our backs but which caused the enemy to tip over and they lose some of their [vessels]."[26] He and Diogo Calvo and many other Portuguese managed to escape back to Malacca, where they founded a "house on the hill" in her honor.

The Chinese sources that detail the fire attack and claim no survivors are not firsthand sources. One, for example, was inscribed on a temple that was erected in honor of Wang Hong. They seem to conflate the battles of 1521, in which Coelho escaped after a miraculous storm, with the battles of 1522, which turned out much worse for the Portuguese.[27]

The Second Sino-Portuguese Conflict, 1522

In 1522, a new Portuguese fleet arrived on the Chinese coast. Leading it was admiral Martim Afonso de Mello, whose orders were to reestablish good relations. He proceeded optimistically up the Pearl River toward Guangzhou but soon found his way blocked by an impressive force. Whereas the Chinese fleet of 1521 had been gathered quickly, this one, as he wrote in a letter to the Portuguese king, "seemed in total to be more than three hundred sails, large and small, and eighty of them were very large junks of two masts [duas gaveas], very well armed with small artillery and many other of the weapons they have."[28]

The two Chinese officers who led the fleet, Ke Rong (柯榮) and Wang Ying'en (王應恩), didn't attack at first.[29] "They just wanted," Mello wrote, "to demonstrate their power . . . doing nothing more than going in front of me and shooting a few shots, [making noise] with their drums and gongs, placing themselves in front of the port that I intended to reach."[30] Mello's goal was peace, so he exercised restraint, although, he wrote, "it pained me that I could not shoot them."[31]

He managed to get near enough to prepare boats to trade on shore, but each day at dawn the Chinese attacked, rowing armed vessels back and forth and firing guns. When he led a party ashore to take on water, he and his men were pinned down by artillery fire for an hour and had to abandon their barrels and make a break for their ships, "coming back with blood instead of water."[32]

The warjunks pressed their attack, firing barrages of such power that de Mello was forced to take extreme measures. He ordered the anchor cords to be cut, the expensive anchors to be abandoned, and the ships to make a run for deeper water. His brother Diogo de Mello led the way with two shallow-drawing vessels, trying, it seems, to sound a passage through the flats. The Chinese fleet approached the sounding vessels and began firing.[33]

The Virgin Mary didn't help this time. As the Portuguese chronicler João de Barros writes, "The first sign that victory would be given to the enemy came in the form of a spark getting into the powder carried by Diogo de Mello, which blew the decks of his vessel into the air. He and the hull went to the bottom together."[34] Diogo's brother, the admiral, was devastated: "I saw one of the vessels burst into flames and go down to the bottom, with nothing left alive or dead that we could see, and it was my brother Diogo de Mello's vessel, and with him went fifteen or twenty members [criados] of my father's household, and of mine, who had gone with him."[35]

The captain of the other sounding vessel, Pedro Homen, saw survivors floating in the water and tried to rescue them. The Chinese attacked, first with artillery and then by sending boarding parties. Pedro was a powerful man, "in stature one of the largest men of Portugal, and his spirit of bravery and physical strength were different from the common man."[36] But the Chinese had a hero of their own: "Pan Dinggou (潘丁苟) . . . was first to board, and the other troops followed and advanced in good order."[37] The combat was intense. Pan's side overcame Pedro's, but the most devastating attacks came not from hand-to-hand combat but from Chinese artillery. According to Portuguese sources, "[Pedro Homen's] fighting was such that if it hadn't been for the shots of [Chinese] artillery, he never would have died, so great was the fear of the Chinese to approach him."[38]

De Mello raced to the rescue, but got to Pedro Homen's vessel too late. Just one sailor and one cabin boy were left, having hidden in a crow's nest (*gavea*). Portuguese chronicles say that the Chinese troops slaughtered everyone on board, "because they show mercy to no-one."[39] Chinese sources corroborate the slaughter: "Pedro (別都盧) . . . and other leaders were captured alive, and thirty five trophy heads were captured, and ten other [living] prisoners were taken, male and female."[40] Pedro and his fellow captives died soon enough, executed by order of the emperor. De Mello escaped, burning Pedro Homen's ship so the Chinese wouldn't get it.[41]

Thus, in this second engagement, the Portuguese encountered a far more effective fleet, and much greater firepower. Whereas in 1521, the Portuguese were able to compensate for Chinese numerical superiority by means of their guns, they couldn't do so in 1522. This suggests that the Chinese had learned from the previous encounter and adapted. The second Chinese fleet was far better armed than the first.

Did it have Western-style guns? It seems likely. In 1517, when the Portuguese ambassadors first arrived in Guangzhou, a scholar named Gu Yingxiang (顧應祥, 1483–1565) had taken careful note of their guns, writing, "On each side of their ships are placed four or five guns, and from within the ship's hold they can secretly fire them. If other ships come near, the bullets burst asunder their planks and the water leaks right in. With them one can rampage across the seas and other countries cannot stand up against them."[42] It seems that the Portuguese were even cajoled into donating one of their cannons to help the Chinese defend against pirates, along with a recipe for powder to suit it.[43]

At around this time, another Ming official also worked to incorporate Western guns. A later Ming source tells the story:

There was a man named He Ru (何儒), the deputy magistrate (巡檢) of Baisha in Dongguan County, who once had to go to a Frankish [*Folangji*] ship to collect tolls. He met some Chinese men—Yang San, Dai Ming, and others—who had lived for years in their [the Portuguese's] country, and these men were entirely familiar with the making of boats, the casting of guns, and the method of making gunpowder. [Wang] Hong ordered He Ru to secretly send people over to them, selling rice wine as a pretext, to clandestinely talk to Yang San and the others, order them to declare their allegiance, and offer them rewards and presents. These men proved willing to become loyal and a plan was devised. At night He Ru secretly came over with a small boat and conveyed them to the shore.[44]

The official *Ming History* also has a version of this story, which differs on some details but concurs that He Ru "obtained their . . . ship guns and other technologies. . . . China's possession of the various Folangji firearms began with [He] Ru."[45]

Sources—at least those known at present—don't say for certain that the advantage in firepower enjoyed by the second Chinese fleet was based on Western-style artillery. What is clear, however, is that the Chinese won not just by means of superior numbers but also because they, too, had effective guns and could use them well, something apparent from Portuguese sources. As Admiral Mello noted, the Chinese fleet was "very well armed with small artillery."[46] Later, his men were pinned down for an hour by Chinese gunfire when they went ashore to gather water. After they made it back to their ships, Chinese gunners blasted them so fiercely that Portuguese guns were incapable of answering, and Mello had to cut and run, leaving his anchors behind. Similarly, in the ensuing battle, Chinese guns killed many Portuguese and directly contributed to the Chinese victory.

Thus, whereas Chinese firepower was inferior during the first set of battles, it was superior—or at least comparable—in the second set. This suggests that the Chinese quickly learned to counterbalance Portuguese firepower with their own.

Indeed, the Sino-Portuguese conflicts mark a watershed in military history, inaugurating a period of deep military innovation in China. Wang Hong, famous for defeating the Portuguese, became a proponent of technology transfer, and he wasn't the only one. Chinese officials at all levels proved eager to learn about and adapt foreign arms. Although today many scholars still argue that China post-1433 was conservative and closed to innovation, that notion does not stand up to the evidence.

PART III

An Age of Parity

CHAPTER 10

The Frankish Cannon

After the Song dynasty, writes a scholar in a recent book, the Chinese "showed little enthusiasm for outside ideas and inventions."[1] This perspective is maddeningly prevalent. Historians have argued variously that "Confucianism [was] slow to mount on the back of technology,"[2] that China's bureaucrats felt that "the mechanics of warfare were beneath their interest,"[3] that "the denizens of the Chinese court looked on gunpowder technology as a low, noisy, dirty business,"[4] that Confucian officials did not want to be associated with the use of "clever devices and wicked tricks,"[5] that "to accept the ways of barbarians as superior and emulate them were deeply distasteful notions to Chinese mandarins,"[6] that Confucianists' "cultural pride stood tenaciously in the way of change,"[7] that China's bureaucrats had a "singular inability to enhance, by implication an indifference to, the destructive capacity of their bombards and cannons."[8] People who hold such views should look at the examples of the Confucian scholars like Wang Hong and his contemporaries, who paid close attention to military matters and avidly adopted Western cannons.

No one was more a member of China's literati class than Wang Hong, who grew up quoting Confucius and memorizing Mencius.[9] In 1502 he passed the highest level civil examinations, held just once every three years and in which only three hundred students from all of China would pass. His degree gave him access to the privileges of highest-level office, but it was after he defeated the Portuguese that he began rising rapidly through the ranks.[10]

In 1529, he wrote a memorial proposing that Frankish cannons be deployed along the Great Wall:

> Today on the strategic borders the fortifications and walls are not fully secured, and when the bandits come, there is ravaging and devastation. The towers (墩台) have been constructed merely as lookout towers, but the walls and fortifications (城堡) lack any capacity to defend at long range, and so frequently there are troubles. It would be suitable to use the Frankish cannons I have submitted. The small ones weigh just twenty pounds [*jin*] or less, and in terms of range they can reach six hundred paces. They can be deployed on the lookout platforms (墩台), with each placement (墩) being equipped with one, with three men to protect it. The large ones can be seventy pounds [*jin*] or more, and they have a range up to five or six li. They should be deployed on the forts (城堡), with each fort being equipped with three, with ten men to protect them. Thus, every five li there will be one lookout tower (墩), and every ten li one fort (堡), and the small and large can back each other up, and the near and far as well. The bandit generals have nothing to counter this sort of thing, such that [if my plan is adopted] one can just sit and wait for them, achieving victory without attacking.[11]

The emperor approved the plan, and the official *Ming History* notes that "this is the point at which [our] guns began to include Frankish cannons."[12] Wang Hong became known as a partisan of Frankish guns, and he maneuvered fiercely in the factional fights that afflicted officialdom.[13] On one occasion, a rival laughed at the writing style he used in a memorial about Frankish guns. He had the man demoted from secretary-general of the Board of War to superintendent of Tongren Prefecture, a massive demotion. Someone joked with the poor guy: "You've been blasted to Tongren by a Frankish cannon."[14]

Ultimately Wang Hong's enemies won. He was dismissed from office and nearly erased from the historical record. The official Ming History doesn't even contain a biography for him, and the *Ming Veritable Records* attribute the importation of Portuguese cannons not to him but to someone else.[15] Today, Wang Hong's reputation is being rehabilitated. A temple built in his honor still exists, and although it's in poor shape, it has a new commemorative plaque, and groups are agitating to restore it.[16] He is being lionized as China's first anti-imperialist champion, "the first to lead troops to defend against the Portuguese western imperialists . . . and also the first person to import into China advanced western military technology . . . and to carry out its large scale promotion and promulgation."[17] Another Chinese article notes that Wang Hong's victory over the Portuguese "opened the Chinese people's struggle against western imperialist invasion, and thus has major historical significance. He was the first military scientist in history to propose 'learning from the [Western] barbarians to control the barbarians.'"[18]

It's true that Wang Hong did much to champion Western cannons, but he wasn't alone in doing so and he wasn't the first. Interest in Western guns was widespread. In fact, before the Sino-Portuguese War, Portuguese guns were incorporated into the arsenal of one of the most famous and influential Confucian scholars of the past five hundred years, the great Wang Yangming (王陽明, 1472–1529).

Wang Yangming and the Frankish Cannons

It's difficult to overstate the importance of Wang Yangming, but I'll give it a shot: He is the most important Confucian philosopher since the Song philosopher Zhu Xi (1130–1200). Although best known for his philosophy, he also made a mark as a military leader, recognized for disciplined troops and wise leadership.

His most important military test occurred in 1519, when he was governor of Jiangxi Province. Jiangxi was home to the Prince of Ning (寧王, Zhu Chenhao 朱宸濠, 1479–1521), an ambitious descendant of the founder of the Ming dynasty, Zhu Yuanzhang. The prince decided that the dragon throne should be his, and so he rose up in revolt. He had prepared carefully, raising money by overseas trade and buying armor and weapons in Southeast Asia. Reliable sources indicate that he even purchased Portuguese cannons as early as 1518.[19]

To counter these weapons, Wang Yangming himself was provided with Portuguese guns. The story goes that a distinguished old scholar named Lin Jun (林俊), sixty-seven and sickly, went to great trouble to cast and send them.[20] Wang Yangming tells the story:

When the honorable Lin heard of the Ning prince incident, it was night-time, but he immediately sent people out to cast tin into Frankish guns.[21]

He even copied out a recipe for gunpowder with his own hands, giving his utmost with extreme loyalty to [help] punish the rebels. At that time it was the sixth month, and the heat was poison. On the roads many were dying of sunstroke. But he sent two servants with their bundles and provisions, who braved the heat, traveling via byways day and night, more than three thousand li, to bequeath their gift. When they arrived, [the rebellion was over and the prince] had already been in captivity for seven days. But upon receiving the letter, I was so moved that tears streamed down my face.[22]

Wang Yangming composed a poem to honor the old scholar and commemorate his "Worthy Deed of the Frankish Gun" (佛郎機遺事). It compares this maker of the Frankish cannon to famous loyal heroes in history:

> The Frankish gun, who made it?
> Removable, like the innards of Bigan,[23] wrapped in smooth leather.
> The blood offerings of Chang Hong did not suffice.[24]
> The fury and hatred of Suiyang remain.[25]
> The outpourings [of the cannon] carry with them the old officials'
>   ardent faith:
> [The sound] shocking for a hundred li, splitting open the guts of
>   the traitorous.
> In vain the Sword of State is requested.
> In the emptiness one hears Lu Yang brandishing his spear [at the
>   sun].[26]
> The writing tablet of the honorable Duan is no longer with us.[27]
> The Frankish gun, who made it?[28]

This poem—stuffed with allusions to famous officials—betrays no hint of derision toward foreign technology, or any sense that war is unworthy of Confucian officials.

The donor of the cannons, Lin Jun, was himself was a top-ranked scholar-official. Born in 1452, twenty years before Wang Yangming, he passed the highest level examinations in 1478 and went on to fill a number of top posts, primarily in Jiangxi Province, where he often needed to field armies against bandits and rebels. In his fifties and sixties, he was sickly and he retired from service.[29] How he acquired the knowledge of Portuguese cannons isn't clear.[30] But there's no doubt of his interest in the technology, an interest he shared not just with Wang Yangming but with a wider circle of highly ranked scholar-officials.

This is clear from the fact that the "Worthy Deed of the Frankish Cannon" became the subject of one of the literati's favorite pastimes: a poetry exchange (唱和).[31] For example, one of Wang Yangming's protégés, a man named Zou Shouyi (鄒守益, 1491–1562), wrote a piece called "Frankish Gun Handscroll Verse Bestowed on Mr. Jiansu Lin [i.e., Lin Jun]" (佛郎機手卷為見素林先生賦), part of which reads as follows:

> The old man Lin Jun, a hero for the world
> A solitary minister, tears of blood dripping into the blue ocean
> With his own hands he tests the Frankish gun
> Sends it far, wending by twists and turns
> Sincerely concerned for his country
> A peal of thunder sounds
> The forces of evil take fright![32]

It's notable that Zou's poem contains the line "the Frankish gun in his hands he tests," which portrays a Frankish gun as a handgun. The Portuguese breach-loading guns that the Ming copied were large pieces, small artillery rather than firearms. We know that the Chinese later made Portuguese-style guns in many different sizes, but Zou's poem is evidence that this kind of adaptation had already begun, and that Lin Jun's guns weren't just simple copies. The guns' small size is also evidenced in a picture that Zou had engraved to commemorate his poem, which shows Lin Jun in the act of presenting Frankish guns to Wang Yangming (see Figure 10.1).[33]

Another poem is by a man named Tang Long (唐龍, 1477–1546), who also ascended to the pinnacle of the scholar-official class.[34] Each seven-character line describes an increasingly powerful blast:

> The first boom rouses the courage of the soldiers
> The second boom flays the skin of the evil officials
> The third boom and raging flames roast the red cliffs
> With the fourth sky[-shaking] boom come the capital [Yan] troops
> The fifth boom: a torrent, and the lakewaters stand up
> The sixth boom and the seventh boom—the wind roars
> Thunder cracks, the waves are everywhere, an iron hammer rings.[35]

FIGURE 10.1 Presenting Frankish guns to Wang Yangming.

This illustration depicts a celebrated episode in the world of letters of sixteenth-century China, when the retired scholar Lin Jun sent Portuguese guns to his friend Wang Yangming, the famous Confucian scholar, who was trying to quell a rebellion. In this scene, Lin Jun's servants present a Frankish gun and a sample of gunpowder to Wang Yangming. From Zou Shouyi, *Wang Yangming xian sheng tu pu*. Courtesy of the National Library of China, Beijing.

Tang Long knew guns. He'd used them to help defeat the powerful bandit brothers Liu Qi and Liu Liu (劉六 and 劉七), and a famous inscription on his tomb describes the varieties of pieces he used: "He fired rice-bowl guns and all kinds of long-handled guns, killing their bravest crack troops."[36] It's interesting that his poem about the Frankish guns emphasizes the seven booms in short succession, perhaps because he was impressed by the way that Frankish guns, being breechloaders with removable cartridges, could fire rapidly.

In the poems of these learned men we discern no reluctance to adopt Western cannons, no notion that war is beneath them. On the contrary, they seem avid. They loved the story of Lin Jun, a Confucian hero, offering foreign technology to help a friend and save his country. And these elite officials, being at the center of wide nets of patronage and friendship, helped spread information about Portuguese cannons widely.

The Ming Adopt Frankish Cannons

Many other Chinese scholar-officials became interested in Portuguese cannons, grasping their utility as soon as they glimpsed them.[37] There is even evidence that Western guns entered China before the Portuguese themselves did, perhaps even before 1510. It is troublesome evidence, and Sinophone scholars tend to doubt it, since the Portuguese didn't even capture Malacca until 1511.[38] Yet Portuguese guns were being adopted in India by 1508, captured from Portuguese ships and quickly copied by local military leaders.[39] Southeast Asians also had occasion to learn about them, and given the density of Asian maritime trade routes during that period, it seems obvious that the guns would have come to the attention of Chinese mariners before the Portuguese arrived in China. Indeed, some evidence suggests that Chinese pirates were using them near Guangdong by 1510.[40] In general, the scholarly consensus in China seems to be trending toward the position that Frankish guns were first adopted by private traders in Guangdong and Fujian and spread to officials later.[41] (There is also evidence—circumstantial but suggestive—that the Ming learned about Frankish cannons from the Ottomans, via the Silk Road.)[42]

It doesn't much matter precisely when or how the new guns were first adopted. What is important is how enthusiastically the scholar-officials welcomed them. Thanks to Wang Hong, Wang Yangming, Gu Yingxiang, and the many other civil and military officials who championed them, Portuguese cannons became a mainstay of Ming defenses. They bristled from the Great Wall. They were integrated with infantry units. They were mounted on carts and used as a sort of armored infantry. They were deployed on ships.[43]

The process of adapting Western guns to China wasn't difficult. Ming bronze-casting techniques were on a par with those of Europe, and Ming iron casting was superior. Evidence also suggests that Chinese and European powder formulas were not appreciably different.[44] Western guns spread rapidly precisely because they were so similar to Chinese guns, the same technology but with ingenious touches, such as breech-loading mechanisms and long barrels that provided greater power and accuracy.[45] Western guns were viewed as variations on a theme, easily incorporated.[46]

The avidity of adoption can be glimpsed in the speed at which the new gun designs were produced by the imperial arsenals in Beijing. It took ninety days just to travel from Guangzhou to Beijing, but the first batch of Frankish guns forged by order of the imperial court was produced in 1523, just a year after the Second Sino-Portuguese Conflict.[47] They were based on the captured guns that Wang Hong sent to the capital, and there were just thirty-two of them, a sort of test run, but soon the central arsenals were producing thousands of Frankish guns of many sizes and types. They were sent throughout the empire, particularly to the most important border defense posts.[48] In 1528, for example imperial arsenals produced four thousand Frankish guns for use on border fortifications.[49] Excavated exemplars of this type weigh only four kilograms each, much smaller than the Portuguese models they had been based on.[50]

Indeed, Frankish guns inspired a wide range of Chinese subtypes. The official Weng Wanda (翁萬達, 1498–1552), for example, who received his jinshi degree in 1526, developed a gun known as the "vanguard gun" (先鋒炮), which was, as he himself described it, "copied from the Frankish gun but with modifications" (仿佛郎機而損益之也).[51] It was a shorter, faster-loading version of the Portuguese gun, equipped with a matchlock and designed so it could be used on horseback against nomads. The famous military innovator Zhao Shizhen (趙士楨, 1552–1611), developed a cross between a Portuguese gun and a Turkish musket.[52] The great general Qi Jiguang (戚繼光,1528–1588) championed a version of the Frankish gun designed to destroy enemy ships.[53]

There were many other experiments, showing that, as the Ming scholar Zheng Ruozeng (鄭若曾, 1503–1570) wrote, circa 1562, "the Chinese people, as they used [the Frankish guns], ingeniously altered them."[54] Historians today concur. As one Chinese author recently noted, the new hybrid guns the Chinese made "possessed the best parts of Chinese and Western gun technology."[55] Indeed, scholars in China have taken to referring to the late Ming period as a period of fusion, during which there occurred a hybridization of Western guns and traditional Chinese guns.[56]

The diversity of Chinese Frankish guns reflected the many uses to which they were put. In the mid-sixteenth century, general Qi Jiguang categorized Frankish guns into six types, by length, weight of ammunition, and powder charge. Type one was eight to nine feet (尺) long, with a sixteen-ounce (兩) pellet and sixteen ounces of powder; type two was six to seven feet long, with a ten-ounce pellet and eleven ounces of powder; and so on, down to one-foot-long specimens that shot fifteen-gram (three 錢) pellets with twenty-five grams (five 錢) of powder.[57] Each had a niche—some for naval warfare, others for defending fortresses, others for field battles, and so on.

The Frankish cannon was, in effect, nativized to China, and although many of the subtypes came to have their own names (Shooting Star Cannon, Peerless General Great Gun, etc.), the term *folangji,* or "Frankish cannon," remained in use, a testament to Confucian bureaucrats' willingness to adopt foreign technologies.[58] Confucian ideology didn't prevent Chinese officials from appreciating, understanding, and incorporating the technologies.[59] The case of the Frankish cannon shows a Ming dynasty open to and curious about the world. And, as we'll see, the Frankish cannons were only the first of many adoptions from the West.

Yet those who argue for the superiority of European warfare do not focus on weapons alone. They also suggest that European gunners were unusually effective because of clever training and painstaking drill, which gave them a decisive edge vis-à-vis other peoples. Here again, we have much to learn from China.

CHAPTER 11

Drill, Discipline, and the Rise of the West

Disciplined troops under an incapable general cannot lose. Undisciplined troops under an able general
cannot win.
—*Zhuge Liang (181–234AD)*[1]

In 1955, when historian Michael Roberts introduced the idea of the military revolution, he described one innovation as being at its heart: the
development in Western Europe of new forms of military discipline and
drill, or rather the return to ancient modes. The Romans had drilled
their infantry in strict formations, but after the barbarian invasions
the practice had died out. Roberts noted that in the late 1500s, ancient
techniques were revived and applied to gun-toting infantry units, in
an attempt "to return to Roman models in regard to . . . discipline and
drill."[2] That's not to say that the medievals hadn't trained. According to
Roberts, individual training was common. But there was no—or little—
drilling in groups, a practice that allowed units to work in cohesion.

Systematic drill solved the problem of handheld guns. By the mid-
1500s, European firearms had improved notably over the primitive
guns of the late medieval period, but they were still dangerously slow.
Under ideal circumstances, they required between twenty seconds and
a minute to load, an eternity under fire.[3] To use them effectively one
had to train soldiers to shoot in turns, a practice that became known
as the countermarch, or, alternately, the musketry volley technique.
The idea was simple. You placed your gunners in rows, one in front of

the other. The soldiers in the first row waited for the command to fire, did so, and then turned and marched to the back of the line, so that the first row became the last row and the second became the first and so on. The soldiers at the back concentrated on reloading, and by the time it became their turn again they were ready to shoot. In this way a formation of gunners could keep up a constant hail of fire.

It worked wonders on the battlefield, but it was very hard to train soldiers to do it properly. The men had to be drilled, exercised, and trained until the sequence became second nature. Otherwise discipline would evaporate once the men faced an enemy. Geoffrey Parker, who adopted Roberts's arguments about the importance of the counter- march, notes that "changing a pike square perhaps fifty deep into a musketry line only ten deep inevitably exposed far more men to the challenge of face-to-face combat, calling for superior courage, pro- ficiency and discipline in each individual soldier. Second, it placed great emphasis on the ability of entire tactical units to perform the motions necessary for volley-firing both swiftly and in unison. The an- swer to both problems was, of course, practice."[4] So the Europeans invented—or reinvented—military drill.

The invention of drill is said to have been epochal. Roberts argues that it revolutionized battlefield tactics and military organization. Parker further argues that it helped lay the groundwork for the rise of Europe in world history: "the combination of drill with the use of firearms to pro- duce volley fire, perfected through constant practice, proved the main- stay of western warfare—and the key to western expansion—for the next three centuries."[5] Although he acknowledges that China, too, had drill, he writes that the most important drilling innovation in modern times, musketry volley fire, developed only twice, in Japan and Europe.

As we'll see, China, too, had volley fire, and well before Japan or Europe. But first let's look at the evidence for Europe.

Volley Fire

According to both Roberts and Parker, the key development happened in the Netherlands in the 1590s. In a letter of 1594, the Dutch count Willem Lodewijk of Nassau-Dillenburg, described how he'd come up with the tactic:

> I have discovered . . . a method of getting the musketeers and soldiers
> armed with arquebuses not only to keep firing very well but to do it ef-
> fectively in battle order . . . in the following manner: as soon as the first
> rank has fired together, then by the drill [they have learned] they will
> march to the back. The second rank, either marching forward or standing
> still, [will next] fire together [and] then march to the back. After that,
> the third and following ranks will do the same. Thus before the last ranks
> have fired, the first will have reloaded.[6]

The letter included a diagram, which is the first extant depiction of
the volley technique in European history (see Figure 11.1). The image
shows nine columns of musketeers, five per column, each musketeer
denoted by a letter, a, b, c, and so forth. The first one, a, fires and then
follows the dotted line to the back of the column to reload his gun.
Meanwhile b fires, and so on.

Willem Lodewijk explicitly based his invention on classical models. The Romans had used countermarch techniques in their infantry
training, and he got the idea from the eminent classicist Justus Lipsius
(1547–1606), whose 1595 book *De Militia Romana* described classical drill in considerable detail.[7] The book influenced not just Willem
Lodewijk but also his cousin Maurice of Nassau, who studied it on
campaign and used it to reorganize the Dutch army.[8]

Willem Lodewijk drilled his troops obsessively, experimenting with
various ways to implement the volley technique effectively. It wasn't
easy. Some people mocked the idea of soldiers moving together in
rhythm like dancers. A few decades later, a Dutch historian recalled
the exercises, describing how the soldiers painstakingly formed and
unformed lines, marching in squares and other shapes, training both in
large and small groups, "man by man bringing the rearmost to the front
and the frontmost to the rear. . . . The beginnings were very difficult,
and many people felt, because it was all so unusual, that it was odd and
ridiculous [*lacherlich*]. They were mocked by the enemy, but with time
the great advantages of the practices became clear . . . and eventually
they were copied by other nations."[9] In fact, in the letter he wrote to
first describe the technique, Willem Lodewijk asked his cousin Maurice
to please not show the new technique too widely, "because it may . . .
give occasion for people to laugh."[10]

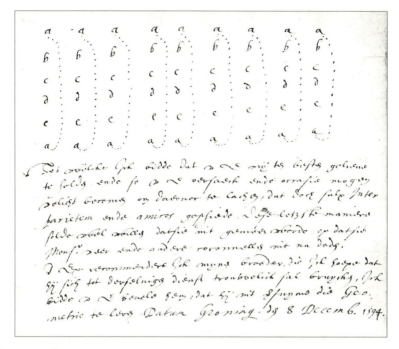

FIGURE 11.1 Schematic representation of the European musketry volley technique, 1594.

From a letter that William Louis of Nassau wrote to his cousin Maurice of Nassau representing his idea for the musketry volley technique (also known as the countermarch). Each of the letters "a," "b," "c," etc. represents one soldier. Willem Lodewijk of Nassau-Dillenburg letter to Maurice of Nassau, 8 December 1594, Courtesy of Koninklijke Huisarchief, The Hague, manuscript A22-19.

Parker's painstaking reconstruction of the emergence of the volley technique in Holland is compelling, although there are hints that the technique emerged earlier. A Spanish military manual written in 1586 describes the practice as clear as could be desired:

> Start with three files of five soldiers each, separated one from the other by fifteen paces, and they should comport themselves not with fury but with calm skillfulness [*con reposo diestramente*] such that when the first file has finished shooting they make space for the next (which is coming up to shoot) without turning face, countermarching [contrapassando]

to the left but showing the enemy only the side of their bodies, which is the narrowest of the body, and [taking their place at the rear] about one to three steps behind, with five or six pellets in their mouths, and two lighted matchlock fuses . . . and they load [their pieces] promptly . . . and return to shoot when it's their turn again.[11]

Similarly, Parker himself cites a 1579 passage by an Englishman named Thomas Digges, who suggested that musketeers should, "after the old Romane manner make three or four several fronts, with convenient spaces for the first to retire and unite himselfe with the second, and both these if occasion so require, with the third; the shot [musketeers] having their convenient lanes continually during the fight to discharge their peces."[12] There is perhaps some evidence—very scanty—indicating that some type of volley fire may have been used in Europe in a battle of 1522.[13] And some historians have suggested that volley fire might have been deployed by the Ottomans at the famous Battle of Mohács in 1526, although not, it seems, with arquebuses.[14]

Yet Parker points out that it's one thing to come up with the idea of volley fire and quite another to implement it. Drill was difficult, and Willem Lodewijk and Maurice of Nassau went through a long period of experimentation. Should each soldier, after firing, march to the back of his individual file? Should the front row of soldiers all walk together to one side of the formation and, in a line, proceed to the back? Or should they divide in half, one half going to the left and one to the right? How far apart should the files be? How many rows did one need? The distance between idea and execution is clear from the many trials and experiments through which the technique was refined, a process that Holland's rich historical sources have allowed historians to reconstruct in minute detail.[15]

The emergence in the Netherlands of the volley technique had wide repercussions. It spread throughout Europe, and historians have suggested that Europeans' disciplined troops—and particularly the volley-firing musketeers—were a key to European dominance overseas as well. Thomas Arnold has written that, wherever they fought, Europeans' victories "depended on tactical doctrines and attitudes, particularly an emphasis on regular formations and the management of firepower, that originated in the sixteenth century. . . . The future belonged to the drill, discipline and tactical doctrine of the West."[16] Geoffrey Parker has argued similarly, although he also notes that Europeans were not alone in having drill. "Only two civilisations," he has written, "have invented drill for their infantry: China and Europe. Moreover, both of them did so twice: in the fifth century BC in North China and in Greece, and again in the late sixteenth century. Exponents of the second phase—Qi Jiguang in Imperial China and Maurice of Nassau in the Dutch Republic—explicitly sought to revive classical precedents, and in the West, marching in step and standing on parade became a permanent part of military life."[17]

Parker was right that the Chinese had a rich tradition of drill, but they did not invent it twice. Whereas Europeans had to rediscover classical Roman drill, the Chinese could draw on a rich and unbroken drilling tradition, which included the volley technique.

The Tradition of Drill in China

Historians have long argued that volley fire for firearms first appeared during the sixteenth century in two separate places, seemingly independently: in Japan during the 1570s and in Europe during the 1590s.[18] Recently, historians have adduced evidence that the Ottomans used volley fire with firearms as early as 1526.[19] In fact, however, the first people to use the volley technique with firearms were probably the Chinese, and its roots run deep.

The volley technique was first used during China's Warring States Period (475–221 BCE).[20] But of course in those days there were no firearms. The missile weapon of choice for the ancient Chinese was the crossbow, a weapon that was quite similar in one respect to the early handgun: it was slow.[21] A text from circa 801 CE, the famous *Tong dian* (通典), by Tang dynasty scholar Du You (杜佑, 735–812), notes the problem: "The crossbow is slow to load, and when battle is near it cannot shoot more than one or two times, and so battle is not a straightforward thing for the crossbow. At the same time, without the crossbow, it is not beneficial to do battle."[22] The solution, Du You wrote, was the volley technique: "[Crossbow units] should be divided into teams that can concentrate their arrow shooting. . . . Those in the center of the formations should load [their bows] while those on the outside of the formations should shoot. They take turns, revolving and returning, so that once they've loaded they exit [i.e., proceed to the outer ranks] and once they've shot they enter [i.e., go within the formations]. In this way, the sound of the crossbow will not cease and the enemy will not harm us."[23]

There is no doubt that Du You is describing a volley formation, and very similar instructions are found in the famous and somewhat earlier Tang dynasty military manual the *Tai bai yin jing* (太白陰經), from circa 759 CE. Its author, a Tang military official named Li Quan (李筌, eighth century), makes a pun on the word "crossbow," *nu,* which is a homophone of the Chinese word for fury, also pronounced *nu.* "The classics," he writes, "say that the crossbow is fury. It is said that its noise is so powerful that it sounds like fury, and that's why they named it this way."[24] By employing the volley fire method, he noted, there is no letup to the sound and fury, and the enemy cannot approach.

He describes the technique clearly in language similar to (but not as beautiful as) that of the *Tong dian* I cited above, and extant versions of the book contain an illustration of the formation (see Figure 11.2), which may be the oldest extant depiction of the technique in history. The illustration shows a rectangular formation, with each circle representing one soldier. The top line is the front of the formation and is labeled "shooting crossbows" (發弩). Below that line are shorter horizontal rows of crossbowmen, two toward the right and two toward the left. They are labeled "loading crossbows" (張弩). The commander (大將軍) is placed in the center of the formation, and to his right and left are vertical lines that are labeled "drums." The drums were used to coordinate the movements of the crossbowmen, who loaded their weapons, stepped forward to the outer ranks, shot, and then retired to reload.

Thus, there is no doubt that the volley technique was known in the Tang dynasty (618–907), more than a millennium after the Warring States Period and eight centuries before the technique was redeveloped in the West. Yet whereas Roman precedents died out in Europe, China's culture of drill remained strong. Indeed, during the Song dynasty (960–1279), the technique was elaborated and systematized further. The author of the famous *Wu jing zong yao* (1044) noted that previously crossbows were not used to their full effectiveness because it was feared that they were too vulnerable to attack by short-range

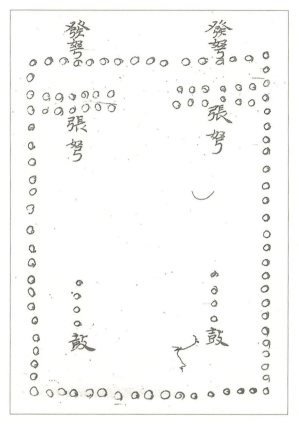

FIGURE 11.2 Representation of Chinese crossbow volley technique, ca. 759 CE.

In this illustration of a countermarch method for crossbows, each circle represents one soldier. The top line faces the enemy and is labeled "shooting crossbows" (發弩). Below that line are shorter lines of crossbowmen, two horizontal rows on the right and two on the left, which are labeled "loading crossbows" (張弩). The vertical lines within the rectangle, toward the bottom, four circles on the left and four on the right, are labeled "drums." From Li Quan 李筌, *Shen ji zhi di tai bai yin jing* 神機制敵太白陰經, Ming-era hand copy, ca. 1644, originally written ca. 759 AD. Courtesy of the National Library of China, Beijing.

troops. "The Tang military thinkers," he wrote, "called crossbows unsuitable for close-range combat."[25] What was his solution? Drilling the volley technique. If a force of spirited cavalry should venture to attack a group of crossbowmen, the latter were not to hide behind shield units but rather "plant the feet like a firm mountain, and, unmoving at the front of the battle arrays, shoot thickly to the middle [of the enemy], and none among them will not fall down dead."[26] He described the volley technique clearly: "Those in the center of the formation should load while those on the outside of the formation should shoot, and when [the enemy gets] close, then they should shelter themselves with small shields [literally side shields, 旁牌], each taking turns and returning, so that those who are loading are within the formation. In this way the crossbows will not cease sounding."[27]

The image (see Figure 11.3) that accompanies this description shows the volley technique in its clearest extant iteration up to that point, a formation that would hold steady for centuries thereafter, eventually being adapted to handguns. There are three clean rows of crossbowmen. And whereas in Tang manuals the rows had only two labels, "shooting" for the foremost line, and "loading" for the other two lines, this one adds a new label for the middle row, "advancing crossbows," which refers to those who have already loaded their weapons and are now making their way to the front of the formation, where they will plant their legs like mountains and shoot.[28]

But how do you persuade troops to plant their legs like mountains when the enemy is advancing and the feet naturally want to run? This was particularly problematic for crossbowmen, who had to face the enemy directly, with no troops protecting them in front. (As the Tang and Song manuals noted, "the accumulated arrows should be shot in a stream, which means that in front of them there must be no standing troops, and across [from them] no horizontal formations."[29]) The only way to make sure the shooters stayed firm was to drill them regularly and intensively.

Regular drill in formation seems to have been rare in medieval Europe, but it was common in China and had been since ancient times, part of a heritage that had never been interrupted. The *Wu jing zong yao* (1044), for example, notes that "although large inspections of infantry and cavalry are not carried out frequently, one should nonetheless adopt a method of daily practice in each garrison [營] in order to teach sitting, rising, advancing, and retreating. . . . One should use drum sounds as signals."[30] The book goes on to describe specific large-scale exercises that combined different types of units—cavalry, spearmen, crossbowmen, archers, flagmen, drummers—whose movements were coordinated by drums, gongs, wooden clappers, and flag signals.

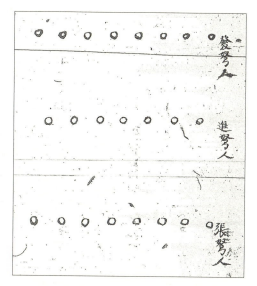

FIGURE 11.3 Teaching the crossbow method, ca. 1044.

In this figure, one can see a further elaboration of the crossbow volley technique. Whereas in Tang manuals the rows had only two labels, "shooting" for the foremost line and "loading" for the other two lines, this one adds a new label for the middle row, "advancing crossbows," which refers to those who have already loaded their weapons and are now making their way to the front of the formation. "Teaching the Crossbow Method" 教弩法, from Zeng Gongliang 曾公亮, Wu jing zong yao qian ji 武經總要前集, Ming-era hand copy, probably based on original from 1231, which in turn was based on the 1044 edition. Courtesy of the National Library of China, Beijing.

In one such drill, infantry archers cover cavalry as they ride forth, shoot three times with bows, and then withdraw, shooting behind their backs while the infantry "opens the door" and welcomes them in with more covering volleys. Another drill has four mixed groups arrayed in ranks, each of which takes a turn going forth, shooting volleys, leveling spears, yelling war cries, stabbing, and then returning, with slight variations between first and second and the third and fourth groups. Another drill has rows of crossbowmen followed by rows of archers who shoot salvoes to the beat of wooden clappers, advancing and withdrawing in time.[31] Often, flagmen were designated to move to certain positions to designate boundaries, allowing the actions of the troops to be choreographed precisely: "Listen for the drum, and then the spears (槍刀) straighten. Another drum beat and they sit, while the bows and crossbows rise, shooting three salvoes of arrows. When this is done, listen for the drumbeat and again stand, droop the head of the spear, wait for the gong (金), and then withdraw to the original position and stop. First beat, straighten spears; second beat, sit and dismiss flags, third beat, again straighten spears; fourth beat and the flag and spears as before, and the drum sounds stop."[32]

As Parker has pointed out, for a commander to come up with the idea of volley shooting is one thing, but to actually implement it is another. When the Dutch implemented the technique in the late 1500s, they had to experiment a great deal before they developed the famous Dutch method that then spread throughout Europe. So we need evidence to prove that the Chinese volley technique was actually used in battle. Fortunately, we have some.

The official *Song History* describes how a famous general named Wu Jie (吳玠) and his younger brother Wu Lin (吳璘) used the volley technique to defend the Song dynasty against Jin invasions in the 1130s. This was a time during which the Jin, now in possession of the Song capital of Kaifeng, were trying to destroy the Song once and for all. In the fall of 1131, the dread Jin commander Wanyan Wushu (完顏兀術) had led a force southward through the Shaanxi region. At a place called He-shangyuan (near present-day Baoji, Shaanxi Province), the Wu brothers attempted to stop him, and their troops employed the volley technique:

> [Wu] Jie ordered his commanders to select their most vigorous bowmen and strongest crossbowmen and to divide them up for alternate shooting by turns (分番迭射). They were called the "Standing-Firm Arrow Teams" (駐隊矢), and they shot continuously without cease, as thick as rain pouring down. The enemy fell back a bit, and then [Wu Jie] attacked with cavalry from the side to cut off the [enemy's] supply routes. [The enemy] crossed the encirclement and retreated, but [Wu Jie] set up ambushes at Shenben and waited. When the Jin troops arrived, [Wu's] ambushers shot, and the many [enemy] were in chaos. The troops were released to attack at night and greatly defeated them. Wuzhu was struck by a flowing arrow and barely escaped with his life.[33]

With half his army destroyed, Wanyan Wushu retreated back to the north. It was the most severe loss he'd ever sustained.

The following year Wanyan Wushu tried again, and this time it was Wu Jie's younger brother, Wu Lin, who deployed the volley technique. Wu Lin was defending a strategic fortress, and the situation was dire. His troops were exhausted, while the Jin were fresh and numerous, having been reinforced by troops with steel armor, and there were many of them, marching inexorably up the hill, an endless stream. According to the *Song History,* Wu Lin "used the Standing-Firm Arrow Teams, who shot alternately, and the arrows fell like rain, and the dead piled up in layers, but the enemy climbed over them and kept climbing up."[34] Although weakened, the Jin kept up the assault and eventually got close enough to attack the northeast tower, which began to tip over. The defenders twisted silken fabric into cables and pulled it straight again. The Jin launched a fire attack. The Song put the fires out with wine. Then the Song counterattacked and managed to drive the Jin away. It was another great victory for the Wu brothers. It's noteworthy that the *Song History* makes specific mention of this volley method, one of the few times that specific tactics are mentioned in the *Song History*, and it's likely that the Standing-Firm Arrow teams fought many other engagements that are lost to history.

The crossbow volley itself certainly wasn't lost to history. Although no one has yet identified references to it from the poorly documented Yuan dynasty (1279–1368), there are numerous references in the Ming period (1368–1644). Moreover, thanks to improvements in printing techniques, Ming books offer us the clearest illustrations of it. For example, the martial artist Cheng Chongdou (程冲斗, 1561–?),[35] who had studied at the famous Shaolin Temple and whose staff and sword postures are still used by Kung Fu students today, was a great partisan of the crossbow and in one of his martial arts manuals he produced a lovely illustration of volley shooting (see Figure 11.4).

His description makes clear that it was an ancient technique, handed down through the ages:

The ancients used ten thousand crossbows shooting in concert to win victories over enemies, and today I will describe it succinctly. Suppose you have three hundred crossbowmen. The first hundred of them have already loaded their arrows and are already arrayed together in the front.

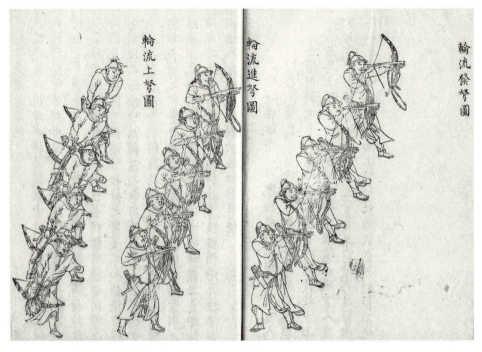

FIGURE 11.4 Depiction of Chinese crossbow volley technique, ca. 1621.

This image illustrates what the author refers to as the ancient technique of "ten thousand crossbows shooting in concert" (萬弩齊發). The crossbowmen on the right are at the fore and are shooting. The ones in the middle are ready to shoot. The ones to the left are in back reloading. "In this way," writes the author, "they revolve and take turns firing a constant stream, and the crossbows sound without cease." From Cheng Zongyou 程宗猷, *Jue zhang xin fa* 蹶張心法, in *Jue zhang xin fa, chang qiang fa xuan, dan dao fa xuan* 蹶張心法1卷長槍法選1卷單刀法選1卷 (1843 [Daoguang 22], woodblock print copy of 1621 original), 17–18. Courtesy of the National Library of China, Beijing.

They are labeled "shooting crossbows." The next hundred crossbowmen have also already loaded their arrows, but they are arrayed together in the next row and are labeled "advancing crossbows." Finally, the last hundred men are arrayed behind them, in [the third and] last row. They are loading their crossbows and are labeled "loading crossbows." The first hundred men, which is to say the "shooting crossbows," shoot. After they are done they retire to the rear, at which the second hundred men, the "advancing crossbows," move to the fore and themselves become "shooting crossbows." The rear hundred men, which is to say the "loading crossbows," move forward and become the "advancing cross-bows." When the first hundred men have fired and returned to the back, they become "loading crossbows." And in this way they revolve and take turns firing a constant stream, and the crossbows sound without cease.[36]

Cheng developed variations on the theme. He stipulated that cross-bowmen should also be trained in either a sword or a lance, and he championed a wearable crossbow that troops could strap to their backs when marching. When it came time to fight, crossbow-men would sheath their swords or lay their lances on the ground, get out their crossbows, shoot together in the volley technique, and then, when the enemy drew near, draw swords or pick up lances to fight at close range. He provided instructions about how to integrate crossbow-swordsmen and crossbow-lancers so that they could carry out the volley technique yet still be in the proper positions to fight at close range.[37]

So there's doubt that the Chinese tradition of the crossbow volley technique stayed strong and vibrant through the Ming period. But when was it adapted for firearms? The first clear evidence is from the late fourteenth century. In 1388, Ming forces were fighting in Yun-nan Province to put down an insurrection by a Tai leader named Si Lunfa (思倫發, d. 1399).[38] The Tai force was huge. It was not the three hundred thousand that the *Ming Veritable Records* suggest (in this case the veritable records aren't so veritable), probably more on the order of one hundred thousand. But it wasn't so much the numbers of Tai fighters that worried the Ming. It was their war elephants, which wore armor and bore on their backs war towers with ramparts.[39]

The Ming commander, Mu Ying (沐英, 1344–1392), devised a plan. The day before the decisive battle, he gathered his officers together and said, "What the bandits are counting on is their elephants."[40] He admit-ted that Ming cavalry attacks had so far failed against pachyderms, but, he said, "I do know what [the enemy] will be unable to withstand."[41] He explained his tactics carefully. The troops were to array themselves in three lines, setting up guns and some kind of gunpowder-fired arrow weapon (神機箭, probably arrow-shooting guns but possibly rockets).[42] "When the elephants advance," he explained, "the front line of guns and arrows will shoot all at once. If they do not retreat, the next line will continue this. If they still do not retreat, then the third line will continue this."[43] The following morning the troops duly divided into three teams and listened as Mu Ying made a rousing speech: "We are deep in enemy territory and both sides are locked together in combat. If we win we will live. If we lose we will surely die."[44] At first the elephants advanced slowly. Then, they broke into a run, charging the Ming lines. The Ming stood firm, "shooting arrows and stones, the noise shaking the mountains and vallies. The elephants shook with fear and ran."[45] The Ming pursued. If we are to believe the *Veritable Records*, half the elephants were killed, thirty-seven were captured, thirty thousand human heads were harvested, and ten thousand men were taken alive.

Scholars have hailed this passage as the first evidence of volley fire with firearms in world history.[46] The evidence isn't unambiguous—Mu Ying doesn't explicitly say that after the third row fires the first fires again, and so on. Yet there's no reason to doubt that a procedure that had been implemented for centuries with crossbows shouldn't immediately have been adapted for guns.

Moreover, other early Ming battles also show evidence of volley fire. One was the main battle of the bellicose Yongle Emperor's 1414 expedition against the Mongols. According to the *Veritable Records*, "The commander-in-chief (都督) Zhu Chong led Lü Guang and others directly to the fore, where they assaulted the enemy by firing firearms and guns continuously and in succession. Countless enemies were killed."[47] The interpretation hinges on two characters: *lian fa* (連發). *Lian* means "connected" or "continuous," one after another. *Fa* denotes "fire" or "shoot." There's no description of taking turns, but the enemy was on horseback, and if the Ming forces weren't using volley fire, there would have been long gaps between shots, or chaos as everyone fired and loaded at their own pace. Moreover, the practice of volley fire was so deeply entrenched that there was no need to describe it in detail. Sinophone historians have rightly interpreted this battle as indicating volley fire.[48]

Another one of Yongle's Mongolian expeditions—that of 1422—has also left sources that some have interpreted as suggesting volley fire, but in this case the evidence is less clear. According to the *Ming Veritable Records*, Yongle instructed his generals to drill carefully to integrate guns and conventional troops:

The emperor ordered that all the generals train their troops outside each encampment by arranging their formations so that the gunnery units (神機銃) occupied the foremost positions and the cavalry units occupied the rear. He ordered officers to exercise and drill in their free time (暇閑操習). He admonished them as follows: "A formation that is dense is solid, while an advance force is sparse, and when they arrive at the gates of war and it's time to fight, then first use the guns to destroy their advance guard and then use cavalry to rush their solidity. In this way there is nothing to fear."[49]

Sinophone historians believe this passage describes volley fire. Wang Zhaochun, for example, writes, "The meaning of this is that when fighting, the gun troops line up in front of the entire formation, and between them there must be a certain amount of space, so that they can load bullets and powder and employ shooting by turns and in concert to destroy the enemy advance guard. Once the enemy has been thrown into chaos, the rear densely arrayed cavalry troops together come forth in great vigor, striking forth with irresistible force."[50] Wang may be right, but there's not enough evidence to prove it. Certainly Yongle's willingness to place thin rows of gunnery units in the front lines of a battle against Mongol cavalry shows that he believed those gunners would offer enough fire to keep the cavalry at bay, which suggests volley fire, but the passage in the *Veritable Records* doesn't in itself make a clear case for it.

Still, the important point is that spreading gunnery units thin—necessary to concentrate their fire—required extraordinary discipline, which is precisely the point Geoffrey Parker made about the musketry volley technique in Europe. To draw out rank-and-file soldiers into thin lines and place them in the front ranks required great faith in the discipline of those soldiers, and that discipline could be conferred only by systematic drill.[51]

It thus seems clear the Chinese had a well-established tradition of drill, that they had developed the volley technique early on, as had the Romans and Greeks, and that whereas that technique had died out in the West, it had stayed strong in China. The volley technique—and drill in general—was thus part of an uninterrupted Chinese tradition from ancient times, and it was applied to gunpowder weapons starting in the 1300s at the latest.

In Europe, on the other hand, it seems that systematic drilling re-emerged only in the early modern period, and this fact has important implications for our understanding of global military history. In fact, historians of Europe, who generally know little about China's military history, have taken precisely the wrong lesson from Europeans' redis-covery of drill. It is a sign not of Europe's modernity—its advance vis-à-vis the rest of the civilized world—but of its backwardness. And this may resolve one of the mysteries of military history: why handheld firearms seem to have been relatively insignificant on the battlefields of late medieval Europe, whereas they formed a key part of Chinese infantry forces at the same period.

Drill and the Classical Heritage, East and West

A key difference between Chinese and European warfare in the 1300s and 1400s was the relative absence of drill in Europe. As military his-torian Michael Prestwich writes in the *Oxford Encyclopedia of Medieval Warfare*, in Europe "there is surprisingly little indication of this type of drill [i.e., "collective training"] taking place until the late fifteenth century."[52] This perspective is supported also in the work of one of the world's foremost experts in medieval military history, who notes that military ordinances from the medieval period say next to nothing about collective drill until the late fifteenth century, when the Burgun-dians began drilling, with the possible exception of Sicilian crossbow-men, who may have drilled in the eleventh century.[53]

There may of course be copious examples of medieval European drill just waiting to be found, but it seems unlikely. The medieval European emphasis on men-at-arms and the general lack of standing armies cre-ated a situation that did not make systematic drilling as feasible as in China, where standing infantry had been the core of military strength almost continuously since the Warring States Period. In one of a series of articles of stunning originality, Stephen Morillo has argued that the reason that European infantries didn't drill in the medieval period is simple: there were no centralized states to make them do it. "Drill," he writes, "may only be instituted where there is a central authority strong enough to gather sufficient numbers of men together, and rich enough to maintain them while they are trained. . . . In effect, strong infantry depends on strong government."[54] European states were undeveloped by the standards of China and many other parts of Asia. It's no wonder that they had poor infantry forces.

This difference in drilling cultures probably explains one of the central mysteries of global military history. Western historians have puzzled over the relative dearth of records describing handguns on Europe's medieval battlefields. In sieges, of course, guns were frequently used, and Europeans became masters of siege artillery. But handguns do not appear nearly so much in medieval European records, which has led some scholars even to question whether early European guns were used on the battlefield at all.[55] There's no doubt that they were, but not in significant numbers, and historians have suggested that they didn't play significant roles in battles.[56] Why? Historians have tended to blame technology: "The technology was not yet there to make the gun an effective battlefield weapon. It was not until the late fourteenth and fifteenth centuries that guns began to appear regularly in battle."[57]

But of course the Chinese managed to make their guns work well enough on the battlefield that by 1380 Ming policies stipulated that 10 percent of troops should be hand gunners; by 1466 the proportion reached 33 percent, a level not reached in Europe until the mid-1500s.[58] Is that because Chinese handguns were better? Perhaps, but probably not appreciably so, and yet the Chinese made them work, using them to kill Mongols, Japanese, Thais, Vietnamese, and, most of all, other Chinese. So technology is not likely behind the difference in handgun use between China and Europe.

Drill, on the other hand, is a very likely factor. As we've seen, in China systematic drill had been a consistent attribute of warfare since ancient times, and the volley shooting technique may date back that far as well. Certainly, evidence shows that it was used in the Tang (618–907), Song (960–1279), and Ming (1368–1644) periods. It seems likely that Chinese armies were able to use handguns effectively on the battlefield not because their handguns were better but because they knew how to deploy them in concert, whereas Europeans learned this skill only slowly.

Evidence from early firearms battles in Europe supports this hypothesis. Whereas Chinese sources rarely suggest that guns were fired all at once and are likely to say they were "fired in succession," the few European sources that describe handgun battles (and there are far fewer than describe artillery battles) usually say that European handguns were fired off all at once. In the Battle of Crécy, for example, there is no indication that guns were fired in turns, and one chronicle even suggests the opposite: "with many guns they vigorously attacked the French camp, firing all the guns at once."[59] Another significant gun battle—this one considerably later—also suggests that guns were fired at once. This was in 1382, at the Battle of Beverhoutsveld. On one side was an army of the Flemish town of Ghent, which was attacking the town of Bruges. The famous chronicler Froissart writes, "The Ghentenaars positioned themselves on a hill and gathered themselves together. Then they fired off more than three hundred cannons all at once and turned themselves about so that the Brugeois had the sun in their eyes. . . . Then they launched themselves into the [Brugeois's] lines, crying 'Ghent!' As soon as the Brugeois heard their voices and the cannons going off . . . they . . . threw down their weapons, turned tail, and ran."[60] Military historian Kelly DeVries hails this battle as "unique and special," one of the only times in late medieval Europe when guns were decisive on the battlefield: "the first such decisive use in the history of western Europe."[61] The firing of guns all at once rather than in turns happened again at another famous early field battle with guns, the Battle of Bulgnéville of 1431, when the victors "shot with fire from their cannons and couleuvres [smaller guns] all at the same time."[62]

Eventually, Europeans did begin drilling regularly, a process that gathered momentum in the mid-1500s. Historians have hailed this "revolution in drill" as a decisive step, a hallmark of incipient modernity and a key underpinning of European dominance. But perhaps these historians' standards are too low. Medieval Northern Europe was a benighted place in global perspective. Its rates of urbanization were low and its states were backward, uncentralized, and lacking in bureaucracies or standing armies. The absence of drill in Europe should probably not be taken as a normative condition, common throughout the civilized world, but rather as an aberration. It is far more likely that most developed regions of the world had drill and Europe lacked it than that most of the world lacked drill and Europeans developed it.

As noted, Geoffrey Parker has suggested that both China and Europe invented drill and did so twice: "in the fifth century BC in North China and in Greece, and again in the late sixteenth century."[63] Yet China did not invent drill twice. It didn't have to because it had never lost its tradition of drill. Whereas Europe's classical traditions were interrupted by the Germanic invasions that ended the western Roman Empire, China's classical tradition continued uninterrupted through the following centuries.

There was no renaissance in China because the traditions had never been swept away. One can speak of various rediscoveries or resurgences of this or that text or practice. The great General Qi Jiguang, for example, whom Parker credits with the rediscovery of Chinese drill, did not see himself as inventing or even reinventing drill but as revivifying ancient traditions handed down and elaborated over the centuries. His wasn't a renaissance moment. He was, rather, a practical man focusing on a particular problem—how to make southern Chinese peasants into soldiers capable of resisting the lethal Japanese troops who were ravaging China's coasts. He turned to the rich resources of classical tradition in the same way that his predecessors in the Song and Tang had done. Moreover, he was just one of many generals writing about drill in the mid-1500s, stimulated by a resurgence of geopolitical tumult: Mongols in the north, Japanese and other maritime invaders in the coastal and southern regions.

European military historians are apt to overplay the renaissance, whether explicitly or implicitly. Tom Arnold has written,

> The difference between East and West lay in the doctrines, the tactics, that Europeans created to harness the revolutionary potential of gunpowder weapons. Unlike the people of any other world civilization (with the possible and temporary exception of late sixteenth century Japan), Europeans were not content to simply retrofit gunpowder weapons to their existing military culture. . . . Outside Europe, in the Ottoman armies—or the Safavid Perian, or the Mughal, or the Ming Chinese—warriors took up gunpowder weapons quickly enough, and appreciated them for their power, but this adoption sparked no basic rethinking on warfare. That happened only in Europe.[64]

For Arnold, then, what lay behind Europe's new art of war was nothing less than the Renaissance itself. "The Renaissance," he writes, ". . . demanded the wholesale reconceptualisation of every custom and art, including the art of war."[65] Other cultures were content to retrofit. Europeans revolutionized everything.

Yet Europeans were starting from a different point—without standing armies, without regular drill, without effective bureaucracies or fiscal organizations. Their social structures were in many ways far behind those of other developed regions of the world. Of course they had to redo everything. The Ming were able to integrate firearms into their armies effectively and quickly. They didn't need to revolutionize their art of war because their structures were already suited to firearms, including their tactics: just substitute guns for crossbows and they were good to go.

And it wasn't just China that had drill. Drill seems to have been part of the cultural patrimony of many of the regions of the world with developed, urbanized, centralized states. In his wonderful book *The Hundred Years War for Morocco*, Weston Cook explores some of the sophisticated battle formations and drilling practices of the Islamic world.[66] Similarly, recent work by historians of the Ottoman Empire has established that Ottoman armies were relatively centralized from an early date, had their own specialized firearms bureaus by the 1390s, and may even have deployed volley fire with arquebuses as early as 1526.[67] In Korea, drill was also a consistent part of military life, and it even seems that a 1447 decree from Korean King Sejong commanded "fire-emitter" troops to drill in the volley technique: "Divide into squads of five and have four men shoot fire-barrels while one soldier swiftly reloads the barrels with gunpowder. Using varieties of fire-barrels such as the two-gun-barrel, three-gun-barrel, eight-arrow-gun-barrel, four-arrow-gun-barrel and the thin-gun-barrel confounds the army because each type of fire-barrel uses varying methods of reloading, so all five members of each squad should carry the same type of fire-barrel to be effective in actual battle. This should be the regular drill regime."[68] How precisely the units fired and whether they took turns is not clear, but there's no doubt about the intent: to drill for combat.

There is much work to do on this front, and non-European military history is a field ripe with possibility. I suspect that in the coming years more and more examples of drilling cultures will emerge as historians increasingly turn their attention to non-Western history. Europe will be seen in many ways to be an aberration, or, perhaps more accurately, as one of a number of relatively peripheral areas whose development lagged behind that of core regions of Eurasia.[69]

Yet if Europeans got a late start, they certainly innovated quickly. Historians have argued that by the 1600s, Europeans had achieved unprecedented power on the battlefield thanks to a lethal combination: the arquebus musket and countermarch drilling techniques. As Geoffrey Parker has written, "the combination of drill with the use of firearms to produce volley fire, perfected through constant practice, proved . . . the key to western expansion . . . for the next three centuries."[70]

Yet the Chinese, the Japanese, and the Koreans also all adopted muskets and employed countermarch techniques. How did East Asian musketry usage stack up against that of Europe?

CHAPTER 12

The Musket in East Asia

Historians have long recognized that the musket revolutionized the battlefield in Europe, becoming the predominant infantry weapon by the middle of the seventeenth century, a position it would hold for the next two hundred years. But what is less known is that the musket was also swiftly integrated into armies throughout Asia, particularly in East Asia. To be sure, the story of the musket in Japan is famous, perhaps because it is so dramatic: a few Portuguese castaways brought arquebuses to Japan in the 1540s, and those guns were rapidly copied, reengineered, and mass produced, so that within a decade or so they were being deployed en masse by Japanese armies. Indeed, some historians have argued that the volley technique was first used in Japan by the 1570s, well before it was used in Europe.[1]

Yet historians have paid less attention to the arquebus's introduction to China, which occurred equally quickly, and at the same time. Moreover, the Chinese—not the Japanese or Europeans—have left the first unequivocal evidence for the application of countermarch techniques to muskets: the practice is referred to multiple times in a famous Ming military manual from 1560. Most intriguing of all, neither China nor Japan was the East Asian state most influenced by the musket. That honor belongs to Korea, which in the seventeenth century developed one of the most effective musket forces in the world, its developments closely paralleling those of Western Europe: an increasing predominance of muskets over other traditional weapons, the relative decline of the cavalry, the growth of standing infantry armies, and the professionalization of the officer corps.

What might most surprise military historians is that whenever Koreans—or other East Asian forces—met Europeans on the battlefield in the seventeenth century, the East Asians triumphed.

The Musket Goes to East Asia

The classic handheld firearm emerged in Europe at the same time that classic artillery did—in the last decades of the fifteenth century. In illustrated chronicles of the 1480s, soldiers fire guns that look recognizably modern (Figure 12.1). They have long, thin barrels, and they are held close to the cheek, one eye peering down the barrel to aim. Although it's not clear in Figure 12.1, these firearms had a lever mechanism that allowed a burning fuse to be lowered into the flash pan by means of a simple movement of the finger. This mechanism, known as a matchlock, was a significant advance because it enabled a soldier to hold the gun at eye level. With its butt resting against his shoulder, he could steady the gun with one hand and fire with the other. In the following decades, trigger mechanisms gained springs and other refinements, and the guns became even more convenient.[2]

Having achieved this classic form, firearms began to appear more regularly on European battlefields. In the 1480s, gunners were still vastly outnumbered by bowmen, swordsmen, and pikemen, but their numbers were growing steadily. Spanish records show that the proportion of matchlock units to crossbow and bow-and-arrow units increased significantly in the late 1480s and early 1490s, a process driven by the constant experimentation of the Granada Wars (1481–1492).[3] Spanish gunners brought their new techniques to Italy during the devastating wars that started in 1494, to decisive effect, as in the famous 1503 Battle of Cerignola. Thereafter arquebusiers became increasingly prominent in Europe, so that by the late 1500s they had become a core component of European armies, reaching proportions of 40 percent of infantry forces.

Portuguese variants of these matchlock arquebuses, known as *espingardas*, found an eager reception in East Asia.[4] The story of their arrival in Japan is famous, partly because it was told in the famous book *Peregrinations*, by Portuguese traveler Fernão Mendes Pinto (1509–1583). He writes that the trouble all started when he and two other Portuguese

FIGURE 12.1 European firearm units, ca. 1483.

This is one of many illustrations of firearm units found in the famous illustrated chronicles of Diebold Schilling the Elder (ca. 1445–1485). Although this scene supposedly illustrates a siege of 1445, the guns reflect the technology of the 1470s and 1480s, when firearms took on their classic form. They are aimed like modern guns, thanks to trigger mechanisms that brought lighted fuses into contact with powder in the flash pan, allowing a stable posture and precise aiming. "Die Österreicher stürmen die Stadt Wil, 1445," Diebold Schilling, Amtliche Berner Chronik, vol. 2 (Bern, 1478–1483), Burgerbibliothek Bern, Mss.h.h.I.2, p. 268. Courtesy of Burgerbibliothek Bern.

took up work with a Chinese pirate. Their ship was attacked by another pirate and then struck by "so great and impetuous a tempest" that they were driven far out to sea.[5] The found themselves on the shores of a new land, Japan. A local lord questioned them and when they informed him that Portugal "was far richer and of a larger extent than the whole empire of China," he showed them special favor, allowing them to wander at will while their pirate boss sold his booty.[6]

According to Mendes Pinto, one of these Portuguese, Diogo Zeimoto, happened to be an ace with the arquebus. One day he shot twenty-six ducks in quick succession, and the Japanese lord was so impressed that he escorted the marksman back to his castle on his own horse, while Mendes Pinto and the other Portuguese man followed on foot "a pretty way after." Diogo Zeimoto presented his gun to the lord, who had it copied. "The effect thereof," writes Mendes Pinto, "was such that before our departure (which was five months and a half after) there was six hundred of them made in the country."[7] Soon there were hundreds of thousands of them.

Mendes Pinto is an embellisher, the Zelig of Portuguese Asia, somehow present at all the great events, yet there is reason to believe certain aspects of his account. A separate Portuguese source does indeed record that three Portuguese were driven by storm to Japan at the time of his story in 1542 or 1543 (although it makes no mention of Mendes Pinto himself).[8] More important, the gist of the account is corroborated by Japanese sources, although with some telling differences. Those sources record that in September 1543, a Chinese ship with some Portuguese arrived in Tanegashima Island, in southwestern Japan.[9] Communicating by writing characters in the sand, a Chinese man said that these odd-looking barbarians were "not very strange and . . . quite harmless."[10] The Portuguese were asked to demonstrate their guns: "A small white target was set up on a bank. . . . The man gripped the object [i.e., the gun] with one hand, straightened his posture, and squinted with one eye. When thereupon fire issued from the opening, the pellet always hit the target squarely. . . . All bystanders covered their ears."[11] Two Portuguese guns were purchased at high prices, and Japanese smiths studied them carefully: "through months and over seasons they worked with the objective of producing a new gun," and, eventually, with help from a foreign blacksmith who had arrived by chance on another ship, the technique was mastered.[12]

There is also evidence that Portuguese-style arquebuses may have reached Japan before this episode, via overseas trade routes. Matchlocks were in use in Southeast Asia by 1540, where thousands upon thousands of Japanese sailed and sojourned. Many of them were mercenaries. It makes sense that some of them acquired the guns and brought them home. Moreover, many Southeast Asians also visited

Japan, as did Chinese who had traveled in Southeast Asia. One should not rule out multiple routes of adoption, even if the evidence of direct Portuguese introduction is compelling.[13]

However the arquebus got to Japan, it found a fertile environment. Japan was divided into scores of warring states. The arquebus—known to the Japanese as the "iron gun," *teppo* (鉄砲), a coinage from an earlier period—spread quickly, and by the early 1580s the proportion of arquebusiers in the most powerful Japanese armies may have reached a third. By the early seventeenth century, arquebusiers significantly outnumbered pikemen, archers, and mounted samurai in the largest armies of Japan.[14]

The Japanese also innovated tactically—many historians believe that they were the first to develop the musketry volley technique.[15] As Geoffrey Parker writes, the great warlord Oda Nobunaga "devised the idea of the musketry volley some twenty years *before* it emerged in the west."[16] Parker even thinks it possible that the idea of volley fire might have reached Europe by way of Japan, that perhaps there is a document in a European archive suggesting that Europeans learned the technique by watching Japanese armies in action.[17] He and many others have argued that Nobunaga employed the technique in the famous Battle of Nagashino in 1575.[18] This is debatable. As two scholars of Japanese history have recently written, "the commonly accepted story that attributes the victory [at Nagashino] to three thousand harquebusiers who, arrayed in three ranks, alternated rank by rank in stepping forward to fire enfilades and rearward to reload their weapons, is a myth."[19] This "myth," they say, originated in a chronicle written years after the battle that is riddled with inaccuracies. An earlier and more accurate chronicle (which these scholars have translated into English) makes no mention of volley fire. On the contrary, when it mentions guns, it usually says they are fired en masse.[20]

Yet the emphasis on Nagashino perhaps misses the point. Evidence suggests that the Japanese did indeed use the technique at other battles.[21] Parker and others are right to suggest that the musketry volley may have been used in Japan before it was used in Europe. Yet even so, the Japanese were not the first in recorded history to use the musketry volley. The Chinese were firing arquebuses in volleys by 1560 at the latest.

The story of the arquebus's arrival in Japan is so dramatic that it has overshadowed the story of the arquebus in China, but it's clear that Chinese were involved in that story from the beginning. Mendes Pinto says that he and his fellow Portuguese were working for a Chinese pirate when they landed on Japan, and Japanese sources even name the Chinese man who interpreted for the Portuguese castaways: Wu Feng (五峰). Some scholars have suggested that this Wu Feng was in fact Wang Zhi (王直, d. 1559), one of the wealthiest and most powerful mariners of the mid-sixteenth century. With thousands of armed adherents, Wang Zhi dominated the illicit maritime trade of China during the 1550s.[22]

There's no way to know for sure, but one Chinese source does credit Wang Zhi with bringing arquebus technology to the attention of Chinese officialdom, saying that after Wang Zhi surrendered to the Ming in 1558, an official asked him to manufacture arquebuses and he obliged.[23] This may be true, but other sources make clear that the arquebus had already taken root in China before Wang Zhi's surrender, and pirates were a vector in its transmission.

The period from the 1540s to the 1560s was a golden age of East Asian piracy, and the pirates were a motley and multiethnic lot. Most were Chinese, but sources make clear that they worked with Japanese, Portuguese, Siamese, "black Malaccans," "black barbarian demons," "white and black mixed types," and various other "barbarians."[24] They exchanged ideas, techniques, and technologies, creating what one scholar has called a "hybrid maritime culture."[25] Although arquebuses weren't widely used by the pirates, they were certainly present, and Ming officials took note.[26] According to one source, a pirate band led by brothers surnamed Xu "lured the barbarians from the land of the Franks . . . and they came in a continuous stream."[27] The Xu brothers established an island outpost, Shuangyu Harbor (雙嶼港), which, according to one scholar, "became the stage for the dissemination to all of East Asia's maritime realms of every kind of gunpowder weapon."[28] The Xu brothers worked with many other pirates, including Wang Zhi himself, as well as a man named Bald Li (李光頭). Some sources suggest that among Bald Li's adherents was "a barbarian chief who was good at guns."[29] A Ming commander captured him and had his guns copied and manufactured, and the resulting muskets (鳥銃) were "as intricate and exquisite as those of the barbarians themselves."[30]

By 1548 and 1549, Ming forces were using arquebuses against the pirates, in small numbers.[31] Over the ensuing years, official interest in the guns continued to grow, with Ming officials on the spot urging the creation of larger arquebus-centered forces.[32] Soon, Ming troops out-gunned the pirates, and Ming arsenals were manufacturing muskets by the thousands.[33] In 1558, for example, the Central Military Weaponry Bureau (兵仗局) ordered the manufacture of ten thousand muskets.[34]

Many questions remain unanswered, because the pirates left few sources, and there is still considerable debate among historians about when and how the arquebus arrived in China.[35] But there's no doubt that the Ming adopted it avidly, and it had soon become a key weapon of Ming infantry armies.

This is clear from the example of the most famous military leader and thinker of the Ming period: the great Qi Jiguang (戚繼光, 1528–1588).

Qi Jiguang and the Arquebus

Qi Jiguang is a national hero of China, and although today he is known primarily for his victories over the pirates and his martial arts techniques, he was also a proponent of the musket. He explained that he first understood the power of arquebuses when he lost his first battles against the Japanese (倭) pirates. "Having suffered setbacks and been thus forced to consider things, [I] used defeat to strive for victory and replaced [our] bows-and-arrows with the tactic of proficiently firing muskets."[36] Perhaps he was predisposed to favor guns because his father had been vice commander of the firearms division of the capital army in Beijing.[37] In any case, Qi became a partisan of the arquebus. "It is," he wrote, "unlike any other of the many types of fire weapons. In strength it can pierce armor. In accuracy it can strike the center of targets, even to the point of hitting the eye of a coin [i.e., shooting right through a coin], and not just for exceptional shooters. . . . The arquebus [鳥銃] is such a powerful weapon and is so accurate that even bow and arrow cannot match it, and . . . nothing is so strong as to be able to defend against it."[38] Arquebuses, used in combination with traditional weapons, allowed him to fight successfully against the pirates.[39]

Qi Jiguang—like other Chinese military leaders—felt that technology (器技) was vital, that going without it was "like fighting a tiger bare-handed."[40] But he also recognized that technology had to be paired with structures, logistical, organizational, and disciplinary, and he became famous for his troops' cohesion and coordination. He based his organization on a twelve-man team (隊), which consisted of two squads of five (伍), a team leader (隊長), and a logistical support unit called a cook (火兵), whose duties went well beyond preparing rice. Today, when people discuss his twelve-man teams, they usually highlight configurations armed with traditional weapons—shields, lances, swords, and so on.[41] But it is clear from his writings that his twelve-man teams could be composed of various types of units depending on their purpose. Some were composed entirely of close-quarter troops like pikemen, shield men, sword men, and the like. Others had two or four gunners supported by close-quarter units. Others were composed entirely of musketeers. In each case, tactics were devised to take advantage of the combinations of units, and teams were trained to be flexible and array themselves in a wide variety of configurations in concert with other teams, all coordinated by horns and drums and flags.[42]

His musketeers were trained in the countermarch technique, and his writings are filled with reference to volley fire, although he never felt he had to explain it in detail, probably because countermarch techniques were so much a part of drilling practices already. We can, for example, discern the countermarch technique in this passage from the earliest version of his most famous manual, the eighteen-chapter edition of the *Ji xiao xin shu*, published in 1560:

All the musketeers, when they get near the enemy are not allowed to fire early, and they're not allowed to just fire everything off in one go, [because] whenever the enemy then approaches close, there won't be enough time to load the guns (銃裝不及), and frequently this mismanagement costs the lives of many people. Thus, whenever the enemy gets to within a hundred paces' distance, they [the musketeers] are to wait until they hear a blast on the bamboo flute, at which they deploy themselves in front of the troops, with each platoon (哨) putting in front one team (隊). They [the musketeer team members] wait until they hear their own leader fire a shot, and only then are they allowed to give fire.

Each time the trumpet gives a blast, they fire one time, spread out in battle array according to the drilling patterns. If the trumpet keeps blasting without stopping, then they are allowed to fire all together until their fire is exhausted, and it's not necessary [in this case] to divide into layers.[43]

The concept of dividing into layers (分層) is key to his drilling patterns, and the layers were trained to fire in turns: "Once the enemy has approached to within 100-paces, listen for one's own commander (總) to fire once, and then each time a horn is blown the arquebusiers fire one layer. One after another, five horn tones, and five layers fire. Once this is done, listen for the tap of a drum, at which then one platoon (哨) [armed with traditional weapons] comes forward, proceeding to in front of the arquebusiers. They [the platoon members] then listen for a beat of the drum, and then the blowing of the swan-call horn, and they then give a war cry and go forth and give battle."[44] Thus, musketeers were placed in the vanguard, fired their volleys, and were then protected by close-quarter units, who marched in front to protect them. If the close-quarter troops drove the enemy back, the musketeers would fire in volleys again, and Qi's manuals detail various drill patterns—withdrawals, advances, the trading back and forth of the vanguard position between missile units and close-quarter units, and so on.

Musketeers didn't always fire volleys in five layers. The configurations were flexible, to suit different contingencies. As Qi wrote in a later edition of the *Ji xiao xin shu* (1584), "Each team has ten muskets. One can divide it into two layers, with each layer having five muskets. Or one can divide it into five layers, with each layer having two muskets. Or one can not divide it at all, putting the ten muskets all in one line."[45] He also described how to arrange musketeers defensively, fortifying them behind stockades or behind gabions. In one passage, he describes a volley fire defense that sounds just like the use of volley fire in the "mythical" version of the Battle of Nagashino, in which Nobunaga supposedly had his arquebuses fire in turns from behind wooden stockades, although in this case Qi Jiguang's defense includes not just arquebusiers but also other cannon and firearm units. The defenders, he writes, are to "wait until the face-the-enemy signal [is given], and then, whether from behind wooden stockades, or from moat banks, or from below abatis (拒馬), [they] open up on the enemy, firing by turns

(更番射賊). Those who are empty reload; those who are full fire again. While the ones who have fired are loading, those who are full then fire again. In this way, all day long, the firing of guns will not be lacking, and there must be no firing to the point of exhaustion [of ammo] and no slipups with guns."[46]

To achieve such coordination required careful training, and Qi Ji-guang felt that drill was of the utmost importance because war is so chaotic. Procedures must become automatic, unconscious, or unit cohesion will break down. In modern times, the great military thinker Carl von Clausewitz famously wrote of "friction in war"—the way that real life tends to ruin well-laid plans.[47] Only one "oil," he wrote, could compensate for that friction: to drill armies in conditions that simulate the exertions of battle.[48] A similar realism underlies Qi Ji-guang's thought. He believed it was vital to drill and test and simulate combat as much as possible because war caused soldiers to lose their training: "If in peacetime martial skills are one hundred percent but in battle one only achieves fifty percent, then that can be counted a success, and if one achieves eighty percent, then there's no enemy on earth (who can stand up to one). But there has never been (a case of an army) able to put forth one hundred percent of peacetime skill (and training) on the battlefield and showing corresponding poise and ease and vivacity. The proverb says, 'When it comes time to fight, the teaching is forgotten.'"[49]

So Qi drilled his troops pragmatically, writing dismissively of training regimes involving lance dances and fancy martial arts moves. The first step was to train recruits in the individual skills of their weapons, and the matchlock arquebus was notoriously tricky. As the great military historian Sir Charles Oman once quipped, "It was said that muskets would be more practical if Nature had endowed mankind with three hands instead of two."[50] The problem was the fuse. It couldn't be allowed to go out, and so one had to keep it burning while pouring powder first into the barrel and then into the flash pan. Careless arquebusiers blew themselves to pieces. European commanders famously divided the task of shooting an arquebus into multiple steps, which authors have considered to be a sign of Europe's incipient modernity.[51]

Qi, too, divided the process of loading and shooting into discrete steps, painstakingly training his musketeers to load and shoot according to a precise sequence. They practiced together in rhythm to a special musket-loading song:

> One, clean the gun.
> Two pour the powder.
> Three tamp the powder down.
> Four drop the pellet.
> Five drive the pellet down.
> Six put in paper (stopper).
> Seven drive the paper down.
> Eight open the flashpan cover.
> Nine pour in the flash powder.
> Ten close the flashpan cover,
> and clamp the fuse.
> Eleven listen for the signal,
> then open the flashpan cover.
> Aiming at the enemy,
> raise your gun and fire.[52]

To facilitate speedy loading, he had them measure out their powder beforehand and keep it in special cartridges: "Whatever weight pellet the arquebus can fit, use the same weight of powder. Cut bamboo tubes, and measure out the proper length for that amount of powder. This should all be done in advance. Fill thirty tubes, and put them in the leather sack, and hang it on the waist."[53]

To make sure his soldiers could carry out the sequence smoothly, he mandated frequent reviews, tests, and inspections. In a musketry exam, for example, a team would be selected, their names called out in a singsong voice. The men proceeded to the front of the ranks and presented their guns for inspection. The gun bores were measured to make sure that they were all the same caliber. (He felt it was vital that weapons be standardized, because to have different muzzle bores in the same unit led to compatibility issues.) Then pellets were examined to see that they were the proper size, that they were polished smooth, and that they fit properly: tightly against the side of the bore, delivered with taps of a ramrod. The ramrod itself must be firm and straight, and "it's best if at the top end it's the same size as the muzzle bore."[54] The rest of the equipment was checked carefully: "The flashpan hole should be small. The fuse should be dry. The powder should be dry and fine and very reactive. One should examine the thickness and length of the fuse, and it must conform to the aforementioned. The powder tube should suit the size of the gun, and it should be filled and suit the caliber. The bullets should weigh no more or less than is proper. Other sundry items, such as the extra fuse . . . the pellet bag, etc., should all be checked and examined carefully in turn."[55] The powder itself should be tested, and sometimes, it seems, they used the hand-burn method, with the soldier setting his powder alight on his hand: good black powder should go up at once without causing burns.[56]

Once the equipment passed inspection, the men demonstrated their mastery of the loading sequence, carrying out the procedure as officials sang the song. Then, guns loaded, they advanced to the shooting range and lined up in ranks, a hundred paces from a target. In the Ming period, a pace was about a meter and a half, which would put the target a hundred fifty meters away.

At the sound of a gong the men began to shoot, displaying not just individual prowess but also collective training. They fired in turns to signals, each man getting nine shots in total and reloading quickly so that "after the first set is finished firing the second has finished loading, shooting again for speed."[57] Target strikes were tallied on an abacus, and the results were recorded with the name of the soldier. The various configurations of layers could be tested, as the commanders deemed suitable: two layers of five, five layers of two, one line of ten.

Incentives and punishments were collective, although individual skill was also rewarded. Qi even included in his manuals sample assessment forms, with blank spaces to be filled in with the names of soldiers and spaces for recording grades. When filling them in, a commander was to consider not just target strikes but also posture and composure. If a gunner flinched while he fired, he got a lower mark, even if he hit the target. Expectations for accuracy seem to have been quite high, and wages depended on performance in trials (and, of course, in combat).

Oddly, many scholars have suggested that Qi Jiguang didn't particularly appreciate the musket or incorporate it into his forces in significant proportions. He is remembered today as a partisan of traditional weapons, who invigorated the Ming military with swords and spears.[58] Historian Ray Huang, for example, has written that Qi "never attempted anything overly ambitious or even truly innovative" and that "even in the later years of his career, he authorized only two muskets for each infantry squad and maintained that each company of musketeers must be accompanied by a company of soldiers carrying contact weapons. Any ratio that favored firearms would be unrealistic and might endanger the army as a whole."[59] Similarly, the French scholar Jean-Marie Gontier has written that Qi Jiguang's tactical methods focused on traditional weapons like lances, shields, and swords and thus "seem to be a hundred years behind those used contemporaneously elsewhere."[60]

But a close reading of his many military writings makes clear that Qi saw himself as a great partisan of the arquebus. More important, there is strong evidence that he incorporated high proportions of muskets in his infantry units, and that the proportion increased through time. In a less-famous manual, the *Lian bing shi ji,* completed in 1571, he prescribes ideal infantry regiments (營) of 2,700 men, of whom 1,080 were arquebusiers, or 40 percent.[61] He didn't always achieve this ratio—and we need more research into his actual battles, as opposed to his military writings—but even so, a comparison with Europe is instructive. In Europe it wasn't until the mid-seventeenth century that the ratio of shot to pike shifted decisively in favor of shot.[62] In the 1570s and 1580s, European infantry ratios were two to one or three to one pike to shot, roughly comparable to Qi Jiguang's ratio of eight to five.

Indeed, some Sinophone scholars are wont to go to the opposite extreme and argue that Qi's use of guns was more than a century ahead of Europe, prefiguring formations and tactics that wouldn't appear in Europe until the famous mid-seventeenth-century reforms of the Swedish king Gustavus Adolphus.[63]

This is too extreme, but one thing is clear. Qi's use of the musketry volley technique suggests considerable sophistication in the use of firearms. If European scholars are correct that the technique was developed in Europe around 1600, then in that respect at least Qi Jiguang was ahead by several decades, using it by 1560, when the first version of his most famous military treatise, the *Ji xiao xin shu,* was published.

Some of the confusion about Qi Jiguang's use of muskets may lie in the apparently contradictory things he wrote about them. At times he seemed to despair of incorporating them in large numbers. But in such cases he blamed not the musket itself but his fellow officers, whom he believed didn't know how to train their troops properly:

The musket was originally considered a powerful weapon, and in attacking the enemy is one that has been much relied upon. But how is it that so many officers and soldiers don't think it can be relied upon heavily? The answer lies in the fact that in drills and on the battlefield, when all the men fire at once, the smoke and fire settle over the field like miasmal clouds, and not a single eye can see, and not a singe hand can signal. Not all [soldiers] hold their guns level, or they don't hold them to the side of their cheek, or they don't use the sights, or they let their hands droop and support it to hold it up, and one hand holds the gun and one hand uses the fuse to touch off the fire, thus failing to use the matchlock grip— what of them? It's just a case of being out of practice and uncourageous, hurrying but not being able to take out the fire fuse and place it in the matchlock grip, trying for speed and convenience. In this way, there is absolutely no way to be accurate, and so how could one value muskets? Especially given that the name of the weapon is "bird-gun," which comes from the way that it can hit a flying bird, hitting accurately many times. But in this way, fighting forth, the power doesn't go the way one intends, and one doesn't know which way it goes—so how can one hit the enemy, to say nothing of being able to hit a bird?[64]

It was not enough to put guns in the field. One had to use them correctly, and that required careful preparation in terms of equipping, training, and drilling. Often the exigencies of warfare and logistics required a departure from ideals.

His most pessimistic discussions of the musket seem to have referred to his experiences in northern China, where he was posted beginning in 1567, after he'd achieved such striking successes in southern China. Whereas he'd been able to start with a clean slate in the south, raising and training his own forces of peasant mercenaries, in the north he found himself in command of soldiers entrenched in their ways. The northern troops stubbornly adhered to the use of older weapons, such as the fast lance (*kuai qiang* 快鎗), a type of gun similar to a fire lance, with a long handle and, in some cases, more than one barrel: "In the north," he wrote, "soldiers are stupid and impatient, to the point that they cannot see the strength of the musket, and they insist on holding tight to their fast lances, and although when comparing and vying on the practice field the musket can hit the bullseye ten times better than the fast-lance and five times better than the bow and arrow, they refuse to be convinced."[65]

To what extent he managed to achieve his ideal proportions of arquebuses and traditional weapons is hard to determine from his manuals alone, and there is much to be learned from looking at other sources. What does seem to be the case is that Qi Jiguang used a wide variety of unit combinations, altering the composition of his teams and platoons and companies as the local situation required. What worked in the south against pirates didn't work in the north against Mongols.

One of the more intriguing units he developed was a sort of armored infantry system based on carts carrying Frankish cannons. These were like the fire lance carts of *Song* times. They could be rolled forth, pulled by horses or donkeys, and then set up in battle array. Troops could fire from within the cart, with teams of musketeers used in a support role, to venture forth when necessary, firing in volleys.[66] These were only useful in the north, however. In the south, in lands that were wetter and hillier, it wasn't possible to use carts like that, so guns had to be smaller. Thus, in his last military treatise, the fourteen-chapter version of the *Ji xiao xin shu*, published in 1584 when he was living again in southern China, he wrote, "In the south, the fields are muddy and the bogs treacherous. Infantry must be light and agile, and heavy weapons are difficult to transport. So [in this region] muskets (鳥銃) are the best."[67]

In any case, numerous passages in Qi Jiguang's voluminous work make clear that Chinese troops were deploying the volley technique with arquebuses well before the Japanese Battle of Nagashino in 1575 or the Dutch Battle of Nieuwport in 1600. And we shouldn't be surprised. We've seen how deeply the volley technique was rooted in China's military tradition, used with crossbows for centuries before being applied to guns in the 1300s. Indeed, a famous military manual of 1639 makes explicit the lineage from the crossbow volley technique to the musketry volley technique. It contains two nearly identical plates. One picture shows crossbowmen shooting with the "revolving and flowing" volley technique, in the same three-row configuration that Chinese manuals used since at least the Tang dynasty: a front row "shooting crossbows" (輪流發弩), a second row "advancing crossbows" (輪流進弩), and a third row of "loading crossbows" (輪流上弩) (see Figure 12.2). Figure 12.3 is the same, except that the crossbowmen have become musketeers. Even the labels are the same, with the term "crossbow" replaced by the term "gun" (*chong*). In the text accompanying the image of the musketeers, the author explicitly notes that "the method . . . is exactly like the revolving flowing crossbow-shooting method."[68] Like crossbows, muskets were slow to load and fire, but, he noted, "the method of taking turns and firing guns alternately allows them to fire in succession all day, so that the sound doesn't cease, and there is no enemy that is not shamefully defeated."[69] This manual doesn't describe the technique in detail, nor does it contain the wealth of practical advice offered by Qi Jiguang's manuals of the 1560s, 1570s, and 1580s. But it does suggest how easy it was to redeploy a technique used for crossbows to arquebuses, which, after all, suffered from the same basic detriment: slow loading.

Qi Jiguang's manuals had enormous influence in China, but they perhaps had their deepest impact in Korea.

The Musket in Korea

Korea is not known as a military power, and most historians will be surprised to learn that this small country, dwarfed by China and Japan, developed one of the most effective musket-based armies of the seventeenth-century world.

Firearms had been used in Korea long before the introduction of the musket in the late 1500s.[70] Korean archaeologists have unearthed many guns from the fourteenth and fifteenth centuries.[71] Some were imported from China, but the Koreans also made their own gunpowder weapons, some of which were impressive enough to be presented as tribute gifts by the Korean court to the Ming emperor.[72] In fact, Koreans seem to have employed some kind of volley principle with guns by 1447, when the Korean king Sejong the Great instructed his gunners to shoot their "fire barrels" in squads of five, taking turns firing and loading."[73] We have much to learn about early firearms in Korea, but what does seem clear is that Korean firearms warfare was revolutionized after 1592, when Japan invaded Korea.

The invasion set off one of the most destructive wars in East Asian history, a conflict that Kenneth Swope has called the First Great East Asian War.[74] For six years, Ming China, a newly unified Japan, and

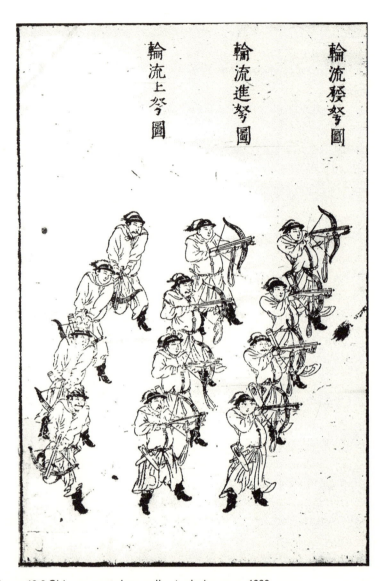

輪流發弩圖　輪流進弩圖　輪流上弩圖

FIGURE 12.2 Chinese crossbow volley technique, ca. 1639.

This image of a crossbow volley formation appears in Bi Maokang's famous illustrated manual of military weaponry, the *Jun qi tu shuo* (軍器圖說). It is nearly identical to an image of musketeers in the same book, thus illustrating the continuity of the tradition of Chinese countermarch techniques, which were swiftly adapted from crossbows to firearms. From Bi Maokang 畢懋康, *Jun qi tu shuo* 軍器圖說, Ming-era woodblock print, ca. 1639. Courtesy of the National Library of China, Beijing.

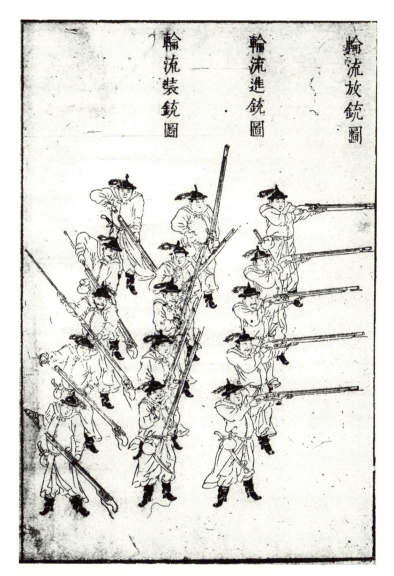

FIGURE 12.3 Chinese musketry volley technique, ca. 1639.

In this image, the author draws an explicit lineage to the earlier Chinese tradition of crossbow volley drill. As the text accompanying this image notes, "the method . . . is exactly like the revolving flowing crossbow-shooting method." From Bi Maokang 畢懋康, *Jun qi tu shuo* 軍器圖說, Ming-era woodblock, ca. 1639. Courtesy of the National Library of China, Beijing.

Korea fought bitterly in the Korean Peninsula and its waters. At first, Japanese musketeers proved overwhelming. As the Korean prime minister Yu Songnyong (柳成龍, 1542–1607) lamented, "When [our] soldiers are lined up against the enemy ranks, our arrows do not reach the enemy while their musket balls rain down upon us."[75] Korean and Chinese sources show that Japanese musketeers employed the volley technique.[76]

Ming forces helped the Koreans push the Japanese back, but the war lasted until the death of Hideyoshi in 1598, and the bitter experience shocked Koreans into military reform, a process that continued well into the tumultuous seventeenth century. At the heart of their reorganizations was the musket. As one of the great reformers put it, Koreans must do precisely as the Chinese had done and learn from the Japanese: "In recent times in China they did not have muskets; they first learned about them from the Wokou pirates in Zhejiang Province. Qi Jiguang trained troops in their use for several years until they [muskets] became one of the skills of the Chinese, who subsequently used them to defeat the Japanese."[77] In the same way, he said, Koreans must learn from foreigners how to improve their military.

Historian Hyeok Hweon Kang compellingly argues that King Seonjo (r. 1567–1608) became a "zealous proponent" of the musket.[78] King Seonjo ordered that Japanese musketeers be captured alive so they could instruct the Koreans, and he established a new standing army called the Military Training Agency (訓鍊都監), whose core units were musketeers. His preference for musketeers irritated archers, who believed that they practiced a venerable and noble art. Once, when the king bestowed upon the musketeers a gift of thirty horses, proclaiming that they had conducted a drill better than the archers, some archers resigned in protest. King Seonjo's interest in the musket extended even to design: he developed a rapid-fire version himself.[79]

Korean musketeers were trained in Qi Jiguang's volley technique. A Korean drill manual of 1607, based closely on Qi Jiguang's *Ji xiao xin shu*, notes that "every musketeer squad should either divide into two musketeers per layer or one and deliver fire in five volleys or in ten."[80] Another manual, first published in 1649, elaborates further, again, based very closely (usually verbatim) on Qi Jiguang's work: "When the enemy approaches to within a hundred paces, a signal gun is fired and a conch is blown, at which the soldiers stand. Then a gong is sounded, the conch stops blowing, and the heavenly swan [a double-reed horn] is sounded, at which the musketeers fire in concert, either all at once or in five volleys (齊放或一次盡舉或分五舉)."[81] Korean reforms built explicitly on Qi Jiguang's work, but his manuals are at times challenging, presupposing a familiarity with the very techniques he proposes. As we've seen, although he refers frequently to musketry volley techniques, he doesn't lay out the procedures in detail.

So Korean military manuals filled in the blanks, interpreting, explaining, and commenting on the Qi manuals. They even contain diagrams that present the clearest explanation of the East Asian musketry volley technique that has yet been discovered. One diagram, for example, shows a team of musketeers halfway through a volley sequence. Just as in Qi Jiguang's teams, this Korean squad has ten musketeers and a team leader (see Figure 12.4). The men stand in two lines, with the team leader standing between them. The two empty circles denote a place where no men are currently standing. They have left their position, marched to the front of their respective lines, and are currently firing at the enemy. When the team leader gives a signal, they will return to their place to reload, while the musketeers behind them will march to the fore and fire. The sequence can go on indefinitely.

The method is different from European methods, in which the musketeer in the front row fired and then went to the back of his line to reload. To be sure, European commanders experimented with various ways of effecting his return to the rear, but in general that's how it worked: shoot, then go to the back and start reloading. In the Korean diagram, however, the musketeers step to the front, fire, and then return to their original position to reload while the next shooters step to the front, and so on. Was this the way that Qi Jiguang's musketry teams worked? It's not clear, but it's likely. After all, the Koreans learned the volley technique from Chinese Southern Troops (南兵), who were trained and organized according to Qi Jiguang's methods. On the other hand, it's quite possible that the Koreans developed this technique on their own or perhaps even conceived and systematized it with the help of other foreigners—Japanese or Dutch. The Korean military reforms were carried out with the help of many foreign experts.[82]

FIGURE 12.4 Korean musketry volley fire.

This plate, titled "Diagram of Musketry Volley Fire" (鳥銃輪放圖), is the clearest diagram yet discovered of the Qi Jiguang–inspired musketry volley technique. It is a snapshot of the team (隊) of ten musketeers and their team leader (隊長) midway through a volley sequence. The top of the diagram is the front. The musketeers stand in two lines, their team leader standing between them. The two empty circles mark places where no men are currently standing. The men have left their original position, marched to the front, and are firing at the enemy. When the team leader gives a signal, they will return to their places in line to reload, at which point the musketeers behind them will march to the fore and fire. The sequence can continue indefinitely. From *Pyŏnghak chinam* 兵學指南, vol. 3, p. 14 (first published 1649). Courtesy of C.V. Starr East Asian Library, Columbia University Libraries.

An early test of Korea's new musketry corps came in 1619, when ten thousand Korean musketeers were sent to help the Ming against the Manchus in the famous Battle of Sarhu. The Manchu cavalry overwhelmed the allies, striking lightning blows to the main Korean musketry corps, who were hindered by unfavorable wind. Yet one division of Korean musketeers, fighting under Ming commander Du Song, managed to fell many Manchus by firing in volleys before being forced to give up the attack because their Chinese allies surrendered.[83] Over the following years, the de facto king of Korea, Prince Kwanghae (r. 1608–1623), strove to learn from this episode, realizing that against such powerful horsemen—and the Manchus had the best cavalry in the world—musketeers had to be supported by traditionally armed support troops. So musketeers trained in concert with spear and cavalry units to create a more robust force. That force was tested when the Manchus invaded Korea in 1627 and again in 1636. The Koreans lost both wars, but their musketeers performed well, inducing respect in Manchu leaders. The first emperor of the newly declared Qing dynasty, Hong Taiji (r. 1626–1643), wrote: "The Koreans are incapable on horseback but do not transgress the principles of the military arts. They excel at infantry fighting, especially in musketeer tactics."[84]

Thus the Koreans, like the Japanese and the Chinese, not only integrated muskets into their armed forces, but also employed the volley technique and had systematized drill. The fact that all three East Asian powers so successfully adapted muskets—with the Chinese employing the musketry volley technique perhaps before the Europeans themselves—suggests that East Asia was far from militarily stagnant in the 1500s. East Asians were eager to learn about new technologies developed in Europe, but they also found instruction and inspiration in their own military institutions and traditions. Some Sinophone historians refer to this period as the era of Sino-Western military hybridization.[85]

It continued into the following century. During the 1600s, even as Japan relaxed into an era of peace (in which, some have famously, if controversially, argued, it "gave up the gun"), China exploded into sustained and bitter conflict, which ensnared Korea as well.[86]

Some of that conflict involved Europeans. The two most expansive European powers of the seventeenth century—the Russians and the Dutch—both fought wars against the forces of China, and they both lost.

we've seen, they were also the inventors of modern drill, and their drill manuals were translated into all the major European languages, while Dutch-trained drill instructors found employment throughout Europe.

Dutch musketeers also proved effective in expanding the Dutch empire. In South and Southeast Asia, musketeers had helped the Dutch win many a battle against Asian forces. In fact, Dutch musketeers had even used the volley technique to defeat a Chinese force that outnumbered them forty to one. This episode shows how effective European drill and discipline could be when deployed against an untrained force.

The clash occurred in 1652 in the Dutch colony of Taiwan, one of the Netherlands' most profitable Asian outposts, inhabited by thousands of Chinese. In September 1652, thousands of Chinese field hands and agricultural entrepreneurs rose up in revolt, "as many Chinese as grass in the field," as one Dutch observer wrote.[6] Waving banners and brandishing spears and swords, they overcame Dutch military posts, chanting, "Kill, Kill the Dutch dogs!"[7] The Dutch garrison on Taiwan numbered only several hundred at that point, and the Chinese numbered in the thousands. Hearing of prisoners tortured, of Dutch heads carried around on bamboo spikes, Dutch families fled their homes and took refuge in the main fortress (see Map 13.1).

The Dutch governor realized he could spare only a hundred twenty musketeers to quell the rebellion. They rode a boat across a bay and had to disembark in waist-deep water, in full view of the rebels. Holding their guns out of the water, they waded toward shore, maintaining formation. As the water became shallow they started shooting in volleys. If the rebels had worked together to rush the Dutch, these musketeers would have been routed, but the rebels fled as the musketeers reached land and kept firing volleys. In a subsequent battle, Dutch musketeers defeated a force of thousands by maintaining tight discipline. In all some four thousand Chinese were killed by the Dutch and their aboriginal allies.

Thus, in 1652, a few disciplined musketeers faced steep numerical odds and won. A decade later, however, Dutch musketeers marched against a professional Chinese army, and the outcome was different. It was 1661, and the famous Ming warlord Zheng Chenggong (鄭成功, 1624–1662) had launched an invasion to take Taiwan from the Dutch.[8]

Map 13.1 Taiwan and the Taiwan Strait.

When he began landing troops on an island just offshore, the Dutch sent musketeers to drive them away.

As the Dutch divided themselves smartly into rows of twelve and prepared to fire, the Chinese troops stood immobile. The Dutch began shooting volleys, but instead of scattering like untrained rebels, these soldiers surged forward in formation, yelling war cries. At first the Dutch kept shooting, supported by vessels in the bay nearby, which emptied cannonloads of shrapnel into the Chinese ranks at point blank range. But the Chinese kept advancing in tight formation. The Dutch lost their composure, their fear inflamed by the fact that the canny Chinese commander had managed to outflank them, sending a smaller force around the side. They dropped their guns and fled. Out of two hundred forty European soldiers, only eighty escaped. The rest were hacked to death, drowned, or captured.

These Chinese troops were trained and experienced. Their commander in chief, Zheng Chenggong, was a stickler for drill. As a youth, he'd studied to be a scholar, learning from one of the most famous men of letters of late Ming China. As the Ming-Qing wars reached his home province of Fujian, however, he burned his scholarly robes and turned his intelligence to war. He developed his own drilling system, the *Five Plum Flower Method*, and published a new drill manual, testing his commanders in its contents. He constructed a special training field, but he didn't stay up in its observation tower: he got down on the ground with the recruits, correcting mistakes and punishing infractions. The details of his training are difficult to reconstruct, because there is no known extant copy of his manual, but descriptions of battles indicate that the drilling patterns were elaborate and effective. Some involved false retreats, for example, which succeeded in tricking his foes, luring them into ambush.

Certainly his troops had no trouble with the Dutch musketeers on that day in 1661, or in other battles in the Sino-Dutch War. In October 1661, for example, several dozen Dutch troops marched against half as many Zheng troops on an island where the Dutch were raiding for provisions. Once again, the Chinese maintained formation and marched inexorably forward. As a Dutch official wrote, "our troops . . . went white with fright and couldn't work their guns."[9] The Dutch tried to flee. Three dozen were killed or captured. The Dutch never managed to defeat Zheng forces in a field battle. The only time they came close was when they used of their infantry as bait to lure the enemy to a fortress and then shot cannons from the walls.[10]

While the Dutch were fighting Ming loyalists in the south, the Russians were fighting the Qing in the north. There, too, Europeans' musketeers provided no discernable edge.

The Cossacks

Like the Dutch, the Russians were masters of the musket. Indeed, their volley fire techniques derived directly from the Dutch: the first nonreligious book published by the Russian imperial press was a translation of a manual by a German man who'd helped the Dutch develop their drilling regimes.[11] The musket was the essential arm of the Cossacks, who, firing in volleys, made their way inexorably eastward across Siberia to the Pacific. Their foes fled, died, or agreed to pay exorbitant tributes in sable and fox furs.

But in the mid-seventeenth century, the Cossacks reached territory claimed by people who also had muskets. As they tried to establish a toehold in the fertile Amur River valley, in Manchuria, they fought a number of engagements against the Qing dynasty and its allies. Two of those engagements involved Korean musketeers, who proved extremely effective.[12]

The first of these engagements occurred in the spring of 1654, when three hundred seventy Russian troops engaged a combined Qing-Korean force about a thousand strong at the mouth of the Songhua River, a tributary of the Amur. Both sides were waterborne, and at first the Cossacks prevailed, forcing the Qing to abandon ship and flee on foot. But Korean musketeers had ensconced themselves up on the riverbanks, in trenches and behind barricades. They opened fire on the Russians, shooting in volleys. The Russians tried storming the Korean positions but couldn't stand the coordinated fire. They gave up and fled, with the Koreans and Qing troops in pursuit.[13]

The second clash occurred in 1658, and we have better data for it because the Korean commander kept a diary.[14] Intriguingly, he describes three practice sessions that Korean musketeers held during the campaign, whose results suggest high levels of accuracy. A target was placed sixty paces away, and it was narrow: just ten centimeters wide, and about a meter and a half high. At sixty paces, the Koreans hit the target 25 percent of the time, an impressive result given its size and the limitations of smoothbore ballistics.[15] As Hyeok Hweon Kang has written:

> These numbers might not seem impressive at first but they were results of shooting an incredibly narrow target, a feat that seems to defy the principles of smoothbore ballistics and that would have been virtually impossible by a contemporaneous European shooter. Further, using standard deviation to extrapolate on ballistic performance, these men would have scored an average accuracy of 66.2% with a roughly man-sized target (1.6 m tall and 30 cm wide) from the same distance and the best of them (those who scored 32.5%) would have had a staggering marksmanship of 79.8% within 72 m of range. Both narrative and quantitative data suggest that Korean musketeers were indeed exceptionally lethal in battle.[16]

The diary notes that the Qing musketeers barely managed to hit the target at all.

This raises an intriguing question. European musket troops generally used smoothbore guns, which impart no spin to the projectile and are thus relatively inaccurate, tending to veer unpredictably after exiting the barrel. Tests have suggested that such inaccuracy is inherent to smoothbore ballistics. Is it possible that the Koreans and other East Asian war makers used rifled muskets? Rifled arquebuses were known in both Europe and East Asia, used for hunting and by snipers. Indeed, the Portuguese gun that famously inspired the Japanese to adopt the musket was a hunting gun, and quite possibly rifled. But rifled guns were slower to load than smoothbore arquebuses, because the pellet had to be rammed down the barrel with force. On European battlefields, smoothbore arquebuses were preferred because they were faster to load. Yet we must take seriously the Korean general's statistics about accuracy, and they are corroborated by other sources, such as the writings of General Qi Jiguang, who continually praised the musket's accuracy. He also spent much time drilling his troops to get them to drive the pellet down the gun quickly. Moreover, in East Asia arquebuses and muskets were known as "bird guns" (hunting guns). So it is possible that Korean and other East Asian musketeer corps may have used rifled weapons. It's certainly a topic worthy of future research.

In any case, after their target practice, the Koreans had a chance to try their aim on Russians. There were a lot more this time: five hundred Russian musketeers. The Qing and Koreans still had numerical superiority: fourteen hundred men, including two hundred Korean musketeers, two hundred Qing gunners (a hundred musketeers and a hundred artillerists), and a thousand traditional units: swordsmen, lancers, archers. Once again, the battle started on water, with the Qing and Russian fleets exchanging cannon fire. The Russians positioned themselves at the riverbanks and the allies attacked, the musketeers shooting volleys. The Cossacks were exhausted and demoralized, and they apparently put up a poor defense. Their lines broke. Some fled inland and others hid in their ships. The Korean musketeers climbed aboard and prepared to set fire to them, but according to the Korean commander's diary, the Qing commander ordered them not to burn the ships because he wanted to capture them as prizes. This hesitation allowed the Russians to regroup, and their counterattack killed Korean musketeers and Qing troops, at which the Qing commander ordered his archers to shoot fire arrows and burn the Russian ships. Some Cossacks took advantage of the confusion to seize a Qing vessel and escape, and others escaped on foot, but nearly half were killed, including their leader, Onufrij Stepanov. It was a major defeat.[17]

Thus, on two occasions, Korean musketeers played a key role in defeating Russian infantry. To be sure, the Cossacks were far from their capital and especially in the 1658 battle were exhausted and demoralized. Yet the Koreans and Qing were also far from their metropoles, and the Korean musketeers were not drawn from the elite troops of the Korean capital but from Korea's less prestigious regional armies. Thus, it seems safe to conclude—as Kang and others have done—that Korean musketeers deserved the deadly reputation they'd gained. Perhaps it's unwise to credit too much the statement of the Korean commander and diary author who claimed that every time the Koreans were mentioned the Russians would "sigh with fear."[18] But it seems safe to say that in the mid-seventeenth century Korean musketeer forces were likely on a par with those of Europe.

Judging relative military effectiveness is difficult. Battles can be affected by many factors—weather, leadership, what's in soldiers' stomachs. And we mustn't presume that the men who fought for the Dutch and Russian empires in Asia were as well trained as their comrades in Europe.[19] Still, we must take seriously the aggregate evidence in the Sino-European infantry battles of the seventeenth century: the forces of China were as disciplined as—probably more disciplined than—the Europeans they fought against. The two great European colonial powers of the seventeenth century found their much-vaunted musketeers ineffective in East Asia, thanks in large part to indigenous East Asian traditions of discipline and drill that were applied to modern arms.

Yet field battles were only one aspect of early modern warfare. The military revolution also posits a coercive advantage to Europeans based on their massive ships and powerful fortresses. How did the forces of China fare in these aspects of warfare vis-à-vis the Russians and the Dutch? Not as well.

CHAPTER 14

A European Naval Advantage

Military historians have argued that during the sixteenth century there occurred a "revolution in war at sea," which made possible European naval hegemony around the world.[1] The key was the broadside sailing ship, which carried two or three rows of heavy cannons jutting through gun ports. Whereas the Portuguese carracks of the early 1500s carried just four or six heavy guns belowdecks, the Dutch vessels that plied the China Seas in the 1600s could carry forty or more. As one Ming official wrote, "The red-haired barbarian ships . . . are called decked-ships because within them they have three layers, all of which have huge cannons facing outwards that can pierce and split stone walls, their thunder sounding for ten miles. . . . Our own ships, when confronting Dutch ships, are smashed into powder."[2] This official recognized that the key to Dutch naval power lay precisely in this lethal broadside ability.

Yet the Chinese proved effective at defending against Dutch naval incursions. Why? There are three reasons. First, they were able easily to adopt the powerful muzzle-loading cannons that jutted out of Dutch cannon ports, just as they had adopted Portuguese guns in the previous century. Indeed, the Chinese versions were in some ways superior to European models. Second, they proved capable of understanding Dutch ships and even making their own broadside vessels, incorporating innovations such as portholes, four-wheeled cannon carriages, and breeching lines. Third, the Chinese found that such naval modernization wasn't actually necessary, because any Dutch advantage on the high seas was counterbalanced by Chinese advantages: the Dutch found themselves outnumbered, outfought, and outled.

Let's start with the Chinese adoption of Dutch cannons, which the Chinese named "red barbarian cannon" (紅夷炮), an appellation they maintained long after the Dutch had ceased to be a threat.[3] These cannons played a key role not just in wars against Europeans but also in the wars between the Ming and the Manchus.

The Red-Haired Barbarian Cannon

We've seen how the Chinese adopted Portuguese "Frankish" guns starting in the early 1500s. During the mid-1500s they also adopted larger, more powerful muzzle-loading cannons, also from the Portuguese.[4] But the cannons that Dutch and English ships brought to the shores of China in the early seventeenth century were far more powerful than any guns in China. As the *Ming History* notes, not only were they capable of destroying other ships; they were also able to "blast holes into and destroy stone walls."[5] These "red barbarian cannon" would change warfare in China, allowing the breaching of Chinese-style walls.

As in the case of Portuguese guns, the first Chinese to adopt the new guns were maritime adventurers, such as pirates and smugglers, who seem to have been deploying and even making them by 1620 or so. But it wasn't long before Ming officials began making them, starting in the coastal provinces. In 1624, for example, the commander in chief (都督) of Fujian and Zhejiang, Yu Zigao (俞資皋) cast a number of iron "red barbarian" cannons.[6]

Other coastal officials obtained red-barbarian cannons by dredging them up from shipwrecks. In 1623, a Chinese salvage team recovered twenty-six large cannons from the wreck of the British *Unicorn*, and the huge guns were dragged, carried, portaged, and poled all the way to Beijing, a voyage of nearly two thousand miles. Such salvage operations were serious undertakings, as we know from an account by an official named Deng Shiliang (鄧士亮), who oversaw one in 1625. He describes how he and his team first had to find the wreck, which they knew must be somewhere near the beach where an iron cannonball had been found. Once they located it they dove and dredged for a month until they found the guns. Only then could the salvage operation begin:

> We set up a rig on a large boat, which we filled with rocks and dirt so it would lie low and heavy on the water. Then we used iron chains and wrapped them around the guns' trunnions (銃耳). Then we removed the earth and rocks and the boat became light and buoyed up on the water, after which we used a crane to wind [the cannons up out of the water]. . . . We obtained two great bronze cannons. They gleamed and shone in the sun, and people thought them marvelous things. It's not clear when they had sunk there.[7]

There were many such salvage operations. In some cases the guns were kept by their discoverers, and some became legendary for their power and accuracy.[8] In most cases, however, the guns were shipped to Beijing.

The Ming court needed cannons, because from the 1610s it was engaged in increasingly intense wars against the Manchu Qing. Aside from reverse engineering salvaged guns, it recruited Chinese artisans who had worked in Western cannon foundries. Macau, for example, had a foundry capable of making large muzzle loaders similar to the new Dutch models—indeed, the city had become one of the most important cannon production centers of all Asia, and some of its products were shipped back to Europe itself.[9] Many Chinese worked there, and others worked in foundries in the Spanish Philippines. Some brought their skills back to China, and the court sought to capitalize on their expertise.[10]

The Ming court focused on cannons because they conferred a clear advantage over the Manchus. Manchu forces were well trained, well equipped, and well led, but they were poor in artillery. To counter their growing power, Ming officials increasingly urged the adoption of red-haired barbarian cannon. In 1626 the famous Christian official Sun Yuanhua (孫元化, 1582–1632) wrote, "Our cannon are not capable of reaching farther than the bows and arrows of our enemies, and therefore we are not able to defeat the enemy. With Chinese cannon it is a matter of getting as close as possible; with Western cannon of staying away as far as possible. Thus it is necessary to use Western cannon."[11] Historians have compellingly argued that in some spheres (such as mathematics), Sun Yuanhua and other Chinese Christians exaggerated the extent of Chinese backwardness, but there's no doubt that they had a point when it came to Chinese cannons.[12]

Their power became clear that very year, 1626, when the Manchu leader Nurhaci attacked the Ming-held city of Ningyuan. Western cannons drove his forces back, "each cannon-shot killing 100 men."[13] Nurhaci himself seems to have been struck by a cannonball, which may have contributed to his death some months later.[14] After the victory, Ming officials made sacrifices to thank the cannons.[15]

In reports to Beijing, Sun Yuanhua urged the widespread adoption of red barbarian cannons. By using proper cannon carriages, telescopes, and targeting instruments, the cannons could make "every shot a hit," and "one of those weapons is worth a thousand [others]."[16] He was not alone. Most officials recognized the might of the new weapons. As the minister of war (兵部尚書), Liang Tingdong (梁廷棟, d. 1636) wrote, "In the Battle of Ningyuan [Western cannons] played a leading role in the defeat of the enemy. Without [these implements] the defenses of the capital . . . will not be adequate to defend against the invaders."[17]

After Ningyuan, Western-style cannons were increasingly sought after. In 1627, the emperor learned that the Portuguese in Macau had captured ten great cannons from a Dutch ship, and he sent an official to purchase them and recruit twenty Portuguese artillerists. Macau sources note his arrival, and the imperial edict he carried: "Since Macau is part of the emperor's domains, during this time of need, [the Portuguese] should provide this service, in order to repay the emperor's favor."[18]

Macau agreed to the request, and the Portuguese experts proceeded to Beijing, well paid for their efforts.[19] It wasn't the first time that Portuguese artillerists had been recruited by the Ming court. An early experiment had taken place in 1623, when two dozen Portuguese went to Beijing to train Chinese artillerists. That experiment had failed—the Portuguese were sent back under the excuse that the "climate didn't suit them" (in fact, a faction of officials had persuaded the court to send them back).[20] In 1627, however, the Portuguese advisors carried out their mission, advising, training, and even fighting for the Ming. To be sure, just as before some officials expressed concern. One wrote,

> I was raised in Xiangshan [the county containing Macau] and I know the barbarians in Macau very well. Their nature is violent, and their motives

cannot be fathomed. . . . Sometimes they display respect and submissive-
ness; sometimes they behave destructively. If they lend us their cannon,
they will not regard it as an act of devoted loyalty from one to the other,
but they will say that the Han Court needs them, and they will crow over
their success in foreign countries! They will not say that they reside in
Macau to trade, but they will say [we] have already conceded important
territory. Their insolence will be indescribable![21]

But we shouldn't infer from these words a Confucian's disdain for foreign technology, or a lack of curiosity. On the contrary, he agreed that
foreign techniques were effective. He just worried that the foreigners would "get insight into our troop concentrations, become familiar
with our circumstances, and deride our Heavenly Dynasty for having
no experts."[22] He advised Beijing to instead recruit artisans from southern China who already knew how to make foreign cannons. Similar
debates occurred in the famous Self-Strengthening Movement of the
nineteenth century: to what extent should one employ foreigners, and
to what extent should the emphasis be on training Chinese experts?

Others, however, were more sweeping in their denunciation of Western learning. The anti-Christian scholar Lin Qilu (林啟陸) inveighed
against the idea that "correct measures and numbers" (a reference
to Jesuits' work in calendrical reform) and cannon casting should be
placed in the hands of foreigners. In a tract that denounced the courts'
dependency on Westerners, he wrote:

> The intrusion into our Great Ming [Empire] of these people who want
> to change the calendrical methods, thus bringing disorder to the system,
> and who spy and plot against the empire, is an immense and unprec-
> edented mistake. . . . How can trivial cannon be a guarantee for 10,000
> years of safety for the country? From the Three Dynasties and from the
> Tang and the Song onwards, it has never occurred that the ordering of
> the calendar and the elucidation of time, the warding off of barbarians,
> and the curbing of bandits have been put in the hands of such green-
> eyed, high-nosed, cunning barbarians! I say, moreover, that this is the
> greatest insult for the country, but it is being presented instead as some-
> thing glorious—is this not disgusting?[23]

These are strong words, and Lin's sentiments were shared by others.
But xenophobic tendencies were outbalanced by openness. Western

learning made a deep impression in the late Ming period, partly because warfare created strong incentives to adopt effective techniques.

Unfortunately for the Ming, the 1627 experiment in employing Portuguese cannoneers died on the battlefield. Sun Yuanhua and his colleagues had been using Western cannons and Portuguese advisors to great effect, but in the winter of 1631–1632, one of Sun's subordinates, Kong Youde (孔有德, d. 1652), mutinied, attacking Sun in the city of Dengzhou.[24] Sun and his troops had twenty large "Red Barbarian" cannons and three hundred smaller "western cannons," and they fought fiercely. Portuguese sources describe the stout resistance they put up, the heavy casualties inflicted. Kong's mutineers won. Some of the Portuguese leapt from the walls into snowbanks and escaped, but Kong captured the city and the cannons.[25] Eventually he defected to the Manchus.[26] The Manchus had been building up their artillery capacities ever since their defeat at Ningyuan in 1627, so Kong's defection was a great boon. His troops had received firearms training directly from the Portuguese and had a reputation for aim as "precise as if at the bull's eye."[27] Sun Yuanhua, for his part, was blamed for the mutiny. He was imprisoned, beaten, and executed, a victim of the fractious court politics of the late Ming.

At this point, the technological advantage shifted toward the Manchus, who raced to incorporate red-barbarian cannons, which they renamed "red-coat cannons" because they found the term "barbarian" insulting. They restructured their military, making cannon units the core of new Chinese regiments.[28] These new units performed admirably, and Manchu leaders credited them with helping turn the tide of battle against the Ming.[29]

It's important to note that the Ming and the Manchus didn't merely copy Western cannon. They improved on them. Ming and early Qing metallurgical practices were in certain ways superior to those of Europe, which allowed Chinese cannon makers to develop new designs. In one composite design, for instance, the interior of the barrel was made of iron, the exterior of brass. Taiwan-based scholar Huang Yilong describes the process: "They ingeniously took advantage of the fact that the melting temperature of copper (which is around 1000C) was lower than the casting temperature of iron (1150 to 1200C), so that just a bit after the iron core had cooled, they could then, using a clay or wax casting mold, add molten bronze to the iron core. In this way, the shrinkage that attended the cooling of the external brass would [reinforce the iron, which would] enable the tube to be able to resist intense firing pressure."[30] The resulting guns, with their iron cores and bronze exteriors, were lighter, stronger, and longer lasting than iron cannons, and they were cheaper than bronze cannons. They also cooled faster.

Chinese artisans also experimented with other variants, such as wrought iron cores with cast iron exteriors. Such iron composite guns were even cheaper than the bronze-iron composites and considerably safer and more durable than standard iron cannons. Both types of composite cannon—bronze-iron and iron-iron—proved enormously successful, "among the best in the world."[31] Indeed, Chinese cannon casting technology was considered so effective that Iberian imperial officials sought to hire Chinese gunsmiths and send them to Goa to impart their methods at Portuguese cannon foundries in India.[32]

The Ming and Qing adoption of red-haired cannons was a concerted and sustained effort at technology transfer, which Huang Yi-long has labeled the "first 'self-strengthening movement' in Chinese modern military history."[33] But making advanced cannons was only one aspect of countering European naval might. Emulating European shipbuilding techniques was more difficult.

The Broadside Sailing Ship in China

In 1637, an English traveler named Peter Mundy described a warjunk he saw near Guangzhou. It had two decks of cannon ports with protruding guns, but Mundy noted that it could carry only light ordnance and judged it flimsy compared to European cannon ships.[34] Statements by Ming and Qing officials suggest that Mundy was right. Although the Chinese had once built huge vessels, by the 1500s European vessels were acknowledged to be larger and more solid than their Chinese counterparts.

As a book of military strategy published in China in 1646 puts it, "The red-hairs [i.e., the Dutch] build their ships tall as mountains and sturdy as an iron bucket, so solid that they can't be destroyed. . . . Ultimately, there's no way to stand up to them. With great ease they traverse the outer seas without worry of being defeated or damaged."[35]

Another Ming official quipped, "Dutch ships are like mountains; ours are like anthills."[36] It wasn't just a matter of solid decks. Other aspects of European ship design, including cannon carriages, cannon ports, breeching lines, and complex rigging, conferred significant advantages. The broadside sailing ship was a complex and sophisticated assemblage of technologies and practices, the product of centuries of evolution.[37]

In the 1630s, however, a Ming official undertook a little-known Westernization project and built a fleet of warships based on European models. His name was Zheng Zhilong (鄭芝龍, 1604–1661), and he is a significant but, alas, underappreciated figure in China. Not only did he end up defeating the Dutch, teaching them that using force to open China's markets was unwise; he also founded an army and navy that, under the leadership of his son Zheng Chenggong, became one of the most effective armed forces in the world.

One of the things that made Zheng Zhilong so powerful was his ability to navigate the multicultural world of seventeenth-century maritime East Asia. He spoke Portuguese, was a Catholic convert (albeit an indifferently doctrinaire one), was married to a Japanese woman, and had close connections to the Dutch, working for a time as their translator. The Dutch and Zhilong did much business together. In his early years, he acted as a privateer for the Dutch East India Company, pillaging under its flag in exchange for a share of spoils.[38] Indeed, Chinese officials liked to blame his piracy on his connections with foreigners.

They were also concerned about the power he gained from foreign techniques. "Zhilong bases his power," wrote one Chinese official, "on barbarian warships and uses all barbarian cannons."[39] In this period, the ships of maritime East Asia were already hybrid things. A vessel might fly a Japanese flag, have a Chinese hull, use European maps with Chinese characters, carry European-built or European-inspired guns, and be piloted by Chinese, Dutch, or Portuguese navigators.[40] But Zheng Zhilong took the practice further, deliberately copying European warships and adopting their armaments. As another Ming source notes, "his ships and weapons are all built like those of foreign barbarians, the warships tall and sturdy, unsinkable in the oceans, even when they encounter reefs; his cannons so effective that they can fire for several dozen li and shatter anything that they strike."[41]

Thanks in part to such adaptations, he could rage with impunity along the Chinese coast, capturing vessels, raiding towns, defeating local militias and imperial forces.

Ming officials didn't need such instability in the south at the very time they were faced with the rise of the Manchu state in the north, so in 1628 they offered him an official position. He was to become an arm of the Ming armed forces, charged with keeping pirates and barbarians at bay. He was given wide latitude to collect tolls and equip his own forces. He was under imperial supervision, of course, but with considerable autonomy.

Thanks to his official status and new sources of income he was able to undertake a systematic program of naval modernization. In 1633, in the port city of Xiamen, he supervised Chinese shipwrights and artisans in the construction of a fleet of sturdy, multidecked vessels like European broadside ships.[42] A painting by Dutch master Simon de Vlieger depicts some of these ships in proximity to Dutch ships, and it is remarkable how similar they were in shape and size, distinguished primarily by the different rigging and flags.[43] Indeed, according to other Dutch sources, Zhilong intentionally built his ships "in the Dutch style [*op sijn Hollants*]."[44] Like most Dutch warships, they were equipped with two cannon decks, which, in contrast to the decks of traditional warjunks, could support the large muzzle-loading cannons used by maritime Europeans in the seventeenth century.

Thus, his ships were armed as well as or better than the Dutch warships in East Asia, carrying thirty or thirty-six large guns. A Dutch description of the fleet notes that the "large, beautiful war junks were equipped with large cannons, some of them having more than our own warships."[45] The Dutch term I have translated as "large cannons" (*grof canon*) usually refers to guns that shot projectiles of at least eighteen Dutch pounds (nine kilograms) which means these were as powerful as Dutch broadside guns.[46] Thus, if these sources are correct—and there's no reason to doubt them—Zhilong's ships were equipped much like the warships of the Dutch.

Equally important, his shipwrights seem to have grasped the details that made European broadside ships so effective. One problem with shipborne artillery was how to load broadside guns after firing. One had to wait for the gun to cool—or cool it oneself—and then swab it, measure out the proper amount of gunpowder, add it, tamp it down with a long rod, add the cannonball, and then push it down securely. Imagine trying to do all of this while astride a cannon that stuck out of a gun port, with the ship swaying, waves crashing, and the enemy perhaps firing a potshot or two. An Icelandic gunner in a Danish fleet described how he'd tried to do so in 1622: "The ship rolled all the starboard guns under, and me on my gun with them. I swallowed much water and was nearly carried away."[47]

To facilitate reloading, Europeans began using special four-wheeled carriages that allowed the cannons to be rolled back within the ship, where they were loaded and then wheeled back into place. It sounds like an obvious solution, but it apparently wasn't. All kinds of subsidiary equipment was necessary, most importantly breeching lines and ringbolts, which prevented the cannons from recoiling too far and aided sailors in pulling them back into place.[48] Historians have argued that one of the reasons the British won the famous Battle of the Spanish Armada in 1588 is that they had developed a means of loading cannons within the ship whereas the Spanish had not.[49]

Zheng Zhilong's new ships had just these features: wheeled carriages and ringbolts with breeching lines. We know this because Dutch officials had an opportunity to examine these ships for themselves. "Never before in this land, so far as anyone can remember, has anyone seen a fleet like this, with such beautiful, huge, well-armed junks, and so well-mounted with cannons, . . . with two solid decks, good cannon carriages [*roopaerden*] and rings for breeching lines [*ringbouts*]."[50]

How did this Dutchman learn so much about these ships? Not by invitation. He destroyed the fleet before it was even able to sail, in a devious attack. The ships weren't even crewed yet but were filled with workers who jumped overboard. He examined the ships and then ordered them burned.

This 1633 sneak attack, which I have described in detail elsewhere, was the opening salvo of the first conflict between the Dutch and the Ming-Zheng family.[51] Zheng Zhilong got his revenge, but not by using Western technology. Instead he used an old standby: fire ships.

It was a masterful plan. With his new fleet destroyed, he cobbled together a fleet of old warjunks and merchant vessels and filled them with gunpowder and incendiaries. But he outfitted them to appear ready for standard ship-to-ship combat, with large crews, full weaponry, and flags and banners. By the time the Dutch discovered the deception it was too late. The fire ships sailed right into the Dutch fleet and then burst into fire. "The junks," wrote a Dutch participant, "went up in an instant in such terrifying tall flames, burning so vehemently, that it was nearly impossible to believe."[52]

It was a terrific defeat. Afterward the official policy of the Dutch was to "keep our main ships away from China and out of harm's way so they won't be exposed to the kind of fury and resolution the Chinese displayed at Liaoluo Bay."[53] The Chinese for their part viewed the victory as a "miracle at sea."[54] Zheng Zhilong rose to preeminence, dominating the rich commerce of maritime China. He kept the Dutch in line not just by means of his military reputation but also by extending trade privileges. In fact, his family and the Dutch became trading partners, although the Zheng were richer and gained more from the trade.[55]

What is curious is that the Ming never tried to rebuild a fleet like the one destroyed in 1633. Perhaps Zhilong's victory in 1634, achieved with conventional vessels, convinced him and his successors that one didn't need to emulate the Dutch to defeat them. Equally important, the Zheng family became the unparalleled masters of the China trade. There were no significant waterborne enemies aside from the Dutch. It simply wasn't necessary to make the huge investments in ship design that had seemed necessary in the early 1630s.

That's not to say that the Zheng were militarily inactive. On the contrary, they soon became embroiled in the most significant conflict of the seventeenth century. When the Manchus took Beijing in 1644 and made it the capital of their Qing dynasty, the Zheng began a decades-long war to try to reinstate the Ming. It was Zheng Zhilong's son, Zheng Chenggong, who became the most famous Ming loyalist, inheriting his father's trading organization and using it to fund a massive military buildup against the Qing.

He also used his army and navy against the Dutch, invading their colony of Taiwan in 1661. As we've seen, he decisively defeated the Dutch in field battles, but he had less success at sea. Dutch ships proved overwhelmingly superior, at least in deep water.

In 1661, for example, three Dutch ships fought against sixty Chinese junks off the coast of Taiwan. It was a gory battle. Hundreds of Chinese soldiers tried to board the Dutch ships but were shot at until "blood flooded out from the gutters."[56] Chinese historians have suggested that the Chinese won the battle by using fireboats, as Zheng Zhilong did in 1634, but this is not the case.[57] In fact, the Dutch used guns to fight off wave after wave of attackers, and just as the battle was ending and the Chinese were withdrawing, a careless Dutch cannoneer allowed a spark to get into the largest Dutch ship's powder room. The vessel was blown to bits.[58] It's quite likely that without this accident the Dutch would have defeated the Chinese, or at least held them off.[59]

This perspective on the superiority of Dutch vessels is corroborated by other battles. One of the most telling occurred in 1663. The Dutch had allied with the Qing to expel the Zheng family from their bases in China. The Zheng had hundreds of vessels, and the Dutch had just fifteen, but upon seeing the Dutch fleet the Zheng sent a letter to the Dutch begging them not to attack: "Our ships cannot fight against your ships. . . . Please, we ask that you and your ships not support the Qing against us but sail to another place."[60] Thus, the Zheng admitted that the Dutch ships were superior. The Dutch demurred, attacked the Zheng, and managed to scatter their fleet. After the victory the main Qing commander wrote admiringly to thank the Dutch admiral: "I watched your ships from a mountain top and rejoiced to see how with their thundering cannon they made the rebel ships flee. . . . I shall not delay to inform the emperor quickly, by special post . . . that the Hollanders are brave and daring in their attacks on our mutual enemy."[61] An Italian missionary, no great friend to the Protestant Dutch, agreed with this assessment: "The Dutch ships equaled all the rest in strength, because the smallest Dutch vessel bore thirty-six pieces of heavy artillery."[62] The victorious Dutch admiral had his own opinion, immodest but probably justified: "on water . . . our own power is (with God's help) sufficient enough to withstand the entire enemy fleet."[63] The results of the battle were clear. Having abandoned the building of broadside fleets after 1634, the Ming found that fifteen Dutch ships were superior to a fleet of hundreds of their warjunks.

The Dutch also seem to have had an advantage in navigation: an ability to sail close to the wind. A seventeenth-century Chinese scholar who traveled to Taiwan and had friends who sailed the seas wrote that Dutch ships "have sails that spiral like a spider's web, receiving wind from eight directions, so there is nowhere they go that is not favorable. Compare this with Chinese sails and masts. When they encounter a contrary wind, they must bend over to the left and then to the right, leaning dangerously, and thus, winding and wending, they must slowly make their way dangerously forward. The two kinds of ships are as different as heaven and earth."[64] A picture of a European ship in a military manual published by Zheng Zhilong circa 1646 focuses on the complex rigging, which is described as "all tangled, forming something that resembles silkworm's silk or a spider web" (see Figure 14.1).[65] It was this rigging that allowed the sails to be configured in many different ways. Chinese rigging, in contrast, was simple.[66] Why this difference? It's possible that the reasons had to do with the environments within which the two maritime traditions had evolved. One didn't need complex rigging to sail long distances in the regular monsoon winds of maritime Asia. European rigging had evolved in the Mediterranean Sea, the North Sea, and the Atlantic Ocean, where wind and current patterns were much more complicated.

The Dutch ability to sail into the wind provided a clear advantage in the Sino-Dutch Wars. For example, after Zheng Zhilong burned the Dutch ships in 1634, he tried chasing down the remainder of the Dutch fleet, but both Dutch and Chinese sources suggest that he couldn't catch them because they were sailing close to the wind.[67]

Decades later, when his son attacked Taiwan, the Dutch capacity to sail close to the wind played a major role in the war. In May 1661, the Dutch were trapped in their fortress in Taiwan. Zheng Chenggong had timed his invasion to coincide with the onset of the southern monsoon so that the Dutch couldn't send a dispatch to their headquarters in Batavia. But a little Dutch yacht managed to take an "entirely unusual route."[68] When a reinforcement fleet arrived in Taiwan later in the summer, Zheng Chenggong was flabbergasted. He couldn't fathom that it was a reinforcement fleet, presuming that it must have been sent for some other purpose, such as attacking the Portuguese at

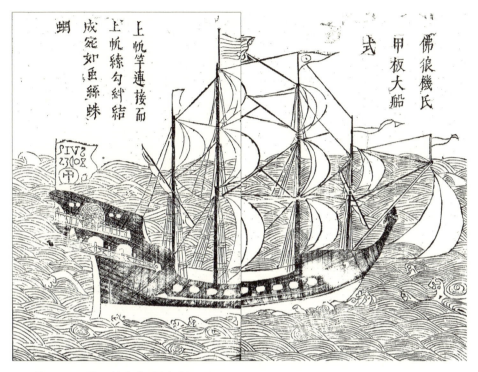

F<small>IGURE</small> 14.1 Frankish decked ship, 1646.

The text on the left calls attention to the complex rigging, which it describes as tangled and resembling a spider's web. Such rigging, along with deep keels, allowed Western ships to sail closer to the wind than Chinese vessels, although Chinese junks were faster sailing with the wind. Zheng Dayu 鄭大鬱, *Jing guo xiong lüe* 經國雄略, "Wu bei kao," juan 8 武備攷卷之八, fols. 20–21. Courtesy of the Harvard-Yenching Library of the Harvard College Library, Harvard University.

Macau. He was deeply acquainted with the Chinese sea routes in East and Southeast Asia, and with the capacities of Chinese vessels. His surprise suggests that this voyage would not have been attempted in a Chinese vessel.

There were other episodes in which the Dutch ability to sail close to the wind—and the Chinese inability to do so—affected the war.[69] Although we still have much to learn about Chinese shipbuilding, it seems safe to say that European vessels were better than Chinese ones at sailing into the wind.

In any case, the Dutch were jubilant when the fleet arrived with fresh supplies and new troops. But Zheng Chenggong, realizing that the Dutch might be able to keep supplying themselves indefinitely, redoubled his efforts to capture their fortress. Fortunately for the Dutch, it was a renaissance fortress.

CHAPTER 15

The Renaissance Fortress

AN AGENT OF EUROPEAN EXPANSION?

China's walls were thick. Europe's were thin and brittle. But in the mid-1400s and early 1500s, Europeans began making walls more like those of China: thick, sloped, and filled with earth. They also began experimenting with new defensive geometries. By the early 1500s, they had codified these experiments into a powerful new design: the renaissance fortress.[1]

From each corner of the renaissance fort jutted an angled bastion, each placed so as to reinforce its neighbors. The bastions could lay out a lethal crossfire, making them nearly impossible to approach. Older fortresses with their round or square bastions had "dead zones," areas where stormers found refuge from fire. The new forts covered all the angles. Storming became difficult, and since the walls were now so thick it was no longer so easy to blast a breach. Sieges became much harder for attackers, and longer-lasting.[2]

Some historians have suggested that the renaissance fortress acted as an "engine of European expansion," allowing small European garrisons to maintain control in settlements far from Europe.[3] Other historians disagree vehemently, suggesting that non-Europeans were able to capture artillery fortresses with relative ease.[4] Neither side in this debate can draw on much evidence, because few historians have examined sieges outside Europe in any detail.

In the seventeenth century, however, the forces of China overcame artillery fortresses belonging to the Dutch and the Russians. In each case, the results marked a geopolitical shift: the Dutch lost Taiwan; the Russians lost their toehold in Manchuria. Should we therefore conclude that the renaissance fortress's reputation is exaggerated? No. The details of these sieges make clear that the renaissance fortress's ability to lay out lethal crossfire, to magnify the power of a small number of defenders, was decisive. In fact, many Ming scholars acknowledged the effectiveness of European fortification designs and attempted to import them into China.

The Renaissance Fortress in China

The most famous proponents of the renaissance fortress in China were the Christian officials Xu Guangqi (徐光啟, 1562–1633) and Sun Yuanhua (孫元化, 1582–1632). Sun Yuanhua's famous military manual *Xi fa shen ji* (西法神機, ca. 1632), contains a section about Western defenses, the "Illustrated Guide to the Artillery Fortress" (銃台圖說), which notes that the key to their efficacy was the angled bastion (銳角).[5] "With the angled bastion," he wrote, "the enemy is kept out beyond the walls, and when subjected to our attack there is nowhere our guns cannot reach and the enemy has no way to approach."[6] Sun Yuanhua sought opportunities to construct angled bastions in northeastern China, to defend against the Manchus. Did he succeed? There is some evidence that he did during the 1620s, although his efforts were impaired by infighting and administrative turnover.[7]

Less known than Sun Yuanhua are two wealthy brothers named Han Yun and Han Lin (韓雲, dates unknown; 韓霖, ca. 1598–ca.1649). Both were Confucian officials. Han Lin in particular wrote a great deal about renaissance fortresses, although, alas, much of his work is no longer extant, including the enticingly titled "Illustrated Guide to the Artillery Fortress" (砲台圖說). It's clear from surviving writings that he and his brother understood the principles of the artillery fortress. As he wrote, "Today, the towns and prefectures are protected only by square-shaped bastions (敵台皆作方形), and although the vertical sides can protect each other, the fronts are subject to enemy attack. Thus, it is necessary to construct angled bastions, which are highly ingenious (作三角形為妙)."[8] Did he and his brother actually manage to construct any artillery fortresses? There is some evidence that they may have, but, as in the case of Sun Yuanhua, it's inconclusive (see Figures 15.1 and 15.2).[9]

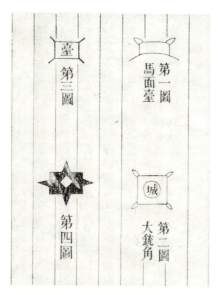

Figure 15.1 The artillery fortress in Ming China, ca. 1632.

This image of forts with angled bastions (銳角) was published in a military manual by Ming official Sun Yuanhua, ca. 1632. It describes how Chinese walls should be refortified in the Western manner. Chinese city walls already had barbicans, massive square protrusions that provided a modicum of defense in depth but without the geometric defense of the angled bastion. Sun Yuanhua proposed that these barbicans be retrofitted with small angled bastions, as in the top right image (as he wrote, 今築城則馬面台宜為小銳角, 如第一圖). Barbicans wouldn't be sufficient at the corners of city walls, however, and so Sun advocated the construction of huge bastions for each corner. Sun Yuanhua 孫元化, *Xi fa shen ji* 西法神機, juan 2, fol. 31. Courtesy of the Max Planck Institute for the History of Science. Creative Commons License: CC-BY-SA 3.0 DE, http://echo.mpiwg-berlin.mpg.de/MPIWG:3YN478NP, retrieved 17 December 2014.

That's not the case, however, with a far lesser-known figure: Ma Weicheng (馬維城, 1594–1659). A scion of a scholarly family, Ma built angled bastions to fortify his home county—Xiong County (雄縣, Hebei Province). According to an extant biography in a seventeenth-century county gazetteer, Ma not only carefully studied the Chinese military classics, but also "was an associate of the Western scholar Adam Schall von Bell."[10] A Jesuit missionary, Schall von Bell was a renowned figure in late Ming China, honored by the Ming Emperor Chongzhen himself for helping cast cannons.[11]

Schall von Bell's teachings on gunpowder warfare were published in 1643 under the title *The Essentials of Gunpowder Warfare* (火攻挈要),

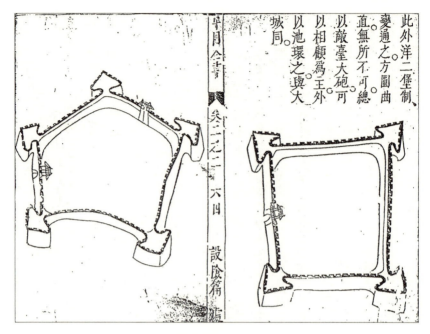

FIGURE 15.2 Late Ming artillery fortress, ca. 1638.

These images are from Han Lin's treatise *Shou yu quan shu* (守圉全書), from ca. 1638. Han Lin and his brother Han Yun propagated the artillery fortress design in China, and there is evidence that they built artillery fortresses, although no traces survive. From Han Lin, *Shou yu quan shu* 守圉全書 (ca. 1638), juan 2 pt. 2, fols. 64a–64b. Courtesy of the National Library of China, Beijing.

which contains a chapter called "Brief Notes on Defending Walls."[12] He explains that angled bastions, by laying out crossfire, "allow few men to defend securely, and small strength to attack powerfully."[13] Ma Weicheng, according to his biography, "received [Schall von Bell's] teachings on gunpowder warfare and angled bastions (火攻銳台)."[14] (Schall von Bell was less successful in passing on his religion—it seems that Weicheng didn't convert to Catholicism.)[15]

Ma Weicheng was placed in charge of building new defenses for Xiong County City, which had recently been sacked by Manchu forces. According to his biography, he "built two large Western angled bastions (西洋銳角大敵台) on two corners of the northern wall."[16] The bastions helped fend off a Manchu incursion in 1638, and over the following years he constructed more fortifications.[17] In 1641, for instance, he "built two western style angled bastions on the southern corners, and then, on each of the eastern and western walls, he built three angled bastions."[18] This brought the number of Western-style bastions on the walls of Xiong County City to ten.

Ma Weicheng's bastion building wasn't limited to his home county. He seems to have built angled bastions in Si County (泗縣) and perhaps even in the city of Yangzhou.[19] In 1645, after Beijing had fallen, he accepted a position with the Qing, working for the Ministry of War. After retiring, and wrote military treatises, including one called "An Illustrated Guide to Artillery Fortresses" (台砲圖說). None of them is extant.[20]

Upon his death in 1659, his son composed a poem called "The Western Fortress" to commemorate his father's work:

> At the end of the Ming, fortresses rose up all over
> Western Angled Bastion Fortresses. . . .
> Created by my late father and bequeathed to those who come after
> far into the future.
> Now, I write these words to commemorate the start of things,
> So there will be no forgetting what he created.[21]

The poem was overoptimistic. Ma Weicheng's efforts were largely forgotten, and no traces of his bastions remain.[22]

Why? Scholars in China have suggested that the answer is simple. Shortly after Ma Weicheng built his fortresses, the Manchus captured northern China, and the pace of warfare there diminished, so these early experiments were abandoned.[23] This may be true, but there was still plenty of warfare in southern China. Why didn't the renaissance fortress take root in the south? Or is it possible that it did and we just don't know about it?

It's certainly possible, but it seems doubtful, because when the Southern Ming tried attacking Dutch renaissance fortresses, they had tremendous trouble understanding how to do so. The same was true when Qing troops attacked a Russian artillery fortress. Europeans, of course, understood that there's no shortcut to capturing a renaissance fort: you had creep closer trench by trench, bombardment by bombardment. It was a long and tedious process.[24] But the Qing and the Ming commanders had no such experience. In both cases, they were overconfident. They knew that the Europeans were greatly outnumbered and operating far from their supply centers, so they launched bold attacks, attempting to bombard and then storm the European forts. This didn't go well.

The Siege of Fort Zeelandia, 1661–1662

Zeelandia was a sea fortress, designed to guard the main entrance to the Bay of Tayouan, the heart of the Dutch colony of Taiwan.[25] It stood on a long, thin peninsula that carved the bay out of the dangerous waters of the Taiwan Strait, its cannons thrusting out over the water (see Figure 15.3). But when Zheng Chenggong arrived in the spring of 1661, he outmaneuvered the Dutch. Instead of trying to sail past Zeelandia's deadly bastions, he rode a high tide through a different passage, wending through twisting sandbars into the bay. It was a brilliant strategy, and soon he'd landed fifteen thousand men. They took up positions in the dunes south of the fortress and in a town across from it, sheltering in stately homes abandoned by Dutch merchants.

Zheng was confident. The numerical odds were twenty to one in his favor, and Fort Zeelandia was small. He'd overcome much larger walls during a dozen years of warfare in China and was certain he'd be able to take the fortress by bombardment and then storm. He wrote messages to the Dutch: "You are," he wrote, "only a handful of people who cannot stand up against my own soldiers. . . . Now all you have left is that little fort, which is like a dead and dried out tree that cannot stand on its own."[26] He acknowledged that the Dutch were skilled with artillery but expressed confidence in his own guns. "It is true," he wrote, "that you people are famous for playing artfully with cannons, but you have never had this many cannons leveled at you. I have brought hundreds of them, ready to use against you."[27] The Dutch were uncowed: "Not even the hundred cannons that Your Highness says are pointed at us can persuade us, because we have even more cannons here in our fort to answer with."[28]

So after careful preparation and various feints, Zheng launched a nocturnal assault. His first salvo demolished the roof of the Dutch governor's house, which stood within the fortress walls. His guns also

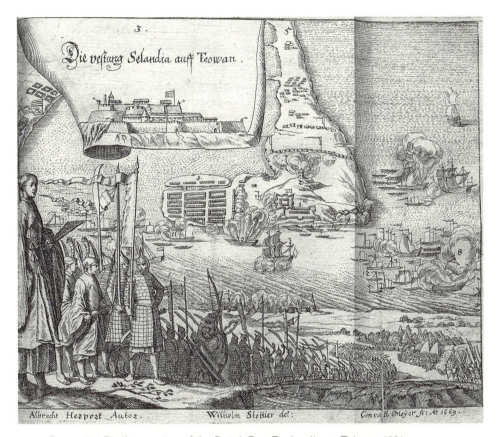

FIGURE 15.3 Bird's-eye view of the Dutch Fort Zeelandia on Taiwan, 1661.

This engraving, based on a drawing by the soldier and artist Albrecht Herport, shows the artillery fortress Zeelandia during the siege of 1661–1662. The fortress is in the very center of the picture, rather small, but the angled bastions are quite clearly depicted. From Albrecht Herport, *Eine kurtze Ost-Indianische Reiß-Beschreibung* (Bern: Georg Sonnleitner, 1669), pp.100 and 101. Courtesy of the Universitätsbibliothek Leipzig, 8-B.S.T.311, Tafel 3.

targeted Dutch cannon positions on the fortress walls, systematically blasting away the crenellations that protected the gunners.

The Dutch had trouble firing back, so effective and accurate was Zheng's attack, but once they gained their composure they exercised their artistry. The Dutch governor surveyed the field from atop a bastion and noted that "the enemy's cannons were placed very poorly, entirely unprotected and easy to destroy."[29] The Dutch gunners re-aimed their cannons and muskets to fire from different angles, the jutting bastions serving as vantage points. The governor later wrote, "with the first charge nearly the whole field was strewn with dead and wounded, the enemy being thus taught the lesson not to expose themselves so readily."[30] A mass of Zheng soldiers who were preparing to storm the walls were also driven away.

When the smoke cleared, Zheng's guns had been silenced, and hundreds of his best troops had been killed. His cannonades had in contrast caused no serious harm to the Dutch—a few houses damaged, some holes in the walls, some crenellations battered, but no significant casualties, although a Dutch artillerist lost an ear and another a hat to Chinese bullets.

The defeat shocked Zheng Chenggong, who gave up his plan of capturing the fort quickly. He withdrew most troops and moved to a long-term strategy: starve them out. But the Dutch, protected by bastions, were able to forage for melons in overgrown gardens, hunt abandoned pigs and seabirds, gather oysters. To be sure, there was hardship. The fort's main church filled with sick people, and there were many burials. But the fortress was on the water, and Zheng hadn't counted on Dutch seamanship. As we've seen, a Dutch yacht managed to sail against prevailing winds and summon help. A Dutch fleet arrived with supplies and reinforcements.

This was another shock to Zheng Chenggong. At this point—it was the fall of 1661—he realized that the Dutch might hold out indefinitely. He understood that he would have to capture the fortress. But how? He tried various tacks, but each time he built a new cannon position, the Dutch responded by putting up a new position of their own. It was a slow dance of sandbags. To be sure, Zheng's commanders were learning. Each new cannon position was better than the last. Yet the Dutch were still able to block each one.

Finally, in December 1661, Zheng had a stroke of luck. A German man, fond of drink, and perhaps frustrated by the fact that alcohol cost the equivalent of five hundred dollars for a six-pack, defected to the Chinese side.[31] He was a high officer who'd fought not just in the colonies but also in Europe. He helped Zheng Chenggong design proper siegeworks.

They were impressive, constructed so as to protect each other from Dutch counterfire and target a Dutch redoubt that stood on a dune overlooking Fort Zeelandia. Zheng Chenggong had tried capturing this redoubt before, understanding that it was the key to Zeelandia, but his attempts had all been thwarted by Dutch engineers and artillerists. The new siegeworks, however, were effective. When his cannons opened fire the Dutch were helpless. The Dutch governor wrote in despair, "We couldn't shoot the enemy anywhere, and so he happily thundered on by himself, and we watched with sadness and grief as our redoubt was destroyed."[32] Shortly thereafter the governor surrendered.

The details of this siege—and I have provided only a few of them here—show quite compellingly that Zheng Chenggong and his commanders, for all their experience and brilliance, did not understand how to approach an artillery fortress. Nine months it took—a three-month blockade followed by several months of experimentation—to conquer the fortress, and Zheng had originally expected to have it in his possession within weeks of his arrival. Moreover, the ultimate solution was provided by a German defector, who showed Zheng that the only way to take a renaissance fortress was to construct extensive protected batteries.

The Dutch case strongly supports the idea that the Renaissance fortress did indeed act as an "engine of European expansion." Nor was Zheng Chenggong's experience unique. The Qing siege of the Russian fortress of Albazin followed a remarkably similar pattern: an overconfident initial attack, failure of the same, a series of deadly European sorties, a long blockade, and a number of experiments in siegecraft that were increasingly systematic. In the Russian case, however, the forces of China never achieved surrender. The Russians held out, despite terrible disease and starvation, until events far away decided their fate.

The Sieges of Albazin, 1685–1689

The Russian settlement of Albazin was located on a bank of the Amur River, within lands that the Manchu Qing considered under their sovereignty. At first the walls were constructed of wood, which is why in 1672, when Moscow formally incorporated Albazin into its empire, the

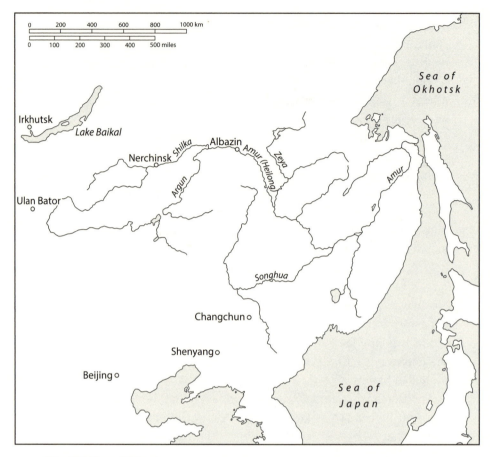

MAP 15.1 Map of Albazin.

settlement was categorized as a fort and not a city. It grew quickly. Whereas other parts of the Russian Far East were too frozen to produce crops, Albazin's lands were fertile (see Map 15.1). Buildings multiplied below the walls and farms spread through the valley. A monastery was founded, and tribute in furs was exacted from nearby peoples.

These tributes, however, were meant to go to the Qing, or at least that's how the young Kangxi Emperor (r. 1661–1722) interpreted the situation. He was determined to counter the Russians' growing power. In 1682, having won the great War of the Three Feudatories (1673–1681), he began preparing carefully, sending a reconnaissance mission to map out routes, acquire informants, assess Russian strength, and study the fortifications.

The reports noted that the Russians were tough and that Albazin's walls, although wooden, were stout. "Without red-barbarian cannon," they concluded, "it is not possible [to capture the fort]."[33] Albazin stood a thousand miles from Beijing as the crow flies, but of course men and cannons can't fly. To get there required a tortuous journey through forbidding lands. Still, the reconnaissance report was optimistic: one could transport huge cannons by moving across land in the winter, when the routes were solid, and over water in spring and summer, when the ice had melted.[34]

The emperor planned assiduously, composing detailed instructions about the sizes of transport boats, the construction of granaries, the staffing of post stations. He studied reports and proposals, sending them back with annotations and demanding rewrites.[35] The preparations took years, but eventually all was ready, testimony to the genius for logistics that was making the Qing such a great power.[36]

It was June 1685 when three thousand Qing troops arrived before Albazin. The emperor had ordered them to try to avoid bloodshed: "We rule . . . by the principle of benevolence and never by bloodthirstiness. . . . Because our army is excellent and our equipment strong, in the long run the Russians cannot resist us, and they must offer up our territories and return our cities."[37] A Manchu general named Langtan (郎坦, d. 1695) was the main commander, and his orders called for restraint: "Whether the Russians surrender right away or fight first and surrender later, you must under no circumstances slaughter or massacre them. With benevolence instruct them to withdraw and return home."[38]

Langtan did as he was told. Arriving at Albazin, he and the other commanders first sent envoys to solicit a surrender. Russian sources suggest that the garrison had only three cannons and three hundred muskets, and that powder supplies were low.[39] Moreover, Albazin was not at this stage a Renaissance fortress. Its wooden walls might be useful against arrows and small guns, but they were not constructed to resist advanced artillery. Nonetheless, the Russians resolved to fight. Or, as the official Qing account put it, "the Russian demons, relying on the stoutness of their lair, refused to surrender."[40]

The Qing advanced troops to the south of the fort, setting up barricades and earthworks and placing bow and crossbow positions on top, "making as though preparing to attack," but this was a feint.[41] They were also secretly moving red-barbarian cannons to the north of the fort, while even more powerful "miraculous-power general cannons" were positioned to the sides, "to carry out a pincer attack."[42] Cannon boats were positioned on the river, to the southeast. How many cannons did the Qing have in total? Chinese sources aren't clear, but European sources suggest an alarming amount, a "great might of guns,"[43] with a generally reliable source saying that there were a hundred or a hundred fifty pieces of light field artillery and forty to fifty large siege guns.[44] The Qing also seem to have had a hundred-man musketeer corps.[45]

The firepower was overwhelming. "In the first days," European sources say, "more than a hundred men [on the Russian side] were lost, struck by enemy shots, and the wooden walls and towers of the fort were badly damaged."[46] Qing sources suggest that the guns themselves didn't work fast enough, and so they tried another method: "The attack went until the next day and it became clear that the fortress had still not quickly fallen, so it was ordered that below the walls on the three [landward] sides firewood and kindling be piled up and the walls burnt, at which the [Russian] chieftain was compelled to dispatch envoys to offer his surrender."[47] The Russian commander later explained that he was compelled by more than burning walls: a petition from the superior of the monastery and the town's inhabitants begged him to surrender, so he reluctantly complied.[48]

Is it true that, as official Qing sources suggest, the Russian officials, grateful for Qing benevolence, "all had tears running down their cheeks as they kowtowed in the direction of the imperial residence [in Beijing]?"[49] European sources mention no tears or kowtowing, but they do agree that the Qing showed mercy. They also say the Qing showed a propensity for long-winded monologues about the emperor's benevolence and the good life that could be had in his service. Many Russians decided to defect, and their descendants still live in China. The rest were allowed to leave, although some complained that their clothes were stolen and they were given barely enough food to survive the trek to Russian headquarters at Nerchinsk.[50]

The Qing soldiers burned Albazin and the nearby villages and monastery, but for some reason they didn't burn the crops as the emperor had instructed. After the soldiers had withdrawn, the Russians returned to reap the harvest.

This time, the Russian commander was explicitly ordered to build more powerful walls.[51] In charge of construction was a Prussian military expert named Afanasii Ivanovich Beiton, who had been captured by the Russians in 1667 and sent as a prisoner to Siberia, where he joined the side of his captors.[52] Some historians suggest that Beiton was a "trained and experienced military engineer," but really we know little about his life before his Russian service.[53] As second in command at Albazin, he was responsible for fortifications. Building the walls wasn't easy. The workers had to forge new tools "because the Chinese had in their thievery taken all of such utensils with them."[54] But according to European sources, the walls eventually reached a height of five and a half meters and a thickness of seven and a half meters (three fathoms high and four fathoms thick).[55] Qing sources suggest that they were perhaps a bit lower and thinner but acknowledged that they were uncommonly strong.[56]

They were also unusual. One of Beiton's subordinates "had learned a way to make walls with clay-earth and tree-roots that were woven and cinched together, worked in such a way that it became as hard as stone, and unbreakable."[57] A Qing reconnaissance mission similarly reported that the thick, sturdy walls "were made from interspersing trees, with a core of earth as the filling . . . and the outside filled in with clay."[58] Another European authority writes that the grass, mortar, and tree roots were "set so well together that it was stronger than a normal wall."[59]

With its new walls, Albazin was given a new status. No longer was it a mere fortress, or ostrog. Now it was a walled city, receiving from Moscow a coat of arms: a stern eagle with a crown, who held a bow in one talon and arrows in the other.[60]

Was Albazin a renaissance fortress? Scholars have suggested that the Russians "never adopted the *trace italienne* to any large degree, but rather used the 'reinforced castle' style of fortification . . . considered . . . in the west to be less modern than the Italian style."[61] They say that Russians built few artillery fortresses and that most of them

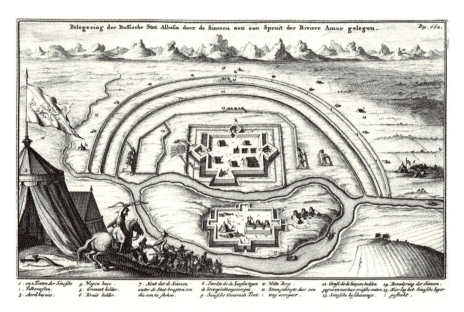

FIGURE 15.4 The Qing siege of Albazin, 1686–1687.

This image depicts the siege of the Russian artillery fortress Albazin by Qing forces in 1686–1687. The Russian fortress is in the center, with four bastions protruding from the walls—the three to landward are of the angled type characteristic of the artillery fortress. On the island below the Russian fortress stands a temporary Chinese fort, with the square barbicans that are typical of Chinese fortifications. From Nicolaas Witsen, *Noord en Oost Tartarye*, p. 662. Courtesy of Göttingen State and University Library, 4 H AS II, 7196:2 RARA.

date from well into the reign of Peter the Great (1682–1725).[62] Yet evidence suggests strongly that Albazin was an artillery fortress. Nicolaas Witsen, a Dutch cartographer (and eventual mayor of Amsterdam), published a geographical treatise about Siberia, based on conversations and correspondence with Russians, Mongols, and Siberians, and in it he includes a detailed plate to illustrate the second Siege of Albazin (see Figure 15.4).[63] Probably based on a sketch by a participant, the plate shows clearly that Albazin had angled bastions. In contrast, it shows the Qing counterfortifications as having the square barbicans characteristic of Chinese walls.[64] Another piece of visual evidence—an image drawn by Beiton himself, the man who oversaw the building of the walls—also depicts Albazin as an artillery fortress.[65] So it seems safe to conclude that Albazin was an artillery fortress, or that it at least employed principles of geometric defense, as did many Russian fortresses built at this time.

The defenses of Albazin certainly were strong enough this time to hold back a long Qing siege. In July 1686, Commander Langtan came back with three thousand troops and dozens of boats filled with supplies and guns, including thirty or forty "newly cast" cannons.[66] Six of his vessels carried nothing but gunpowder and ammunition.[67] In contrast the Russians had just eight hundred men, and only eleven large cannons, although they did have bombs and grenades.[68]

Langtan informed the Russians that the imperial patience was not inexhaustible. If they surrendered immediately, they would be treated well, but if they decided to fight, they would be punished.[69] Once again, the Russians were defiant. They resolved "to hold the fortress as long as there was food, and that then they would melt down all the cannons, destroy any remaining weapons, and then, armed with just hand and side weapons, see if they could [fight their way out] and get through to safety."[70]

The battle began on 18 July 1686.[71] Jeremy Black, who has argued that artillery fortresses were not as effective vis-à-vis non-Europeans as some might suggest, has asserted that the Qing won by blockade: "in capturing Albazin, the Manchu allowed hunger, backed up by superior numbers, to do their work."[72] But in fact, European and Chinese sources show clearly that the Qing actually tried many different times to penetrate the walls but failed. Moreover, the Russians, with few guns and a small and sickly garrison, inflicted serious losses.

Sources from both sides agree that over the first weeks of the battle, the Qing attacked vehemently a number of times, trying various tacks, but were driven back repeatedly. For example, Qing sources state that on 23 July 1686,[73] Langtan ordered a two-pronged nocturnal assault. From the north he supervised bombardment with red-hair cannons, but the real attempt was made on the south, where his subordinates led troops to try to storm the walls.[74] As Russian sources report, "the Celestials [Bogadaiskii—i.e., the Chinese Emperor's People] fired on the town repeatedly with cannon and then these Celestials suddenly advanced on Albazin. A large-scale barrage of cannons from the town occurred and in the smoke neither the people nor the town could be seen, and the enemy, unable to do anything, retreated and stood in small groups below the town behind their gabions."[75] The famous historian and ethnologist G. F. Müller (1705–1783) wrote, basing his account on Russian sources, that the Chinese "attempted a storm but were driven back with great losses [*mit grossem Verluste*]."[76] Afterward, the Russians conducted a series of sally attacks, during which they sometimes took prisoners. "During all of this," writes Müller, "the losses on the Russian side were very slight.[77] Some Russian participants gave numbers: one sortie, for example, killed a hundred fifty enemy troops, including two commanders.[78] In contrast, the Russians claimed, their own side lost no more than twenty-one men.[79]

This pattern—an initial attempt to bombard and storm the walls, followed by deadly sorties by the defenders—is precisely what happened in the Siege of Zeelandia. In both cases, the forces of China underestimated the offensive ability of the artillery fortress. Even a minor prefectural capital of China looked far more imposing. But Chinese walls, with their square barbicans, couldn't lay out the same deadly crossfire.

Unable to take Albazin by storm, the Qing tried other tactics but each time were stymied. For example, after the failed storm they bombarded the town all night, but according to Qing sources "the walls stood strong and could not be reduced."[80] A few days later (27 July 1686) Langtan launched another nocturnal assault, in an attempt to capture defenses to the south of Albazin. This attack, too, failed.[81]

After this, he tried building siegeworks on the shore of the river close to the walls. The Russians shot fiercely to prevent this, and the Qing fired back: "Our troops," Qing sources say, "used cannons and arrows and, shooting upwards, attacked all night."[82] The Qing managed to finish their works and left before dawn. Expecting that the Russians would emerge and try to dismantle the siegeworks, Langtan hid troops within them. The following day the Russians indeed emerged, under cover of a thick fog, and according to Qing sources the ambush worked. The Russians withdrew, although two days later, another foggy day, they attacked again.[83]

Such attacks—and there were many—are described in Chinese sources as Qing victories because in each case Russian troops were driven back into the fortress. But Russian sorties were not intended to hold positions outside the walls. The aim was to destroy Qing siegeworks, and European sources suggest that they were successful: "Since the cannons [being fired] from the town damaged the enemy in no small degree, the enemy sought at first to build a wall out of spruce trees and then [a network of] extended structures made out of nassem wood, to protect themselves behind them, but the first was shot into flames and the second was blown up by mining."[84] As some Russian fugitives later reported, "the town had been constantly shot by cannons, but the enemy could not gain an advantage, because the besieged defended themselves so bravely."[85]

These are telling details. They suggest that the Qing had trouble determining where to place their batteries and siegeworks. An artillery fortress, of course, is designed to strike with flanking fire, to hit the enemy from various angles, and also to cover forces that sally forth. For those accustomed to traditional fortifications, this capacity for crossfire comes as a surprise. Each time the Qing constructed batteries or siegeworks the Russians worked to destroy them with cannon fire or sorties. The Qing were forced to move their positions, and the new positions also proved vulnerable. The parallels with the Dutch case are clear. Zheng Chenggong and his officers also kept trying new placements for their batteries and bulwarks and they too were consistently outmaneuvered by the Europeans.

Eventually, the Qing established walls that stayed up. In early August, Langtan "advanced troops directly against the enemy's walls, digging a long moat and setting up ramparts to surround them [the Russians]."[86] These new structures weren't designed to capture the fort, however. They were intended to close off the Russians' access to the river. The Russians tried to prevent this. Qing sources record that "the enemy was anxious and feared losing their water route, so they fought fiercely for four days and four nights."[87] Langtan had switched strategies. Instead of trying to take the city by storm, he was surrounding it to starve the Russians out.

His network of blockading walls and moats grew and grew. Russian reports note that "the Chinese fortified themselves and put up bulwarks, setting up gabions that were eleven meters [six fathoms] high, and on each bulwark were three cannons, in addition to another fifteen guns, which stood on the batteries. Around the city they had also dug trenches, as well as various places to live, behind, under, and within their works or fortifications."[88] As is clear in Figure 15.4, the

Qing counterdefenses were more extensive and massive than the walls of Albazin themselves. By the end of August the siege had transformed into a full-scale blockade.

Here again the parallels with Zeelandia are clear. After Zheng Chenggong failed to take Zeelandia by force, he set up a blockade. It didn't work, because the Dutch fortress remained accessible by sea and because in subtropical Taiwan the besieged could harvest melons and vegetables through the fall and shoot seabirds and gather mussels in the winter.

There were no such opportunities in subarctic Albazin. By early October, the river had ice in it, and soon it was frozen across. But there was in any case nowhere to go. The Qing had built a fortress on the opposite bank. The other three sides of Albazin were also tightly invested, walls and moats stretching all the way around. Moscow had sent elite musketeers to relieve the fort, but the Qing controlled all approaches. No sleigh or dogsled could slip past.

The Russians began dying. When the siege had begun in July 1686, Albazin's walls held more than eight hundred men and an unknown number of women and children. By the beginning of November, no more than a hundred fifty men were alive, a mortality rate of more than 80 percent. They had enough grain. What they lacked was fresh food. Many were killed by scurvy, caused by a deficit of vitamin C, and which Müller described as "an evil that in such situations is more feared than the enemy himself."[89] The Dutch in their fort had also suffered from scurvy, although for them the more significant nutritional disease was beriberi, associated with eating only rice and caused by a lack of vitamin B1. But the Dutch had much more access to fresh food, thanks to the climate and access to the sea.

The Dutch also had another advantage. Fort Zeelandia contained brick houses with windows and tile roofs—a slice of Amsterdam. In Albazin, only ten or so buildings had been completed when the Qing arrived, so its residents had dug themselves holes in the ground. It was believed that these poor dwellings caused illness: "The people of Albazin, because they had to live underground in the dankness . . . became very sick or died."[90] The most deadly killers were probably diseases of poor sanitation such as typhus and cholera. The Dutch had outhouses on piers that stuck out over the ocean, although sometimes Chinese took potshots at poopers. What did the Russians do with their excrement? It was difficult to bury in the frozen ground, and people at the end of their lives couldn't be expected to leave their dugouts and defecate outside. Roommates had to deal with full night pans and soiled blankets. Dutch sources discuss at length the stench of urine and feces and vomit that pervaded the air around the church that served as a hospital. The Russian fortress must have been worse, although frozen feces is better than warm feces. In any case, it's no wonder that in Albazin "many brave people were continually lost, because in the fall and winter bad illnesses occurred in those dank, unhealthy houses."[91] By the end of November, "there were no more than a hundred and fifteen healthy men, and fifty-five children and women."[92]

The Qing, too, suffered. A Qing defector revealed to the Russians that "toward the end of the siege many men in the Chinese camp were dying of hunger, and that they even ate each other."[93] European sources say that Albazin's commander even sent taunting gifts of meat, which were refused, "but which they really wanted to accept."[94] It seems that by the end of November "the toll of dead besiegers exceeded fifteen hundred," or around 50 percent.[95]

Somehow, the Russians, their garrison depleted, many too sick to work, remained on alert. "Thirty held the watch," writes Witsen, "and fifteen worked on the works."[96] He attributed the miraculous defense to the Prussian officer Beiton: "With just twelve healthy men left, Beiton managed miracles. He was able with these few people to keep the cannons firing, making it seem as though there were still many people within the fortress."[97]

Indeed, the siege was ultimately decided not by storm or starvation but by decree. In October 1686, Russian envoys arrived in Beijing with news that Moscow wanted peace. The Kangxi Emperor sent a messenger to Albazin, who arrived in December, just as Langtan was preparing a major assault. People on both sides of the walls watched as the imperial scroll was read out, an ostentatious occasion. As a Russian source noted, "whenever a letter arrived in the Chinese camp before Albazin, from the Emperor of China, all of the commanders and soldiers stood bareheaded as the letter was read, from which we can see what kind of great reverence these people have for the orders of their king."[98]

of warfare."[105] "They didn't," he wrote in a report, "have more than four pieces of artillery. It seemed that they didn't think it was worth the trouble to do anything but try to take the fortress by storm."[106] Instead, de Meijer felt, they should have set up proper siegeworks:

> If the Chinese had used proper means of warfare, then they would have had us. . . . By creating a little more alarm for us in the fortress, they would have exhausted all of our people and it wouldn't have taken more than a few days for us to use up all our lead, of which we had very little. I won't even mention that if they had fired at us with cannons out of batteries we would have quickly run out of cannonballs, because most of our cannons were three or four pounders, for which we had very little ammunition or shrapnel in our armory.[107]

Again, just as in the cases of Zeelandia and Albazin, the forces of China foundered against the artillery fortress, with its powerful bastions.

Of course, we can't conclude from Müller's and de Meijer's words that the commanders they faced were inexperienced. The commanders who led attacks against Dutch and Russian forts had undertaken plenty of sieges, had captured walled forts and towns, most of them far larger and with more defenders than either Fort Zeelandia or Albazin.

But the many walls that the Qing and Zheng forces had previously attacked had, at best, only square bastions with ninety-degree angles, which were called barbicans, and which couldn't lay out a web of mutually reinforcing lines of fire as European bastions did. The Qing capital of Beijing, for example, had massive walls, with huge barbicans but no angled bastions. Similarly, Zheng Chenggong's headquarters, the city of Xiamen had walls more massive than most European cities, but a Dutch admiral who got a close look at them in 1663 found them "uncommonly high" but unsophisticated: "They have four gates that stick out beyond the walls but no bastions or bulwarks."[108]

Walls without angled bastions could be stormed much easier than walls with angled bastions, and since Chinese walls were so thick, storming was far more common than blasting a breach. To be sure, Chinese artillerists did sometimes breach walls. The Qing's artillerists (most of whom were Han Chinese) became experts at using red-haired barbarian cannons to destroy walls in their drive against the Ming in the 1640s.[109] But wall smashing was never as prevalent as storming. In fact, the most common way the armies of China got through walls was by walking calmly through their gates. Data compiled from a decade of Zheng Chenggong's assaults against walled fortifications—forts, villages, towns, and cities—indicate that two-thirds of the cities that he took were opened to him from within by surrenderers or conspirers.[110] Indeed, the traditions of Chinese warcraft strongly dissuaded one from besieging walls. The words of Sun Zi were quoted approvingly: "The best policy for winning wars is to use stratagems. The next best policy is to use diplomacy to destroy the enemy's alliances. The next best policy is to launch an armed attack against the enemy. The worst way of all is to storm walls and seize territory. Sieges should be used only as a last resort."[111] Zheng Chenggong's father, Zheng Zhilong, specifically advised him not to lay siege to walls if it was avoidable. As one historian writes, avoiding sieges was "a golden rule of the clan."[112] But it was not always possible to persuade defenders to open their gates. So the next most common way Zheng forces got through walls was by means of mass assault, usually by storming with ladders. About a sixth of his sieges were decided by this method. Bombardment decided sieges only 6 percent of the time.[113]

Even then, it seems, Chinese bombardment techniques were quite different from those of Europe. Whereas Europeans had learned by experience that the best way to destroy an artillery fortress was by building siegeworks around the walls and creeping carefully closer position by position until one was finally in a position to batter the walls, Chinese besiegers tended to focus on gates. This was partly because Chinese walls were so thick that they were difficult to breach, but it is also partly because Chinese walls were not designed to fire back as effectively. With a gate battered down, one could enter the fortification without being sliced from all sides by artillery and musket fire. To be sure, a gatehouse usually had an outer gate and an inner gate, with a courtyard in between that was designed to frustrate an enemy's advance, with defenders shooting down from the walls above. For this reason, even when gates were captured it was usually best to also secure the walls above, usually accomplished by storming.

It's interesting that even the Dutch used Chinese techniques when facing Chinese walls. In 1662, they attacked a small city in Fujian Province against whose walls their cannons could make no headway. So they retargeted their guns to shoot at the gates, battered them down, and then entered through a hail of "stones, filth, nightsoil, . . . and also some dead dogs."[114] This was just what a Chinese commander would have done.

Tactics of this sort weren't possible against angled bastions. The success of Russian and Dutch defenses suggests that the renaissance fortress did indeed confer a significant advantage on Europeans. Even in East Asia, whose military forces were among the most powerful in the world, it acted as a force multiplier, allowing small garrisons to stand up against more numerous foes.

Despite this advantage, however, the forces of Europe were relatively evenly matched against those of China. The forces of China easily matched European artillery firepower, having adopted, adapted, and improved upon Western guns. Chinese forces neutralized any putative European advantage in musketry tactics by means of effective drill, and by adopting European muskets. (Indeed, as we've seen, the musketry volley technique was used in China before its first proven appearance in Europe.) To be sure, in deep water and behind the walls of their fortresses, Europeans had an advantage, but East Asians had another advantage: logistics.

It's not that Europeans weren't good logisticians. The Russians and Dutch, for example, were fighting effectively thousands of miles from their metropoles. But the Manchu Qing were the masters of logistics in the seventeenth-century world.[115] The Kangxi Emperor's careful planning helped defeat the Russians, and in subsequent years he and his heirs conquered some of the most forbidding regions of the planet, the Central Asian areas that had resisted Chinese imperialism for millennia. Historian Peter Perdue has masterfully shown how Qing logistics made possible these great conquests, expanding China's borders to the farthest extent in history and establishing dominance in continental East Asia.[116] The great Qing became the largest, most powerful country in the world, by far.

Paradoxically, however, the Qing's tremendous success may have led to China's later weakness. The Qing Peace was so overwhelming that it removed the stimulus of war. The next time China and a European power went to war, the balance had shifted sharply in favor of the Europeans.

PART IV

The Great Military Divergence

CHAPTER 16

The Opium War and the Great Divergence

Whereas European forces and those of China were evenly matched through the early 1700s, there's no doubt that a Great Military Divergence opened up over the following century. By the time of the Opium War of 1839 to 1842, the divergence was huge, enabling the British, who were severely outnumbered and far from home, to overpower Qing forces in nearly every battle at sea and on land.[1] The most systematic study of weaponry used in the war concludes that the Chinese and British were in two different historical eras: the British in the Fire Weapon Era and the Chinese in the Mixed Era, when traditional arms, or "cold weapons" (冷兵器), comprised the majority of arms, while gunpowder weapons, or "hot weapons" (熱兵器), were used in small numbers.[2]

Some historians call for caution about such assessments. Peter Lorge, for example, has suggested that "Western military technology had been absorbed into the Qing military as it became available over the course of the nineteenth century."[3] Elsewhere he argues that China was never more than a decade or two behind the West.[4] This was certainly true through the first part of the eighteenth century, and we historians must be careful when making judgments about European superiority—often new data force us to revisit those judgments. But it seems clear that by the mid-1700s a military gap was opening, and by the Opium War the British had an overwhelming military edge.

What underlay this edge? Part of the answer of course has to do with industrialization. Steamships destroyed warjunks, towed long trains of traditional vessels into position, reconnoitered shallows and narrows, and, equally importantly, decreased communication times, allowing for minute, systematic coordination of the war effort.[5] Similarly, industrial ironworks made strong, supple metal for muskets and cannons, and steam power was used to bore cannons and mix, crumble, and sort gunpowder.

But industrialization isn't the only answer. Many of the innovations that most helped the British weren't about steam power or the division of labor or mechanized factories. They stemmed, rather, from the application of seventeenth- and eighteenth-century experimental science to warfare. During the mid-1700s, new scientific discoveries enabled Europeans to measure the speed of projectiles, understand the effects of wind resistance, model trajectories, make better and more consistent gunpowder, develop deadly airborne missiles, and master the use of explosive shells. These innovations as much as the use of steamships and industrial manufacturing techniques underlay the British edge in the Opium War.

Yet there is also another reason for the Great Military Divergence of the nineteenth century. Even as Europeans were making rapid strides in the science of war, China's military power was atrophying because of lack of practice. By the outbreak of hostilities in 1839, Qing China had undergone a long period of relative peace, and its armed forces, once among the best in the world, had become weak and ineffective.[6]

Rusty Swords: The Great East Asian Peace

If we examine the number of battles recorded in dynastic histories per year for the period 900 to 1900 CE, we see that the period 1760–1830 has the lowest level of armed conflict in the whole series (see Graph I.1 and Appendix 2).[7] There were major military actions, of course: wars in Southeast Asia (Burma, 1766–1770, and Vietnam, 1788–1789) and campaigns against rebels within China and on its borders, most notably the Lin Shuangwen Rebellion in Taiwan (1786–1787), the White Lotus Rebellion of Central China (1795–1804), and the Eight Trigram Uprising, which actually breached the gates of the Forbidden City.[8] But none of these, with the possible exception of the White Lotus Rebellion and its associated Eight Trigram Uprising, were considered existential wars from the perspective of the Qing state. As a prominent scholar of China's military history puts it, most of these engagements were "restricted to limited areas within China proper or the . . . imperial periphery."[9]

Compared to the Ming dynasty at a similar stage—that is, a century and a half or so after dynastic founding—the Qing during this period faced no significant external threats. In contrast, the Ming experienced a difficult middle period. A hundred seventy-five years after founding it faced a resurgence of Central Asian power and vehement and sustained raids by the Wo (Japanese) along its coasts. The latter may not have been an existential threat, but the former certainly was, and one reason that Ming officials were so eager to experiment with new weaponry in the 1500s and 1600s was that they feared that their capital might fall to an invasion from people beyond the Great Wall, as indeed it eventually did. By a comparable period of the Qing, however—the mid-1700s—the Qing had few such worries. They had established an unprecedented hegemony in Central Asia, decisively ending the threat from horse-born nomads.

China specialists Peter Perdue and Frederic Wakeman have both suggested, in separate publications, that the Qing were, in a way, victims of their own success.[10] The period of Qing conquest, consolidation, and expansion had been exceedingly violent, with devastating wars that wracked East and Central Asia and corresponded with a significant decrease in China's population. But once the Qing had established its dominance, expanding China's borders to their largest extent in history, it remained virtually unchallenged until the mid-nineteenth century. In those generations of relative peace, 1760 to 1839, military leaders in China had little need to focus on innovation or incorporate new methods and technologies from beyond East Asia. Korea and Japan were also generally at peace during this period. East Asians had access to the new technologies and techniques of war that were being forged on the other side of Eurasia, but they had few incentives to adopt or incorporate them on a significant scale.

The resulting military gap became clear to observers before the Opium War. In 1836, an anonymous British correspondent prepared a report about China's military strength and concluded that if the art of war was the most "infallible criterion of the civilization and advancement of societies," then China was in the lowest state of civilization.[11] Its gunpowder was coarse, uneven, and liable to spoil. Its cannons were old-fashioned, with uneven bores and primitive carriages, "mere blocks of wood, or solid beds on which the gun is lashed down with rattans, so that it must be impossible to fire any but point blank shots, and very difficult to direct the gun to an object, except that immediately in front of the embrasure whence fired."[12] For firearms it had only "ill-made" matchlock muskets and no flintlocks, pistols, or any of the other "tribes of fire-arm."[13] In fact, he observed, China's soldiers still relied heavily on the bow and arrow, which, given how poor the rest of their weapons were, was "the most efficient of their arms."[14]

Chinese defenses were, the reporter noted, mere "samples of fortification in its infant state; without fosses, bastions, glacis, or counter defences of any kind; being, in fact, but such lines as the engineers of a disciplined army would throw up, as temporary defences and to cover their guns, in the course of a single night."[15] Chinese naval vessels were so laughable that they were "beyond the power of description or ridicule to portray."[16] Indeed, the correspondent wrote, he wouldn't be surprised if a couple of New Zealand war canoes wouldn't outmatch the entire Chinese navy.[17] (Charles Dickens would later describe a Chinese junk, which he saw at the Crystal Palace in 1848, as a "ridiculous abortion.")[18]

But it wasn't just technology and engineering that the Chinese lacked. The reporter discerned a marked deficiency in military readiness. When garrison troops in Guangzhou mustered for duty, he wrote, they

> come in, one by one, undressed, unarmed, unprepared, and half asleep; while piles of brown felt caps, and heaps of shabby looking red and yellow long jackets, bearing the character "courage" . . . are brought through the gates, for the adornment of the heroes of the hour; by and bye, straggles in an officer, generally the largest sized man that can be found; some bows, sheaves of arrows, and rusty swords, make up the warlike show; evidently got up for the nonce to astonish and awe "the barbarians," who might, did they please, be in the governor's harem before the guard could awake from their slumbers.[19]

On occasion European travelers had observed that Chinese swords were so rusty that the soldiers could scarcely draw them.[20]

At the end of his report, the correspondent expressed surprise himself at the extent of China's military backwardness. "We have now gone through the subject which we sat down to discuss, and although we were well aware that the military force of the Chinese empire was much overrated, we rise astonished at the weakness, the utter imbecility. . . . It seems indeed strange that the whole fabric does not fall asunder of itself. Of this we are convinced; that, at the first vigorous and well directed blow from a foreign power, it will totter to its base."[21]

He was wrong about how much the Qing would totter, but modern research corroborates his views about Qing military capacity. Historians Liu Hongliang and Zhang Jianxiong have conducted an exhaustive and detailed comparison of Chinese and European guns circa 1840 and conclude, "At the time of the Opium War, the difference between British and Chinese cannon technology and capacity is an objective fact. . . . The British military had made innovations and improvements in all aspects—design, ammunition, powder technology, firing mechanisms, and especially in the quality of the iron, the production, the finishing and other such key technologies—such that their cannons' range, speed of firing, accuracy, and lethality were superior to Qing cannons."[22] The Qing had not made such improvements. As Liu Hongliang notes in a different work, "At the time of the Opium War, the Qing military's front-loading cannon form was the same type as that of seventeenth century Europe, and . . . the design hadn't seen any kind of change."[23] Qing cannons were heavier, clumsier, slower to load and fire, and far less efficient in terms of powder use. Indeed, many of the cannons deployed in coastal forts were actually forged or cast in the seventeenth or early eighteenth century. To be sure there were local exceptions. Artisans in coastal regions—particularly in Guangdong Province—could produce more up-to-date ordnance based on Western models, but they were still not as effective as the advanced guns of Britain, and in any case they were outliers.[24]

Modern research also shows that Qing infantry forces were also backward. Liu and Zhang note that troops "were equipped with sixty or seventy percent traditional weapons, of which the most important were the long lance, the side sword, the bow and arrow, and the rattan shield, and only thirty or forty percent [of their armament consisted of] gunpowder weapons, of which the most important were the matchlock musket, the heavy musket, the cannon, the fire arrow, and the earth-shaking bomb and such things."[25] The Qing matchlock musket was constructed according to a design that hadn't changed much since the seventeenth century.[26] (It's interesting to note that Qing armies weren't the only non-European forces clinging to matchlocks. They were still in use in the Levant and Iran, for example.)[27]

European armies had long since switched to flintlocks, and the British were undergoing a transition to percussion cap muskets, which required no externally applied sparks at all. In contrast, the Qing matchlock guns were slow, unwieldy, and dangerous, as British observers noted with empathy and derision. "Every soldier," wrote naval officer William Hutcheon Hall, "has to carry a match or port fire to ignite the powder in the matchlock when loaded. Hence, when a poor fellow is wounded and falls, the powder, which is very apt to run out of his pouch over his clothes, is very likely to be ignited by his own match, and in this way he may either be blown up at once, or else his clothes may be ignited; . . . it is therefore not surprising that they should regard the matchlock with some little apprehension."[28]

Many Qing soldiers preferred to fight the British with bow and arrow, a matchup that did not usually end well, as this same William Hutcheon Hall found to his good fortune. One of Hall's subordinates records how a Chinese officer, "with cool determination and a steady aim, deliberately discharged four arrows from his bow at Captain Hall, fortunately without effect. Had they been musket-balls, however, he could scarcely have escaped. A marine instantly raised his musket at the less fortunate Chinese officer: the aim was unerring, and he fell."[29] Someone tried to rescue the fallen Qing officer, "for his coolness and courage,"[30] but the attempt failed because "in the heat of an engagement it is impossible to control every man."[31]

Historians have suggested that Manchu leaders privileged the bow because of its traditional role in Manchu culture.[32] Indeed, Manchu banner forces devoted more time to archery practice than to firearms practice.[33] Moreover, the Manchu court at times actively suppressed firearms, reserving them for hunting and prohibiting their use by fishing boats and coastal vessels.[34] Firearms were even restricted within the military itself, as when Qing leaders at times tried to prevent Han Chinese divisions from using the most powerful types of handguns, reserving them for Manchu units.[35] Similarly, provincial officials were sometimes even discouraged from arming local militias with firearms, fearing that those militias might rebel. In 1778, for example, the Qianlong Emperor severely rebuked the governor of Shandong Province for training militia forces in firearms.[36] Another provincial official was instructed to take his militia units' muskets, "and exchange them for bows and arrows."[37] This sort of suppression was only possible because the Qing Pax was so complete, just as in Japan the Great Tokugawa Peace supposedly made it possible to "give up the gun."[38] The Qing didn't give up the gun, of course, and we mustn't exaggerate the suppression of firearms. Indeed, sometimes Qing officials actively stimulated firearms use, as for example in the early eighteenth century, when the Kangxi Emperor encouraged the casting of Western-style cannons to combat pirates.[39]

Yet the problem for the Qing wasn't just antiquated weapons; its forces also suffered from ineffective drill. Historians have found that by the early nineteenth century, China's once vibrant tradition of drill had withered, becoming "highly formalized and ritualistic, with little attention given to practical problems of warfare."[40] In Beijing's banner armies, for instance, it seems that musketeers drilled only five times a month, and although they did perform volley fire maneuvers, their exercises were, according to an American observer named Emory Upton, "mere burlesque of infantry drill."[41]

Upton describes how twelve hundred musketeers formed themselves into a dense column and awaited a signal from their officers, who were not even on the training field but sat under tents to the side. When the signal was given, the troops arranged themselves into lines, but "there was no order, nor step; the men marched in twos, threes, and fours, toward the line, laughing, talking, and firing their pieces in the air."[42] They shot and then, to the clamor of gongs, drums, and cymbals, faced to the rear and shot again. This was repeated by another unit, with heavy matchlocks, and then the drill was over and the men, "individually and in squads, wandered back to the city."[43] Emory Upton's description is from 1877, by which time some forces in China had improved drilling techniques, adopting Western practices and revivifying those of the past (Qi Jiguang's drilling manuals were an inspiration), but Upton's account is just one of many that indicates the feebleness of Chinese drill in the nineteenth century. By the eve of the Opium War, drilling standards had fallen well below those of the early Qing, even as European drilling patterns had altered to suit the more effective weapons being produced in the West.[44]

Qing military readiness on the eve of the Opium War can be summed up in an image from our anonymous British writer of 1836: a sword so rusty it couldn't be removed from the scabbard. The Europeans, of course, hadn't had the luxury of such tranquility and order. During the eighteenth and early nineteenth centuries, the period of the Great Qing Peace, Europeans had continued fighting each other. Their eighteenth century wasn't as warlike as their seventeenth, but conflagrations regularly rocked the subcontinent—the War of Austrian Succession (1740–1748), the Seven Years' War (1754–1763), and, most devastating of all, the Revolutionary and Napoleonic Wars (1792–1815), which convulsed Europe from Madrid to Moscow and provided a massive stimulus for European warcraft.

This warfare spurred rapid and continuing improvement in gunpowder and associated technologies, but geopolitical friction wasn't the only underpinning of Europe's Great Military Divergence. Equally important was a strong tradition of experimental science, whose roots lay firmly in the seventeenth century.

Experimental Science and European Warcraft

Today many prominent historians downplay the role of science in the rise of the West, and the topic has aroused considerable discussion.[45] As usual most of this debate has focused on economic history, and it's been hard for either side to sway the other, largely because the links between science and economic growth are difficult to pin down for the period when the Great Divergence was opening up, to wit the 1700s.

But if the links between science and eighteenth-century economies remain unclear, there's no doubt about the links between science and the eighteenth century military divergence. European advances in gunpowder manufacture and gun design were based on discoveries from experimental science, and those advances played a key role in the British victory in the Opium War.

Before the mid-eighteenth century, people did not understand some very basic things about guns and gunpowder. What was the precise relationship between the amount of gunpowder used, the shape of the barrel, and the velocity of a projectile of a given mass and size? How much air resistance did the projectile face once it exited the barrel, and how did that resistance affect the trajectory?

In the seventeenth century, Galileo and others had developed a theory of ballistics and put together tables to help artillerists—Galileo had even developed instruments for aiming cannons, which brought him significant income.[46] Over the ensuing generations, others had refined these tables and instruments, but by the mid-eighteenth century these tools were still inaccurate, useful for a limited range and only in certain conditions.

In order to develop more effective models one needed to know how fast projectiles came out of guns. It wasn't an easy problem. Enter Benjamin Robins (1707–1751). A disciple of Isaac Newton, Robins developed an instrument that transformed the science of guns: the ballistic pendulum. It was a tripod the height of a tall man with a heavy pendulum hanging down from it. On the pendulum was affixed a target. The experiment started with the pendulum at rest. When struck by a projectile, the pendulum swung upward. By measuring how high it went one could determine the projectile's momentum, and using Newtonian models one could calculate its velocity.

The ballistics pendulum revolutionized gunnery. The most exciting findings had to do with the effect of air pressure on projectiles. Galileo had dismissed the effects of air pressure in his work on ballistics, and Newton, too, underestimated it, or, rather, expected that its effects were linear at increasing speeds. But Robins showed that air resistance was incredibly significant. Whereas then-current models predicted that a twenty-four-pound cannonball should, at the muzzle velocity Robins had measured, fly sixteen miles, in actuality it flew only three. Air resistance was thus *much* higher than expected. Even more surprising was the nonlinearity of the results. The higher the muzzle velocity, the greater the effect, with extreme drag as you approached the speed of sound.[47] His research thus revealed a hitherto invisible threshold: the speed of sound, at which air resistance increased greatly. No one could have predicted this phenomenon. Only careful experiment could have revealed it.

Robins's slim book, *New Principles of Gunnery*, was translated and emulated.[48] The great Swiss mathematician Leonhard Euler (1707–1783) produced a German edition with the support of the Prussian king Frederick the Great, converting Robins's hundred fifty pages into more than seven hundred and providing even more complex equations, which took into account such factors as the rate of the gunpowder reaction itself (Robins had postulated an instantaneous expansion of gas) and the effects on barrel pressure of the gas that inevitably blew through the touchhole or past the projectile.[49] The result was a set of equations of unprecedented efficacy, which were quickly adopted by artillerists to compute new ballistics tables.[50] Robins in turn responded to Euler's work, further refining his own,[51] and all over Europe dozens of other scientists, mathematicians, and artillerists built on Robins and Euler's models: the Irishman Patrick d'Arcy (working for France), the Piedmontese Papacino d'Antoni, the Frenchman Charles de Borda, the Englishman Charles Hutton, the Prussian Georg Friedrich Tempelhoff, the Austrian Georg Vega, and the Frenchman Jean-Louis Lombard, to name a few of the most important.[52]

Their research programs were often sponsored by governments, and the governments were motivated by war. The War of Austrian Succession (1740–1748) stimulated ballistics research in Austria, France, Britain, and, perhaps most notably, the Piedmontese state, whose leader Charles Emanuel III sought advice from Robins himself (Robins advised him to employ low muzzle velocities).[53] During and after the war, the Piedmontese used the ballistic pendulum and other instruments to produce data that led them to develop new guns that optimized muzzle velocity. They also developed a method to estimate muzzle velocity in the field, without instruments: fire projectiles into compacted earth and compare the depths of penetration to the depths produced by a calibrated musket that fired pellets at a known muzzle velocity.[54]

The new ballistics science revolutionized gun design. Artillerists had generally believed that faster projectiles led to greater power. But the new science indicated that air resistance was such an important variable that it made sense in many cases to *lower* the power of guns, to attain the lowest possible muzzle velocity necessary for one's objectives. This meant that cannons could be made smaller relative to projectile weight.

Robins himself put the principle into practice. Working with the Royal Navy, he developed a proposal for a new gun with short barrel and thin walls, which would use smaller charges of powder to fire heavy rounds at low velocities.[55] The Royal Navy's adoption of the carronade in the late eighteenth century was based on these ideas.[56] And the carronade proved enormously useful. A short, light cannon used for close range antiship combat, it was far more destructive than traditional guns of the same size. Moreover, its rate of fire was also higher because its walls were thinner and cooled quickly. In addition, it was light enough to sit on a sliding carriage that absorbed recoil, which meant that it kept its aim after each shot, whereas cannons on traditional carriages had to be wheeled back into place and re-aimed. A carronade also required fewer hands to operate.[57]

The carronade played a major role in the Opium War from the very first battle. In early November 1839, two British sailing vessels were confronted by a Qing fleet of sixteen warjunks and thirteen fireboats guarding the river passage to Canton. HMS *Volage* carried twenty-six guns, of which at least eighteen were carronades, and HMS *Hyacinth* carried eighteen guns, of which sixteen were carronades.[58] Taking advantage of the carronades' quick-fire capacities, they sailed in close and shot devastating broadsides, destroying six junks and throwing the rest into flight, except for the Qing flagship, which the British decided to stop shooting after a good barrage. The Qing ships had guns, but they were older-style cannons. The two British ships sustained little damage.

The carronade played a key role in nearly all subsequent naval battles. For instance, in January 1841 it helped the British capture three fortified islands that guarded the approaches to Guangzhou (see Map 16.1).[59] The British vessels in the battles carried far more carronades than traditional artillery: the *Algerine* carried ten guns, of which eight were carronades; the *Conway* carried twenty-eight guns, of which twenty-six were carronades; the *Herald* carried twenty-eight guns, of which twenty-six were carronades; and so on.[60] The Qing defenders were overwhelmed by the fast and powerful barrages. It's not that they

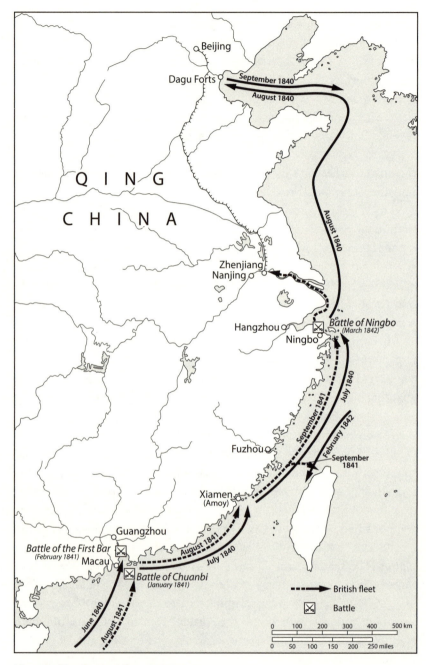

Beijing

Dagu Forts — September 1840 / August 1840

QING
CHINA

Zhenjiang
Nanjing

Hangzhou
Ningbo — *Battle of Ningbo*
(March 1842)

August 1840

July 1840

September 1841

February 1842

September
1841

Fuzhou

Xiamen
(Amoy)

August 1841

July 1840

Guangzhou

Battle of the First Bar
(February 1841)

Macau

Battle of Chuanbi
(January 1841)

June 1840

August 1841

→ British fleet

⊠ Battle

| 0 | 100 | 200 | 300 | 400 | 500 km |
| 0 | 50 | 100 | 150 | 200 | 250 miles |

MAP 16.1 The Opium War, 1839–1842.

lacked cannons; it's just that theirs were old-fashioned, difficult to aim and fire (although they had managed to obtain one or two carronades). Surveying the guns captured in one fortress, for example, British naval lieutenant John Bingham wrote, "The guns were very long Chinese twelve and twenty-four pounders, with the exception of two carronades, evidently old English ship guns."[61] He also noted that the gun carriages were primitive: "Their carriages were of the most ordinary description, only a few of them having trucks, the others being merely beds of wood on which the guns rested."[62] Carronades, able to hurl massive amounts of iron at close range, in rapid succession, and with relatively little powder, were a key armament of the war.

The new ballistics science also underlay the development of new field guns, which, like the carronade, were shorter, thinner-walled, faster, and far more portable than previous models. Small field guns and related guns called howitzers transformed land battles in Europe, and, like the carronade, played key roles in the Opium War. The most striking example—and the saddest—was the Battle of Ningbo in March 1842. The British had captured Ningbo several months before, in October 1841, and the Qing were determined to take it back. After long preparations, the Manchu nobleman Yijing (奕經, 1793–1853) led thousands upon thousands of Qing troops to attack from two directions at once. They scaled walls and began pouring through gates.

A British force of a hundred men, armed with muskets, four field pieces, and a howitzer, opened fire. "The slaughter," wrote one British participant, "was quite horrible; the mangled bodies lay in huge piles, heaped one upon another; and old Peninsular officers present declared that, the breach of Badajos alone excepted, they never in a similar small space saw such a mass of slain."[63] (The Siege of Badajoz of 1812 was one of the bloodiest battles of the Napoleonic Wars.) Another account notes that "the howitzer only discontinued its fire from the impossibility of directing its shot upon a living foe, clear of the writhing and shrieking hecatomb which it had already piled up."[64] In the Ningbo battles, the British decisively repulsed the most important Chinese offensive in the war, losing only twenty-five men. As Scottish surgeon Duncan MacPherson noted, "the salutary effect produced by the above engagements was very evident, no further molestation being offered to us during our occupation of this city."[65]

Not only were the new field guns and howitzers powerful. They were also able to be transported by human beings, whereas traditional cannons of equivalent power required teams of horses or oxen.[66] Sometimes the new guns were even pushed on wheelbarrows, "it being easier with these to transport guns over the narrow paths which intersect the paddy grounds, and which present such continual difficulties to the movement of troops through the entire cultivated districts of this country."[67] In many cases, the British simply made use of China's excellent roadways. On approaching Nanjing, for example, British lieutenant John Ouchterlony noted, "the road was so broad and straight, that a field-piece could be run along it with ease until within a short distance of the gates."[68] For cases in which there were no good roads or paths, some pieces, like mountain howitzers, could be disassembled and the parts carried separately.[69]

The evolution of carronades and light field pieces wasn't of course due to science alone. A multitude of formal and informal experiments played a role, as did new methods of casting and boring.[70] But the new science of ballistics provided the theoretical and mathematical basis, and the Chinese had no equivalent knowledge. They were unprepared for the overwhelming advantage the British had in terms of firepower.

The British also excelled in accuracy, because the new ballistics revolutionized the calculation of trajectories and times to impact. Such calculations were highly technical, requiring trigonometry and calculus, and so in the course of the eighteenth century, European states had increasingly funded military education systems focusing on the mathematics of artillery, such as the Piedmontese Royal Artillery and Military Engineering Academy (established in 1739) and, even more famously, the artillery schools of France.

The French artillery schools, particularly the Ecole Royale d'Artillerie, were famous not just for their exacting curricula, but also because of their alumni, most notably Napoleon Bonaparte. As a student, he took detailed notes on Robins and Euler, paying special attention to air resistance and the fact that Robins's work showed one could make effective field guns by shortening barrels and decreasing weight. As a student he even conducted his own research into ballistics, writing a treatise on the use of standard cannons to fire mortar rounds.[71] In fact, Napoleon so enjoyed his studies that he later said that if his military career hadn't worked out he would have been content as a math professor.[72] Some have suggested that his mathematical background may have been key to his wider success, giving him a scientific understanding of warfare.[73] That may be overreaching, but there's no doubt that his mastery of scientific ballistics helped him in battle. His field cannons decimated enemies in precisely the way that British field cannons would later annihilate Chinese forces.

The British refused to be outdone by the French and invested in their own military academies. An academy at Woolrich was established in 1741, to instruct "the raw and inexperienced People belonging to the Military Branch of this (Ordnance) Office, in the several parts of Mathematicks necessary to qualify them for the Service of the Artillery, and the business of Engineers."[74] Robins's *New Principles of Gunnery* became the basis of the curriculum and was even used as a textbook.[75]

As a result of such education, the British artillerists who fought in the Opium War were able to use ballistics models that took into account the expansion of gas in the gunpowder reaction, the loss of pressure due to the leaking of gas through touchholes and past projectiles, and the effects of wind resistance. The Qing gunners had no such resources. Renaissance ballistics models had been imported into China in the late sixteenth and the seventeenth centuries, and data from the Sino-Dutch War of 1661 to 1668 suggest that Chinese artillerists were as effective as the Europeans, perhaps more so.[76] (As the Dutch governor of Taiwan once lamented, during an artillery battle, "The enemy . . . is able to handle his cannon so effectively. . . . They put our own men to shame.")[77] But in the mid-eighteenth century, while Europeans were experimenting with the ballistic pendulum, the Chinese were making no significant investigations into ballistics, and this gave the British an overwhelming advantage. In fact, Qing gun carriages usually didn't even allow for easy rotation or changing elevation, whereas British guns had all manner of aiming devices.

But calculations weren't just for aiming. They were also about timing. The new ballistics science revolutionized the use of explosive shells. Chinese and Europeans had fired explosive rounds for centuries, but thanks to the new science of ballistics—and to considerable experimental data concerning the speed at which fuses burned—European artillery officers were able to time the explosion of shells with unprecedented precision. Success was measured in hundredths of seconds. When firing mortars, for instance, the object was to make the shell explode just after it had landed. When firing against human targets, the shell needed to explode in the air above the enemies' heads. The new artillery manuals contained detailed tables classified by gun type, size of gunpowder charge, and so on, and these tables could be used effectively only if one possessed the requisite mathematical training.[78]

Like carronades and howitzers, explosive shells played a key role in the Opium War. In the Second Battle of Chuanbi (穿鼻), for example, shells were lobbed into a Chinese fort, exploding "with great precision . . . much to the astonishment of the Chinese, who were unacquainted with this engine of destruction. . . . The Chinese could not long withstand the fire of the 68-pounder of the *Queen*, and the two 32-pounder pivot-guns of the *Nemesis*, the shells from which could be seen bursting within the walls of the fort."[79] Field pieces also used exploding shells, especially the dreaded howitzers, which, as we've seen, caused so much carnage in Ningbo that its handlers had to stop shooting because the corpses piled too high. Howitzers, placed in batteries and fired in concert, to deadly effect, are referred to repeatedly in British sources on the Opium War.[80] In general, explosive shells were one of the technologies most marveled at by Chinese.[81]

The ballistics revolution may have been the most important scientific advance of the eighteenth century as regards war, but it was far from the only one. Europeans also conducted research into gunpowder.[82] Perhaps the greatest innovations came after 1783, when William Congreve the Elder (1742–1814) was placed in charge of gunpowder manufacture at England's Royal Powder Mills. He conducted systematic experiments and built dedicated testing ranges, new saltpeter refineries, and special proving houses.[83] Among his findings was the discovery that charcoal made in sealed iron cylinders produced superior powder. During the Revolutionary and Napoleonic Wars, this "cylinder powder" gave British gunpowder a reputation as the best in the world, nearly twice as powerful as traditional powders and far less vulnerable to spoilage.[84]

In contrast, in the 1830s the Chinese were still using the same methods for producing gunpowder that had been used in the early Qing period.[85]

The British recognized its inferiority. Lieutenant John Elliot Bingham captured some Chinese powder in 1841 and wrote that "though the proportions in Chinese powder are very nearly ours, it is a most inferior article."[86] He and his comrades threw several thousand pounds of it into the ocean. Sometimes the British condescended to use Chinese powder to blow up captured ships or forts, but even then it was found wanting.[87]

Even as European powder got better, it got cheaper and more plentiful. The Napoleonic Wars created demand for gunpowder and attracted funding for new equipment and personnel, which William Congreve the Elder used to increase experimentation and production.[88]

He died in 1814, but his son, William Congreve the Younger (1772–1828), continued the experiments. He developed a machine that mixed the ingredients of powder in the correct proportions and another machine that could granulate powder, with toothed rollers and filters that sorted granules by size.

He was also good at the main task that scientists face: gaining financial support. A tireless lobbyist, he made his case on the basis of warfare. Napoleon, he wrote, controlled realms that were so vast that Britain had to invest in technology to even the odds: "England has now, with ten millions of population, to wage war against ten times that number—what man can do, Englishmen will accomplish! But there is a limit to all physical force; and when the difference in number is so enormous, it is no disgrace to have recourse to every aid that human ingenuity can support. He, therefore, that strives to supply the deficiency of real power by mechanical combinations, cannot but deserve well of his country."[89]

Congreve the Younger was particularly excited by rocketry. His famous "Congreve rocket"—whose "red glare" features so prominently in the USA's National Anthem—was actually inspired by Indian rockets. In the late eighteenth century, the Sultanate of Mysore, located in what is today southern India, fought against Britain in a series of conflicts known today as the Anglo-Mysore Wars (1767–1792). Although the British eventually prevailed, the sultanate's forces proved effective, and among their weapons were large iron rockets, which the British began trying to copy. Congreve didn't like to admit this. He merely noted, in an aside, that rockets were invented by some "heroes of Chinese antiquity."[90]

His rockets, however, were unusually effective. By means of experiments he improved their range, accuracy, and power, and he lobbied the Royal Navy to use them as a lighter alternative to shipborne mortars. He had to overcome skepticism. As one naval commander wrote, "Mr. Congreve, who is ingenious, is wholly wrapt up in rockets, from which I expect little success."[91] Yet Congreve had powerful patrons. The Prince of Wales himself read Congreve's plans at the Royal Pavilion in Brighton, a mock Mughal temple whose interiors were decorated with Chinese dragons, miniature pagodas, and paintings of mandarins in official robes.[92] The prince ordered expensive sea trials. They didn't go terribly well, but Congreve was persistent, and eventually his rockets were adopted by the Royal Navy.[93]

They played a devastating role in the Opium War. In the Second Battle of Chuanbi (1841), for example, a Congreve rocket helped defeat a Chinese fleet of fifteen warjunks (or perhaps eleven, depending on which source you believe). A British participant later recalled the flying body parts:

> One of the most formidable engines of destruction which any vessel . . . can make use of is the Congreve rocket, a most terrible weapon when judiciously applied, especially where there are combustible materials to act upon. The very first rocket fired from the *Nemesis* was seen to enter the large junk against which it was directed, near that of the admiral, and almost instantly it blew up with a terrific explosion, launching into eternity every soul on board, and pouring forth its blaze like the mighty rush of fire from a volcano. The instantaneous destruction of the huge body seemed appalling to both sides engaged. The smoke, and flame, and thunder of the explosion, with the fragments falling round, and even portions of dissevered bodies scattering as they fell, were enough to strike with awe, if not with fear, the stoutest heart that looked upon it.[94]

The effect was so terrifying that everyone paused for a moment, frozen with shock. The Qing abandoned the rest of their ships. Thirteen warjunks were destroyed.[95]

Congreve rockets were also useful on land. On 27 February 1841, they helped the British capture an island guarding the approaches to Guangzhou. One British account notes that "operations commenced by throwing a few rockets into . . . the . . . custom-house, situated at the entrance of the North Wang-Tong fort; and such was the precision with which these were directed, that the place was soon in a blaze of fire, which rapidly communicated with the encampment, and presented an animating and inciting appearance."[96] Again, the precision and destructive power of the rockets created shock and awe: "The panic created by the bursting of the shells and rockets, which were quite new to them, evidently threw them into great disorder. It was reported, and there is reason to believe with truth, that the Chinese officers abandoned the place at the first commencement of the firing, and ran down to their boats."[97] At nearly every major engagement in the war, rockets proved enormously effective, and, as a British account noted, "amused the enemy."[98]

Examples of Britain's deadly use of rockets, carronades, field cannons, explosive shells, and howitzers abound in Opium War sources, and all of these weapons were based on experimental science. Robins's ballistics revolution, which developed from the work of Newton, Boyle, and Bernoulli, and which was carried forward by Leonhard Euler and dozens of other scientists, mathematicians, and artillerists, represented a deep transformation in the understanding of how guns worked. The experiments were painstaking, the results far from intuitive. Without the experimental culture and heritage that made them possible, the knowledge would never have been won, and it turned out to be a very practical knowledge, which directly influenced the work of war makers. When British observers noted how bad Chinese guns were, or how poor at aiming the Chinese artillerists were, they were drawing a clear and objective contrast. British gunnery was based on experimental science. Chinese gunnery wasn't.

To be sure, the Opium War was also decided by more typical tools of industrialization. The steamer *Nemesis* was the war's workhorse, paddling against the wind and towing sailing vessels upriver. Nor was steam power the *Nemesis*'s only edge. It also had a very shallow draft. In the 1500s and 1600s, the Chinese had used shallow-draft vessels against the Dutch and Portuguese, outmaneuvering them by sailing on flats and shallows. Such tactics didn't work against the *Nemesis*, which drew only five feet (one-and-a-half meters) with keel retracted. In the Second Battle of Chuanbi, for example (1841), a fleet of warjunks took refuge in shallows. She maneuvered right up to them, and when they tried fleeing into an even shallower channel, she simply towed them away from their moorings and destroyed them. One British officer records the words of some Chinese who watched the *Nemesis* maneuver where, at low water, they were accustomed to wade: "He-yaw! how can! My never see devil-ship so fashion before; can go all same man walkee."[99]

The Opium War was an industrial war: steamers like the *Nemesis* played key roles, and industrial manufacturing techniques helped make steel, bore cannon, and mix powder, even as they made those products cheaper. Nonetheless, it was the science developed by Robins and others that played the greatest part in Britain's Great Military Divergence vis-à-vis China, combined, of course, with the fact that China had undergone a long period of relative peace.

But now that the Great Qing Peace had been overturned, how would the leaders, statesmen, and scholars of China react? In the Ming and early Qing periods, China had adapted quickly and effectively, maintaining parity with European powers. The nineteenth century proved more challenging.

CHAPTER 17

A Modernizing Moment

OPIUM WAR REFORMS

They are much too clever a people not to be sensible
of their inferiority as regards the art of war.
—*Alexander Murray, 1843*

During the 1500s and 1600s, Chinese officials quickly adopted Western guns, which spread widely throughout the Middle Kingdom. In the
period 1839 to 1850, during and immediately after the Opium War,
there were similar attempts to adopt Western innovations, but historians have suggested that they were "a collection of largely isolated
incidents,"[1] or the work of "only a few exceptionally alert men."[2] Most
textbooks barely even mention these early adoptions.[3] Or when they
are mentioned, it is usually in an attempt to explain China's failure
to adapt, which is blamed variously on China's Confucian culture, the
character of the reformers, the personality of the emperor, the structure of the Qing bureaucracy, or factions within the Qing court.[4]

Certainly these first attempts to design new ships, cast modern ordnance, and understand steam power appear paltry compared to the
reforms of the post-1860 period, but in fact they were significant. Not
only did they achieve a degree of success and generate a literature for
later reformers to build on. They also illustrate the challenge of military reform in the nineteenth century.

Whereas it had been a relatively straightforward process to adopt
Portuguese cannons, Japanese muskets, and red-hair cannons, it
proved far more difficult to adopt nineteenth-century technologies.

Historians have of course long recognized this, but the details are important. Precisely what knowledge, skills, practices, and tools did would-be modernizers lack? And how did they come to understand their ignorance? The answers are surprising. A lack of technical drawing and the absence of machine tools, for example, proved to be important impediments.

Adaptations

The British noticed signs of innovation even during the war, especially toward the end and in places they had attacked more than once—Xiamen, Zhoushan, Wusong. One British participant noted in an account published just after the war that "the Chinese are already beginning to perceive their defects, and have attempted to profit from the models of our ships."[5] In Guangzhou he saw Chinese gunboats based on European designs, armed with new cannons, although the *Nemesis* easily chased them away, an "amusing occupation."[6] In Xiamen, he found hybrid warjunks modeled on a British man-of-war. One of his comrades described them: "Some large men of war junks were found in the inner harbour, nearly completed; these had two decks, mounting upwards of twenty guns on carriages, made like those of our own ship guns."[7] (Other sources say they were armed with thirty guns.)[8] It's intriguing that Xiamen is just where Zheng Zhilong had built his own double-decked hybrid warjunks two hundred years before, the ones that the Dutch had destroyed during their sneak attack of 1633. These new vessels suffered the same fate: captured before they could even put to sea; most were still under construction in dry dock.[9]

In Zhoushan in June 1842, the British found a cannon foundry that was producing carronades copied from pieces salvaged from a British wreck. As one English-language account noted, these guns "were better made and finished than any we had as yet seen. All these improvements must have been begun during the last year; for the guns at Chusan [i.e., Zhoushan], when first we visited that city, and even at Canton, were old rotten machines, with touch-holes which you might put two fingers into."[10]

The gun carriages had likewise improved, and many guns had been fitted with sights.

The guns were good, and had been cast very lately. Nearly all of them were mounted on carriages with a peculiar sort of wooden swivel, which enabled them to train them better. They had sights, such as they were, fitted on, showing they were open to improvement, and conscious of the advantage of them. Round the breech of the gun they had fastened an iron band, with an upright sight in the centre, with a hole to look through, and another sight fastened in the same way round the muzzle, having a sharp spike on it. Some had a hollow bamboo fastened along the centre of the gun, through which they looked to take aim; this was an ingenious plan for point blank range.[11]

These new guns were more effective than the British had expected. "The Chinese fire [at Zhoushan]," wrote Lieutenant Alexander Murray, "was better than any . . . as yet encountered. The [British] Flag ship was hit several times, besides receiving three shot in her mizzen mast. The *Blonde* was hulled fourteen times, Lieutenant Hewitt, Royal Marines was killed on board her by a round shot. The *Sesostris* was hulled eleven times, and the other ships were hit several times. It appears extraordinary that the casualties were so few, for the fire was good."[12]

Lieutenant Murray was struck by these adaptations: "So far from being bigoted to their old customs and ways of doing things, we have remarked a great improvement in many of their arms since we first met them."[13] As he put it, "They are much too clever a people not to be sensible of their inferiority as regards the art of war."[14] Others were also impressed, and they even suspected that the Chinese must have sent spies to make sketches of British equipment.[15]

Yet there were signs that the copying wasn't effective. Describing one of the bronze carronades, for example, a British aide-de-camp wrote:

This gun was almost a facsimile of our own; but the tangent screw for elevation and depression, in the original, had no doubt become corroded by the action of the salt water, it having lain some short time at the bottom of the sea. Adhering closely to the model, they had cut their screw and gun all in one piece; with all their ingenuity being totally at a loss to divine its use or meaning, but being determined to act steadily up to the old maxim, of fighting the barbarians with their own weapons; they therefore stuck rigidly to the pattern they had received.[16]

Similarly, the new Qing vessels couldn't match British ones. The Chinese tried, for example, building boats that emulated steamers, replacing steam power with human power. An official named Gong Zhenlin (龔振麟, d. 1861) describes his experiments:

> In the summer of the gengzi year [1840], when the British invaded and occupied Zhoushan, I was summoned to Ningbo. . . . There I saw the enemy sails standing like a forest, and among them were ships which stored fire in a cylinder and churned the water with wheels. These were surveying the beach, reconnoitering the situation and guiding the other vessels, appearing and disappearing in the waves, and going where they would. People marvelled at their strangeness and wondered at their being powered by fire. But it occurred to me to copy the pattern of these wheel-ships simply replacing steam by man-power. So I asked some artisans to build a small model, and when this was tested on a lake it proved to be quite fast. Hearing of this, the Governor [of Zhejiang], Liu Yunke [劉韻珂], authorised me to build several full-scale warjunks according to my design; they were ready in a month or so, and proved very maneuvrable at sea.[17]

There were other, similar experiments, and some human-powered paddle wheel boats saw action against the British.[18] Murray describes them with some admiration: "large junks (fitted with wooden paddles like those of a steamer, worked by a cog wheel from the inside), mounting several brass guns, and capable of going about three knots an hour against the tide."[19] Still, they were no match for steamships. Murray describes how four of them "were taken a little way up the river by the *Nemesis*: she destroyed three, and kept the other to show the fleet."[20]

Perhaps the Chinese were "much too clever a people not to be sensible of their inferiority as regards the art of war," but an acknowledgment of weakness is only the first step. Matching British military technology would not be easy. How deep did this first stage of modernization go?

The First Modernization Movement

In fact it went deeper than is usually recognized. Consider the case of Lin Zexu (林則徐, 1785–1850). He is arguably the man who sparked the war in the first place, and historians have castigated him for a blinded adherence to Confucianism, a wrongheaded insistence that China could beat Britain with righteous peasant militias, a rigid public morality combined with a disturbing tendency to lie for the sake of his career.[21] There is truth to such judgments, but Lin also oversaw a systematic attempt to understand the West and its innovations.

When he arrived in Guangzhou in March 1839 to end the opium trade, he immediately set up a translation bureau. One source says it employed twenty or thirty employees who read Western newspapers and documents and drafted daily reports.[22] Other sources say there were four main translators, all Chinese who had acquired English. One, Yuan Dehui (袁德輝), had studied English and Latin in Southeast Asia.[23] Another had been educated at a Foreign Mission School in Cornwall, Connecticut, in the 1820s, although his knowledge of English was perhaps not so strong.[24]

Historians have cast aspersions on these translators and their knowledge of English, and Lin himself may have been wary of their work, since he often had others check it.[25] But at least one of his translators was considered by Westerners as being "able to read and translate papers on common subjects with much ease, correctness, and facility."[26] This boy, who has been identified as Liang Jinde (梁進德, 1820–1862), son of the famous Chinese Protestant minister Liang Fa (梁發, 1789–1855), had been a promising student, and his teachers were disappointed that he'd chosen to join Lin Zexu when his education was not yet complete, although they understood why: Lin had made "the strongest persuasions and promises."[27] Indeed, they were impressed by Lin Zexu's dedication: "The efforts made to secure the services of this youth . . . are good evidences that the Chinese, even in the highest stations, appreciate the value of an acquaintance with foreign languages and literature. The youth was kindly treated by the commissioner, well remunerated."[28]

Liang Jinde and his colleagues mostly translated newspapers and magazines, but they also tried their hands at more scholarly works, including international law and, most importantly, geography, translating sections of Hugh Murray's fifteen-hundred-page *Encyclopedia of Geography*.[29] These translations were widely propagated later in books by Lin Zexu and others.[30]

Lin Zexu also showed interest in Western guns, buying scores of them to try to defend Guangzhou.[31] He also purchased at great expense a British ship, the *Cambridge*, which mounted thirty-four cannons. The British were impressed by how well it had been prepared for battle, "the guns being in perfect order, fire-buckets distributed about the decks, and everything very clean and well-arranged."[32] It was a pity to have to blow it up, but this was necessary to "strike terror into the Chinese, far and wide."[33] Also "she was an old and useless ship."[34] It took an hour for the fire to reach the powder magazine, but the explosion was satisfying.

As the fate of the *Cambridge* suggests, few of Lin's procurement activities made a difference during the war. The British easily overcame his new gunboats, his useless English ship, and his newly purchased cannons.

But Lin himself understood that military modernization would not be fast. In 1840, he wrote a secret memorial to the emperor outlining a long-range plan.

> Take for instance ships and guns, which are the essential means for maritime defense. Although we cannot possess them immediately, in the long run we must prepare ourselves for future occasions. The advantage of Canton lies in its good position for foreign trade. From 1821 to the present time [1840] revenues from the maritime customs have amounted to more than thirty million taels. . . . If formerly we had used ten percent of this sum for making guns and building ships we could have controlled the foreigners effectively without any difficulty. . . . From now on we must manufacture effective guns and build strong ships.[35]

This idea of using customs receipts from foreign trade to underwrite military modernization was precisely the sort of arrangement that the Qing would adopt two decades later.

Unfortunately, this memorial was the last Lin sent before learning he'd lost the emperor's confidence. The emperor was shocked when the British showed up at the mouth of the Yellow River, uncomfortably close to Beijing, and he felt that Lin should have warned him. He stripped Lin of his commission and sent him to Kazakh lands, nearly two thousand miles from Beijing. Lin's translation work, his procurement work, his incipient modernization were cut off.

He was later rehabilitated, and in the mid-1840s he once again turned to Western guns. As governor general of Shanxi and Gansu, he used Western-inspired cannons mounted on Western-style carriages to fire Western-style explosive shells. As he wrote, "I have seen foreign guns with explosive shells, and secretly explained to the mechanics how to manufacture them. The experiment has been conducted in my Yamen under my personal supervision. . . . One gun of this kind is just as good as a dozen ordinary guns. . . . I have measured the mouth of the guns, made many casts, and manufactured such guns for military use."[36]

Perhaps more important, Lin's friends and supporters propagated his ideas. The most important was Wei Yuan (魏源, 1794–1857), to whom Lin gave his notes and translations and who prepared the famous *Illustrated Treatise on the Maritime Countries* (海國圖志), which went through three metastasizing editions, more than doubling in size between its fifty-chapter first edition in 1842 and its one-hundred-chapter third edition in 1852. Wei Yuan's recommendations built on Lin's own: docks and arsenals should be established near Guangzhou; French and American experts should be hired to teach navigation and artillery and oversee teams of Chinese gun makers and shipwrights; funds should be set aside to build steamships. He even suggested that naval knowledge—including the construction of Western steamers—be tested in the official examinations. For just two and a half million taels of silver, he wrote, "all the superior skill of the West would become the skill of China."[37] This book wasn't solely about modernization. Wei Yuan also believed that China should try to use diplomacy to destroy Britain's Indian Empire.[38] Yet Westernization projects were a key part of his plan.

Wei Yuan is the best-known early proponent of Westernization, but he wasn't the only one. Lin Zexu had shared his materials with many people, who made their own contributions. In Ningbo, for instance, where Lin sojourned for a month before his exile, he had a meeting with the Ningbo magistrate, Gong Zhenlin, the man who had built human-powered paddle wheel vessels.[39] Gong's boats were perhaps inspired by pictures Lin had brought of British steamers. After the war, Gong tried to add steam power to the scheme, working with two colleagues to build a steam engine and writing in detail about their experiences.[40] He also developed new methods for casting iron cannons by using molds made of iron, methods that were probably more advanced in some ways than those then used in the West.[41] He recorded the results of his experiments in a book that itself became a part of Wei Yuan's *Hai guo tu zhi*.[42]

There were many others. Wang Zhongyang (汪仲洋) built paddle wheel boats near Zhenhai. Chang Qing (長慶) made paddle wheel boats near Guangzhou, and also worked with officials and scholars to develop more effective gunboats.[43] Another denizen of Guangzhou, Pan Shicheng (潘仕成), built a hybrid double-decker warjunk with a copper-plated hull, which he armed with British-made guns, and he also experimented with gun casting, trying to emulate British techniques. Most intriguingly, he developed an underwater mine called the water-thunder.[44] Also in Guangzhou, the admiral Wu Jianxun built a hybrid warjunk based on an American three-master, which used Western rigging and mounted fifty guns.[45]

But the man who gained the most thorough understanding of Western naval technology was Ding Gongchen (丁拱辰, 1800–1875), the first Chinese person to correctly describe steam power in writing. While living in Guangzhou in 1841 he began experimenting with steam engines, and he managed to build a model, which he describes in his book *Yan pao tu shuo* (演炮圖說): "It was a small fire wheel boat, four feet two inches long and one foot one inch wide. [We] placed it on the inner river and let it run. It went quickly, but because it was small and the steam was weak, it wasn't able to go far. But although it was small the spectacle was great, and it is a first step on the route to imitating [Western] methods."[46]

Ding's description was a milestone because the mechanism had baffled most of his countrymen. The Manchu commissioner Qiying—the man who took over the position that Lin Zexu had once held—examined a steamship, and in his confused attempt to explain the mechanism, he speculated that it might secretly be driven by human or animal power: "The ship is fitted with a water and a fire cylinder. When coal is burnt [in the fire cylinder], fire flares and smoke rises. Both inside and outside [of the water cylinder] there are gears, which are agile. [The fire cylinder] is roughly based on the law of clock. Hence [the ship] can cruise fast without the sail. It is rumored that there are men or oxen driving the gears. But this is speculation."[47] In their bewilderment, officials sometimes sought help from charlatans. In 1841 a domestic servant in Ningbo claimed he understood steamships, demonstrating by making a wood and bamboo model with a candle in the middle. It seemed to work, but when the governor-general of Jiangsu, Jianxi, and Anhui hired him to build a larger model, the man didn't deliver, claiming that he lacked good workers. The project was abandoned.[48]

Even Ding couldn't build a full-sized steamer. Why? "The artisans of Guangdong," he explained, "have no machines for making machines (無制器之器) and it is thus not possible to make a large one."[49] This phrase, "machines for making machines," is significant. As historian Wang Hsien-chun argues, a lack of precision machine tools turned out to be a tremendous obstacle for Ding Gongchen and his successors.[50] Precision lathes, planers, and shapers had developed in Britain in the late eighteenth century, and by around 1815 the sophistication and prevalence of machine tools were increasing dramatically.[51] Engineers used them to manufacture pistons and cylinders that fit together with unprecedented exactness, and screws and threads that were minutely aligned. Handicraft labor, no matter how skilled, was no substitute. Small imperfections led to major losses of efficiency.

Another missing piece was technical drawing, by which European engineers communicated designs to manufacturers. In contrast, Chinese images were nearly useless for artisans. Ding's images showed the working parts of Western technologies, and they adopted certain Western conventions (such as dotted lines for interior bits), but it would have been impossible for an artisan to make a steam engine from his plans.[52] In fact, his friend Zheng Fuguang (鄭復光) struggled to understand the drawings and text.[53] Only after examining a working engine—perhaps supplied by Ding—did Fu grasp the mechanism, and the diagram he provided in his own treatise of 1846 was even cruder than Ding's.[54]

To be sure, it was possible to make working steamships without machine tools and technical drawing, but they ran poorly. In Guangzhou, a man named Pan Shirong hired foreign workers and managed to build a small steamer, about which we know little except that it didn't work well.[55] Even more intriguingly, some fifteen years before Pan Shirong and Ding Gongchen were building their engines, a Bengali blacksmith built a steam engine without help from Europeans. A report in the *Calcutta Gazette* of 1828 notes, "A curious model of a Steam Engine, made by Goluk Chunder, Blacksmith of Tittaghur, near Barrackpur, without any assistance from European artists, was likewise exhibited; and . . . was considered so striking an instance of native ingenuity and imitative skill as to deserve encouragement."[56]

It's important to note that these various efforts of Chinese to build cannons and steamships were not isolated events, the work of "only a few exceptionally alert men."[57] The question of military and naval reform began to obsess the court of the emperor. For example, textual analysis shows that discussions of cannons took on an unprecedented significance in court records in the early 1840s. In the *Qing Veritable Records*, whereas the dynasty-wide average occurrence of the character for cannon (炮 or 砲) is about 0.02 percent, in 1842 its use shot upward to 0.19 percent, or nearly 2 occurrences per thousand characters, the highest level in the entire dataset (see Graph 17.1). Although we can't deduce a great deal from such basic analysis, this jump in frequency indicates that the court was discussing ordnance as never before.

Indeed, court records and correspondence make clear that it was precisely at this time that the emperor himself began grasp the necessity of reform. In the spring of 1842, the British were preparing to drive up the Yangtze River, and he began sending out a series of edicts. Many demanded information. When he learned, for example, that a certain Cantonese prisoner had experience building barbarian ships, he wrote to provincial officials and ordered them to investigate and send a report. When he heard about Ding Gongchen's experiments with cannons, he asked for more information. When he received news of the "fire wheel boat" constructed in Guangzhou, he demanded a picture of it.[58]

He also exhorted his officials to make new ships and guns, making clear that he wanted new ideas, a break with the past: "The mere following of the conventional way of building warships is useless. The imperial commander [in Guangzhou] and other officials are instructed to study plans, to engage shipwrights, and to build as rapidly as possible large and small warships."[59] He sent pictures of ships to officials in coastal provinces and ordered them to choose plans that suited their regions and report back. He ordered interior provinces to send building materials to coastal provinces. This flurry of edicts didn't end with the war. After the peace he ordered his officials not to become complacent: "The sizes, structure, and equipment of the warships . . . must not be confined to the old methods and conventional practice."[60]

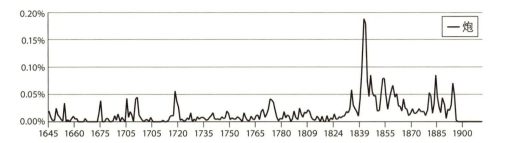

GRAPH 17.1 Incidence of the term "cannon" in the *Qing Veritable Records*, 1644–1911.

This chart shows the incidence of the term "cannon" (炮) in the *Qing Veritable Records* throughout the entire dynasty, expressed as a percentage. Thus, in 1842, 0.19 percent of the characters were the character for *pao*. Most of these occurrences appear in reference to the British threat. These data suggest that the war stimulated an unprecedented discussion of the use of cannons. The veritable records consist of court records and correspondence that have been selected and redacted for posterity after the death of each emperor. They are not a primary chronicle but contain considerable amounts of primary materials and are generally considered a reliable source.

And yet there were few results. Within a few years the ambitious projects had fizzled out. Why?

Why Did the Early Reforms Fail?

Historians have tended to blame the "Confucian mind-set." John Rawlinson produced the most thoughtful treatment of early reform available in English, and although his explanation is nuanced, he concluded that the most important impediment was Confucianism: "The explanation is not that China did not have enough money to sustain experimentation; nor is it that China lacked skills. . . . The main problem was that official attitudes militated against experimentation."[61] Confucian values, he wrote, focused too much on morality and the upright official and gave short shrift to techniques, tactics, and technologies. "Alien technical considerations such as were involved in military steamships were looked down upon."[62] Rawlinson published these words in 1967, when the idea that Confucianism was to blame for China's failure to modernize was widely shared. In the 1970s and 1980s, however, this orthodoxy began to relax among China specialists.[63]

It's certainly clear that Confucianism didn't stop Lin Zexu and Wei Yuan from being interested in foreign techniques and technologies, and we've seen many other examples in this book of Confucian officials who had little trouble conceiving an interest in foreign ways and technological solutions.[64] So if Confucianism as a philosophy was an impediment to reform, it was probably a slight impediment, no more detrimental than Christianity was to Western science, or European aristocratic values were to the adoption of guns and cannons. Moreover, there were so many strands of Confucianism to choose from, to say nothing of the myriad other philosophies and ideologies that float in the great ocean of Chinese culture. Wei Yuan, for example, although a Confucian, was influenced by the statecraft school of the New Text Movement, which drew inspiration from a Chinese tradition with affinities to legalism and which saw statecraft in terms of money and power and not just in terms of moral example.[65]

Others have blamed the failure of reform on the emperor himself, and there's certainly no reason to excuse him. He had a tendency to vacillate, to issue confusing directives, and to cycle through officials, naming, demoting, punishing, pardoning, and reinstating. Lin Zexu was removed from office in 1840 and banished to Xinjiang, only to be rehabilitated in 1845. His successor in Guangzhou, Qishan (琦善, 1786–1854), found his position undermined when the emperor sent three officials whose power overlapped with his own; he barely had time to protest before he was thrown into chains, brought to Beijing, and sentenced to death. The sentence was commuted to banishment, and in 1842 he was rehabilitated.

To be sure, the emperor sometimes had good reason to punish officials. He often caught them withholding information or even lying. Lin Zexu fell from grace because he failed to warn the court about British plans to move northward after they stopped fighting in Guangzhou. Qishan was replaced for negotiating a truce with the British and not telling the emperor about it. But at other times, lies were rewarded. In 1841, Yishan (奕山, 1790–1878) had agreed to pay the British six million silver dollars not to capture Guangzhou, but he knew he couldn't tell the emperor that. So he represented the incident to the emperor as an act of generosity on his part, saying that the English had humbly begged him for money so they could pay their debts:

The foreigners outside the walls waved at us, as if they had something to say. . . . Apparently, they wanted to petition me with their grievances. "How could our Generalissimo possibly agree to see you?" my general roared. "His only orders are to make war." The foreign officers immediately removed their hats and made an obeisance. . . . Apparently, because the English hadn't been allowed to trade and their goods haven't been allowed to move freely in and out of the city, they were facing bankruptcy . . . so they had come to beg the General to communicate sincerely to the Great Emperor that he should take mercy on them, permitting trade and ordering the [Chinese] merchants to make good their debts [to the English]. Then they would immediately leave the river . . . and not make any more trouble.[66]

In this way, Yishan portrayed a shameful ransom as an act of generosity, and the emperor rewarded him with the Order of the White Jade Feather.

Similarly, in 1842, the Manchu nobleman Yijing (奕經, 1793–1853) made up a fake naval victory, reporting that dozens of British vessels had been sunk and hundreds of British soldiers had been burned and drowned. The emperor conferred a double peacock's feather.[67] Later the emperor changed his mind. Then he changed it again, issuing confusing commands: Yijing must come to Beijing for a reckoning; no, actually Yijing should stay in the south; well, no, he should come to Beijing after all, and in chains. Yijing was sentenced to death, and then the sentence was commuted.[68] He was subsequently imprisoned, pardoned, given a post in Xinjiang, discharged, banished, reinstated again, and finally died of malaria.[69]

This kind of waffling impaired reform. Scholars have suggested that the emperor's "passing enthusiasm for a little-understood naval reform accomplished no more than to persuade a few officials that it would be tactful for them to pay a visit to a foreign war vessel, which several did."[70] This is too pessimistic, and we must remember that the emperor stood atop a sprawling bureaucracy—the largest in the world—and often couldn't tell when his top officials were lying, or when their denunciations were based on fact rather than faction.

Consider what happened with Lin Zexu. After the emperor demoted him, Lin defended himself in a campaign of letters to friends and patrons. He'd been accused—quite rightly—of failing warn the court that the British had left southern China and were heading northward. Their arrival at the mouth of the Yellow River seemed to imperil the empire, and the emperor was shocked. But Lin claimed in his lobbying campaign that he had in fact sent warnings but that other officials had ignored them, particularly Qishan, his rival and replacement. Qishan had been in charge of the forts guarding the entrance to the Yellow River, and Lin accused him of failing to prepare them for an assault that Lin claimed Qishan knew all about. He further claimed that after the emperor had sent Qishan to Guangzhuo to replace him, Qishan had failed to defend Guangzhou. If only, Lin said, the emperor had left Lin in place: the British would have been defeated and China would have avoided humiliation. Instead, with treasonous officials like Qishan and others in charge, the war effort had collapsed, sabotaged from within.

In fact, the Qing would have lost the war even if Lin had remained in office. The British advantages were overwhelming. A group of aristocratic Manchu and Mongol officials understood this and opposed the Lin narrative, arguing that the treaty with Britain was a necessary expedient and that China should use the peace to strengthen herself. Historian James Polachek calls this group a "praetorian guard of reform."[71] Unfortunately for China, the praetorians lost the debate. Lin's supporters created a literati version of the political echo chamber effect, repeating their false interpretations so much that they were eventually accepted as reality.[72] The Lin faction argued, in effect, that China lost the war because of treachery from within, not because of military backwardness. In 1850, Lin's faction succeeded in ousting the top praetorian and the rest soon succumbed. In this way, historians have argued, Lin's faction squashed reform. After they won the debate there was less attention paid to making the expenditures and efforts necessary to keep the new shipbuilding and ordnance-casting programs running. Cash-strapped governments let them die.

So was the fizzling of reform caused by factionalism? Partly, but we must also keep in mind the sheer difficulty of reform. The technological gap circa 1840 was much steeper than that of a century before. Most Chinese officials had trouble even understanding their own ignorance. As Hsien-chun Wang has argued, Chinese officials "understood the superiority of Western firepower, and there was little delay in their . . . obtaining firearms from the West. Beyond this, however, they had no idea that the paddlewheel boats . . . were the products of a string of technological developments. Steam power was beyond their imagination."[73] Of course, as we've seen, Ding Gongchen and Zheng Fuguang did manage to understand steam engines and write cogent explanations of their mechanisms. But neither could build effective machines. Understanding the mechanism was not enough. They also needed technical skills and tools, most notably technical drawing and machine tools. Moreover, although Chinese understood how to make new types of Western guns, they didn't know how to deploy the advanced mathematics that allowed Western artillerists to shoot them effectively. For instance, Ding Gongchen's treatise contains descriptions and diagrams of the new lighter field cannons and carronades, but the sections that discuss aiming and trajectory calculation seem to be based on techniques that predate the ballistics revolution.[74]

Wang believes that it just took time: "it took the Chinese two decades of experimentation to finally appreciate that they had to import from the West both its technology and its engineering tradition."[75] This may be too generous. The period 1840 to 1860 did not see constant experimentation. Interest in reform flared in the 1840s but burned out around 1850. If the experimentation had been persistent through the 1850s, technical obstacles could have been overcome faster.

Why did reform stop in 1850? There are probably many reasons—including factionalism—but beneath them is one key factor. After such a long period of unprecedented peace, the Opium War was not in itself significant enough to shock the Qing into the deep-seated reform it needed. The British investment of Nanjing in the summer of 1842 caused Qing officials to *fear* dismemberment, but only temporarily, and once it became clear that the British could be mollified with concessions—an indemnity, the right to trade in certain ports, the retention of Hong Kong—the fear lifted. As the anti-reform faction succeeded in propounding the idea that defeat was caused by treasonous officials, the focus of reform shifted from technology to personnel.

It takes significant and consistent insecurity to foment reform, because interest groups that support the status quo are difficult to dislodge.[76] Reformers can create momentum for change when there is a shared perception among policy makers and elites of what social scientists call "systemic vulnerability."[77] Geopolitical insecurity is key to this process, and it is little wonder that in the second half of the twentieth century, South Korea, Taiwan, and Singapore, all states that have lived with a justified fear of annihilation, were among the most successful models of the "developmental state." As one expert notes, "security made a huge difference, if not the *whole* difference."[78] Indeed, one can argue that if in the period 1500 to 1945 Europe's states tended to be unusually focused on military, economic, political, and technological reform it was because they, like twentieth-century South Korea and Taiwan, faced a nearly constant threat to their security. In the first half of the nineteenth century, the Qing did not.

But we don't need twenty-first-century social scientists to tell us that. In 1843, just after the Opium War ended, a British newspaper editor recalled Napoleon's prophecy that the Chinese would, if attacked, "get artificers, and ship-builders, from France, and America, and even from London; they would build a fleet, and in the course of time, defeat you."[79] The editor acknowledged widespread reports that China was building new, European-style ships, constructing better fortresses, and hiring Europeans to teach gunnery and other skills, but he didn't think this would amount to much. He wrote, with imperial condescension,

> The late struggle, was too short . . . and the national humiliation too local, to engender the widely-spread conviction among the Chinese of their inferiority in the warlike, or in any other arts, to the foreigners. . . . Experience tells us that very rarely has the pettiest rajah or predatory chieftain in British India, been content with the first drubbing he has received at our hands. Hence we deem another war with China sooner or later inevitable, in which case we shall, of course, be successful; but then we think the Chinese will be constrained thoroughly to feel and acknowledge their inferiority; and if so, their next defeat will, perhaps, be the precursor of their social advancement.[80]

According to this Victorian, China simply needed another drubbing. In the mid-1850s, the drubbings began coming in rapid succession.

CHAPTER 18

China's Modernization and the End of the Gunpowder Age

The second half of the nineteenth century saw warfare of a frequency and scale not seen in China since the seventeenth century. Some conflicts involved external enemies, most notably the Second Opium War (1856–1860), the Sino-French War (1884–1885), and the Sino-Japanese War (1894–1895). But the fiercest wars were fought against internal enemies: the Nian Rebellion (1851–1868), the Islamic Rebellions (1855–1877), and, most devastatingly, the insurrection of the Taiping Heavenly State (1851–1864), whose neo-Christian troops swept from their homeland in China's Southwest to the heart of the Great China Plain, seizing Nanjing and holding it for more than a decade.

These wars stimulated reforms, which later became known as the Self-Strengthening Movement.[1] China built huge shipyards, modern arsenals, massive factories. It produced repeating rifles, advanced artillery, exploding shells, and an armored steam fleet that by the 1880s was considered one of the top ten in the world. Yet these efforts have generally been considered a failure.

Why? Largely it was because China was humiliatingly defeated by Japan in 1894–1895.[2] This loss to an Asian neighbor a tenth its size threw its modernization attempts into harsh relief. China's failure to modernize—and Japan's success—became a key topic of twentieth-century Sinologists, who blamed Confucianism, culture, and conservatism.[3] More recent work has called into question such interpretations, yet they still persist, even among China experts.[4]

As we've seen, Confucianism proved no obstacle to innovation or adoption during other periods of Chinese history. All manner of Confucian officials were enthusiastic about Frankish cannons, Western muskets, red-barbarian cannons, and so on, including Wang Yangming himself, perhaps the most prominent Confucian thinker of the past five hundred years. Was the nineteenth century different?

No. All the great reformers of the mid-nineteenth century—men like Zeng Guofan, Zuo Zongtang, and Li Hongzhang—were Confucian scholars par excellence. They found no impediment in Confucian philosophy or Chinese culture to the adoption of Western devices, Western learning, and thoroughgoing reforms of education, commerce, fiscal structures, and military organization.[5]

In fact, scholars have recently come to a more favorable perspective on the 1860 to 1895 reforms, sometimes to their surprise. As Meng Yue wrote in a seminal article, "During the course of my research I was surprised to find, in terms of the technological details of its products, that the [Chinese] Jiangnan Arsenal was in many respects in the leading position in late nineteenth-century Asia."[6] As she and others have pointed out, from 1868 through the 1880s China built warships that were better than those being built in Japan: wooden-hulled and iron-hulled; paddlewheel, single-screw, and double-screw; single-engine, compound-engine, and triple-compound-engine. China's firearms and artillery were similarly state-of-the-art for Asia, as good as or better than those of Japan. The adaptations and innovations that took place in China suggest that the period of self-strengthening was more dynamic and formative than historians had believed.[7]

If that is so, then why did China lose the war against Japan? The answer is that China's problem wasn't technical or technological—it was political. Japan's reforms were made possible by revolution. After the Tokugawa Regime died in 1867, the new Meiji regime was able to undertake reforms that would have been impossible under the old order, with its entrenched interests. In contrast, the Qing dynasty stumbled in the nineteenth century but did not die until 1911. Indeed, it's an odd coincidence of history that the Tokugawa order lasted precisely as long as the Qing dynasty—267 years.[8] It's just that the Japanese got rid of their *ancien régime* four decades earlier.

The problem for an old state isn't so much embracing the new as getting rid of the old. Qing subjects got good at manufacturing steamships and training rifle corps, but the Qing government had to spend enormous sums on armies it had established in the seventeenth century. By the mid-nineteenth century, those forces, hundreds of thousands of men, were nearly useless. The court couldn't abolish them or even change them in any fundamental way—they were powerful interest blocs invested in the status quo. But it also couldn't afford them. If the Qing had been able to devote to new armies the funds it was expending on decrepit ones, it would have done far better.

The problem for the Qing wasn't a lack of technology or know-how. It was a lack of focus. Old institutions drained resources. Rulers balanced interest groups instead of creating a centralized military structure. And we can't forget that Japan was an unusually effective enemy. "China," wrote two experts, "did not simply lose the war through weakness; Japan won it through strength."[9] A decade after defeating China, Japan defeated another huge old state: Russia.

Self-Strengthening

Self-strengthening is said to have begun in 1861, after the end of the Second Opium War, but the sparks for reform were actually early and manifold. The key stimulus was the Taiping Rebellion. Inspired by a prophet who believed he was the younger brother of Jesus, the Taiping marched and floated from their homeland in the far Southeast through the center of China, seizing cities and winning adherents. In 1853, they captured the city of Nanjing, the original Ming capital.[10]

The Taiping made use of Western arms. In May 1853, it was reported that a hundred or so Westerners and six hundred Cantonese equipped with Western arms and uniforms were fighting for the Taiping, using vessels purchased or leased from Westerners.[11] In these early days of the rebellion, however, they didn't need modern weapons because the Qing forces they faced were poorly armed and trained. One Taiping commander boasted in 1853, "I am beginning to get old now but give me a good spear, and I am still not afraid to meet any ten of them."[12]

But as the Taiping wars intensified, they stimulated the most significant military experimentation in China since the seventeenth century. In 1852, the Qing emperor ordered officials to raise local armies to resist the rebels, giving them considerable autonomy. The most famous of these officials was Zeng Guofan (曾國藩, 1811–1872), who began purchasing Western artillery as early as 1852.[13] By 1856, he was manufacturing his own Western-style ordnance.[14] In response, the Taiping increased their use of Western weapons and vessels, hired more foreign advisors and officers, and established factories and arsenals to repair and maintain equipment.[15] Some scholars have suggested that the Taiping thus laid essential groundwork for China's subsequent modernization.[16] This may be overstated, but there's no doubt that a challenge-response dynamic led both sides to seek new weapons.

Both sides also focused on drill. Taiping armies were famous for their rigorous formations and their command structures. In response, Zeng Guofan turned to the practices of Qi Jiguang. He felt that he had an affinity with the Ming general. Just as Qi had found it expedient to recruit and pay his own local forces instead of relying on ineffective imperial forces, so Zeng did the same, declining to use the standard Qing banner forces.[17] Zeng even adopted Qi Jiguang's unit organization.[18] And Zeng instituted daily drill for his armies, using Qi Jiguang's tactical formations as his model.[19] He urged others to do the same.[20]

Zeng Guofan's troops and commanders were Qing subjects, mostly Chinese, but other officials began hiring Westerners. From a political standpoint, this was a risky proposition, because even as the Qing contended with the Taiping, they were fighting against the British and French in the Second Opium War (1856–1860). In this environment, it seemed dangerous to trust Westerners, but some provincial officials were so worried about the Taiping that they were willing to take the chance. In May 1860, for instance, the Qing governor of Zhejiang Province, Wang Youling (王有齡, 1810–1861), asked a subordinate to help him acquire aid from the foreigners, promising that he would personally accept the "infamy" and "even the crime" if things went wrong.[21] Higher-ups balked at the idea, at which Governor Wang lamented that "we will watch our cities fall and our people die."[22] Indeed, the following year, the Taiping captured Governor Wang's capital, Hang-zhou. He hanged himself in his garden.[23]

Others had more success. The Shanghai governor Wu Xu (吳煦, 1828–1860) and his wealthy associate Yang Fang (楊坊, 1810–1865), for example, sought British and French help to defend Shanghai from advancing Taiping armies, organizing, in the spring of 1860, the Foreign Arms Corps.[24] The man they put in charge was Frederick Townsend Ward (1831–1862), an American adventurer. At first, Ward's forces primarily comprised Filipinos and Western officers, and they weren't very successful. But they got better, and events soon made the employment of Western officers much more acceptable.

During the summer of 1860—even as Ward and his Foreign Arms Corps were fighting on behalf of the Qing—British and French forces marched on the Qing capital, and the Qing were forced to capitulate and sign the Convention of Beijing. This treaty created a new climate in the imperial court. Forced to appreciate the effectiveness of Western arms and faced with mounting losses to the Taipings, the court countenanced Western military help. Ward's Foreign Arms Corps morphed into the famous Ever-Victorious Army (常勝軍), whose soldiers were Chinese and whose officers were European and American.[25] Ward renounced his American citizenship and was made a Qing official. Today he is still honored in China.[26] In addition to his Ever-Victorious Army there was the Ever-Triumphant Army (常捷軍), a Sino-French force of the same type.[27] Both forces fought effectively against the Taiping.[28]

Other new Qing armies also did well, most notably those led by Zeng Guofan, Li Hongzhang (李鴻章, 1823–1901), and Zuo Zongtang (左宗棠, 1812–1885). In the summer of 1864, Zeng Guofan's Western-style artillery blasted a breach in the walls of Nanjing and captured the city.[29]

The new Chinese armies chased down the rest of the Taiping and then went on to more victories, putting down the Nian Rebellion and stamping out Muslim Rebellions. They even saw success against Western armies. In 1878, Zuo Zongtang's army exchanged fire with relatively poorly equipped Russian forces and intimidated the Russian Empire. In 1884, Chinese forces under Liu Mingchuan (劉銘傳) and Sun Kaihua (孫開華) fought the French to a standstill in Taiwan. The Qing, to be sure, lost the overall war against the French, but some individual forces, such as Liu and Sun's, did very well, much to the surprise of many Westerners.[30] Of these new armies, the most significant was Li Hongzhang's Huai Army, which later came to be known as the Beiyang Army, and which, as China's most effective defense force, would fight against the Japanese in 1894–1895.[31]

The development of these new armies was paired with broader calls for reform, some of which went deep. Scholar Feng Guifen (馮桂芬, 1809–1874), for example, outlined a set of proposals that included a system of foreign language education; the establishment of shipyards and arsenals; a route to officialdom and promotion based on science and industrial production; a translation program for works of mathematics, mechanics, chemistry, geography; and even elements of representative government, including popular elections at the local level.[32] All of this, he said, should be done toward the goal of self-strengthening.

Many of Feng's proposals were taken up by reformers, as early attempts to incorporate Western armaments gave way to sustained attempts at modernization.

Machines to Make Machines

Ding Gongzhen had complained in 1843 that he couldn't make a full-sized steamship because he lacked "machines for making machines" (制器之器). In the summer of 1863, Zeng Guofan addressed this deficit. He summoned to an audience China's first graduate of an American university, Yung Wing (容閎, 1828–1912). At first, Yung reacted with fear. At that point, the Taiping wars were still raging, and he'd recently offered to help the Taiping modernize their military and banking systems. What if Zeng knew and wanted to behead him for treason?[33] Yung's friends said Zeng just wanted help, so Yung went to the great official's headquarters. In their first meeting, Zeng sat in silence for a few minutes, staring at Yung with a slight smile, and then asked a series of personal questions. When Zeng sipped his tea, Yung knew the audience was over. At a second meeting, Zeng asked Yung what China most needed at present. Yung, having been coached by his friends, replied that China needed "a mother machine shop, capable of reproducing other machine shops."[34]

Zeng liked this answer and liked Yung Wing. He gave him 68,000 taels of silver (about 2,500 kilograms) and full autonomy to buy a modern factory and transport it back to China, a task he could carry out wherever and however he saw fit. Yung went to America, arranged to purchase a machine shop, attended his tenth class reunion at Yale, volunteered to fight for the Union in the Civil War (his service was declined), and, finally, in 1865, returned to China on a Nantucket bark of dubious seaworthiness (the captain's six-year-old son swore like a sailor).[35] He was rewarded with an official rank in the Qing bureaucracy, and the factory he purchased became the heart of the famous Jiangnan Arsenal.

The Jiangnan Arsenal is often considered a failure, but in fact the strides made there were impressive.[36] It produced steamers from scratch—every part, from the engines to the hulls to the screw propeller mechanisms.[37] It produced guns of advanced designs, copying or reverse engineering Western models.[38] Testing and experimentation were an important part of the production process, and high officials were closely involved.[39]

It wasn't the only modern factory in China. There were many such experiments. The most significant was started by Zeng's contemporary, the great general Zuo Zongtang (famous in the United States for the chicken dish named after him). Working with the Frenchman Prosper Giquel (commander of the Sino-French Ever-Triumphant Army), General Zuo established an institution that historians usually call the Fuzhou Shipyard, although the term is too modest.[40] It was a huge complex, occupying 118 acres of land, with forty-five buildings, including factories, workshops, a foundry, offices, and dormitories. It even had its own tramway system. Dozens of Europeans worked there as technicians, teachers, and foremen, as did scores of Chinese administrators and thousands of Chinese workers.

The Fuzhou complex also had schools. Most of China's new arsenals did, too, but the Fuzhou Shipyard's were particularly ambitious, and they focused on precisely the skills that had prevented Ding Gongchen and other would-be modernizers of the 1840s from achieving success: technical drawing, mathematics, and engineering. The French advisor Prosper Giquel explained, in a report on the first five years of the Fuzhou Shipyard, the rationale for such schooling:

In order to calculate the dimensions of a piece of machinery or of a hull, it is necessary to know arithmetic and geometry; in order to reproduce that object on a plan it is necessary to understand the science of perspective, which is descriptive geometry; in order to explain the pressure exerted on engines and ships as well as on still bodies, by gravity, heat, and other phenomena of nature, it is necessary to understand the laws of physics. Next in order come the increments a body undergoes under the impulse of the forces to which it is subjected; the resistances which it will need to overcome, the strain which it is able or ought to bear, which is the science of statics and of mechanics; and for these the calculations of ordinary arithmetic and geometry no longer suffice; it is necessary also to possess the knowledge of trigonometry, of analytical geometry, of the infinitesimal calculus, so as not to be any longer bound down to reason as to objects of determinate form and size, but be able to arrive at general formulae applicable to all the details of construction.[41]

High Chinese officials were becoming cognizant of the close link between science and military production. As Governor-General Ding Richang (丁日昌, 1823–1882) wrote, "The Westerners . . . have been expending their intelligence, energy, and wealth on things that were completely vague and intangible for hundreds of years; the effects are now suddenly apparent."[42] Shen Baozhen (沈葆楨, 1820–1879), the director of the Fuzhou Shipyard, wrote in 1870, "The ships and guns of the West are making such extraordinary improvement that they almost defy imagination; this is the result of a capacity for computation that reaches smaller and smaller decimals; if the calculation is finer by the slightest degree, the performance of the machinery will be ten times more adroit."[43] He later recommended that Chinese students be sent to Europe so that they could continue mastering Western learning, and "peep into [its] subtle secrets."[44]

Fuzhou Shipyard students got a good opportunity to peep in 1877, when the first cohort was sent to France. Others followed, and the education programs were enormously important. As Hsien-chun Wang has recently written, "We cannot overemphasize the significance of the [Fuzhou Shipyard's] School of Naval Construction. It was China's first engineering school that systematically imported from the West a technology from its scientific principles to the engineering application. . . .

Compared to other new educational institutions in China that introduced Western knowledge in the period between the 1860s and 1880s, the schools of the Fuzhou shipyard were much more technical."[45] Students learned about every part of steamship design, and graduates had careers lasting well into the twentieth century.

The Fuzhou Shipyard produced guns, ammunition, and steamships. At first the steamships were basic models: a 150-horsepower transport, an 80-horsepower gunboat. But the quality was high. A British merchant noted that the vessels were "admirably fastened and particularly well finished outside and inside. They could not be better finished in London or New York."[46] The third vessel to launch—an 80-horsepower gunboat—was even better, fast and solid, perhaps even a little too solid, according to the merchant: "somewhat unnecessarily strong for the tonnage and weight, but the faults are good and unusual."[47] Other early vessels were also considered effective. By 1873, the British observer noted, Fuzhou-produced gunboats were better than contemporary British vessels of the same type. "No navy," he wrote, "has better vessels."[48] Other Western observers corroborated these judgments.[49]

Yet steamer technology was changing rapidly. In 1853, the Scottish shipwright John Elder (remembered today as a master draftsman, among other things) had patented a design for a compound engine for marine use. Instead of a single condenser, Elder's engine had two. The steam first entered a high-heat, high-pressure condenser. Then it was shunted to a lower-pressure, lower-heat condenser. At each stage it drove pistons. The result was a significant increase in efficiency, and by 1858 Elder patented a triple-compound version, even more efficient.[50] By the 1870s, iron-hulled vessels driven by compound engines were being widely adopted throughout Europe.[51]

The Fuzhou Shipyard followed. By 1877 it was producing iron-hulled vessels with compound engines. Its first success, a sloop launched in May 1877, was impressive: at 1,200 tons, it was driven by a composite 750-horsepower engine. By December 1880, the shipyard had built four such sloops. In 1883, it launched a powerful cruiser: 2,200 tons, with a 2400-horsepower triple-compound engine and a cruising speed of fifteen knots. General Zuo Zongtang ordered two more. In May 1888, a ship called the *Longwei* was completed, and it was the most technologically sophisticated vessel yet: 2,100 tons with twenty-centimeter-thick steel armor, and a turret whose armor was even thicker. It was driven by two 1,200-horsepower triple expansion engines, which enabled a cruising speed of fourteen knots. It featured electric lighting, a searchlight, and a telephonic communication system.[52]

Yet still the pace of change accelerated. By the 1880s, European cruisers could reach nine thousand tons and cruise at twenty-two knots. Triple expansion engines of eight thousand horsepower were by then common, and hulls were made of steel.[53] Never before had technology moved so swiftly. In 1903, a historian of the British navy wrote, "It may be said with little or no fear of exaggeration that the best ship existing in 1867 would have been more than a match for the entire British fleet existing in 1857, and, again, that the best ship existing in 1877 would have been almost, if not quite, equal to fighting and beating the entire fleet of only ten years earlier. By 1890, the ships of 1877 had become well-nigh obsolete; and by 1900 the best ships, even of 1890, were hardly worthy of a place in the crack fleets of the country."[54]

So when we assess the performance of the Fuzhou Shipyard and the Jiangnan Arsenal, we must keep in mind that China was not just closing a gap. It was embarking on a new phase of continuous revolutionary improvement, and that phase was not new to Asia alone: it was new in world history. To appreciate the rapid development of mechanical technologies, one can chart the number of specialized engineering societies that were founded in the course of the nineteenth and early twentieth centuries. There is certainly a lag between East Asians and Europeans, but what is surprising is how new Great Britain's were as well.[55]

China and Japan were modernizing swiftly, but so were all their Western rivals, and it is the trajectory that is important. Within its first two decades of existence, the Fuzhou Shipyard had vaulted forward in technological capacity, able to follow the continual technological revolution. In fact, the Fuzhou Shipyard compares favorably to Japan's famous Yokosuka Shipyard well into the 1880s.[56] The Yokosuka Shipyard was smaller than that of Fuzhou, and its budget was lower, just a third of that of Fuzhou in 1871. It produced far fewer vessels—just thirteen between 1876 and 1894, whereas the Fuzhou Shipyard produced thirty-three vessels before 1895. The Yokosuka Shipyard also trailed the Fuzhou Shipyard in terms of technology, building its first iron-hulled vessel after Fuzhou.[57] Experts now believe that the relative maritime performance of

Japan and China was much closer than historians had tended to assume up through the 1880s.[58] Moreover, China and Japan seem to have been unusual: with the possible exception of the Ottoman Empire, no other non-Western states mastered steamship technology so well.[59]

Unfortunately, by the late 1880s the Fuzhou Shipyard ran into problems. The issue was not conservatism or lack of know-how or a supposed Chinese indifference to engineering and preference for Confucianism, as scholars have suggested. It was a lack of dedicated funding.[60] Yokosuka Shipyard received clear and consistent allocations, having been placed under Japan's Naval Department in 1872. The Fuzhou Shipyard didn't. When Zuo Zongtang had set it up, he'd arranged for funding to be shared by several provinces, of which the most important was Fujian, where the shipyard was located. Other provinces were supposed to contribute, but their allocations weren't automatic. Moreover, Zuo Zongtang hadn't taken into account steam vessels' high maintenance costs, which consumed an increasing portion of the budget. Each year, funding had to be cobbled together from multiple sources. The shipyard's directors spent as much time wrangling funding and lobbying officials as directing operations.[61]

For a time, powerful officials kept the shipyard flourishing. The great Shen Baozhen, for example, had supported it as viceroy of Liangjiang. But he died in 1879. Zuo Zongtang, the shipyard's founder and greatest patron, died in 1885. Afterward, it became harder and harder for directors to cobble together the funding. Morale suffered, as evidenced by high turnover for the position of shipyard director: between 1875 and 1890, three resigned and four moved to other posts.[62] By the late 1880s, the shipyard was faltering.

Japan's Yokosuka Shipyard was on the opposite trajectory. Although its early years had been rough, by the late 1880s it had dedicated funding that allowed it to invest in multiyear projects and make continued capital investments, vital in this time of constant technological change.[63] It increased its commitment to innovation, hiring Western experts to build the latest designs, although its advanced cruisers were less effective than once believed.[64]

Indeed, on the eve of the war between China and Japan, many experts believed with good reason that China's fleet had advantages over that of Japan and that China would win the war.[65]

The Sino-Japanese War

In the summer of 1894, a reporter for the London newspaper *Pall Mall Gazette* asked British naval expert Sir Edward J. Reed to compare the navies of China and of Japan. Sir Edward had helped design Japanese ships, but he believed China had the advantage because it had wisely invested in armored ships, whereas Japan had focused on weakly armored cruisers.

"Can't stand much knocking about then?" asked the reporter.

"They have no power," replied Sir Edward, "to resist even the smallest machine-guns."

"Then they could easily be knocked into a cocked hat?"

"These ships," said the imperturbable Sir Edward, "may be regarded as having their powers of flotation entirely without defence even against the smallest guns afloat. . . . I have no doubt whatever that Japan has made an immense mistake by investing all its recent expenditures in new ships on vessels without any armour."[66]

Sir Edward admitted that Japan might have an advantage early in the war, but he believed Japan's failure to invest in heavy armored vessels of the type possessed by China would turn out to be a major mistake.

Many others agreed. British admiral George Ballard wrote that Japan had "a less powerful fleet than that of her opponents."[67] Other Western military experts concluded that the Jiangnan Arsenal was "certainly capable of constructing war-like material on a more extended scale than can be done by Japan."[68] The opinion that China's great arsenals were superior to Japanese ones was widespread, and the Japanese were deeply concerned about China's growing technological might.[69]

So why did Japan win the war? Even after the fact, most observers felt that the reasons were not technological. The secretary of the US Navy analyzed the results and concluded that "the ships of China, including armaments were, in offensive and defensive power, superior to those of Japan."[70] The famous naval theorist A. T. Mahan (1840–1914) noted that the thirty-centimeter shells—manufactured in the Jiangnan Arsenal—fired by Chinese ship artillery were so effective that their destructive power "showed how complete might have been the victory of the Chinese, had their gunners been able to fire with full judgment and sight."[71]

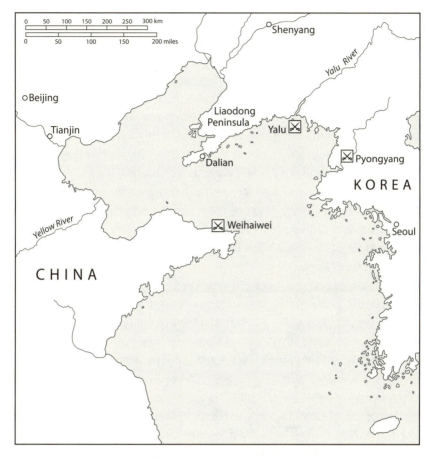

Map 18.1 Selected Battles of Sino-Japanese War, 1894–1895.

Japan won through leadership and cohesion. For one thing, Japan had a sophisticated and flexible war plan that took account of what one scholar of Japan has called "the enormous naval superiority of the Chinese fleet."[72] War leaders in Japan decided that they must quickly seize control of the Yellow Sea in order to be able to land troops wherever they wished, because they envisioned, from the start, taking the war to Beijing itself. They wanted a clear demonstration of Japanese military superiority. But they also realized that China might use its powerful navy to take control of the Yellow Sea, so they had an alternate plan: to secure control in Korea while protecting the Japanese coast (see Map 18.1).[73]

China had no cohesive military plan. Li Hongzhang, who was in control of most of the relevant Qing forces, tried at first to avoid battle, hoping to paint Japan as the aggressor so that Westerners would intervene on China's behalf. When Japan began transporting troops across the Yellow Sea to Korea, he could have used his powerful ships to stop them. He didn't, and the Western nations didn't respond as he'd hoped. His inaction allowed the Japanese to quickly take control of Seoul, after which they marched on Pyongyang, which was defended by fifteen thousand troops of his Beiyang Army. The Qing's Beiyang troops fought well, and sources suggest that "the Chinese army was not quite as cowardly or incompetent as historians believe."[74] Nor was the Japanese army as effective, being hampered by poor logistics.[75] The Japanese did capture Pyongyang, thanks to bold leadership and to the fact that Chinese leaders failed to attack while Japanese troops were crossing the river.[76] The Beiyang Army was badly defeated and withdrew from Korea.

The Japanese also attacked at sea. On 17 September 1894, the day after the Battle of Pyongyang, a Japanese fleet confronted the core of China's Beiyang Fleet at the famous Battle of Yalu River. The Qing fleet was imposing, especially its two main battleships, which were precisely the sort of vessel that Sir Edward Reed thought would knock Japanese ships into a cocked hat. The Japanese flotilla was much more weakly armored. Moreover, the Qing had more huge guns: eight guns with a caliber of thirty centimeters, compared to three on the Japanese side.[77] Yet the Japanese fleet was considerably larger in total displacement: 36,462 tons versus the Beiyang flotilla's 32,915 tons.[78] Moreover, the Japanese had many smaller guns that were new and easy to aim (see Figure 18.1).[79]

The Chinese probably could have won, but they fought poorly. As analysts at the time recognized, the Chinese admiral, Ding Ruchang (丁汝昌, 1836–1895), adopted an ill-advised formation, placing his great battleships in the center and the weaker vessels on the wings.[80] This exposed the weaker vessels to Japanese firepower and prevented the huge ironclads from using the full strength of their gunnery.[81]

People have also criticized Admiral Ding's standing orders. According to British admiral George Ballard (1862–1948), these orders were "of the crudest description, based the principle that when once engaged each captain was to act as he considered best under the circumstances."[82] Such orders, Ballard continued, "make it obvious that he exercised no effective control over his force for tactical purposes and either understood very little of fleet maneuvering himself or placed no reliance on his captains for working together."[83]

Ding was perhaps right to have little faith in his officers, whom historians—both Chinese and Western—have accused of ineptitude.[84] An officer on Ding's own flagship fired the large guns while Ding was still standing on a moveable platform before them. Ding's leg was crushed and he couldn't walk for the rest of the battle.[85] Two captains in his fleet simply fled, their fellow officers cursing at them in Chinese.[86]

Taking advantage of this disorder, the Japanese quickly disabled Ding's weakest vessels and turned their attention to the ironclads. The American soldier of fortune Philo McGiffin (1860–1897) commanded one of these ironclads and described how the Japanese kept strict formation and, ignoring the smaller Chinese vessels, "steamed around our two ironclads, pouring in a storm of shell."[87]

McGiffin lauded the discipline and bravery of the Chinese crews but lamented that they were hampered by insufficient ammunition, particularly a lack of explosive shells. Nonexplosive shells, no matter how well aimed, did far less damage. In one instance, for example, a Japanese vessel found itself between the two great Chinese ironclads and was barraged at point blank. "It was impossible to miss," wrote McGiffin. "We considered her 'done for'—as doubtless she would have been had we used shell—one shot, for instance, passing diagonally through the ship from one bow to the opposite quarter, doing various minor damages. Had it been a live shell the result may be imagined."[88] The lack of proper ammunition was a problem throughout the war, and it was reported that some shells were even filled with sand instead of gunpowder.[89]

McGiffin and his comrades kept shooting until they had just three shots in the guns "for the last moment."[90] They thought they were done for, but the Japanese stopped shooting. McGiffin felt that "this withdrawal . . . has always been a mystery."[91] But we know today that the Japanese admiral, Itō Sukeyuki (伊東祐亨, 1843–1914), called off the attack because he didn't know the enemy was out of ammunition and doubted that his fleet would ever sink the two battleships.[92] In the sudden calm, the two ironclads gathered the other surviving vessels

COMPARISONS OF VESSELS ENGAGED
BATTLE OFF YALU RIVER

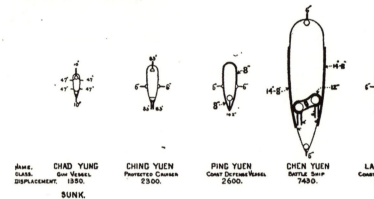

NAME.	CHAD YUNG	CHING YUEN	PING YUEN	CHEN YUEN	LAI
CLASS.	Gun Vessel	Protected Cruiser	Coast Defense Vessel	Battle Ship	Coast
DISPLACEMENT.	1350.	2300.	2600.	7430.	2
	SUNK.				

CHINESE FLEET

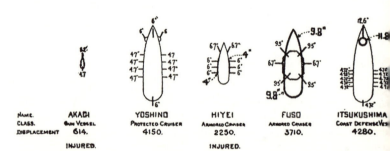

NAME.	AKAGI	YOSHINO	HIYEI	FUSO	ITSUKUSHIMA
CLASS.	Gun Vessel	Protected Cruiser	Armored Cruiser	Armored Cruiser	Coast Defense Vessel
DISPLACEMENT.	614.	4150.	2250.	3710.	4280.
	INJURED.		INJURED.		

JAPANESE FLEET

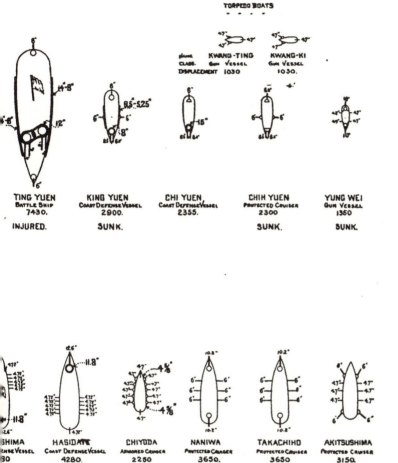

FIGURE 18.1 Schematic representation of Chinese and Japanese fleets, 1894.

This image is a pictorial representation of the Chinese and Japanese fleets that met at the Battle of Yalu River in September 1894. Although the Chinese had two massive, heavily armored battleships, the Japanese fleet was larger in terms of total displacement: 36,462 tons to 32,915 tons on the Chinese side. The Chinese had more of the largest type of gun (eight 12-inch guns, as compared to three 12.6-inch guns on the Japanese side), but the Japanese had more medium-sized guns, and they were newer and more effective. From Herbert, H. A., "The Fight off the Yalu River."

and steamed toward port. Admiral Itō made no attempt to reengage. In retrospect, we say that the Japanese won, but McGiffin felt it was a stalemate: "both fleets had fought themselves to a standstill."[93] The US secretary of the Navy similarly described the Battle of the Yalu as "nearly a drawn battle."[94]

The ironclads would fight again, but not McGiffin, who'd been so badly wounded he had to return to America. From his hospital bed, he dictated an account of the battle that remains invaluable.[95] His injuries were so severe that he never fully recovered. One account suggests that "he would sit on the porch . . . , be in a conversation with someone and say, 'Excuse me,' when a splinter from the Yalu River fight worked its way to the surface of his skin. . . . [He] would take out a pen knife, roll up his shirt, and lift out the splinter, or whatever it was, with no great ceremony."[96] Eventually he shot himself.[97]

The ironclads, in contrast, were repaired and ready to play a major role in the war. As George Ballard noted, these two vessels "should have been more than a match for the six best ships of the Japanese Navy."[98] But the Qing didn't use them.[99] Bold commanders could have sent them to attack Japanese troop convoys or support the defense of ports in Liaodong, but Beijing wanted the ships kept nearby and wasted them in convoy duty. One of them—the one that McGiffin had commanded—struck a reef and was beached for the remainder of the war. As the *New York Times* rightly opined, "With the loss of . . . her greatest battleship, China becomes practically powerless on the sea."[100] Its captain, Lin Taizeng (林泰曾, 1851–1894), was the grand nephew of Lin Zexu. He took an overdose of opium. At the funeral, people spat on his coffin.[101]

So the Japanese quickly captured the Qing's major ports in Liaodong, meeting little effective resistance. Sometimes they even found Qing strongholds abandoned, still full of provisions and ammunition. The Japanese forces were not only well led and well trained. They also had more ample provisions and better medical care, with official commissariats for provisioning and medical units for taking care of the wounded. Qing forces had neither. On land, Qing troops probably suffered less from inferior equipment than from inferior support.

In February 1895 the Japanese captured the heavily fortified port of Weihaiwei, whose defenses had been designed with the help of

German military advisors and were armed with powerful new guns. The remaining vessels in the Beiyang Fleet were captured or destroyed. The Qing were prostrate. Admiral Ding Ruchang took an overdose of opium. The court decided to enter into peace talks.

The negotiations were long and ridiculous. In an attempt to demean the Japanese, the Qing sent low-level negotiators. They were sent back. Eventually the Qing dispatched Li Hongzhang, who was then shot in the face by a Japanese nationalist. This was, wrote Western diplomat John W. Foster, "the most effective shedding of blood on the Chinese side during the entire war, as it brought to him the sympathy of the world, and made the Japanese plenipotentiaries more considerate of him."[102] Li Hongzhang didn't fare much better among his own countrymen. He was demoted and stripped of honors (although they were restored for his trip to Japan), and it seems he was even forced to pay huge bribes to his political enemies.[103]

Today, many historians blame Li Hongzhang's poor leadership for the Chinese loss, describing him as "militarily inert."[104] Li himself tried to manage his reputation during and after the war by leaking documents (or someone leaked them on his behalf) demonstrating how he had long urged the Qing court to prepare for war with Japan, how he had requested funds for military preparations, and how those funds had not been provided.[105] These and other documents make clear that the blame isn't all his. In April 1894, on the eve of the war, he was still warning about the need for warships, improved fortresses, and better military training, and during the war he complained bitterly about the court's reluctance to grant his continued requests for funding and materiel.[106]

Most significantly, he had long called for a unified military command. In 1874–1875 there had even been a major debate on the topic. Li, with the support of many others, had proposed that there be a single commander in chief (統帥) to oversee all forces—land and naval—as well as to take charge of procurements and manufacturing.[107] The commander in chief would lead a unified navy and a central army, rather than the divided forces that then existed. But after eight months of debate, the proposals failed. Instead, the Qing created two regional commands, north and south, and the funds allocated were insufficient.[108] Li tried again in 1884 to urge the creation of a national navy, but again to no avail.[109]

So when war arrived, Li Hongzhang found himself facing the Japanese navy with just the Beiyang Fleet, receiving little support from the rest of China's naval forces. As Ben Elman has noted, "the lack of coordination between the northern and southern navies became the chief disadvantage of the Chinese fleets vis-à-vis their counterpart in Japan, which was a unified fleet stationed in Yokosuka under a central command."[110]

Why didn't the Qing court institute a centralized command? Because it was afraid of revolt.[111] Decentralization was baked into the Qing state, the result of a "carefully devised system of checks and balances."[112] Officials' responsibilities and chains of command were intentionally kept ambiguous so that nobody acquired too much power. This dysfunction was not due to conservatism or Confucianism. As historian Richard Smith has written, the obstacles were "less ideological than institutional."[113]

Li Hongzhang's forces were also underfunded. Between 1871 and 1892, allocations for the Beiyang army had dropped by more than a third.[114] The navy, too, was chronically short of funds, and, as experts have recently shown, in this period "navies required vast amounts of annual funding to purchase, construct, and maintain warships, land-based infrastructure, naval institutions, and personnel."[115] To supplement insufficient funding, Li Hongzhang constantly had to seek support on an ad hoc basis from the central government, and to cajole other provincial governors to contribute funds as well.[116] He wasn't always successful.

The Qing court failed to provide adequate support not only because it was worried about putting too much power into his hands, but also because it faced revenue problems. At the end of the nineteenth century, Qing central governmental revenues probably came to around two percent of China's GDP, and this includes the court's share of the new transit and customs taxes that had been instituted to fund military expansion during the Taiping Rebellion.[117] This is less than half the average of other late nineteenth-century states for which data are available.[118] To make matters worse, the new toll and customs receipts, which had helped fund the promising reforms in the 1860s and early 1870s, were by the 1880s committed to other projects, both civil and military.[119] At the same time, the Qing lacked a fiscal state, so unlike

Japan it had little capacity to borrow money for military investments.[120] Some historians suggest that China's earlier failure to develop the fiscal state stemmed from a relative lack of warfare compared to Europe, and recent work suggests that the warfare of the mid-nineteenth century did indeed stimulate the development of a fledgling fiscal state.[121] Whatever the case, it seems clear that by the 1880s, the Qing state was under significant economic constraint.

Moreover, many of its resources flowed to old, nearly useless armies. Li Hongzhang and others had proposed reducing their size and using the savings to develop modern armies, but to little avail.[122] The Qing court was afraid to upset vested interests, especially in the military.[123] Only after the turn of the twentieth century did the Qing court finally begin dismantling its old banner systems.[124]

In contrast, Japan started fresh. In the late 1860s and early 1870s, it swept away old military structures, abrogating feudal lordship and the samurai system. This left it free to focus on new structures.[125] In fact, if we compare Japan's reforms before its Meiji revolution to those of the Qing, we find that they were quite similar: decentered, ineffectively coordinated. In China, most reforms were carried out by provincial officials such as Zeng Guofan, Zuo Zongtang, and Li Hongzhang, rather than by the Qing court in Beijing. Similarly, in the years 1853 to 1867, before the Tokugawa shogunate had been replaced by the Meiji State, Japan's main experiments with reform occurred in the feudal domains, particularly in the Satsuma, Mito, and Chōshū domains.[126] When the shogunate itself attempted centralized reforms, the results were uneven. As Richard Smith writes, these late Tokugawa reforms were "no more effective than those of [China's] Tongzhi era [1862–1874]."[127] But with the growth of central power in the Meiji Period (1868–1912), Japan's reforms became focused and centralized, whereas Qing reforms became increasingly ad hoc and decentered.

It's not that historians are entirely wrong to blame conservatism for Qing failures. Consider, for example, the events of 1866–1867, when the reform-minded court officials Prince Gong (奕訢, 1833–1898) and Wenxiang (文祥, 1818–1876) proposed creating an imperial department of astronomy and mathematics, to foster teaching and research not just in mathematics but also in chemistry and physics. It was a bold plan: the new department would serve as a sort of institute of advanced studies, to educate members of the Hanlin Academy, the most prestigious imperial academy of scholarship.[128] But the plan was opposed by a group of Confucian scholars headed by Grand Secretary Woren (倭仁, 1804–1871), who denounced the idea of honoring barbarians as teachers, particularly barbarians who burned summer palaces (Woren himself was of Mongol extraction). He argued that it was more important to cultivate morality and righteousness than to study "numerical arts" (術數).[129] Prince Gong, Wenxiang, and others argued back forcefully, but Woren and his allies managed to call the endeavor into question, even inciting rumors of treason. As a result, prominent scholars declined to apply to the program, which withered.[130]

Yet the arguments that Woren spouted were no more deeply rooted in Confucianism or "Chinese culture" or even Qing political culture than the arguments of his opponents. Both sides made arguments in Confucian terms. Moreover, the powers that be—most importantly the Empress Dowager—did not so much choose Woren's side in the debate as refuse to choose either side. With her own legitimacy in doubt, she was disinclined to take a stand.[131] Conservatism itself wasn't the problem. The problem was the increasing dysfunction of the Qing state.

Military power depends closely on state power, especially in the modern age. Historians have shown, for example, how the United Kingdom became a great imperial power not just because it had good guns and ships, but also because the British state financed, provisioned, and controlled its armies and navies effectively.[132] Japan's military rise in the 1890s and 1900s demonstrates the same point. So although in 1894 most observers felt that China's fleets were on a par with those of Japan—perhaps even better—and although many of China's infantry soldiers were armed with guns superior to those of Japan, China's government was divided and incapable, which meant that China's forces were poorly provisioned and badly led. Japan's military acted with cohesion. China's was in disarray.

The Sino-Japanese War was an epochal event in the late nineteenth-century world. After its victory, Japan was recognized as a major military power, the "Yankees of the East."[133] The Chinese were increasingly viewed as weak and laughable.

Even more important for our purposes, the war was also the last major conflict of the gunpowder age. In the 1880s, chemists had developed new smokeless powders, which were cleaner and more powerful than gunpowder.[134] China's reformers worked hard to make smokeless powder, and there's even some evidence that they used it against the Japanese in 1894, causing one observer to conclude that Chinese arms were "superior to the enemy."[135]

But it was after the Sino-Japanese War that smokeless powder became widely adopted, particularly after the Spanish-American War (1898) and the Boer War (1899–1902). Leaving less residue, it facilitated the development of rapid-fire guns, even as it reduced the danger of misfires. Equally important, soldiers armed with smokeless powder didn't reveal their position with telltale puffs of smoke. The Boers famously used their smokeless guns by hiding and sniping at British soldiers, and in response the British quickly went smokeless.

The Qing did too, and during the Boxer Rebellion (1898–1900) American soldiers complained about how hard it was to locate the Chinese and Manchu gunners who shot at them.[136] When the Americans tried blocking the export to China of smokeless powder, the Chinese simply made it themselves.[137] The Japanese, too, rapidly embraced the new technology, and in the Russo-Japanese War of 1904–1905, smokeless powder conferred a significant advantage on them. The great Russian chemist Dmitri Mendeleev, inventor of the periodic table, had developed a very effective type of smokeless powder in the 1890s,[138] but the Russians generally relied on what observers called "brown powder," or "partially smokeless" powder.[139] This was a mistake. As a British analyst wrote, "the Russians, by not using smokeless powder, always revealed the position of their guns, whereas it was almost impossible to locate the Japanese guns."[140] He concluded that "not to use smokeless powder is a criminal neglect of first principles."[141]

By the early 1900s, the gunpowder age was over, but black powder continued to be used for fireworks. In fact, this was a golden age of "pyro-spectacles." One of the most popular was "War Between China and Japan," which played in New York and New England, and which a critic described as "the most brilliant and picturesque work ever offered to the public in an open air theatre."[142] Seated behind an artificial lake, the audience watched actors re-create the war, starting with sedate scenes in Japan and culminating in a huge firework version of the Battle of Weihaiwei, whose display was, according to one reviewer, "so true to life, so picturesque, and so appalling; the sinking of the Chinese men-of-war, the scream of terror of the drowning sailors, the shouts of triumph of the victorious Japs, . . . the belching of the cannon, the rattle of musketry . . . ; smoke, fire, and flame were mingled together in admirable confusion."[143]

China, the birthplace of gunpowder, had become an object of entertainment, and of derision. As a front-page article in the *New York Times* proclaimed in 1895, "China is an anachronism, and a filthy one on the face of the earth."[144]

It didn't remain an anachronism for long.

Conclusions

A NEW WARRING STATES PERIOD?

In 1863, Li Hongzhang had written that if China worked hard to acquire Western military technologies "she will be able to stand on her own feet a hundred years from now."[1] His timing was spot-on. In 1964, the People's Republic of China tested an atomic bomb, signaling its ability to pursue advanced military programs without foreign aid (the Soviet Union had withdrawn support in 1960). Since then, China has continued improving its military capacities, and today it is investing heavily in battleships, nuclear submarines, missile systems, military satellites, stealth bombers. Its power is increasing so fast that its leaders feel compelled to offer reassurances. "Napoleon," its president has stated, "said that China is a sleeping lion, and when it wakes the world will shake. Today, the Chinese lion has indeed woken up. But it is a peaceful, kindly, and civilized lion."[2]

Many are wary. After all, in the past two dynasties—the Ming and the Qing—domestic consolidation was followed by huge wars of expansion. Using state-of-the-art gunpowder troops, the bellicose Yongle Emperor (r. 1403–1424) undertook expeditions southward against Vietnam, northward against the Mongols, and across the oceans, intervening in lands far beyond China's borders. Similarly, in the early and mid-Qing periods, the Kangxi Emperor and his successors invaded Tibet, marched into Central Asia, and, later, attacked Vietnam, Burma, and Nepal.[3] Thanks in part to such wars, both the Ming and Qing dynasties managed to overawe potential rivals and establish lasting hegemonies.

It's impossible to know how the People's Republic of China will use its military might, but it seems unlikely that it will achieve the same level of hegemony as its predecessor, the Qing dynasty. Indeed, some Chinese thinkers today suggest that their country is entering a new warring states period, this time on a global scale.[4] That is perhaps too pessimistic, but it does seem that the modern period—from the mid-nineteenth century through today—is a return to a more standard pattern in Chinese history, in which wars were more frequent and military innovation deep and vibrant. Indeed, the situation today is perhaps less like the original Warring States Period (475–221 BCE) than like the period I have called the Song Warring States Period (960–1279). During that time, warfare was not so frequent as during the ancient Warring States Period, but the Song dynasty and its neighbors nonetheless co-existed in strained and sustained geopolitical rivalry.

As a result, the Song Warring States Period was a time of military innovation, when the polities that existed in what we today call China held the global lead in gunpowder technology—and indeed many other technologies. This lead persisted throughout the first five hundred years of the gunpowder age, from the 900s through the mid-1400s. Although Europeans had received guns by the 1320s, for the following century and a half they used them less effectively on the battle-field than did the Chinese, which is why Ming armies of the 1300s and 1400s contained a much higher proportion of gunners than did those of Europe. To be sure, Europeans and Ottomans took the lead in gunpowder artillery after 1380, but that's probably because European walls were an order of magnitude thinner than those of China; it made sense for European leaders to allocate the huge sums necessary to manufacture, maintain, and deploy artillery, whereas in China large guns were simply not worth the investment. After 1480, European guns of all sizes did become more effective than those of China, but by the 1520s, China had already closed the gun gap, and that gap didn't open again until the eighteenth century, when the Great Military Divergence occurred.

What caused that Great Divergence? Historians have tried to explain it by referring to deep-seated cultural characteristics, suggesting that Chinese culture emphasized words over war, or that Confucian scholars felt that military matters were beneath them, or that Chinese literati were disdainful of the idea of borrowing from foreigners, or that China's "epic mistake" was to turn inward, to cut itself off from the world after the early Ming period.[5] As we've seen, such explanations are insufficient at best.

There was tremendous military innovation during the imperial period before the 1700s, a time during which Confucianism was firmly ensconced. And there's ample evidence of openness on the part of Chinese officials after the supposed "turning inward" of the 1400s. When Chinese literati first encountered the "classic gun" of Europe in the early 1500s, they immediately began to adopt and adapt it, making new sizes and styles but keeping the term "Frankish guns." In the 1550s, Chinese leaders adopted large muzzle-loading cannons and arquebuses with alacrity, and they drilled their arquebusiers in the famous volley technique by the 1550s, well before the commonly accepted date of the technique's emergence in either Europe or Japan. In the early 1600s, the "red-haired cannons" brought by the Dutch and English were also adopted, as were similar models acquired from the Portuguese and Spanish. China's advanced casting techniques allowed these guns to be constructed so effectively that in certain respects they were superior to European models, and European colonial officials even sought Chinese cannon makers for their foundries.

Thanks partly to such borrowings, the early modern period, from the early 1500s through the early 1700s, was an Age of Parity between East Asians and Europeans. Yet we must acknowledge that Europeans did have two key advantages. First, on the high seas, European broadside vessels proved superior to Chinese warships. To be sure, this wasn't an overwhelming edge. Chinese admirals defeated Europeans by sailing into shallows, launching sneak attacks, and deploying fireboats. Moreover, in the mid-1600s, Chinese war makers were able to construct broadside warships similar to those of Europe. This naval modernization program was abandoned not for technical reasons but for geopolitical ones. After the Ming admiral Zheng Zhilong defeated the Dutch in 1634, there was no longer any need to develop a deep water navy, and in any case the Ming were much less worried about Europeans than about Manchus, who were so weak on the water that traditional warjunks were sufficient. Europeans' naval advantage played a role in the Sino-Dutch War of 1661–1668, but the Chinese won anyway. Second, Europeans benefitted from advanced fortress design. Although Chinese literati experimented with European-style artillery fortresses in the 1600s, those experiments did not bring lasting changes to China's wall-building culture. So when East Asian forces attacked Russian and Dutch fortifications in the mid-seventeenth century, they were stymied. Ultimately, the East Asians overcame the forts, but at steep cost, and the details of battles suggest that Chinese commanders had a difficult time understanding how to take them.

Thus, proponents of the military revolution model are correct about the significance of the broadside ship and the renaissance fortress.[6] This suggests that recent attempts to label the military revolution model "passé" are premature.[7] The military revolution paradigm continues to help frame and generate research questions.[8] We must be careful, of course, when we make comparisons between Western and non-Western warfare, and some scholars have argued that the military revolution model doesn't apply outside Western Europe because it adopts a one-size-fits-all perspective on military effectiveness, focusing on a package of techniques and technologies (ships, cannons, muskets, forts, and drill) that were effective in Western Europe but not elsewhere.[9] But although it's true that the world was a complicated place and each context demanded local solutions, what's intriguing is that East Asian military developments showed surprising parallels with those of Western Europe. The forces of China defeated European forces not so much because they did things differently but because they did the same sorts of things as well or better.

As we've seen, the forces of China—and, even more effectively, their allies the Koreans—used muskets in formations similar to those of Europe, and, equally intriguingly, these new developments in drill were expressed in a spasm of military printing in the 1500s and 1600s, just as in Europe. Between 1550 and 1644, Chinese presses put out at least 1,127 military manuals, at a steadily increasing clip, with 42 manuals published each year of the warlike Chongzhen reign (1627–1644).[10] Historians of Europe tend to portray Europe's print revolution as unique and unprecedented, and maybe it was, but we certainly need to be aware of the rich history of East Asian printing.[11] In other ways, too, selective pressures seem to have led to similar outcomes in both Europe and East Asia: an increase in the ratio of officers to enlisted men; a tendency to reexamine reliance on cavalry; a closer integration of firearm units with traditional units.[12]

These parallel developments were complemented by an unprecedented level of transnational borrowing. During the Age of Parity,

Ming, Qing, and Korean leaders welcomed foreign expertise. Jesuits published Chinese books on European military arts; Dutchmen served alongside Chinese and Japanese in Korean armies; Germans and Danes offered Ming generals advice on tactics and strategy; and of course there were the many technological exchanges we've detailed in this book. Huang Yi-long is on firm ground when he draws a parallel between China's borrowing during the seventeenth century and its nineteenth-century Self-Strengthening Movement.[13] But whereas the self-strengthening of the nineteenth century has been viewed as a failure, there's no doubt that the self-strengthening of the Age of Parity was effective.

Some scholars have argued that all this adoption is itself evidence of European military superiority.[14] This is too simple. Everyone was adopting and adapting from everyone. Europeans had adopted the gun from China, through Asian intermediaries, and they then passed designs back and forth among themselves—Spanish to Italian to French to Burgundian, and so on—and with significant interborrowing between Western Europe and neighboring regions, most notably North Africa and Western Asia.[15] Asians adopted European guns rapidly, not just the East Asians, but also Ottomans, South Asians, and Southeast Asians, and they traded these gun designs back and forth, just as Europeans did. Areas on the eastern coast of the Indian subcontinent, for example, became prime producers of cannons and arquebuses, a process that seems to have begun even before the Portuguese arrived in the Indian Ocean, or at the very least, shortly thereafter, and very rapidly.[16] Arquebuses spread quickly throughout Asia, and there's evidence that they first arrived in East Asia not via Europeans but via Southeast Asians, or via Japanese and Chinese who traded in Southeast Asia.[17] Similar evidence can be found for larger European guns.[18] In any case, whatever military edge Europeans possessed didn't last. During the Age of Parity, East Asians innovated swiftly and successfully, and whenever Europeans went to war with East Asian forces they found themselves outmatched, even controlling for the fact that they were usually outnumbered.

The forces of China were effective not just because they'd achieved technological parity, but also because of statecraft, which made possible large standing armies, intensive drilling practices, and sophisticated logistics. This was particularly true of the Qing Empire, whose logistical innovations made possible not just victory over the Russians but also the conquest of some of the most forbidding reaches of the planet, ending for all time the nomadic menace from Central and Northern Asia.[19]

Maybe the Qing were too successful. As Peter Perdue and Frederic Wakeman have argued, the Qing's unprecedented hegemony removed the stimulus for military innovation.[20] During the Great Qing Peace, 1760 to 1839, China's military atrophied, and this was a period during which European militaries were undergoing an unprecedented increase in size, organization, and technological sophistication. The result was the Great Military Divergence, whose timing corresponds closely to the economic Great Divergence described in the work of revisionist historians like Kenneth Pomeranz, Robert Marks, and R. Bin Wong.[21] Recent work suggests that this periodization may also work for other regions of Asia, such as the Ottoman Empire and the Indian Subcontinent.[22]

Yet the timing of the Great Divergence is perhaps less important than its roots. Traditionalist scholars believe that those roots stretch deep into the past and are related to a whole complex of developments in Europe: private property, independent cities, the rise of the bourgeoisie, renaissance humanism, and so on.[23] These deep cultural and institutional differences, they argue, were the source of Europe's unique dynamism. Are they right? Perhaps, but if we focus on military history, it seems clear that dynamism followed the pulse of warfare. During the first half of the gunpowder age, from 900 or so to about 1450, warfare was relatively frequent and intense in East Asia, and East Asia was an epicenter of military innovation. From 1450 to 1550, a period of relative peace for the Ming dynasty, China's military innovation slowed even as Western Europe's surged, stimulated by war. After 1550, as East Asia erupted into warfare, rapid innovation and interadoption occurred on both ends of Eurasia, and this Age of Parity lasted until the mid-eighteenth century. From 1760 to 1839, however, warfare decreased dramatically in East Asia, and China's military effectiveness diminished relative to that of Europe.

Rates of warfare thus correlate with military effectiveness, but we mustn't forget the many other factors that come into play: statecraft, knowledge networks, economic organization, fiscal structures, communications and transportation infrastructure, and so much more. Warfare explains a lot, but not everything.

Indeed, I came to believe during the writing of this book that one extra-military factor in particular played a vital role in the Great Military Divergence. I used to teach, in my lectures in Chinese history, that arguments about a lack of Chinese science in the Ming and Qing period were overwrought, that indigenous discourses such as the *kaozheng* school of evidentiary research were analogous to Western science, and that people have been too quick to discount the many writings on nature within the sea of Chinese thought.[24] Certainly there's still a tendency to underrate the dynamism of intellectual life in Late Imperial China, but today I find myself agreeing with China specialist Mark Elvin, who writes of his own conversion to the view that "something dramatic" was happening in Europe in the seventeenth century:

> I will not easily forget my awareness of this when first studying [Rudolf Jakob] Camerer's *De sexu plantarum epistola* (Letter on the sex[uality] of plants) of 1694. This is a miniature masterpiece of summarized and analyzed observations and experiment directed at testing a conceptual model, in a context of breathtaking honesty about both what he had done and also failed to do. The book is the foundation text of modern plant science—and I found myself saying to myself, almost in a state of shock, something like "so that was when and how it happened!" . . . With three centuries of hindsight, one knows as one reads that the door to Darwin is now starting to swing open.[25]

Elvin believes the roots don't run as deep as many traditionalists say—we don't need to trace the divergence back to Aristotle and Archimedes—but they certainly predate the nineteenth century.

I'll leave the discussion of science's influence on Europe's economic divergence to others, but its influence on the Great Military Divergence seems clear.[26] The discoveries of scientists like Benjamin Robins and Leonhard Euler, based in turn on seventeenth-century models, most notably Newtonian physics and Boyle's gas laws, facilitated the development of the carronades and howitzers that proved so lethal in the Opium War. Those discoveries also allowed British gunners to calculate trajectories with equations that modeled wind resistance and the expansion of gasses in the gunpowder reaction itself. They could time the explosion of their shells with uncanny—and lethal—precision. Qing gunners lacked these tools. Britain's military advantage was due in part to Europe's tradition of experimental science.

One might of course suggest that the triumph of science in Europe was itself contingent, as Jack Goldstone has argued: it might have been stamped out or at least held back by religious and political orthodoxies, and luck played a role.[27] This is a compelling argument, but by the end of the seventeenth century, experimental science was firmly established in Europe, increasingly supported by formal institutions such as the scientific societies that were founded in the mid-seventeenth century. Goldstone is perhaps correct to suggest that only in England did there exist the conditions that linked science to industrialization, but I believe one can speak of the "autonomy of science" just as scholars speak of the "autonomy of politics."[28] Science, especially once institutionalized, follows its own path. In the case of military innovation, it played an unpredictable and increasingly central role. Robins's discovery about the enormous effect of air resistance on projectiles was stunning precisely because it couldn't have been foreseen. It surprised Robins himself.

East Asian reformers understood that military advances were based on science and on the mathematics that underlay it. As Shen Baozhen, the director of the Fuzhou Shipyard, wrote in 1870, "The quality of steamships and guns is founded in mathematics, . . . the result of a capacity for computation that reaches smaller and smaller decimals; if the calculation is finer by the slightest degree, the performance of the machinery will be ten times more adroit."[29] The schools and study abroad programs that he and his colleagues developed were designed to enable students to master Western science and "peep into [its] subtle secrets."[30]

Thanks to such programs, both China and Japan were perhaps the most effective modernizers of Asia in the nineteenth century. To be sure, by the end of the nineteenth century, Japan proved more successful, although this is probably because it was more fortunate in the timing of the collapse of its *ancien régime.* But the message that science and engineering underlie a country's influence and power still resonates powerfully in East Asia, which is one reason that China and other East Asian states are increasing their research and development budgets faster than Western nations.[31] They are competing not just with the West, but also with each other.

So the "challenge-response" dynamic continues to operate today. We may not be in a new warring states period, but there's no doubt that China's current leaders are determined to make their country competitive, and they have the support of most citizens. "Never forget national humiliation" (勿忘國恥) is the rallying cry, inscribed on monuments, intoned at rallies, taught in classrooms.[32] Although Chinese leaders insist that China's will be a "peaceful rise" (和平崛起), the Chinese lion is watchful, and it's possible that China's leaders will try to acquire the kind of hegemony that the Ming and Qing states each fought to achieve.

Some scholars of international relations believe this to be highly probable. International relations are anarchic, they say, and rising superpowers inevitably use their new power against old superpowers.[33] Certainly, China's leaders feel that China is unfairly constrained by other countries, particularly the United States. Taiwan, for example, a close ally of the United States, has been described as a huge "unsinkable aircraft carrier" that exposes China's "soft, weak underbelly."[34] "Solving the Taiwan issue," a top Chinese military strategist has written, "will remove the last stumbling block for China's peaceful rise."[35] There are many other potential flashpoints, particularly in maritime areas. Will the People's Republic of China undertake expansive military campaigns like those of the early Ming and Qing dynasties?

The warring states dynamic has operated throughout history, and there's no good reason to expect it to stop, except for one thing: human beings today have an unprecedented and urgent need to work together on global issues. Some analysts—such as Hu Angang (胡鞍鋼)—predict that China will be "a new type of superpower," cooperating with the United States and other states to "cope with global challenges in economics, politics, energy, and the environment."[36] Let's hope so, and let's hope that China finds willing partners. We human beings have gotten extraordinarily good at war. We need to get even better at peace.

Acknowledgments

This book would not have been possible without the support of many people and organizations. The most significant institutional support came from the John Simon Guggenheim Foundation and the Harry Frank Guggenheim Foundation, which provided fellowships invaluable for research and writing. At Emory University, Dean Robin Forman helped arrange and subsidize leave time based on those fellowships, and Emory's Woodruff Library purchased books and databases and borrowed and wheedled rare editions and theses from all over the world. I'd like to thank in particular Alain St. Pierre, Guo-hua Wang, and, perhaps most important, Marie Hansen and her colleagues in the Interlibrary Loan Department.

Other libraries and archives were also generous, providing access to their collections and granting permission to reprint images, especially the National Library of China in Beijing; the Shanxi Library of Taiyuan, Shanxi; the Statens Historiska Museum of Stockholm; the Library of the Georg-August University of Göttingen; the Johann Christian Senckenberg University Library of Frankfurt; the Universitätsbibliothek of Augsburg; the Universitätsbibliothek Leipzig; the Max Planck Institute for the History of Science of Berlin; the Burgerbibliothek of Bern; the Koninklijke Huisarchief of The Hague; the Christ Church Library of Oxford, England; the Harvard-Yenching Library of Cambridge, Massachusetts; and the C.V. Starr East Asian Library of Columbia University, New York.

This work was also deeply inspired by many scholars of China's fascinating military history. It's impossible to name them all, but perhaps the most suitable starting place is Ho Ping-yü (何丙鬱, 1926–2014), who drafted the manuscript that became Joseph Needham's *The Gunpowder Epic* (SCC5 pt. 7), a work of world historical scholarship both deeply foundational and enjoyable. Wang Zhaochun (王兆春) wrote several hugely influential books on gunpowder warfare, which laid the groundwork for this book. Among the other scholars of China who have inspired and informed my research and writing are Zheng Cheng (鄭誠), Zhong Shaoyi (鍾少異), Huang Yi-long (黃一農), Nicola Di Cosmo, Harriet Zurndorfer, Sally Paine, Peter Perdue, Peter Lorge, Kenneth Swope, and Sun Laichen, the last three of whom also read drafts of this book and gave valuable feedback. In particular I wish to thank Sun Laichen, whose perspective on Ming military history set me off on the path that has led me here—his innovative and deeply sourced work is a paragon of cross-cultural scholarship.

I must also acknowledge the work of scholars of European medieval military history, especially Kelly DeVries, Kay (formerly Roger) Smith, Bert Hall, Stephen Morillo, and Clifford Rogers, whose brilliant research, based in turn on stunningly comprehensive work of nineteenth-century scholars such as Henry Brackenbury, has established that many of the key transformations in Europe's military history, the ones that set Western Europe off on a separate path, occurred not during the early modern period (1500–1750), as most historians have suggested, but during the late medieval period, particularly in the 1400s. I believe that placing their work on Europe in juxtaposition with data from China strongly corroborates their perspective. Many of their arguments in turn would not have been possible without the seminal work of Geoffrey Parker, with whom they may sometimes disagree but whose model of the military revolution has remained an essential touchstone. Parker has in a real way helped bring about this book, not just because he has been such a wonderful mentor to me but also because his writings have proven so effective at stimulating debate and framing research questions.

A number of Emory students have helped in the research that underlies this difficult project, and it has been a joy to work with them. In particular, I wish to thank Dan Zhao, Hewei Shen, Alice Qiu, Xiaotian Qi, Jing Zhu, Christina Welsch, and, especially Kirsten Cooper and Hyeok Hweon Kang, whose enthusiasm and research brought insights that became essential.

The editors of the *Chinese Journal of Military History*, *Journal of Early Modern History*, and *Journal of Medieval Military History* accepted portions of three chapters of this book for publication, and their impressive peer-review process greatly strengthened those chapters. They also generously granted permission for those pieces to appear here.

Friends and colleagues also helped, listening patiently as I discoursed about gunpowder. Mark Ravina is a delightful and savvy interlocutor, and the survey course in East Asian history I coteach with him at Emory has been a constant source of intellectual stimulation. Matt Payne reads widely and deeply, and he helped with ideas and translations for the bits about Russia. Phil Hoffman shared his stimulating manuscript *Why Did Europe Conquer the World?* and gave thoughtful and warm comments on a draft of this book. Ari Levine, a good friend who also happens to be a Song specialist, read parts of this manuscript, and provided valuable perspective about the Song period. Tristan Mostert is undertaking fascinating research into military innovation in Southeast Asia, and his comments on a draft of this book were deeply helpful and stimulating. Jared Diamond has inspired me with his thoughtful and stimulating work, and a conversation with him (and subsequent correspondence) helped guide me as I set off on this challenging project. Another early conversation, with an old family friend, Dr. John Hibbs, was also formative. After hearing my initial ideas, he urged me not to neglect the role of science. As is clear, I took his advice to heart. Princeton University Press has also been great to work with. With her alacrity and patience, my editor, Quinn Fusting, kept the process moving smoothly. Jenny Wolkowicki's amazingly thorough production management and proactive style of communication helped us avoid many an error. Dimitri Karetnikov did his magic with the illustrations, even going so far as to redraw tables and charts. David Cox prepared the lovely maps. Carmina Alvarez created the cover. Joseph Dahm carried out the detailed and assiduous copy-editing, catching many mistakes (the remaining inconsistencies in units and measures are my fault alone). Heather Jones generated the index. Last but certainly not least, editor-in-chief Brigitta van Rheinberg saw the promise in this project nearly a decade ago, when I first conceived it. Through the years she stayed supportive, and flexible, even letting me write another book in the interim, and then accepted with enthusiasm a manuscript quite different from the one we'd originally planned. She also helped me gain an editor's perspective on the importance of holding to one overall argument throughout a work. I hope this book justifies the faith she has in me.

I know it's perhaps odd to thank parents in one's third book, but mine continue to inspire me. My father's openness—nay, his enthusiasm—for my decision to abandon science for the humanities has helped me embrace history, just as my mother's interest in and support for language learning has helped me gain the linguistic skills central to the multilanguage work this book has entailed. They are also both avid writers, and we confer about composition and encourage each other to keep at it.

My nuclear family is the center of my life, and at its core is my relationship with my wife, Andrea, whose warmth, brilliance, and sense of humor enliven my days and brighten my nights. I could not have written this book without her. My daughters, Amalia, Sylvia, and Josephine, were also a source of delight and, increasingly, intellectual stimulation. As I wrote I found myself thinking in particular of my middle daughter, Sylvia. This book turned out to be an exercise in mediation, between scholarly perspectives, revisionist and traditionalist, and between discourses about civilizations, Chinese and European. Any attempt at mediation is tricky, and success is not guaranteed. Sylvia, positioned between a demanding four-year-old and a focused eight-year-old, inspired me with her patience and thoughtful attention to both sides—indeed, to all sides. She understands all of us better than any of the rest of us does, and in her quiet, wise way, she keeps the peace. I dedicate this book to her.

The timeline A.1.1. is a guide to the periodization arguments in this book. The terms on the timeline are explained in the main text of the book, with one exception: "neutral divergence." By "neutral divergence," I refer to the period from 1380 to 1480, during which China excelled at firearm use on the battlefield (and Europe didn't) while Western Europe and its neighbors (most notably the Ottoman Empire) excelled at siege artillery (and China didn't). See in particular chapters 4, 5, and 6.

Appendix 1: Timeline

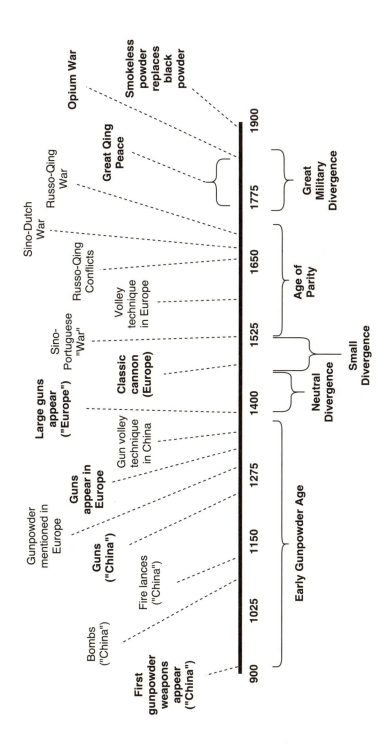

Appendix 2: Datasets

Most of the arguments of this book are based on textual and archaeological evidence—the standard sort of data relied upon by historians—but the book also uses several databases.

The first is a simple tabulation of warfare per year culled from a publication by the People's Liberation Army Press.[1] (See, for example, Graph I.1 and Graph A2.1.)

Tabulating wars is a very difficult business.[2] What counts as a war? Does one treat all wars as equal? If not, how does one gage the intensity of a conflict? Does one use casualty figures? Numbers of troops involved? And how does one compensate for the fact that not all enemies are the same, that wars against weak foes have different effects than wars against strong foes? Most problematic of all is the problem of sources. Certain periods are better documented than others. So are certain regions. And even when sources appear abundant, it's often difficult to gage their reliability or their commensurability with sources from other periods or regions.

The tabulations in this book are intentionally rudimentary. They leave the judgment about what counts as a war to others, merely graphing data presented in the People's Liberation Army Press lists.[3] Other scholars have used these data, or subsets thereof, for their own ends. Some have been interested in proving that the Sinocentric state system was more peaceful and stable than the more evenly balanced system of Europe, others in proving that the Chinese did not have a culture of peace but engaged in frequent wars when expedient, others in showing that China's ancient Warring States Period was similar to Europe's early modern period.[4] Our purpose here is simpler: to use the frequency of warfare as a contextual aid, tying it to the history of military innovation. Where there is more warfare, we find more military innovation.

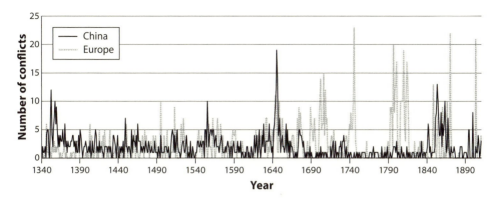

GRAPH A2.1 Warfare by year in Western Europe and China.

The solid line represents China, the dotted line Europe. For more information on this graph, its dataset, and other corroborating datasets, as well as for caveats about their use, see Appendix 2. Data from Zhong guo jun shi shi bian xie zu, *Zhong guo li dai*, vol. 2; and Dupuy, *Encyclopedia of Military History*.

Paired with this tabulation of Chinese warfare is a cruder tabulation of European warfare culled from the influential encyclopedia of military history by Trevor Dupuy.[5] The caveats about what counts as a war, and so on, are even more important for this dataset, which was compiled by me and some students at Emory University, particularly Dan Zhao, Hewei Shen, and Xiaowei Qi. It's impossible to avoid judgments in the selection of these data, and so we must be particularly cautious in using them.

Most important, the Chinese and European warfare frequency data cannot be compared in terms of their magnitudes, at least not with any commensurability. Thus, we can't say with any certainty that Europe saw more wars per year in a given period than did China. Yet they do allow us to compare the patterns of warfare. For example, we can draw inferences about the relative frequency of warfare compared to other periods within each region. We can infer, for example, that Europe's eighteenth century was slightly less warlike than its seventeenth century, whereas China's late eighteenth and early nineteenth century was a period considerably less warlike than its seventeenth century.

These two databases are based on the judgment of the compilers—in the first case the group of researchers who put together the tabulation of Chinese wars for the People's Liberation Army Press and in the second case a small research team at Emory University. So it's important to try to corroborate the results with a second type of database, whose results are less dependent on the judgment of the database creators and thus more objective, or at least more reproducible: word frequency counts of imperial Chinese sources. The most important such database used in this book counts the incidence of terms related to warfare in the two greatest historiographical resources of the Late Imperial Period, the *Veritable Records of the Ming Dynasty* (明實錄) and the *Veritable Records of the Qing Dynasty* (清實錄), which consist of chronicles and correspondence created in the imperial court and edited and compiled (sometimes with considerable alteration) at the death of each emperor.

When we express the incidence of a group of terms as a percentage of total characters per year, we find that the resulting graph rises and falls in rhythm with the tabulation of wars from the People's Liberation Army publication, with significant peaks at dynastic transitions and lower incidences at other points (see Graph A2.2). Of particular interest is the period from the mid-eighteenth century through 1839, which shows a lower frequency, although the effect is not as marked as that in the graphs based on tabulations. To be sure, the correlations are not precise. Nor should one expect them to be, because talking about warfare and actually fighting are quite different activities.

Both types of graph are crude tools. They serve merely as a guide to the interpretation of more detailed historical evidence, and this book is primarily concerned with using the traditional tools of historiography (chronicles, reports, correspondence, memorials, etc.) to shed light on the dynamics glimpsed in such graphs. But what seems clear from these and other such quantitative evidence is that in the early part of the gunpowder age, from gunpowder's emergence around 800 or so until 1450, patterns of warfare in Eastern and Western Eurasia were in many ways quite similar: there was a lot of it on both sides of the supercontinent. Between 1450 and 1550, however, there was a small divergence: warfare in China decreased even as it increased in Western Europe. After 1550, there was a convergence again, which lasted until 1700 or so, and which we refer to as the Age of Parity. In the mid-1700s, a Great Military Divergence opened up, as Chinese warfare fell to its lowest sustained period in history. The consequences of this Great Qing Peace were profound. While

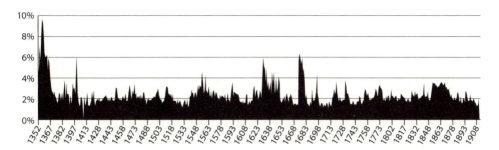

GRAPH A2.2 Terms pertaining to warfare in the *Ming* and *Qing Veritable Records.*
Percentage of total characters per year. The terms are as follows: 起兵, 攻, 亂, 守,
率兵, 兵復, 降, 兵勢, 兵驟, 兵圍, 率師, 獮戮, 滅, 戰, 爭, 逼, 降, 虐, 征, 掠, 寇, 焚, 逼迫, 獲,
捷, 軍需, 搗, 獲,敗, 破, 擊, 陷, 謀反, 增募, 倭, 設伏, 取勝, 民兵, 民壯, 軍餘, 兵眾, 調募, 克
敵, 客兵, 應役, 給軍, 戮梟, 游兵, 守兵, 調兵, 召募, 驍勇, 募兵, 禦敵, 陸戰, 水戰, 異賊,
兵臨, 俘, 調兵選將, 淨絕根株, 肅清, 鎮壓, 剿, 拏, 驅逐, 禍變, 鏟除, 水師, 唬船, 戰船, 軍
機, 營, 器械, 駐, 槍, 炮, 火藥, 扼守, 殲, 撤, 抗拒.

Europeans continued their war-driven military innovation, Qing military innovation slowed considerably, even as its military atrophied.
The relative rates of warfare during this period may thus help explain
one of the great puzzles of world history: when and why China fell
behind the West.

Abbreviations

JS	Tuo Tuo et al., *Jin shi*
LX	Liu Xu, *Zhong guo gu dai huo yao huo qi shi*
MS	Zhang Tingyu et al., *Ming shi*
MSL	*Ming shi lu*
QSL	*Qing shi lu*
SCC	Needham, *Science and Civilisation*
SS	Tuo Tuo et al., *Song shi*
WJZY	Zeng Gongliang, *Wu jing zong yao*
WZC	Wang Zhaochun, *Zhong guo huo qi shi*
WZC2	Wang Zhaochun, *Zhong guo ke xue ji shu shi*
WZC3	Wang Zhaochun, *Shi jie huo qi shi*
YS	Song Lian et al., *Yuan shi*

Notes

Abbreviations are listed on page 317

Introduction

1. The quote has never been traced in direct form to Napoleon. It is probably derived from a conversation Napoleon had with his Irish surgeon, Barry O'Meara, who recorded it in his memoir. See O'Meara, *Napoleon*, 471–72.

2. A Google book search for "China sleeping giant" yields dozens of results from the past decade, many of which go on ominously: China is now "awake and roaring" (Myers and Kent, *New*, 21) or "wide awake . . . and creeping up behind us" (Navarro, *Coming*, 59) or "wide awake . . . and aggressive [and] unrelenting" (Ulsch, *Cyber*, chap. 2).

3. Xi Jinping, Paris, 27 March 2014, cited in Teddy Ng and Andrea Chen, "Xi Jinping Says World Has Nothing to Fear from Awakening of 'Peaceful Lion,'" *South China Morning Post*, 28 March 2014, http://www.scmp.com/news/china/article /1459168/xi-says-world-has-nothing-fear-awakening-peaceful-lion?page = all, accessed 2 December 2014.

4. Among the most important works on the revisionist side are Pomeranz, *Great Divergence*; Wong, *China Transformed*; Rosenthal and Wong, *Before and Beyond*; Frank, *(Re)Orient*; and Marks, *Origins*. On the traditionalist side, see esp. Duchesne, *Uniqueness*; Bryant, "West and the Rest"; Landes, *Wealth*; Landes, "Why Europe"; Ferguson, *Civilization*. But see also Huff, *Intellectual Curiosity*; Justin Yifu Lin, *Demystifying*. See also an important debate in the *Canadian Journal of Sociology*, touched off by the thoughtful but highly critical article Bryant, "West and the Rest": Goldstone, "Capitalist Origins"; Elvin, "Defining"; Bryant, "New Sociology"; Andrade, "Accelerating." The best recent overviews and syntheses of the debates can be found in Ghosh, "Great"; Vries, "Challenges"; and Brandt, Ma, and Rawski, "From Divergence."

5. But see Goldstone, "Capitalist Origins"; Bryant, "New Sociology"; Andrade, "Accelerating"; and Andrade, *Lost Colony*.

6. O'Meara, *Napoleon*, 472.

7. Many scholars have inspired this book, and among the most influential to it are, on the Chinese side, Sun Laichen, Peter Lorge, Kenneth Swope, Kenneth Chase, Nicola Di Cosmo, Peter Perdue, Wang Zhaochun, Zheng Cheng, and Huang Yi-Long. Key studies include Lorge, *Asian*; Sun Laichen, "Ming-Southeast Asian"; Sun Laichen, "Military Technology Transfers"; Swope, "Crouching"; Swope, *Dragon's Head*; Swope,

Military Collapse; Di Cosmo, "Did Guns"; Chase, *Firearms*; Filipiak, *Krieg*; van de Ven, *Warfare*; WZC; WZC2; Huang, "Ming Qing du te"; Huang, "Ming Qing zhi ji"; Huang, "Ou zhou chen chuan"; LX; Li, *Da Ming*; Zheng Cheng, "Fa gong kao"; Shi Kang (Kenneth Swope), "Ming-Qing zhan zheng"; many pieces by Zhong Shaoyi, for example "Zhong guo qing tong"; Li Yue, "Ming dai huo qi"; Feng Zhenyu, "Lun Fo lang ji." On the Western side, the most influential are Geoffrey Parker, Kelly DeVries, Kay (formerly Robert) Smith, Bert S. Hall, and Clifford Rogers.

8. To this end, I apply to military history the "reciprocal comparison" method that the revisionist historians R. Bin Wong and Kenneth Pomeranz have applied so fruitfully to economic history: Pomeranz uses the term "reciprocal comparisons"; Wong uses the term "symmetric perspectives." Pomeranz, *Great Divergence*, 8; Wong, *China Transformed*, 1–7. See the discussion in Cohen, *China Unbound*, 5–6.

9. In his recent book on Chinese education, for instance, Yong Zhao writes that "gunpowder stopped at a level good enough for fireworks, but not for the modern weaponry that gave the West its military might" (Yong Zhao, *Who's Afraid*, 35). For other examples, see Malanima, *Pre-modern*, 64; Smith, *Dragon*, 17. Peter Lorge discusses the myth in "Development and Spread," 819–20. The idea that the Chinese invented gunpowder but didn't use it in warfare is found in a famous and much cited essay by Lu Xun (Lu Xun, "Dian," 15).

10. In Archer et al., *World History of Warfare*, the section on early Ming wars doesn't even discuss guns or gunpowder weapons, despite the fact that by the early Ming period, some 10 percent of soldiers were likely armed with guns, or around a hundred thousand men. Archer et al., *World History*, 194–98. A similar neglect is found in Neiberg, *Warfare*, 38–41. In Dupuy's still-influential *Evolution of Weapons and Warfare*, China is barely mentioned in a section called "The Age of Gunpowder;" Dupuy, *Evolution*, 91–168, see esp. 92–95. Even in works by China specialists this neglect holds, as in the otherwise illuminating work of Robert Marks, which, in looking at military developments in Europe and the perfection of gunpowder weapons, ignores Chinese developments and ignores the Ming. See Marks, *Origins*, 58–59 and 156.

11. See chapter 8.

12. Montesquieu was, to be sure, less concerned about geopolitical competition than about geographic constraints on state power, which he believed allowed law and liberty to flourish in the small states of Europe, whereas the huge Asian despotic states (most notably China) were able to extinguish liberty in the service of state power. See, for example, the famous passage in Montesquieu, *The Spirit of the Laws*, book XVII, pt. 6, Montesquieu, *Spirit*, 269; Weber, *General Economic*. On Marx and Engels's "Asiatic Mode," see McFarlene, Cooper, and Jaksic, "Asiatic," pts. 1 and 2.

13. Diamond, *Guns* (esp. "Epilogue" and "2003 Afterword"); Wallerstein, "Rise"; Landes, *Wealth*; Parker, *Military Revolution*. For other intriguing or influential treatments, see Jones, *European Miracle*; Tilly, *Coercion*; Vries, "Governing Growth"; Turchin et al., "War, Space"; Cosandey, *Secret*; Hoffman, *Why Did*.

14. Mo, "Effective Competition"; Rosenthal and Wong, *Before and Beyond.*

15. See Hartman, "Chinese," esp. 38–40, and Levine, "Review of Yuri Pines."

16. Hui, *War*; Parker, *Military Revolution.*

17. Parker, *Military Revolution*, 2–4. Parker's outstanding and nuanced work has been a key inspiration and scaffolding for this project.

18. Sun Laichen, "Century."

19. Snooks, *Dynamic Society*, 315–24; Mielants, "Europe and China."

20. Parker, *Cambridge*, 5–8.

21. For sources and reasoning, see the beginning of chapter 4.

22. Sun Laichen, "Ming-Southeast Asian," 31. The term "gunpowder empire" is of course drawn from McNeill, "Gunpowder Revolution"; McNeill, *Pursuit*; and Hodgson, *Venture* (particularly vol. 3). Their work is built upon admirably in the wonderful comparative volume, Streusand, *Islamic.* Recently, Stephen Haw has suggested that the "first gunpowder empire" was the Yuan dynasty (1279–1368). Haw, "Mongol." By his logic one might even apply the term to the Jin dynasty (1115–1234).

23. Economic historians have also used the term "little divergence," such as Jan van Zanden, who locates it in late sixteenth- and early seventeenth-century Northern Europe. Van Zanden, *Long Road*, esp. 95–100. Cf. Gorski, "Little Divergence."

24. On other early mentions of volley fire, including Ottoman examples, see chapter 11.

25. See esp. Roy, *Military*; Ágoston, *Guns.*

26. This perspective is indebted to the work of previous scholars, particularly Peter Perdue and Frederic Wakeman, who suggested, in separate publications, that China's military weakness in the nineteenth century was due to the unprecedented military success of China during the seventeenth and eighteenth centuries. Wakeman, *Great Enterprise*, 1125–26; Perdue, *China Marches*, 526–27.

27. On approaches to quantifying warfare, see Thompson, *On Global*, 5–14 and 87–111; Levy, *War*, 50–92; Singer, *Correlates*, vol. 1; Cioffi-Revilla, *Scientific*; and "Bibliographic Essay," Correlates of War Project, www.correlatesofwar.org, retrieved 19 May 2014.

28. For a discussion of the current debate on this topic, see Jacobsen, "Limits," esp. 388–89.

29. Dickens, *Works*, 110–13. Other observers described the junk as fast and seaworthy. See Anonymous, *Description*, esp. 8–9. On Dickens's views about China, see Witchard, *Thomas Burke's*, 46–48.

30. Duchesne, *Uniqueness*, 179. See also Ferguson, *Civilization*, esp. 26–33; Landes, "Why Europe," 11, 14, 15, 21.

31. The least subtle of the traditionalists, David Landes, describes China as "a singularly bad learner," with an "indifference to technology," an "almost instinctive resistance to change," a deep-seated "intellectual xenophobia," and a "near terminal case of cultural superiority." Landes, "Why Europe," 11, 14, 15, 21. Other traditionalists are less provocative but say similar things. Niall Ferguson suggests that

China made a great mistake when it decided to "turn inwards" in the 1430s, leading to isolation and stagnation. Ferguson, *Civilization*, 26–33. Cf. Mielants, "Europe and China." Mielant's argument is sophisticated and compelling: structural issues lay below China's decision, to wit the influence of merchants in the political realm, and he explains the relative power of European merchants vis-à-vis their Chinese counterparts in quite intriguing ways. Ricardo Duchesne suggests that the Chinese "showed little enthusiasm for outside ideas and inventions." Duchesne, *Uniqueness*, 173.

32. Duchesne, "Reply," 386.

33. Kelly, *Gunpowder*, 99.

34. Arnold, *Renaissance*, 25.

35. Neiberg, *Warfare*, 39. According to the *World History of Warfare*, "Confucian teaching stressed the classical ideal of the individual who attained his ends without violence. . . . In this atmosphere, military technology was seen as a low priority." Archer et al., *World History*, 204.

36. See, for example, "What the Collapse of the Ming Dynasty Can Tell us about American Decline," *The Week*, 6 March 2014, http://theweek.com/article/index/257266/what-the-collapse-of-the-ming-dynasty-can-tell-us-about-american-decline, retrieved 9 March 2014; Dyson, "Case."

37. Elvin, *Pattern*; Deng, *Premodern*; SCC7 pt. 2, 209; Rosenthal and Wong, *Before and Beyond*; see also the exceptionally informative extended essay Brandt, Ma, and Rawski, "From Divergence."

38. For the historiography around this issue, see chapter 16 and Conclusions.

39. Huang, "Sun," 258.

40. Huang, "Ming Qing du te," 77.

41. See chapters 13, 14, and 15.

Chapter 1: The Crucible

1. Zhou Mi, "Pao huo" 炮禍, in Zhou Mi, *Gui xin za shi* 癸辛雜識. The "Pao huo" entry is contained in the first juan (前集), available at http://zh.wikisource.org/zh/%E7%99%B8%E8%BE%9B%E9%9B%9C%E8%AD%98, retrieved 26 September 2012.

2. Zhou Mi, "Pao huo."

3. Bacon's reference to gunpowder dates to 1268. SCC5 pt. 7, 50.

4. The *Qi dong ye yu* 齊東野語, cited in SCC5 pt. 7, 134–35. This was actually a "ground rat."

5. Zeng Gongliang 曾公亮, *Wu jing zong yao* 武經總要 (1044). There are many published editions of this work. The one closest to the original is Zeng Gongliang 曾公亮, *Wu jing zong yao qian ji* 武經總要前集 (1506–1521, based on original from 1231, which in turn was based on the 1044 edition). This edition, originally published in the late fifteenth or early sixteenth century, is considered to be the most reliable version still available, since it was made from blocks recarved from tracings of a now-lost 1231 edition. See SCC5 pt. 7, 20. A more accessible version is Zeng

Gongliang 曾公亮, *Wu jing zong yao qian ji* 武經總要前集, *Zhong guo bing shu ji cheng* 中國兵書集成, vol. 3 (Beijing: Jiefangjun Chubanshe, 1988).

6. The term "medieval" is of course a loaded one. Many historians consider the Song "early modern." For an illuminating look into how seriously the Chinese took their history during the "medieval" period, see Chan, "Compilation"; and Hartman, "Chinese."

7. See Neiberg, *Warfare*, 39; Morris, *Measure*, 203; Daly, *Rise*, 276–77; Kristinsson, *Expansions*, 258–59; Petrucci, "Pirates," 63; Delbruck, *Dawn*, 24; Dupuy, *Evolution*, 93; O'Connell, *Soul*, 113–14.

8. The great John King Fairbank once wrote, "It is a striking fact . . . that gunpowder had been created by Chinese alchemists in the ninth century. . . . [But] this great breakthrough in military technology evidently had little significance for the classically trained Song statesmen. Here we find Confucianism slow to mount on the back of technology." Fairbank and Goldman, *China*, 115.

9. Kuhn, *Age*, 276.

10. Deng, *Premodern*, 322. Some estimates of Song urbanization rates reach above 15 percent. See Deng, *Premodern*, 183.

11. See Chandler and Fox, *3000*, 12.

12. Fairbank and Goldman, *China*, 89.

13. Fairbank and Goldman, *China*, 92.

14. Ibn Battuta, *Travels*, 216.

15. Fairbank and Goldman, *China*, 89. On the extent of Song water infrastructure, see Liu, "Song China's."

16. The term "Song Industrial Revolution" is from Kuhn, *Age*, 276. The idea of a Song "economic revolution" or a "medieval economic revolution" recurs throughout the literature on the Song, from Mark Elvin to E. L. Jones, John Fairbank, and Gang Deng. The most foundational works along these lines are Hartwell, "Revolution," and Hartwell, "Cycle."

17. These estimates are rough and controversial. For an analysis, see Wright, "Economic Cycle."

18. Elvin, *Pattern*, 86.

19. Wang Zhen 王禎, *Nong shu* (農書), cited in Elvin, *Pattern*, 195.

20. Jones, *European Miracle*, 202.

21. Sharaf al-Zamān Ṭāhir al-Marwazī, cited in SCC5 pt. 7, 94.

22. Emperor Gaozong (1127–1162), cited in Lo, "Emergence," 499.

23. See SCC7 pt. 2, 217–24.

24. On Song military technology, see Su, *Nan Song*, 82ff.

25. Brace, "Egg," 696.

26. Fairbank and Goldman, *China*, 88

27. The Chinese term *wen* means, in essence, writing. It stands for civilization, culture, diplomacy, language. *Wu* stands for arms, soldiers, warfare.

28. John Haeger quotes scholar Li Chi, who writes that in Song times, "a kind of 'peaceful culture developed to an especially advanced degree, which made the physical strength of the Chinese daily weaker until they were no longer able to face

bows, soldiers, and horses from the north. When you add that since the late T'ang, Chinese women had developed an exaggerated preference for small feet . . . , that the custom of sitting on chairs was even more habitual in Sung, and that after the southern retreat officials did not ride horses to court, but rode sedan chairs, [you see that] these things contributed to the weakening of the Chinese, which was shown clearly on the battlefield." Haeger, "1126," 160.

29. For a great overview of this historiographical transition, see Ari Levine, "Review of Don Wyatt." See also Wyatt, *Battlefronts*; Di Cosmo, "Introduction"; Wang, *Harmony*. Marcia Butler shows how Song thinkers conceived of *wen* and *wu* as complementary principles, like *yin* and *yang*, and how the Song court paid careful attention to military ritual and display. See Butler, "Reflections." For an outstanding treatment of military ritual in the Ming period, see Robinson, *Martial*.

30. Wang, *Harmony*, 74.

31. Wyatt, "Introduction," in Wyatt, *Battlefronts*, 1–11, 1.

32. See Zurndorfer, "Meaning."

33. SS, "Bing zhi," cited in Su, *Nan Song*, 82.

34. SS, juan 197, Bing 11, cited in Su, *Nan Song*, 82.

35. Smith, "Eurasian."

36. Smith, "Introduction," 17.

37. Others have suggested that Song florescence might have been related to geopolitical insecurity. See Deng, *Premodern*, 301–5. Deng believes that other factors are more important than geopolitical pressures, pointing out that China had faced such pressures before and never experienced a comparable period of florescence. He also admits, however, that the frequency of conflict between the Song and its neighbors was higher than for any other dynasty in Chinese history.

38. Hartman, "Chinese," 37.

39. On Chinese economic influences on the Xi Xia, see Lu Yidong 鲁亦冬, *Zhongguo Song Liao*, 211–12.

40. Liu and Mao, *Zhongguo Song Liao Jin Xia*, 192.

41. Liu and Mao, *Zhongguo Song Liao Jin Xia*, 182–85; Galambos, "Consistency."

42. Liu and Mao, *Zhongguo Song Liao Jin Xia*, 181. Elsewhere they write, "The tremendous flourishing of military study during the Song-Liao-Jin-Xi Xia period, this mutual blending and mutual stimulation, was the reason the Song period was the second high water mark of military science in Chinese history." Liu and Mao, *Zhongguo Song Liao Jin Xia*, 194.

43. Some members of the Xi Xia ruling elite established successor states. See Mote, *Imperial*, 256–57.

44. Victoria Tin-Bor Hui, for example, dates the "onset of system formation" to 656 BCE. See Hui, *War*, 51, 54–59.

45. Ebrey, *Cambridge*, 87.

46. Ebrey, *Cambridge*, 86.

47. On the ways that this period of interstate competition laid the ground for the Song, see Smith, "Introduction."

48. P.H.H. Vries observantly writes, "China under the Song resembled Europe far more than under Ming or Qing." Vries, "Governing Growth," 90.

49. Su, *Nan Song*.

50. Su, *Nan Song*, 92.

51. Su, *Nan Song*, 90.

52. See Parker, "Western Way of War," in Parker, *Cambridge*, 1–14.

Chapter 2: Early Gunpowder Warfare

1. SCC5 pt. 7, 15.

2. SCC5 pt. 7, 115.

3. SCC5 pt. 7, 113.

4. As for earlier formulas, it seems that the first recorded recipe came in 804, in Qing Xuzi 清虛子, *Qian gong jia geng zhi bao ji cheng* 鉛汞甲庚至寶集成. See Lorge, *Asian*, 32.

5. See SCC5 pt. 7, 117–26.

6. LX, 21.

7. LX, 21.

8. 發機飛火，燒龍沙; Cited in Su, *Nan Song*, 89.

9. Xu Dong 許洞, *Hu Qianjing* 虎鈐徑 (ca. 1004), juan 6, 火利第五三, cited in LX, 13. The interpretation of the 904 source is controversial. See Su, *Nan Song*, 89. Liu Xu believes firmly that the "flying fire" does indeed refer to gunpowder arrows, and his reasoning can be found on 13–14. I find it convincing.

10. Sawyer, *Fire*, 3–237.

11. WZC, 13.

12. WZC, 13–14.

13. WZC, 14.

14. Although completed around 1044, the *Wu jing zong yao* remained, it seems, in manuscript form until 1231, when it was published in a woodblock edition, presumably by order of the Southern Song court. See SCC5 pt. 7, 19–21.

15. SS, juan 197 (Bing Section, no. 11, "Qi jia zhi shi"), cited in WZC3, 22.

16. *Song hui yao* 宋會要, "Zhi guan No. 37" 職務官三十之七, cited in WZC, 13.

17. WZC, 13.

18. WZC, 20–21. See also Su, *Nan Song*, 89.

19. SS, juan 186 [zhi 139], cited in Haw, " Mongol," 8.

20. As Frederick Mote wrote, "The abrupt rise and triumph of the Jurchen state [the Jin Empire] was one of the most unexpected and explosively upsetting events in all of East Asian History." Mote, *Imperial*, 211.

21. Mote, *Imperial*, 195.

22. For nuanced analyses of the Jin and Song alliance and subsequent events, see Thiele, *Abschluss*; Tao, *Two*; Levine, "Reigns."

23. A group of Liao partisans fled and formed a new state far to the west, the Western Liao (西遼, 1125–1218).

24. Aguda had died in 1123.

25. See Ari Levine's superb discussion in Levine, "Walls."

26. Li Gang 李綱, *Jing kang chuan xin lu* 靖康傳信錄, cited in SCC5 pt. 7, 165. Cf. WZC, 21. A weapon called the thunderbolt bomb appeared in WJZY in 1044, nearly a century before the Jin Siege of Bianliang, but it was likely a less powerful weapon: the gunpowder was merely a conflagrative encasing airtight bamboo, and the detonation was caused by the expanding air heated by the gunpowder. In 1044, gunpowder seems not to have been capable of explosions, but in the mid-1100s, it had become so. See Turnbull, *Siege*, 7–8. Cf. SCC5 pt. 7, 165–66.

27. See Franke, "Chin," 228–29.

28. WZC, 21.

29. The most detailed account of the siege in a Western language is Werner, *Belagerung*.

30. WZC, 22.

31. WZC, 21.

32. Li Dao 李燾 and Huang Yizhou 黃以週, *Xu Zi zhi tong jian chang bian shi bu* 續資治通鑑長編拾補, juan 58, cited in WZC, 22.

33. SCC5 pt. 7, 154.

34. SCC5 pt. 7, 223–25.

35. For refutations of Needham's 950 date, see Yang Hong, "Xiang mo"; Li Yue, "Ming dai huo qi," 40; and Cheng Dong, "Zhong guo gu dai huo pao." Some Chinese authors do accept Needham's argument about the 950 appearance of the fire lance. See Dang Shoushan, *Wu wei*, 107–8. On the early mentions of fire lances in Chinese sources, see LX, 27; cf. Haw, "Mongol," 3.

36. Tang Shou 湯璹, "De'an shou yu lu" 德安守禦錄, traditionally included within Chen and Tang, *Shou cheng*, as juans 3 and 4. See Balazs and Hervouet, *Sung Bibliography*, 237.

37. Tang, "De'an shou," juan 4.

38. Experts in Song fortifications translate the term *zhan peng* (戰棚) as "gate house," "gate tower," or "barbican tower," but I employ the more neutral term "defensive structure." See Huang, "Defensive Structures," 51.

39. Tang, "De'an shou," juan 4.

40. Tang, "De'an shou," juan 4.

41. Tang, "De'an shou," juan 4.

42. Tang, "De'an shou," juan 4.

43. Lorge, *Asian*, 36.

44. "Biography of Chen Gui," in SS, juan 377, lie zhuan 136.

45. Tang, "De'an shou," juan 4.

46. WZC, 28.

47. Fa, "Effects"; Turnbull, *Hussite*, esp. 23–24; Joregensen, Niderost, and McNab, *Fighting*, 108–10.

48. On the Chinese successors to the fire lance carts, see Zhou Weiqiang, "Ming dai."

49. "Biography of Li Bao" 李寶傳, in SS, juan 370, Lie zhuan 129.

50. Noted in WZC, 27–28.

51. "Biography of Li Bao" 李寶傳, in SS, juan 370, Lie zhuan 129.

52. On paddle wheel ships, see SCC4 pt. 2, 418–26. See also SCC4 pt. 3, 476.

53. SCC5 pt. 7, 165–66.

54. See Haw, "Mongol," 8.

55. Zhao, *Xiangyang*. A good English translation is Avery, "Record"; German translation Franke, *Studien*. I do not discuss here another simultaneous siege at which gunpowder weapons figured prominently: the Siege of De'an, 1206–7. The best work in a Western language on that siege is Hana, *Bericht*.

56. Avery suggests that huo jian (火箭) and huo pao (火炮) refer not to gunpowder arrows and bombs, respectively, but to more traditional incendiaries, since there are other points in the text where the author refers specifically to gunpowder arrows (火藥箭). Avery, "Record," "Glossary."

57. Zhao, *Xiangyang*. Avery's translation, Avery, "Record," 66–67.

58. WZC, 28.

59. Zhao, *Xiangyang*. Avery's translation (with slight changes), Avery, "Record," 77.

60. Zhao, *Xiangyang*.

61. WZC, 28–29.

62. Yuan Haowen 元好問, Xu yi jian zhi 續夷堅志 (thirteenth century), juan 1, cited in WZC3, 34.

63. For more on the name and the relationship of Zhao Yurong to the Song dynasty imperial line, see Qi, "Zhao."

64. Zhao, *Xin si*, 22.

65. Zhao, *Xin si*, 20.

66. Zhao, *Xin si*, 23.

67. Cited in Qi, "Zhao"

68. The commander's name was Pusan'anzhen 僕散安貞. Like most famous last words, this utterance is likely apocryphal.

Chapter 3: The Mongol Wars and the Evolution of the Gun, 1211–1279

1. Kate Raphael, for example, sifted through an array of Arabic, Persian, and Chinese sources and concluded that "gunpowder did not arrive in the Middle East with [the Mongol] army." Raphael, "Mongol," 362. Timothy May reaches the same conclusion, admitting that the Mongols may have used gunpowder in China but arguing that there is no evidence that they did so outside of East Asia. May, *Mongol*, 152. On the other side of the debate is historian Stephen Haw, who argues not only that the Mongol Empire used gunpowder weapons but that it even deserves the moniker "the first gunpowder empire." His analysis is compelling, and, indeed, before his article was published I had independently sorted through many of the same sources (he found some I had not) and come to similar conclusions. I discuss the evidence below. See Haw, "Mongol."

2. See, for example, May, *Mongol*, 149.

3. Raphael, "Mongol," 362; May, *Mongol*, 152ff.

4. On the paucity of Mongol records, see LX, 47 and Mote, *Imperial*, 534.

5. One of the best accounts of the fall of the Jin in English is Franke, "Chin," esp. 259–65.

6. LX, 47.

7. Liu Qi, *Gui qian*, juan 11 ("Lu da liang shi" 錄大梁事). Cf. the German translation, in Haenisch, *Zum Untergang*, 7–26.

8. Liu Qi, *Gui qian*, juan 11 ("Lu da liang shi" 錄大梁事).

9. JS, juan 113 ("Lie zhuan No. 51"). Cf. Needham's translation, in SCC5 pt. 7, 171.

10. He, *Xu dong*, juan 5. Part of this is cited in WZC, 31.

11. He, *Xu dong*.

12. WZC, 30.

13. JS, juan 113 ("Lie zhuan No. 51").

14. JS, juan 116 ("Lie zhuan No. 54") (biography of Pucha Guannu 蒲察官奴傳).

15. JS, cited in SCC5 pt. 7, 225.

16. JS, cited in SCC5 pt. 7, 225.

17. JS, juan 116 ("Lie zhuan No. 54") (biography of Pucha Guannu). See also WZC, 32.

18. On this melting bomb-making episode, see SCC5 pt. 7, 173.

19. Goodrich, *Short History*, 173. Cf. Mote, *Imperial*, 460.

20. Feng and Chen, *Song shi ji shi*, juan 93.

21. Fang, "Military," 54.

22. Chen, *Song-Yuan*, 100.

23. Some scholars believe that the elipao may not have been a gunpowder bomb. See Yang and Wang, *Nan Song*, 139.

24. Chen, *Song-Yuan*, 100–101. Another siege around the same time similarly provides evidence of the Mongols' use of gunpowder bombs. See Chen, *Song-Yuan*, 98–99.

25. "When I was in Jingzhou," he wrote, "they were making one or two thousand [iron bombshells] each month, and they would dispatch ten or twenty thousand of them at a time to Xiangyang and Yingzhou." Li, *Ke zhai*, cited in SCC5 pt. 7, 174. I have altered the translation slightly and updated the transliterations to Pinyin. See also WZC, 34.

26. Li, *Ke zhai*, cited in SCC5 pt. 7, 174. See also WZC, 34.

27. The identification of these hundred vessels as paddle wheel boats is based on Needham, although it seems possible not all of them had paddle wheels. SCC4 pt. 2, 423–24.

28. SS, biography of Zhang Shun (張順), juan 450, Lie zhuan 209.

29. SS, biography of Zhang Shun (張順), juan 450, Lie zhuan 209.

30. Cited in SCC5 pt. 7, 174.

31. WZC, 35.

32. On the other hand, I think Needham is wrong to add into his translation of the *Song Shi* passage that on the Zhangs' boats were "trebuchets and bombs." SCC5 pt. 7, 175.

33. Haw, "Mongol," 11. The passage in question does not necessarily imply that the boats had catapults, but it also doesn't say anything about guns.

34. SS, biography of Zhang Shun (張順), juan 450, lie zhuan 209.

35. Cited in SCC5 pt. 7, 174.

36. SS, biography of Zhang Shun (張順), juan 450, lie zhuan 209.

37. SS, biography of Zhang Shun (張順), juan 450, lie zhuan 209.

38. Chen, *Song-Yuan*, 214.

39. See SCC5 pt. 7, 574.

40. Cited in Rossabi, "Reign," 433.

41. SCC5 pt. 6, 221.

42. Mote, *Imperial*, 463.

43. Shayang 沙陽 was located in present-day Hubei Province.

44. YS, juan 127, Lie zhuan 14, biography of Bayan 伯顏.

45. "Li Yanxian shou xia" 李彥仙守陝, in Hong Mai 洪邁, *Rong zhai wu bi* 容齋五筆, juan 6. See LX, 44.

46. Mote, *Imperial*, 464.

47. Cited in Wright, "Mongol," 111.

48. YS, juan 127, lie zhuan 14, biography of Bayan.

49. Wright, "Mongol," 112.

50. SS, biography of Ma Ji 馬曁傳, cited in WZC, 35.

51. In modern gunnery, the term "windage" refers to the side-to-side adjustment of a sight for aiming purposes. For premodern guns, "windage" refers to the amount of space between a projectile and a barrel. See Watson, *Eight Lectures*, 62–65.

52. SCC5 pt. 7, 9.

53. On early precursors to the *Huo long jing* and speculation about the layers of texts within it, see SCC5 pt. 7, 24–33. There are significant doubts about its dating and provenance, which I discuss at greater length in chapter 4.

54. SCC5 pt. 7, 233.

55. SCC5 pt. 7, 235.

56. SCC5 pt. 7, 238.

57. On the paucity of Mongol records, see LX, 47.

58. WZC, 23–24.

59. SS, cited in WZC, 33.

60. This is a position that Feng Jiasheng 馮家昇 took in the 1950s. See Feng, *Huo yao*, 25. Wang Zhaochun agrees (WZC, 33).

61. LX, 53.

62. Zhong et al., "Nei," 65–67.

63. Zhong et al., "Nei," 65–67.

64. Another gun may have an earlier inscription, which reads, roughly translated, "Made by bronzesmith Li Liujing in the year Zhiyuan 8 (直元), ningzi

number 2565." An expert suggests that Zhiyuan (直元) should actually be zhi-yuan (至元), which would put the date in the Western calendar at 1271 CE. Like the Xanadu Gun, it has a serial number (2565), which suggests that thousands of similar pieces were manufactured. There is reason for caution about the dating, because the reign name used is not a standard form, but the timing is not improbable. See "Ningxia fa xian shi jie zui zao you ming que ji nian de jin shu guan xing huo chong" 寧夏發現世界最早有明確紀年的金屬管形火銃, *Xinhua News Net*, 9 June 2004, http://www.nx.xinhuanet.com/newscenter/2004-06/09/content_2278435. htm, retrieved 20 September 2012.

65. Needham says the gun can be dated to 1288. Lu Xu says it is from around 1290. Wang Chong says between 1287 and 1289. SCC5 pt. 7, 289, 290. LX, 50–51. Wang, "A cheng," 33–34.

66. That's the argument of Wang, "A cheng." On Nayan's rebellion, see Biran, *Qaidu*, 45–46.

67. Needham says thirty-five centimeters long. Lu Xu says thirty-four. SCC5 pt. 7, 289, 290. Cf. LX, 50–51. See also Wang, "A cheng."

68. The best archaeological overview is Dang Shoushan, *Wu wei*, 103–13. See also Niu and Niu, "Xi Xia," esp. 51–52; and Liu Xiaolei 劉小雷, "Wuwei tong huo pao: shi jie shang zui gu lao de jin shu guan xing huo qi" 武威銅火炮：世界上最古老的金屬管形火器, *Gansu Daily* 每日甘肅, 17 February 2012, http://gansu.gansudaily .com.cn/system/2012/02/17/012373433.shtml, retrieved 21 September 2012.

69. Dang Shoushan, *Wu wei*, 109–11.

70. The ball is also, however, highly corroded, suggesting that it used to be larger. Thanks to Ben Sinvany for this perspective and for alerting me to an error in the manuscript of this book. See Dang Shoushan, *Wu wei*, color plates (圖板戊二 鐵彈丸).

71. Niu and Niu, "Xi Xia," 52. There is ambiguity about when the weapon was discovered, which may cast doubt on the contextual data used to date it.

72. Dang Shoushan, *Wu wei*, 106–7; Niu and Niu, "Xi Xia," 52.

73. Chen Bingying argues that there were no guns before 1259. Chen Bingying, "Gan su chu tu." Stephen Haw believes that guns were developed by 1200. Haw, "Mongol." Dang Shoushan believes that the Xi Xia guns indicate an origin for guns by 1220 or so. Dang Shoushan, *Wu wei*, 109

74. Sun Laichen, "Military," 516. Cf. WZC5, 103 and 122. But see Haw, "Mongol."

Chapter 4: Great Martiality

1. See, for example, Li, *Da Ming*; WZC3, 103ff.; Li Yue, "Ming dai huo qi," 5ff. and 92; WZC5, 85–122.

2. MSL, *Tai zu shi lu*, juan 129, Hongwu 13, cited in WZC, 103.

3. Wang Zhaochun estimates that the total number of soldiers in that period (Hongwu 1380 to 1393) was around 1,800,000, meaning there would have been 180,000 gun units or more. Other evidence from the *Ming Veritable Records* suggests

that toward the end of the year Hongwu 25 the Ming military had 1,215,000 men, which means that "those equipped with firearms would have numbered more than 125,000." WZC, 103; see also WZC3, 103ff. According to Liew Foon Ming, "during the early Ming period Zhu Yuanzhang had a total of 1,304,923 military men." Liew, *Treatises*, 74.

4. For example, scholars have estimated that during the Ming dynasty's massive Luchuan-Pingmian Campaigns (麓川平緬戰爭), from 1436 to 1449, which involved as many as 150,000 Ming soldiers, some 20 percent of soldiers were armed with guns. WZC3, 114.

5. WZC, 106.

6. *Da Ming hui dian*, juan 1936, Gong bu 13, "Huo qi." Cf. WZC, 75–76.

7. *Da Ming hui dian*, juan 1936, Gong bu 13, "Huo qi."

8. WZC, 88.

9. Jiao Yu 焦玉, *Huo long jing* 火龍經 (date unknown). See *Huo long shen qi zhen fa* 火龍神器陣法, in Liu Lumin, *Zhong guo*. On the controversy, see below and also Li, "*Huo long*"; WZC, 63–66; Xu, *Zhong guo bing shu*, chap. 10, sec. 2; SCC5 pt. 7, 24–27; and Ho and Ling, "Karyukyo."

10. Cited in SCC5 pt. 7, 30–31.

11. Cited in SCC5 pt. 7, 31.

12. Cited in SCC5 pt. 7, 31.

13. See, for instance, Li, "*Huo long*"; and WZC, 63–66. Cf. Xu, *Zhong guo bing shu*, chap. 10, sec. 2. On the *Huo long jing* as a product of the early Ming, see SCC5 pt. 7, 24–27; and Ho and Ling, "Karyukyo."

14. The best English-language account is Dreyer, "Poyang."

15. As Wang Zhaochun writes, "Zhu and Chen, in this Poyang Lake Decisive Battle, were the first in Chinese history to use guns [*huo chong*] (namely the earliest naval cannons) to engage in water-based warfare." WZC, 57.

16. Nanchang (南昌) is the capital of Jiangxi Province.

17. MSL, *Tai zu shi lu*, juan 12, guimao year, fourth month (p. 153). Rong, *Ming shi*, juan 3, contains an identical passage. Late Ming scholar Qian Qianyi includes the passage from the *Veritable Records* in his "Han Chen," 98.

18. On this drama, see http://en.wikipedia.org/wiki/Founding_Emperor_of_Ming_Dynasty, retrieved 12 October 2012.

19. See Cui, "Nei." The Ming were certainly capable of making huge guns. But, as we'll see, they tended not to do so, and below we will explore some reasons why.

20. The inscription notes that it was produced for the Left Guard Advance of the Naval Forces and also that it was the forty-second exemplar of this type of gun produced for this unit (水軍左衛進字四十二號). WZC, 73.

21. WZC, 73.

22. WZC, 86.

23. This list is from Qian, "Han Chen," 103. I differ from Dreyer translations of some weapons. See Dreyer, "Poyang," citation on 358n36. The Qian Qianyi work from which this passage is excerpted was produced nearly two centuries after the

battle, but the author sourced his information carefully, and I follow other historians in treating it as trustworthy. See, for example, WZC, 57.

24. Qian, "Han Chen," 103.

25. Rong, *Ming shi*, juan 3.

26. Rong, *Ming shi*, juan 3. MSL, *Tai zu shi lu*, juan 12, is quite similar.

27. Rong, *Ming shi*, juan 3.

28. WZC, 57. See also WZC3; cf. LX, 58.

29. MSL, *Tai zu shi lu*, juan 12, 1363 [guimao 癸卯], fall, seventh month (秋七月),
Chenzi Day (戊子) [August 30] (p. 158). Identical passage in Rong, *Ming shi*, juan 3.

30. MSL, *Tai zu shi lu*, juan 12, 1363, [guimao 癸卯], fall, seventh month (秋七月),
Chenzi Day (戊子) [August 30] (p. 158).

31. LX, 99.

32. Dreyer, "Poyang, 358n38.

33. For a good summary, with descriptions drawn from the *Huo long jing* and the
later *Wu bei zhi*, see LX, 89–132. See also 60 for a useful tabulation of the numbers
of gunpowder weapons discussed in major Ming military manuals.

34. Cited in Dreyer, "Poyang," 225.

35. Gu, *Ming shi ji shi*, juan 3. (Although published in 1658 the book is based on
older sources.)

36. MSL, *Tai zu shi lu*, juan 12, 1363 [guimao 癸卯], fall, seventh month (秋七月),
Jichou day (己丑) [August 31] (p. 159).

37. MSL, *Tai zu shi lu*, juan 12, 1363 [guimao 癸卯], fall, seventh month (秋七月),
Jichou day (己丑) [August 31] (p. 159).

38. Dreyer, "Military Origins," 93.

39. Lorge, *Asian*, 74. Cf. Lorge, *War*, 105.

40. Lorge, *Asian*, 74; elsewhere Lorge writes that "Suzhou was not a notably
strong city" (Lorge, *War*, 105). But sources, like Yu Ben's account, suggest Suzhou
was stoutly defended.

41. Yu Ben 俞本, *Ji shi lu* 記事錄, in Qian, "Zhou Zhang."

42. Figures, converted from Chinese units, are in Xu, *Chinese City*, 114. Cf. Mote,
"Millennium," 53.

43. Xu, *Chinese City*, 113. Rubble was also included at least in some parts of the walls.

44. Xu, *Chinese City*, 113.

45. Lorge, *Asian*, 74.

46. Yu Ben, *Ji shi lu*.

47. MSL, *Tai zong shi lu*, juan 21, bingwu year, eleventh month (p. 309).

48. MSL, *Tai zong shi lu*, juan 21, bingwu year, eleventh month (p. 309).

49. The Official *Ming History* uses "fire tube" (火筒). MS, juan 125, lie zhuan no
13, "Xu Da" 徐達: "[On the towers] were placed bows and crossbows and fire-tubes.
On the towers they also placed huge catapults, and everything they struck was burst
into pieces. Within the town there was fear and shock."

50. Yu Ben, *Ji shi lu*.

51. Li Yue, "Ming dai huo qi," 31–32.

52. See WZC, 73–97; and LX, 106–7. Some historians—including Needham—have suggested that a collection of old cannons known as the Zhou cannons, and which weighed between a hundred and five hundred pounds (forty-five to two hundred and twenty-five kilograms), were forged by Zhang Shicheng in the 1350s or 1360s. These pieces certainly are inscribed with the dynastic term Zhou (週), which Shicheng used, but recent work establishes that those guns were from the short-lived Zhou dynasty of Wu Sangui (吳三桂, 1612–1678) in the 1670s. SCC5 pt. 7, 290–92. Discussion of controversy in WZC, 58–63.

53. Cheng Dong, "Ming dai qian qi," 74. Cheng Dong argues compellingly that the outcroppings were handles and not trunnions. For pictures, see Cheng and Zhong, *Zhong guo*, 238 (figures 11–34) and (cai ban 彩版 30).

54. Wang Zhaochun, "Hong wu," 183.

55. Cheng Dong, "Ming dai qian qi," 74; Wang Zhaochun, *Zhong guo gu dai bing qi*, 170–71. See also Wang Fuzhun, "Gu dai da tie pao," 48.

56. Xu Mianzhi 徐勉之, *Bao yue lu* 保越錄 (1359). There is an excellent German translation. Herbert Franke, "Belagerung," 122–214.

57. Xu Mianzhi, *Bao yue lu*, cited in WZC, 56.

58. Xu Mianzhi, *Bao yue lu*.

59. Xu Mianzhi, *Bao yue lu*. Cf. Franke, "Belagerung," 176. Franke comes to a slightly different interpretation, because he is using a different version of the text.

60. Franke, "Belagerung," 213. Cf. Franke, "Siege," 191.

61. MSL, *Tai zu shi lu*, juan 24, 1367 (Wu Year 1), sixth month (p. 344).

62. Yang Weizhen 楊維楨 (1296–1370), "Tong jiang jun" 銅將軍, written ca. 1367 and excerpted in Qian, "Zhou Zhang." Qian comments that the poem was meant to mock Zhang Shixin, "who was attacked in 1367 [dingwei year] by a long-jing gun and was killed." Note that the line I translate as "a thousand metal bodies" in the original refers to "gilded Buddhas," a metaphor for the combatants' metal armor.

63. Qian, "Zhou." WZC, 56. Cf. LX, 56; WZC3, 74.

64. Yu Ben, *Ji shi lu*.

65. Wu Kuan 吳寬, *Huang chao ping Wu lu* 皇朝平吳錄. This text is also known in a slightly different version attributed to Wu Kuan, *Ping wu lu* 平吳錄, http://www .guoxue123.com/other/gcdg/gcdg/010.htm, retrieved 15 November 2012.

66. Biography of Zhang Shicheng, MS, juan 123, lie zhuan no. 11.

67. Qian, "Zhou Zhang."

68. Yu Ben, *Ji shi lu*.

69. There is a description of them in the WJZY, juan 12, and Needham discusses them briefly in SCC5 pt. 6, 212–13.

70. MS, juan 125, lie zhuan no 13, "Xu Da" 徐達.

71. Yu Ben, *Ji shi lu*.

72. MSL, *Tai zu shi lu*, juan 21, bingwu year, eleventh month (p. 309).

73. Gu, *Ming shi ji shi*, juan 4, "Tai zu ping wu" 太祖平吳. Other sources use slightly different language, saying that the defenders built a "flying catapult" (飛礮). MSL, *Tai zu shi lu*, juan 25, Wu 1, month 9, Xinsi day (p. 363).

74. Gu, *Ming shi ji shi*, Juan 4, "Tai zu ping wu" 太祖平吳.

75. Xu, Chinese City, 115–22.

76. Yang, "Tai fu."

77. Gu, *Ming shi ji shi*, juan 4, "Tai zu ping wu" 太祖平吳. The description in the *Ming Veritable Records* is almost identical. MSL, *Tai zu shi lu*, juan 25, Year of Wu 1, month 9, Xinsi day (p. 363).

78. Yang Weizhen 楊維楨 (1296–1370), "Tong jiang jun" 銅將軍, written ca. 1367 and excerpted in Qian, "Zhou Zhang."

79. See WZC, 73–97; and LX, 106–7; SCC5 pt. 7, 290–92.

80. Although these pieces do indeed carry inscriptions bearing the dynastic term Zhou, which Shicheng did use, it seems clear that the guns were actually from the short-lived Zhou dynasty of the seventeenth-century warlord Wu Sangui. See Wang Fuzhun, "Gu dai da tie pao," 48 and WZC, 58–63. On the size of extant guns from Zhang Shicheng's rule, see Lu Wenbao, "Xin fa xian."

81. McNeill, "Gunpowder Revolution," 8.

Chapter 5: The Medieval Gun

1. There are still a few dissident views. Some scholars, for example, have recently written that guns were invented independently in Europe and China. See Morillo, Black, and Lococo, *War*, 237, 259, and 286; and Khan, *Gunpowder*, 3 and 41. Other scholars have argued that guns were first used in the Islamic world, drawing their support from a passage by Ibn Khaldun on the Marinid Siege of Sijilmassa in 1274: "[The Sultan] installed siege engines . . . and gunpowder engines . . . , which project small balls of iron. These balls are ejected from a chamber . . . placed in front of a kindling fire of gunpowder; this happens by a strange property which attributes all actions to the power of the Creator." Ibn Khaldun, cited in al-Hassan and Hill, *Islamic Technology*, 112–13. Scholars have dismissed this interpretation of Ibn Khaldun's passage as anachronistic. See Cook, *Hundred*, 63.

2. Cook, *Hundred*, 65; and McJoynt, "Appreciation," 243. Cf. DeVries, "Gunpowder Weapons," 352.

3. Allsen, "Circulation," 275.

4. Although, as Kelly DeVries notes, compilers of early recipes for gunpowder in Europe noted that if an instrument could be enclosed on one end, the reaction of gunpowder inside would produce "flying fire." See DeVries, "Sites," 308.

5. SCC5 pt. 7, 568.

6. See the brilliant charts prepared by Joseph Needham and his team in SCC5 pt. 7, 346–47.

7. Contamine, *War*, 139.

8. Hall, *Weapons*, 42.

9. There is a record of a very early gun, dated 1322, that was discovered in the nineteenth century but subsequently lost. See Angelucci, *Documenti*, 75; and Gohlke, *Geschichte*, 11.

10. Preserved at Christ Church College, Oxford, MS 92, fol. 70v. On the dating of the manuscript, see Blair, "Milemete," 7; and DeVries, "Reassessment." On early depictions of guns, see Serdon-Provost, "Débuts."

11. Walter de Milemete, "De secretis secretorum Aristotelis" [Concerning the secrets of Aristotle], British Library, London, Add manuscript 47680, image at fol. 44v.

12. See Blair, "Milemete," 5.

13. Blair, "Milemete," 7; Dondi, "Terzo."

14. DeVries and Smith, *Medieval Military*, 138; Rogers, "Military Revolutions of the Hundred," 258; Hall, *Weapons*, 43–44; Contamine, *War*, 139.

15. Blair, "Milemete," 13.

16. Partington, *Greek Fire*, 104.

17. Strickhausen, "Bemerkungen," 50; Essenwein, *Quellen*, 8.

18. Contamine, *War*, 139.

19. Strickhausen, "Bemerkungen," 51.

20. Place St. Brice still exists, suggesting that the quarrel traveled almost half a kilometer. Blair, "Milemete," 9.

21. Bonaparte, *Etudes*, 357–58; Brackenbury, *Ancient, Part I*, 18–19.

22. Petrarch, "De remediis utriusque fortunae," cited in Brackenbury, *Ancient, Part I*, 10. I have altered his translation slightly and excised the last two words from the phrase "thrown from an infernal instrument of wood." Alternate editions of the dialogue replace the word "ligneo" (wood) with "igneo" (fire), which makes more sense in context: there's no evidence of wooden cannons in this period in Europe.

23. Petrarch, "De remediis utriusque fortunae," cited Brackenbury, *Ancient, Part I*, 10.

24. Hartley and Aldridge, *Johannes*, 90–91.

25. Contamine, *War*, 138.

26. Brackenbury, *Ancient, Part I*, 5–6.

27. Blair, "Milemete," 11.

28. One early European gun, dated to 1322, was found in the mid-nineteenth century but subsequently lost. See Angelucci, *Documenti*, 75; and Gohlke, *Geschichte*, 11. On the dearth of European guns, see Smith, "Artillery," 154. For a list of extant fourteenth-century Chinese guns, see LX, 106–7 and 123–25. On the gun that has been dated before 1399, see Strickhausen, "Bemerkungen," 52.

29. For more information on the gun, see the information page of the Swedish Historical Museum of Stockholm: http://mis.historiska.se/mis/sok/fid.asp?fid =114743, retrieved 3 January 2013. Kelly DeVries has challenged the dating of the gun. See DeVries, "Reassessment."

30. Zhong et al., "Nei."

31. On the controversy, see Tittmann, "Eltzer"; Tittmann, "Guns"; Leibnitz, "Fitting." For replica testing, see Smith, *Rewriting*, 115–18.

32. See Smith, *Rewriting*, 115–18. Leibnitz, "Fitting."

33. Clephan, *Outline*, 27.

34. Brackenbury, *Ancient, Part I*, 17; Tout, "Firearms," 670–74.

35. Tout, "Firearms," 670.

36. Tout, "Firearms," 670.

37. Brackenbury, *Ancient, Part I*, 8.

38. Brackenbury, *Ancient, Part I*, 21.

39. See Rathgen, *Geschütz*, 6–7 and 151ff.; see also DeVries, "Technology."

40. Smith, "Artillery," 153

41. Brackenbury, *Ancient, Part I*, 21.

42. DeVries and Smith, *Medieval Military*, 144.

43. Villani, *Seconda*, 185.

44. See DeVries, "Technology," 290.

45. Brackenbury, *Ancient, Part I*, 14–17; Tout, "Firearms," 670–71. Similar but later records distinguish between small and large shot and between small and large guns (although these were still very small compared to later European guns), yet it seems that raw lead was always provided, again to allow flexibility.

46. Villani, *Seconda*, 186.

47. Villani, *Seconda*, 186.

48. DeVries, *Infantry*, 169–70; Prestwich, "Battle," 148.

49. Anonymous, "Storie pistoresi," 223, http://books.google.com/books?id=ov FVAAAAYAAJ&source=gbs_navlinks_s, retrieved 30 January 2013. Cf. Brackenbury, *Ancient, Part I*, 13. Note that Brackenbury mistranscribed the word "scoccare" for "soccare."

50. Among the best and fairest recent attempts to reconstruct the battle are Prestwich, "Battle," 159–252; DeVries, *Infantry*, 155–75; Rogers, *War*.

51. Still one of the best overviews of the evidence for and against guns at Crécy is Burne, *Crecy*, 192–203, but see also Tout, "Firearms," 670–72; and Brackenbury, *Ancient, Part I*, 13–17.

52. See Brackenbury, *Ancient, Part II*, 21. He believes they were but feels there is room for doubt.

53. DeVries and Smith, *Medieval Military*, 144; DeVries, "Forgotten Battle."

54. Ayton and Preston, *Battle*, 154–55.

55. Anonymous, "Storie pistoresi," 223.

56. Froissart, *Chroniques*, vol. 5 (1868 ed.), 376.

57. Froissart, *Chroniques*, vol. 5 (1868 ed.), 377.

58. Froissart, *Chroniques*, vol. 5 (1868 ed.), 389; Brackenbury, *Ancient, Part II*, 39.

59. Haldon, "Greek," 291.

60. Haldon, "Greek," 290.

61. Extracted in Reinaud and Favé, *Histoire*, 224. This type of recipe has a long pedigree in Europe. Consider, for example, the recipe for Greek fire given by Marcus Graecus, probably written up in the late 1200s: "Take live sulfur, tartar, sarcocolla and pitch, boiled salt, petroleum oil, and common oil. Boil all these well together and then immerse tow in it. . . . When the fire is kindled it cannot be extinguished except by urine, vinegar, or sand." Partington, *Greek Fire*, 50.

62. To be sure, we cannot be certain that the "cannons throwing fire" were intentionally being used as incendiary weapons, because all black powder weapons

from the late medieval and early modern periods shot out considerable amounts of fire along with their projectiles. Moreover, even if the cannons were being used as incendiary weapons, it is possible that the quarrels themselves were incendiary—perhaps tipped with burning gunpowder and other conflagratives, much as Chinese fire arrows were.

63. See SCC5 pt. 7, 259–62.

Chapter 6: Big Guns

1. The classic work in English on Philip the Bold, still authoritative, is Vaughan, *Philip the Bold*.

2. DeVries and Smith, *Artillery*, 16.

3. DeVries and Smith, *Artillery*, 17–18.

4. Brackenbury, *Ancient, Part II*, 30.

5. Froissart, *Chroniques*, vol. 8, 1370–1377 (1888 ed.), 249.

6. Froissart, *Chroniques*, vol. 8, 1370–1377 (1888 ed.), 249. Actually, what Froissart writes is that they shot quarrels (*quariaus*) of two hundred pounds, but it seems likely that Froissart uses the term "quarrels" in a generic way, to mean projectiles. See Brackenbury, *Ancient, Part II*, 39; Froissart, *Chroniques*, vol. 1 (1835 edition), 33–34.

7. Froissart, *Chroniques*, vol. 1 (1835 ed.), 716.

8. Brackenbury, *Ancient, Part II*, 33.

9. Froissart, *Chroniques*, vol. 8, 1370–1377 (1888 ed.), 249.

10. Froissart, *Chroniques*, vol. 8, 1370–1377 (1888 ed.), 249.

11. Froissart, *Chroniques*, vol. 8, 1370–1377 (1888 ed.), 249.

12. Brackenbury, *Ancient, Part II*, 39; Froissart, *Chroniques*, vol. 1 (1835 ed.), 34.

13. Froissart, *Chroniques*, vol. 2 (1835 ed.), 214.

14. Froissart, *Chroniques*, vol. 2 (1835 ed.), 214. That "53 pouces" refers to circumference and not diameter is convincingly argued by Brackenbury. Brackenbury, *Ancient, Part II*, 37.

15. Froissart, *Chroniques*, vol. 2 (1835 ed.), 214.

16. Schmidtchen, "Riesengeschütze," pt. 1, 164–66.

17. Gibson, *Pieter Bruegel*, 124–28.

18. Schmidtchen, "Riesengeschütze," pt. 2, 221–22.

19. Hale, *Renaissance*, 393.

20. Cunningham and Grell, *Four*, 119.

21. Cited in Rogers, "'Military Revolutions' and 'Revolutions in Military Affairs,'" 22.

22. DeVries, "Facing," 41.

23. Clifford Rogers suggests that the triumph of artillery came slightly later than DeVries and Smith argue, to wit starting in the middle of the 1420s. He writes, "the many long sieges of the 1410s and early 1420s show that artillery was not yet then capable of rapidly battering its way into a strong fortress garrisoned by determined defenders." Rogers, "Military Revolutions of the Hundred," 262. Smith and DeVries offer convincing evidence, however, of artillery battering walls regularly before

then. See DeVries, "Use of Gunpowder," 4–5; and Smith, "Artillery," 157. Rogers has responded to their critiques in Rogers, "Artillery." See also DeVries, "Facing" and Salamagne, "Attaque." For another counterpoint, see Curry, "Guns," 182–83.

24. DeVries, "Facing," 41.

25. DeVries and Smith, *Medieval Military*, 142.

26. DeVries and Smith, *Artillery*, 25.

27. DeVries, "Use of Gunpowder," 8.

28. Duc d'Alençon, cited in DeVries, "A Woman," 9.

29. DeVries and Smith, *Medieval Military*, 159.

30. Paschalidou, "Walls," 172.

31. A monumental and exceedingly detailed book evaluates the various sources on Urban and concludes that they prove "beyond doubt the historicity of Urban." Whether he was actually Hungarian remains debatable. Philippides and Hanak, *Siege*, 390n112.

32. DeVries, "Technology," 285.

33. Philippides and Hanak, *Siege*, 390. Cf. the translation in DeVries, "Technology," 285.

34. How much bronze is hard to establish. Kritoboulos said that the copper and tin weighted as much as 1,500 talents, which Philippides and Hanak estimate would be 38,790 kg. Philippides and Hanak, *Siege*, 416–17.

35. This is from the historian Doukas (ca. 1400–after 1462), who lived through the siege and is one of the most important sources on it. Cited in and translated by Philippides and Hanak, *Siege*, 394.

36. Philippides and Hanak, *Siege*, 417–18.

37. Philippides and Hanak, *Siege*, 419. In a separate piece, Hanak inclines toward the lower figure, 1,200 pounds. Hanak, "Sultan." His estimate is probably low: in more recent times, a similar but smaller bombard of this type was test fired and found to shoot an 1,100-pound stone ball. Philippides and Hanak, *Siege*, 419.

38. Philippides and Hanak, *Siege*, 419n89.

39. Michael Kritoboulos (ca. 1410–ca. 1470), cited in and translated by Philippides and Hanak, *Siege*, 416.

40. Philippides and Hanak, *Siege*, 423.

41. Philippides and Hanak, *Siege*, 423.

42. This according to Doukas. Philippides and Hanak, *Siege*, 425.

43. Nestor-Iskander, cited in Philippides and Hanak, *Siege*, 419.

44. Bishop Samuel, cited in Philippides and Hanak, *Siege*, 477n10.

45. Eparkhos and Diplovatatzes, cited in Philippides and Hanak, *Siege*, 477n10.

46. Michael Kritoboulos, cited in DeVries, "Gunpowder Weapons," 357–58.

47. Kritoboulos, cited in Eparkhos and Diplovatatzes, cited in Philippides and Hanak, *Siege*, 483.

48. Eparkhos and Diplovatatzes, cited in Philippides and Hanak, *Siege*, 483.

49. Contrary to the arguments of many military historians, there was no significant divergence in size or power of Ottoman and Western European artillery

through the seventeenth century. See Ágoston, "Ottoman," esp. 45–46; and Ágoston, *Guns,* 184ff.

50. Doukas, cited in DeVries, "Gunpowder Weapons," 358.

51. Barbaro, *Diary,* 67.

52. Howard, *War,* 35, cited in DeVries, "Gunpowder Weapons," 345.

53. Paschalidou, "Walls," 172–78, 174.

54. Gibbon, cited in DeVries, "Gunpowder Weapons," 343.

55. Gibbon, cited in DeVries, "Gunpowder Weapons," 343.

56. Ágoston, *Guns.*

57. Kritoboulos, cited in DeVries, "Gunpowder Weapons," 355.

58. Kritoboulos, cited in DeVries, "Gunpowder Weapons," 360.

59. Gibbon, cited in DeVries, "Gunpowder Weapons," 343.

60. See "The Siege of Suzhou, 1366" section in chapter 4.

61. See "The Siege of Suzhou, 1366" section in chapter 4. Cheng Dong, "Ming dai qian qi," 74; Wang Zhaochun, "Hong wu," 183; Wang Zhaochun, *Zhong guo gu dai bing qi,* 170–71.

62. McNeill, "Men," quote on 14.

63. Toy, *History,* 181.

64. *Wu Yue chun qiu,* cited in Xu, *Chinese City,* 45.

65. For a perspective on the importance of European walls to civic identification, see Koller, "Mittelalterliche," esp. 9–11.

66. Xu, *Chinese City,* 45.

67. Sit, *Chinese City,* 39.

68. Sawyer and Sawyer, *Ancient,* 125.

69. DeVries and Smith, *Medieval Military,* 189. They were "built on a standard of .25 meters of width for each 1 meter of height. Thus an 8 meter high wall would be 2 meters thick." Kaufmann, Kauffman, and Jurga, *Medieval Fortress,* 35.

70. Kaufmann, Kauffman, and Jurga, *Medieval Fortress,* 35; DeVries and Smith, *Medieval Military,* 191.

71. DeVries and Smith, *Medieval Military,* 191.

72. To be sure, some ancient Northern European ringforts were much thicker than Roman-style walls, such as the Ringwall of Otzenhausen, a Celtic fort in Saarland, Germany, parts of which were forty meters wide at the base. This was exceptional, however, and in any case Celtic fort-building practices died out during the early medieval period.

73. See Paschalidou, "Walls," 172–78.

74. Paschalidou, "Walls," 172–78, 172.

75. Tomlinson, *Mycenae,* cited in Tracy, "Introduction," 10.

76. DeVries and Smith, *Medieval Military,* 269. This is perhaps an understatement, though, since it is not always easy to tell whether towns had walls or not. See Planitz, *Deutsche Stadt,* 231–35.

77. Planitz, *Deutsche Stadt,* 260.

78. Kenyon, *Medieval Fortifications,* 186.

79. For France, see Allmand, *Hundred*, 77; for England, see Kenyon, *Medieval Fortifications*, 183–84. For the German lands, see Planitz, *Deutsche Stadt*, 229–42.

80. Kenyon, *Medieval Fortifications*, 187.

81. Kenyon, *Medieval Fortifications*, 187.

82. DeVries and Smith, *Medieval Military*, 248–49.

83. DeVries and Smith, *Medieval Military*, 270. My italics.

84. Kaufmann, Kauffman, and Jurga, *Medieval Fortress*, 36.

85. Kiang, *Cities*, 19.

86. Xu, *Chinese City*, 113.

87. See Huang, "Defensive," 39–40.

88. DeVries, "Facing," 48.

89. Contamine, "L'artillerie."

90. Cited in Contamine, "L'artillerie."

91. The huge bombards used in the Siege of Constantinople probably required up to three hundred pounds of powder per shot. See Philippides and Hanak, *Siege*, 423.

92. Kelly, *Gunpowder*, 78

Chapter 7: The Development of the Classic Gun in Europe

1. Smith, "All Manner," 137.

2. Smith, "All Manner," 137.

3. Hall, *Weapons*, 92; DeVries and Smith, *Medieval Military*, 154; DeVries and Smith, *Artillery*, 42. Hall dates the development to a few decades later than does Smith, saying that it occurred in the early 1500s and suggesting that the "modern ordnance" synthesis was also about muzzle loading and casting and that breech-loading guns and forged iron guns were old-fashioned and abandoned. Smith disagrees, and makes a convincing case. See DeVries and Smith, "Breech-Loading," 251–65.

4. We don't know the precise dimensions of Mehmet's monster, but we can get an idea from the Dardanelles Gun, an Ottoman bombard from 1464. It was 518 cm long with a caliber of 63 cm—a length-to-bore ratio of roughly 8 to 1. Schmidtchen, "Riesengeschütze," pt. 2, 226–28.

5. See, for example, Shi and Li, "Nei," 36. The article discusses archaeological excavations that found, among other things, iron bullets from the early Ming period, ca, 1370. Europeans had experimented with iron ammunition beforehand, but it was in the late 1400s that iron cannonballs replaced stone.

6. On vinegar and water, see Bradbury, *Medieval Siege*, 286; and Irwin, "Gunpowder," 126. On oil, see Philippides and Hanak, *Siege*, 483. On firing rates, see Ágoston and Masters, *Encyclopedia*, 219. Sources suggest that Mehmet's monster could fire once every three hours, when cooled by oil. Philippides and Hanak, *Siege*, 483.

7. Tallett, *War*, 33.

8. This evidence is taken from French sources, as reported in Hall, *Weapons*, 90. See also Rogers, "Military Revolutions of the Hundred," 268–69.

9. Hall, *Weapons*, 87.

10. See esp. Smith, "All Manner," 136; cf. DeVries and Smith, *Artillery*, 42.

11. The length-to-bore ratios of Chinese guns differed greatly according to the weight class, with smaller guns having higher ratios, something that was just as true for Europe.

12. See Li Yue, "Ming dai huo qi," 13.

13. Hall, *Weapons*, 69–104.

14. Shi and Li, "Nei," 36.

15. See Dang Shoushan, *Wu wei*, 111.

16. DeVries and Smith, *Artillery*, 46.

17. Smith, "All Manner," 137.

18. Smith is also committed to a promising way to learn more: to spend less time in the archives and more time on the shooting range. Smith has collaborated closely with the extraordinary Center for the Study of the Middle Ages (Middelaldercentret) of Sunby Lolland, Denmark, which is devoted to assiduous reenactments of medieval life. Smith has helped them attempt to make saltpeter from chicken pee (it didn't work), manufacture powder with medieval tools (it did work), and fire replica medieval guns, most notably the Loshult gun. These experiences have been written up in a delightful account, which includes a trip to a traditional saltpeter refining operation in India. Smith, *Rewriting*. Alas, this book is difficult to obtain. At the time writing there seems to be just one copy in a US library, in the Smithsonian, signed by Smith.

19. Lorge, *Asian*, 17.

20. This argument is also put forth in Allsen, "Circulation," 286.

21. See esp. quotes from He Rubin (何汝賓) and the MSL, *Xiao zong shi lu* (Hongzhi reign), cited in Li Yue, "Ming dai huo qi," 16 and 31.

22. Feng Zhenyu, "Lun Fo lang ji," 59.

23. Wang Zhaochun writes that "the Ming . . . was an advanced feudal autocratic despotic dynasty and exerted strict control over the manufacture and use of firearms." WZC, 111–12. He believes that Europe, on the other hand, with its many states, had a sort of market-based evolutionary environment, in which competition led to faster selection. WZC3, esp. 132.

24. Ferguson, *Civilization*, 31–33.

25. Cipolla, *Guns*, 117; Landes, "Why Europe," 13, 19, 20; Duchesne, *Uniqueness*, 173–74; Kelly, *Gunpowder*, 99; Arnold, *Renaissance*, 25; Neiberg, *Warfare*, 39; Archer et al., *World History*, 204.

26. Key works in English on Ming dynamism in general are Clunas, *Empire*, and Brook, *Confusions*. On Ming military dynamism, see Swope, *Dragon's Head*; Swope, *Military Collapse*; Shi Kang (Swope), "Ming-Qing zhan zheng"; Li Yue, "Ming dai huo qi"; Di Tema, "1514–1683"; and Li, *Da Ming*.

27. In Musée Condé, Chantilly, manuscript 1561, fol. 10v, cited in Contamine, *War*, 125.

28. Cook, *Hundred*, 71.

29. Tallett, *War*, 13.

Chapter 8: The Gunpowder Age in Europe

1. See Hall, *Weapons*, 2. For the roots of the military revolution idea, see Rogers, "Idea."

2. Smith, *Inquiry* (1869 ed.), 292.

3. Smith, *Inquiry* (1869 ed.), 292.

4. Smith, *Inquiry* (1869 ed.), 292.

5. Marx, "Division."

6. A small sampling of uses of the gunpowder revolution model is as follows: Landers, *Field and Forge*; Bulliet et al., *Earth*, 628; Harari, *Special*, 1–52; Truxillo, *Crusaders*, 35–77; Thornton, *Warfare*, 61–64; McClellan and Dorn, *Science*, 192–95. To be sure, the usage of the term varies, with some using it to refer just to military changes and others to wider changes in society. Parker, for example, uses it to refer to military changes, reserving the term "military revolution" for social changes, which in any case he sees as occurring rather later than medievalists do. See Parker, *Cambridge*, esp. 2–11 and 106–19. Max Boot uses the term more capaciously, in Boot, *War*, 19–105. Many scholars who don't use the term nonetheless subscribe to the idea itself. Luc De Vos, for example, notes that artillery played an important role in helping different princes "succeed in diminishing feudalism." De Vos, "La bataille," 145.

7. DeVries, "Gunpowder Weaponry and the Rise," 145. England bucks the trend to a certain extent, according to DeVries. Anne Curry agrees, Curry, "Guns."

8. On culture, see, e.g., Arnold, *Renaissance*, 18–19; on styles of warfare, see McNeill, "Gunpowder Revolution," 8.

9. Lorge, *Asian*, 20–22; Lorge, "Development and Spread," 819, 822–23.

10. Lieberman, *Strange Parallels*, vols. 1 and 2. See Andrade, "Victor." Other scholars similarly suggest that China was too advanced for a gunpowder revolution. See, e.g., Cullen, "Reflections," 20.

11. Crone, *Pre-industrial*, 148.

12. Zhang Wen, "Huo qi," esp. 86–89.

13. Hale, *War*, 248–51, cited in DeVries, "Gunpowder Weaponry and the Rise," 129. See also Downing, *Military*, 63–64n26.

14. See esp. Hall, *Weapons*, esp. 1–8 and 201–35; cf. Stone, "Technology."

15. See esp. Parker, *Military Revolution*.

16. Ayton and Price, *Medieval*, 17; Mortimer, "Introduction," 3. Mortimer writes that the military revolution debate has "outlived its usefulness." Yet in the book in which he publishes these words, there are many articles discussing the military revolution. See esp. the insightful de León, "Spanish."

17. Hall, *Weapons*; Black, *Military Revolution*; Rogers, "Military Revolutions of the Hundred." Some dispute the link between the state and the military revolution. Parrott, "Had a Distinct."

18. Roberts, *Military Revolution* (1956 version).

19. See Rogers, "Military Revolutions of the Hundred," 243; and Rogers, "Artillery." Cf. Salamagne, "Attaque," and DeVries, "Facing."

20. See esp. Black, *Military Revolution*.

21. De León, "Spanish," 26.

22. Van Nimwegen, *Dutch Army*, 17.

23. Cook, *Hundred*; Börekçi, "Contribution"; Ágoston, "Military"; Eaton and Wagoner, "Warfare"; Stavros, "Military"; Kang, "Big Heads"; Andrade, Kang, and Cooper, "Korean." On India's gunpowder revolution, see Khan, *Gunpowder*, esp. 48–49.

24. Andrade, *Lost Colony*; Sun Laichen, "Ming-Southeast Asian," 31, 75.

25. For the population dynamics of Guangdong, see Marks, *Tigers*, 84–133.

26. In fact his comrade Cristovão Veyra also wrote a detailed account, and one suspects that Vieyra was helped by Calvo, since Vieyra apparently didn't read Chinese as well, if at all (Vieyra refers to Chinese as the "Devil's writing"). Letter of Cristovão Vieyra, 1534, Guangzhou, China, to unknown recipients, translated in Ferguson, *Letters*, 103–43.

27. Most Europeans who wrote about China knew so little about the language that their transliterations of Chinese terms and place names are often impossible to discern, but Calvo's are clear, reflecting his understanding of Chinese phonologies.

28. For a good overview of Iberian plans, see Ollé, *Invención*. For Dutch wars against China, see Andrade "Company's Chinese Pirates"; Blussé, "V.O.C."

29. Letters of Vasco Calvo, October and November 1536, Guangzhou, China, to unknown recipients, Ferguson, *Letters*, 158–66, quote on 160.

30. Letters of Vasco Calvo, October and November 1536, Guangzhou, China, to unknown recipients, translated in Ferguson, *Letters*, 158–66, quote on 157.

31. See Newitt, *History*, 14–15.

32. Correa, *Three Voyages*, 367, cited in Garett, *Defences*, 1.

33. Letters of Vasco Calvo, October and November 1536, Guangzhou, China, to unknown recipients, translated in Ferguson, *Letters*, 158–66, quote on 164.

34. Letter of Cristovão Vieira, 1534, Guangzhou, China, to unknown recipients, translated by Ferguson, in Ferguson, *Letters*, 103–43, quote on 124–25.

35. Letters of Vasco Calvo, October and November 1536, Guangzhou, China, to unknown recipients, translated in Ferguson, *Letters*, 158–66, quote on 161.

36. Letters of Vasco Calvo, October and November 1536, Guangzhou, China, to unknown recipients, translated in Ferguson, *Letters*, 158–66, quote on 150.

37. Cited in Parker, "Artillery Fortress," 393–94.

38. Cited in Parker, "Artillery Fortress," 394.

39. Duffy, *Siege Warfare*, 8–57; Parker, *Military Revolution*; Parker, "Artillery Fortress."

40. Parker, "Artillery Fortress."

41. Parker, "Artillery Fortress," 416.

42. Letter of Vasco Calvo, 10 November 1536, Guangzhou, China, to unknown recipients, translated in Ferguson, *Letters*, 158–66, quote on 145.

43. Letters of Vasco Calvo, October and November 1536, Guangzhou, China, to unknown recipients, translated in Ferguson, *Letters*, 158–66, quote on 146.

44. Letters of Vasco Calvo, October and November 1536, Guangzhou, China, to unknown recipients, translated Ferguson, *Letters*, 158–66, quote on 150–51.

45. Letters of Vasco Calvo, October and November 1536, Guangzhou, China, to unknown recipients, translated Ferguson, *Letters*, 158–66, quote on 144.

46. Letters of Vasco Calvo, October and November 1536, Guangzhou, China, to unknown recipients, translated Ferguson, *Letters*, 158–66, quote on 149.

47. Letters of Vasco Calvo, October and November 1536, Guangzhou, China, to unknown recipients, translated by Ferguson, *Letters*, 158–66, quote on 150.

Chapter 9: Cannibals with Cannons

1. On the appellation "Sino-Portuguese War," see Yongjin Zhang, "Curious," esp. 63–64; Wang and Pan, "Ming chao"; and Wilson, "Maritime," 281n61. In my book *Lost Colony* I suggested that the term "war" was too grand to be applied to these Sino-Portuguese conflagrations. Andrade, *Lost Colony*, 337n23. I'm not so sure anymore.

2. The most detailed account in English is still that of Chang, *Sino*, 54–60; but see Gruzinski, *Eagle*, 96–100; the most complete in Chinese is Wang and Pan, "Ming chao." Histories of Portuguese expansion often leave it out altogether, as in Newitt, *History*; and even histories of Macau tend to gloss over it quickly, as in Hao, *Macau*, 11–12.

3. Black, *European*, 173; Black, "Conclusion," esp. 437–38.

4. Kolb, "Excursions," 454.

5. See Peng, "Wo guo," 66. See also "Gan tang liu yong : ming huan ci si" 甘棠留泳：名宦祠祀, *Shenzhen yuan zhu min wang* 深圳原住民網, 15 October 2012 (originally published in the *Bao'an guo xue tang* 寶安國學堂), http://www.szyuan zhumin.com/a/culture/local_focus/history/2012/1015/20073.html, retrieved 5 March 2013. Roderich Ptak calls the adoption a case of "technology transfer." Ptak, "*Wugongchuan.*"

6. For more on this mission and early Sino-Portuguese relations, see Chang, *Sino*; Wills, "Relations"; Chang, "Malacca"; Ptak, "Macau"; Ptak, "Early Portuguese"; Pelliot, "Hoja"; Lévy, "L'arrivée"; and Ng, "Trade."

7. MS, juan 325, "Foreign Countries Part 6" (外國六), section on "Fo lang ji." See also Pelliot, "Hoja."

8. MS, juan 325, "Foreign Countries Part 6" (外國六), section on "Fo lang ji." See also Pelliot, "Hoja."

9. MS, "Foreign Countries Part 6" (外國六), juan 325, section on "Fo lang ji."

10. Yan, *Shu yu*, 320. Yan used an earlier source, Li Wenfeng 李文鳳, *Yue shan cong tan* 月山叢談, which contains an almost identical description. That section of the *Yue shan cong tan* is also excerpted in Gu, "Tian xia," 3831.

11. MS, juan 325, "Foreign Countries Part 6" (外國六), section on "Fo lang ji," which notes that the Portuguese (*Folangji*) "captured small children and ate them" (掠小兒為食). References to cannibalism also occur in the *Guangdong fu zhi* 廣州府志,

juan 107, "Huan ji" 宦績, in Zhang Haipeng, *Zhong Pu*, 206; and Li Wenfeng 李文鳳, *Yue shan cong tan* 月山叢談, excerpted in Gu, "Tian xia," 3830–32; and the "Dou xian Wang gong yi ai ci ji" 都憲汪公遺愛祠記, in *Xin'an xian zhi* 新安縣志, juan 23, "Yi wen er" 藝文二, excerpted in Zhang Haipeng, *Zhong Pu*, 206–7, 206. Other references occur in the *Ming shan cang* 名山藏; see Fukuda, "Relations," 1.

12. The chronicler Barros notes the rumors about Portuguese eating children and suggests that many of the children taken as slaves had been given in surety for debts. De Barros, *Da Asia*, Decada Tercera, Parte Segunda, 14–17. See also Ferguson, *Letters*, 15.

13. The phrase "sound of their cannons" is from a petition to the emperor by Imperial Censor He Ao, which is excerpted in both the *Ming Veritable Records* and the official *Ming History*. See *Ming Shi*, juan 325, "Foreign Countries Part 6" (外國六), section on "Fo lang ji."

14. Gu, "Tian xia," 3831.

15. Wang Hong has no biography in the official *Ming History*, which reflects the fact that he ran into scandal toward the end of his career. Nor does his biography appear in Carrington and Fang, *Dictionary*. A synopsis of his career is in Peng, "Wo guo," 66–67.

16. His official title might best be translated as "chief provincial prosecutor" (按察使). See Wang and Pan, "Ming chao," 142. I base my translation of official titles on Lin and Zou, *Zhongguo*, with reference to Hucker, *Dictionary*. Another title one finds in the sources is deputy marine commissioner (海道副使)—See Chang, *Sino*, 54. Other accounts suggest that his official title at the time of the first war was *xun dao* (巡道): http://www.szyuanzhumin.com/a/culture/local_focus/history/2012/1015/20073.html, retrieved 5 March 2013.

17. He received disciplinary action for his actions when superintending the fight against pirates. Wang and Pan, "Ming chao," 142.

18. *Guangdong tong zhi* (Wanli period), cited in Chen, "Ming dai," 90. Some Sinophone scholars suggest that Wang Hong first attacked with Portuguese cannons and then with fireboats. See Peng, "Ming kang," 115.

19. De Barros, *Da Asia*, Decada Tercera, Parte Segunda, 21–22.

20. De Barros, *Da Asia*, Decada Tercera, Parte Segunda, 21–22.

21. See Li Wenfeng 李文鳳, *Yue shan cong tan* 月山叢談, excerpted in Gu, "Tian xia," 3832, 3831. Other sources suggest that Wang Hong used a ruse to defeat the Portuguese but don't specify what kind. See Wu Guifang, "Yi zu."

22. Wang Hong, "Zou chen yu jian yi mi bian huan shi" 奏陳愚見以弭邊患事. This memorial appears in various sources, this particular version from Yao, "Xi pao," 16.

23. "Dou xian Wang gong yi ai ci ji" 都憲汪公遺愛祠記, in *Xin'an xian zhi* 新安縣志, juan 23, "Yi wen er" 藝文二, excerpted in Zhang Haipeng, *Zhong Pu*, 206–7. Cf. Jin Guoping, Xi li, 2; and Chen Botao 陳伯陶, "Wang Hong," 205. Balfour adduces this and a similar account, without naming his sources, in Balfour, "Hong Kong," 172–73.

24. De Barros, *Da Asia*, Decada Tercera, Parte Segunda, 22–23.

25. "Dou xian Wang gong yi ai ci ji" 都憲汪公遺愛祠記, in *Xin an xian zhi* 新安縣志, juan 23, "Yi wen er" 藝文二, excerpted in Zhang Haipeng, *Zhong Pu*, 206–7.

26. De Barros, *Da Asia*, Decada Tercera, Parte Segunda, 23.

27. Indeed, like a similar source, it notes, "In this battle the troops set forth in Zhengde 18 xinsi 辛巳 [1521] and they returned and celebrated victory in Jiajing renwu 壬午 [1522]." "Dou xian Wang gong yi ai ci ji" 都憲汪公遺愛祠記, in *Xin'an xian zhi* 新安縣志, juan 23, "Yi wen er" 藝文二, excerpted in Zhang Haipeng, *Zhong Pu*, 206–7. In fact, the two battles occurred a year apart, one in 1521 and one in 1522, and there's no reason that Wang Hong would have stayed on campaign for a year in 1521 and wait to declare victory until the following year. The Portuguese had certainly been chased away and only came back the following summer, and in subsequent years, the Chinese anti-Portuguese fleet came out annually after the monsoon winds began blowing from the south.

28. Letter from Martim Afonso de Mello Coutinho to the King, Goa, 25 October 1523, in Costa, "Coroa," appendix, 75–81, 76. Mello's letter is also in Smith, *Martim*.

29. MSL, *Shi zong shi lu*, juan 24, Jiajing 2, 3rd month (p. 693).

30. Letter from Martim Afonso de Mello Coutinho to the King, Goa, 25 October 1523, in Costa, "Coroa," appendix, 75–81, 76.

31. Letter from Martim Afonso de Mello Coutinho to the King, Goa, 25 October 1523, in Costa, "Coroa," appendix, 75–81, 76.

32. Barros, *Da Asia*, Decada Tercera, Parte Segunda, 285.

33. Barros, *Da Asia*, Decada Tercera, Parte Segunda, 286.

34. Barros, *Da Asia*, Decada Tercera, Parte Segunda, 286.

35. Letter from Martim Afonso de Mello Coutinho to the King, Goa, 25 October 1523, in Costa, "Coroa," appendix, 75–81, 78.

36. Barros, *Da Asia*, Decada Tercera, Parte Segunda, 286.

37. MSL, *Shi zong shi lu*, juan 24, Jiajing 2, 3rd month (p. 693).

38. Barros, *Da Asia*, Decada Tercera, Parte Segunda, 286.

39. Barros, *Da Asia*, Decada Tercera, Parte Segunda, 286. De Mello wrote that he "found everyone dead with Pedro Homen." Letter from Martim Afonso de Mello Coutinho to the King, Goa, 25 October 1523, in Costa, "Coroa," appendix, 75–81, 78.

40. MSL, *Shi zong shi lu*, juan 24, Jiajing 2, 3rd month (p. 693).

41. The fight took a toll on the Chinese as well. The commander Wang Ying'en was killed in action, and Chinese sources suggest that many Chinese soldiers were killed when de Mello scuttled Homen's ship. From MS, juan 235, "Foreign Countries Part 6" (外國六) section on "Fo lang ji."

42. Gu Yingxiang 顧應祥, cited in Zheng Ruozeng, *Chou hai tu bian*, 1257. See also Gu Yingxiang 顧應祥, "Jing xu zhai xi yin lu" 靜虛齋惜陰錄, excerpted in Zhou Weiqiang, "Fo lang," 95–125, 102.

43. Gu Yingxiang, "Jing xu zhai xi yin lu," 102.

44. Yan, *Shu yu*, 321–22.

45. MSL, *Shi zong shi lu*, juan 154, Jiajing year 12, ninth month (pp. 3494–95), cited and translated by Geoff Wade, "Portuguese," 295–96.

46. Letter from Martim Afonso de Mello Coutinho to the King of Portugal, Goa, 25 October 1523, in Costa, "Coroa," 11–84, quote on 76. (Mello's letter appears as an appendix to this article, on 75–81.) The letter is also contained in another edition: Smith, *Martim*.

Chapter 10: The Frankish Cannon

1. Duchesne, *Uniqueness*, 173

2. Fairbank and Goldman, *China*, 115.

3. Arnold, *Renaissance*, 18–19.

4. Kelly, *Gunpowder*, 99.

5. Fan Chuannan, "Gong ma," 102.

6. Kelly, *Gunpowder*, 99.

7. Cipolla, *Guns*, 117.

8. Landes, "Why Europe," 19.

9. On Wang Hong's genealogy and schooling, see Peng, "Ming kang," 114–15.

10. Portuguese cannons weren't the only thing that helped propel him through the bureaucracy. He also chose the winning side in a great factional debate and rode a wave of preferment when that side won. Of course, when the faction fell, he also fell. See Wu and Li, "Lun Wang Hong."

11. MS, juan 235, *Foreign Countries Part 6*, section on "Fo lang ji."

12. MS, juan 235, *Foreign Countries Part 6*, section on "Fo lang ji."

13. On Wang Hong's involvement in the factional fighting around the Great Rites Controversy, see Wu and Li, "Lun Wang Hong."

14. The man was Wu Jin (吳縉). The story appears in the *Yue shan cong tan*, excerpted in Yan, *Shu yu*, 322.

15. MSL, *Shi zong shi lu*, juan 154, Jiajing year 12, ninth month (pp. 3494–95), translated in Wade, "Portuguese," 295–96.

16. See Wang Shilin, "5 ceng."

17. Peng, "Wo guo," 66. Peng has made it his mission to raise the profile of Wang Hong, as in Peng, "Wang Hong yu Folangji" and Peng, "Ming kang."

18. "Gan tang liu yong: ming huan ci si" 甘棠留泳：名宦祠祀, *Shenzhen yuan zhu min wang* 深圳原住民網, 15 October 2012 (originally published in the *Bao'an guo xue tang* 寶安國學堂), http://www.szyuanzhumin.com/a/culture/local_focus/history /2012/1015/20073.html, retrieved 5 March 2013. Almost identical language was used to introduce him in the Chinese wiki-encyclopedia site Baike. See "Wang Hong," Baike, http://baike.baidu.com/view/1452345.htm, retrieved 5 March 2013.

19. Scholars have cast doubt on this idea, since, as Wang Zhaochun points out, the main source from which the data come, Rong, *Ming shi*, was written well after the fact. See WZC, 120–25; and WZC2, 198ff. Cf. Lin and Guo, "Ming Qing," 165–78. But a compelling article by Zhou Weiqiang adduces some compelling additional sources, including official punishment board documents that include testimony from a participant in the rebellion, who testified that in Zhengde 12 (1518) they did indeed send people to Guangdong to buy Frankish guns. Zhou, "Fo lang ji chong," 105

20. Lin Jun, 1452–1527. A collection of his writings is Lin Jun, *Jian su*.

21. The guns were certainly not made just of tin but rather of bronze, an alloy of copper and tin. Tin, however, was a rare and expensive ingredient, which may be why it was singled out by Wang Yangming.

22. Wang Yangming, "Shu Fo lang ji."

23. This refers to the way that the Frankish guns were constructed: breech-loaders, each consisting of a main gun and several removable cartridges that could be individually loaded. Wang compares the cartridge to the entrails of the legendary minister Bigan, who remonstrated against the last king of the Shang dynasty for corruption and cruelty and was sentenced to having his heart ripped out.

24. Chang Hong (萇弘, d. 492 BCE), a famous scholar of the Zhou dynasty. Zhuangzi has a story in which Chang Hong was falsely accused and died in exile, and his blood was kept in a small box and found three years later to have turned to jade.

25. The Battle of Suiyang (757 CE), in which the people of Suiyang fought loyally against a would-be usurper's army. They lost the fight, and many died of starvation, but in holding back the rebels they greatly weakened them, helping the Tang dynasty to survive the devastating An Lushan Rebellion (755–763).

26. Lu Yang (probably fifth century BCE), who is the subject of the story "Lu Yang brandishes his spear" (魯陽揮戈). The story goes that one day Lu Yang was in battle, and when the sun began to set, he raised his spear and shook it at the sun, demanding more time to defeat his enemy.

27. Duan Xiushi (段秀實, 719–783), who died while attacking a rebel leader with a writing tablet.

28. Wang Yangming, "Shu Fo lang ji."

29. Zhou, "Fo lang ji chong," 112–14.

30. He was from Putian, a city on the coast of Fujian Province, which is where he retired and was living when he heard of the rebellion. In 1517, a Portuguese expedition under Jorge Mascarenhas, sailed up the Fujian coast, stopping in Quanzhou to trade, just sixty kilometers from Putian. It's possible that Lin Jun learned about Portuguese guns from this exchange. See Ng, "Trade," 386. See also Zhou, "Fo lang ji chong," 117. Zhou cites in turn Liao, "Zao qi," 72. Xu Qingsong believes that Lin Jiansu got the folangji in Fujian from a man named Wei Sheng. It was supposedly used in quelling a pirate incident in Zhengde 1 (1507). Zheng and Xu, "Fo lang ji."

31. In a remarkable article, Zhou Weiqiang has pieced together the relationships between these men and the older Lin Jun, and my discussion here is deeply indebted to his pathbreaking work. Zhou, "Fo lang ji chong."

32. Zou Shouyi 鄒守益 (1491–1562), "Folangji shou juan wei Jiansu Lin xian sheng fu" 佛郎機手卷為見素林先生賦 [literally "Frankish Gun Handscroll verse bestowed on Mr. Jiansu Lin [i.e., Lin Jun]"], from Zou Shouyi 鄒守益, Dongkuo Zou xian sheng wen ji 東廓鄒先生文集. Reprinted in Zhou, "Fo lang ji chong," 109.

33. The guns depicted here are exceedingly small, although this may simply mean that Zou Shouyi wasn't aware of the true size of Frankish guns. Evidence suggests that Zou was quite ill when the rebellion broke out but followed along

anyway, so perhaps he never saw a Frankish gun himself. On the other hand, it is quite possible that the guns that Lin Jun had cast for Wang Yangming were quite small. After all, they seem to have been carried by two servants.

34. The date of his birth is not entirely clear, with some sources giving 1475 instead of 1477.

35. Tang Long, "Folangji gong suo wei," poem in Tang Long, *Yu shi ji* 漁石集, reprinted in Zhou, "Fo lang ji chong," 112. Great thanks to Sun Laichen, who helped me translate the fourth stanza.

36. "Guang lu da fu tai zi tai bao lib u shang shu zeng shao bao shi wen Xiang Tang gong Long mu zhi ming" 光祿大夫太子太保吏部尚書贈少保諡文襄唐公龍墓誌銘, cited in Zhou, "Fo lang ji chong," 112. The inscription is dated to 1553. See Clunas and Wen, *Elegant Debts*, 116–18.

37. Well, perhaps not "as soon as." There were some small visits by Portuguese to Guangzhou before the great tribute fiasco that began in 1517, of which the first and the most famous was the visit of Jorge Alvares, who arrived on islands downriver from Guangzhou in 1513. See Braga, *China Landfall* and Smith, *Projected*.

38. Roderich Ptak buys the idea, as does Needham, who writes, "The Frankish breech-loaders were a fairly familiar weapon in the south [of China] as early as +1510. If this is the case, it cannot have reached China directly from the Portuguese, because Malacca did not fall until +1511." See SCC5 pt. 7, 369–72. Needham is drawing on Pelliot, "Hoja." See also Ptak, "*Wugongchuan*," esp. 76. Others are more skeptical of this idea, such as Fukuda, "Relations," 102; WZC, 120–25; WZC2, around 198; Lin and Guo, "Ming Qing"; Zhou, "Fo lang ji chong," 97.

39. Eaton and Wagoner, "Warfare," 26.

40. Yin and Yi, "Ming mo," 504.

41. See Li Yue, "Ming dai huo qi," 62; Li Bin, "Ming Qing huo qi," 154–55.

42. See Di Cosmo, "Did Guns," 131–32.

43. Wade, "Portuguese," 300.

44. Zhou, "Fo lang ji chong," 97.

45. Gu Yingxiang, perhaps the first high official to get a close look, noted that a Frankish gun had a "belly with a long cavity, into which one can insert a cartridge [literally "little gun"], of which there are five or six [per large gun], loaded with powder, which can be interchanged." Zheng, *Chou hai*, juan 13 (1990 edition), 1257. A related and similar account is Gu Yingxiang 顧應祥, "Jing xu zhai xi yin lu" 靜虛齋惜陰錄, excerpted in Zhou, "Fo lang ji chong," 102. On the advantages of Frankish cannons, see Li Bin, "Ming Qing huo qi," 155–56.

46. Swope, "Crouching," 20.

47. See WZC, 127.

48. Feng Zhenyu, "Lun fo lang ji," 59.

49. WZC, 129.

50. WZC, 129.

51. Weng Wanda, "Zhi zao huo qi shu," in Weng Wanda, *Weng Wanda ji*, 378–79, cited in Feng Zhenyu "Lun Fo lang ji," 59.

52. Feng Zhenyu, "Lun Fo lang ji," 59–60.

53. Feng Zhenyu, "Lun Fo lang ji," 60–61.

54. Zheng, *Chou hai*, juan 13, section on Folangji, 1990 edition, quote from 1264.

55. Li Yue, "Ming dai huo qi," 32.

56. WZC3, 159ff. See also Li Yue, "Ming dai huo qi."

57. WZC, 126.

58. On the nativization of the Frankish cannon, see the brilliant article by Feng Zhenyu, "Lun fo lang ji." On the varieties of Frankish cannons and the process of reengineering, see WZC, 126–34.

59. Not all Confucian gentry were effective military leaders. Many failed to become good commanders. See Zhang, "Role."

Chapter 11: Drill, Discipline, and the Rise of the West

1. Zhuge Liang, *Bing yao* 兵要, in Zhuge Liang, *Zhuge liang ji*, juan 2, 43. The phrase seems to predate Zhuge Liang.

2. Michael Roberts, cited in Eltis, *Military*, 8.

3. See Hall, *Weapons*, 149.

4. Parker, *Military Revolution*, 20.

5. Parker, *Cambridge*, 391.

6. Willem Lodewijk letter to Maurice of Nassau describing the "countermarch," December 1594, in Koninklijke Huisarchief, The Hague, MS A22-1XE-79, last two pages, Parker's translation, in Parker, "Limits," 339. Note that when he wrote this letter he was not yet a count. He inherited the title only in 1607.

7. Lipsius, *militia* (copy held at Manuscript, Archives, and Rare Book Library, Emory University). For more on classical models in European war making, see Scott, "Victory." (For her examination of the volley technique, see 116–22.)

8. Landtsheer, "Justus," 101–22; Dear, "Mechanical"; Parrot, *Business*, 97–99; and, most important, Parker, "Limits."

9. Van Reyd, *Histoire*, 162. I found this through Parker, "Limits," a wonderful article.

10. Willem Lodewijk letter to Maurice of Nassau describing the "countermarch," December 1594, in Koninklijke Huisarchief, The Hague, MS A22-1XE-79, last two pages, cited in Parker, "Limits," 339.

11. De Equiluz, *Milicia*, 69. I found this source through the excellent de León, "Spanish," 25–42.

12. Parker, "Limits," 337. He cites a couple other examples.

13. De León, "Spanish," 28, citing Oman, *History*. De León seems to overinterpret the Oman passage, suggesting that the Spanish arquebusiers kneeled to reload, yet Oman doesn't include that detail. Oman, *History*, 181.

14. Ágoston, *Guns*, 93–94; Ágoston "Firearms," 16–24; Börekçi, "Contribution," 407–38.

15. See van Nimwegen, *Dutch*, 100–112; and Parker, "Limits." But see also Puype, "Victory."

16. Arnold, "War," 35.

17. Parker, *Cambridge*, 3.

18. Parker, "Limits," 140; Stavros, "Military."

19. Ágoston, *Guns*, 93–94; Ágoston "Firearms," 16–24; Börekçi, "Contribution," 407–38.

20. A passage in Sun Bin's *Art of War* may refer to the practice: "Long range units should be in front, short-range behind, and the crossbows should flow to help their rapidity." The passage appears in the section of the *Sun Bin bing fa* 孫臏兵法 called "Questions of the King of Wei" 威王問. It's a short and enigmatic passage and certainly admits to other interpretations. Indeed, the translation in the best English edition is quite different (Lau and Ames, *Sun Bin*, 100). My interpretation is informed by that of an enigmatic young Taiwanese blogger who writes under the name Shuo Xuehan 朔雪寒, and whose website on Chinese military thought, *Ce lüe yan jiu zhong xin* (策略研究中心) was an incredible resource, filled with original sources and ruminations on China's military history. Alas, that website is now gone, and at present it seems not to have been rebuilt, which is a pity. I wish nonetheless to acknowledge that good parts of what I write about Chinese drill were inspired by it, particularly an article from the website on drill in history, in which Shuo Xuehan reflected on the film *Zulu*—the same film that Geoffrey Parker alludes to in his article "Limits to Revolutions in Military Affairs." The URL was http://www.cos.url .tw/tacticspattern/id10001.htm, retrieved 26 March 2013.

21. People had tried with multishot crossbows, including one designed by the great military genius Zhuge Liang, but they proved weaker and less effective than standard crossbows. See Cao Huabin, "Zhong guo," 35–36.

22. Du, *Tong Dian*, vol. 4, 3818 (juan 149, "Warfare Part 2").

23. Du, *Tong Dian*, vol. 4, 3818 (juan 149, "Warfare Part 2").

24. Li Quan, *Shen ji*, 147. English editions of the *Tai bai yin jing* focus on the first half of the work, on strategy and philosophy. See Sawyer, *Strategies*; and Liu and Zhu, *Tai bai*. We need a complete translation, one that includes the fascinating discussions of weapons, formations, and tactics.

25. "Teaching the Crossbow Method" 教弩法, WJZY, juan 2 (1959 edition, juan 2 fol. 28r; 1988 edition), 103.

26. "Teaching the Crossbow Method" 教弩法, WJZY, juan 2 (1959 edition, juan 2 fols. 28r–28v).

27. "Teaching the Crossbow Method" 教弩法, WJZY, juan 2 (1959 edition, juan 2 fol. 28v; 1988 edition), 104.

28. It's not clear whether the three lines had already appeared in the no-longer-extant 1044 CE version or even in the no-longer-extant 1231 CE version. It seems likely that at the very least they were in the latter, since the edition published in the Zhengde reign (1506–1521), which is our most authoritative extant version, was printed with blocks made directly from the then-extant tracings of that 1231 edition.

29. This is from Li, *Shen ji*, juan 6, "Jiao nu tu bian" 〈教弩圖篇〉第七十. The WJZY says almost precisely the same thing.

30. WJZY, juan 2, "Ri yue fa" 日閱法 (1959 edition after fol. 23 or so).

31. These and other exercises are described in detail (although with plates that don't always seem to match the text) in WJZY, juan 2 (1959 edition, juan 2 fols. 17–26; 1988 edition), 83–106.

32. WJZY, Juan 2 (1959 edition, fol. 25v; 1988 edition), 98.

33. Biography of Wu Jie, in SS, juan 366, "Lie zhuan 125."

34. Biography of Wu Jie, in SS, juan 366, "Lie zhuan 125."

35. Cheng Chongdou was also known as Cheng Zongyou (程宗猷).

36. Cheng, "Jue zhang," 17r.

37. Cheng, "Jue zhang," 17–21.

38. For a good recent overview of the Si Lunfa rebellion in a Western language, see Filipiak, *Krieg*, 28–33.

39. MSL, *Tai zu shi lu*, Hongwu 11, month 3, juan 189 (pp. 2858–59).

40. MSL, *Tai zu shi lu*, Hongwu 11, month 3, juan 189 (p. 2859), my translation, having consulted Wade, *Southeast*, entry 2876, accessed 26 October 2012.

41. MSL, *Tai zu shi lu*, Hongwu 11, month 3, juan 189 (p. 2859), my translation, having consulted Wade, *Southeast*, entry 2876, accessed 26 October 2012.

42. Sun Laichen suggests that they were rockets, and he is one of the world's experts on the topic. Sun Laichen, "Military," 500.

43. MSL, *Tai zu shi lu*, Hongwu 11, month 3, juan 189 (p. 2859). My translation is different from Wade, *Southeast*, entry 2876, accessed 26 October 2012.

44. MSL, *Tai zu shi lu*, Hongwu 11, month 3, juan 189 (pp. 2859–60). My translation is different from Wade, *Southeast*, entry 2876, accessed 26 October 2012.

45. MSL, *Tai zu shi lu*, Hongwu 11, month 3, juan 189 (p. 2860). My translation is different from Wade, *Southeast*, entry 2876, accessed 26 October 2012.

46. WZC, 109–10; Sun Laichen, "Military," 500.

47. MSL, *Tai zong shi lu*, juan 152, Yongle 12, sixth month (p. 1764).

48. WZC, 110.

49. MSL, *Tai zong shi lu*, juan 262, Yongle 21, month 8, bingyin day (22 September 1423) (p. 2396).

50. WZC, 110.

51. Parker, *Military Revolution*, 20.

52. Prestwich, "Training," 372.

53. Rogers, *Soldiers' Lives*, 68–69.

54. Morillo, "Age," 52.

55. See Brackenbury, *Ancient, Part II*, 21. He believes they were but feels there is room for doubt.

56. DeVries and Smith, *Medieval Military*, 144.

57. Ayton and Preston, *Battle*, 154–55.

58. WZC, 103 and 106.

59. Anonymous, "Storie pistoresi," 223.

60. Froissart, *Chroniques*, vol. 10 of 1870 Lettenhove ed., 31. With thanks to DeVries, whose translation informed mine. DeVries, "Forgotten Battle," 300.

61. DeVries, "Forgotten Battle," 303.

62. Enguerrand de Monstrelet, *Chronique*, cited in DeVries and Smith, *Artillery*, 105.

63. Parker, *Cambridge*, 3.

64. Arnold, "War," 36–37.

65. Arnold, "War," 37.

66. Cook, *Hundred*, 42ff.

67. Ágoston, *Guns*, 93–94; Ágoston, "Firearms," 16–24; Börekçi, "Contribution," 407–38.

68. *Chosŏn wangjo sillok* 朝鮮王朝實錄, Sejong Sillok 世宗實錄 (1447:11:15), cited in Kang, "Big Heads," 42–43.

69. Lieberman, "Protected."

70. Parker, *Cambridge*, 391.

Chapter 12: The Musket in East Asia

1. Parker, *Military Revolution*; Parker, "Limits."

2. For an overview of the development of trigger mechanisms, see Daehnhardt, *Espingarda*. The overview chart appears in the front matter.

3. McJoynt, "Appreciation," 245.

4. On the espingardas' equivalence to the arquebus, see McJoynt, "Appreciation," 245. Mendes Pinto also refers to the guns as "espingardas" in Pinto, *Peregrinação*, 242–45. For more on Portuguese guns and their reception in Asia, see Daehnhardt, *Espingarda*. He is excellent on the guns, not so good on the history of Japan.

5. Pinto, *Voyages*, 258–60.

6. Pinto, *Voyages*, 262.

7. Pinto, *Voyages*, 258–60.

8. António Galvão, *Tratado dos diversos e desvayrados caminhos*, excerpted in Murai, "Reconsideration," 22.

9. For translations of the two major Japanese accounts, see Lidin, *Tanegashima*, chaps. 2 and 3.

10. *Teppoki* 鐵炮記 (1606), translated in Lidin, *Tanegashima*, chap. 2, 37.

11. *Teppoki*, Lidin, *Tanegashima*, chap. 2, 38.

12. *Teppoki*, Lidin, *Tanegashima*, chap. 2, 40.

13. Udagawa, *Teppo*. One of Udagawa's pieces of evidence—that Portuguese guns' serpentines were reversed—is intriguing, but Daehnhardt has shown in considerable detail the diversity of Portuguese-style matchlocks in production and use in South and Southeast Asia. See Daehnhardt, *Espingarda*. For a discussion of Udagawa's arguments and counterarguments thereto, see Nakajima, "16 shi ji," 34–35.

14. Brown, "Impact," 239. For a detailed discussion of units and their proportions in the seventeenth century, see Keith, "Logistics," esp. 90–91.

15. For a recent example, see Stavros, "Military," 250–51.

16. Parker, "Artillery Fortress," 414. See also Parker, *Military Revolution*, 140–41, italics original.

17. Parker, "Limits," 336–37.

18. Parker, *Military Revolution*, 140–41; Stavros, "Military," 248–52; Brown, "Impact," 239; Perrin, *Giving*, 17–20; Haskew et al., *Fighting*, 54–62, 94, and 189.

19. Ōta, Elisonas, and Lamers, *Chronicle*, 42. In another work, Jeroen Lamers is a more circumspect, writing, "whether or not Nobunaga actually operated with three rotating ranks cannot be determined on the basis of reliable evidence." See Lamers, *Japonius*. See also Conlan, *Weapons*, 170.

20. Ōta, Elisonas, and Lamers, *Chronicle*, 34, 42, 222–27; Lamers, *Japonius*.

21. Conlan, *Weapons*, 170.

22. So, *Japanese Piracy*, 148. Maria Petrucci says that the ship that brought the arquebus to China belonged to Wang Zhi. Petrucci, "Pirates," 63. Cf Murai, "Reconsideration," 21–22.

23. So, *Japanese Piracy*, 149.

24. These data are from Zhu Wan 朱紈, *Bi yu za ji* 甓餘雜集, 12 juans, originally published in the Jiajing Period, probably around 1549, cited in Nakajima, "16 shi ji," 35–38.

25. Shapinsky, "Polyvocal."

26. Fan and Quan, *Ming dai*, 159–60. Nakajima, having combed through the sources, believes that the evidence of Chinese smugglers deploying arquebuses is slight, although they did use other types of Portuguese weapons, and they fought alongside the Portuguese, suggesting that they were at least familiar with arquebuses. Nakajima, "16 shi ji," 37.

27. Zheng Shungong 鄭舜功, *Ri ben yi jian* 日本一鑑, "Qiong he hua hai" 窮河話海, excerpted and translated in Murai, "Reconsideration," 23.

28. Nakajima, "16 shi ji," 34.

29. Zheng, *Chou hai*, section on "鳥嘴銃" (2007 edition), 909. See also SCC5 pt. 7, 431.

30. Zheng, *Chou hai*, section on "鳥嘴銃" (2007 edition), 910. See also SCC5 pt. 7, 431.

31. Nakajima, "16 shi ji," 43.

32. So, *Japanese Piracy*, 149. So Kwan-wai doesn't provide the date of this letter but says he gets this information from *Ming jing shi wen bian* 明經世文編, juan 245, 2568, which cites a letter from Grand Secretary Hsü Chieh to Commander in Chief Yang I.

33. Fan and Quan, *Ming dai*, 160.

34. *Da Ming hui dian*, juan 193, fol. 3, 2620.

35. Ming scholar Lang Ying (郎瑛, 1487–1566) wrote that "During the Jiajing Period [1521–1567], when the Japanese invaded Zhejiang, the bird beak wood gun (鳥嘴木銃) was acquired from Japanese who were captured, and since then it has spread and been manufactured." Lang Ying 郎瑛, "Qi xiu lei gao" 七修類稿,

juan 45, "Wo guo wu" 倭國物, cited in Nakajima, "16 shi ji," 34. Other scholars see things precisely opposite: it was Chinese sea traders who introduced the arquebus to Japan. Yan Su'e, "Guan yu Ming dai." For good general discussions, see Yin and Yi, "Ming mo," 505ff.; Nan Bingwen, "Zhong guo," 64ff.; and WZC, 134–37.

36. Qi Jiguang, *Lian bing*, "Za ji, juan 2" 雜集卷二, "Chu lian tong lun" 儲練通論 (2001 edition), 242.

37. Fan and Quan, *Ming dai*, 259–60.

38. Qi Jiguang, *Ji xiao xin shu: shi si juan ben* (2001 edition), 56.

39. It's important to note that he adopted the arquebus to counter not other arquebuses but the heavy arrows of the enemy. The greater range of the arquebus provided an advantage. Qi Jiguang, *Lian bing*, "Za ji, juan 2," "Chu lian tong lun" 儲練通論 (2001 edition), 241.

40. Qi Jiguang, *Lian bing*, "Za ji, juan 2," "Chu lian tong lun" 儲練通論 (2001 edition), 242.

41. See, for instance, Huang, *1587*, 168–69; Archer et al., *World History*, 198; Turnbull, *Pirate*, 52; Whiting, *Imperial*, 449.

42. Wang Zhaochun has shown how the teams were altered for the conditions of northern China, with more guns and different tactics. See WZC3, 202–4.

43. Qi Jiguang, *Ji xiao xin shu*, 18 juan version, juan 2 (p. 38, 1999 edition).

44. Qi Jiguang, *Ji xiao xin shu*, 18 juan version, toward the end of juan 8 (p. 94, 1999 edition).

45. Qi Jiguang, *Ji xiao xin shu: shi si juan ben* (2001 edition), 136. For more on the fourteen-juan version of the *Ji xiao xin shu*, see Fan Zhongyi, "*Ji xiao xin shu*"; and Werhahn-Mees, "Neue," 19–20.

46. Qi Jiguang, *Ji xiao xin shu: shi si juan ben* (2001 edition), 152–53.

47. Clausewitz, *On War*, esp. 119–21. I'm indebted to Sally Paine for helping clarify Clausewitz's thought for me.

48. Clausewitz, *On War* 122.

49. Qi Jiguang, *Ji xiao xin shu: shi si juan ben* (2001 edition), 124–26.

50. Charles Oman, cited in Kelly, *Gunpowder*, 71.

51. Smith, "Meaning," esp. 285ff.

52. Qi Jiguang, *Ji xiao xin shu: shi si juan ben* (2001 edition), 59.

53. Qi Jiguang, *Ji xiao xin shu: shi si juan ben* (2001 edition), 59. Europeans, too, measured out musket shots in advance. See, e.g., WZC3, 137.

54. Qi Jiguang, *Ji xiao xin shu: shi si juan ben* (2001 edition), 135.

55. Qi Jiguang, *Ji xiao xin shu: shi si juan ben* (2001 edition), 135.

56. Qi Jiguang, *Ji xiao xin shu: shi si juan ben* (2001 edition), 135.

57. Qi Jiguang, *Ji xiao xin shu: shi si juan ben* (2001 edition), 135.

58. See, for example, Haskew et al., *Fighting*, 44.

59. Huang, *1587*, 172, 171.

60. Gontier, "Qi," chap. 1, sec. 3.3.

61. Qi Jiguang, *Lian bing*, Za ji juan 6, "Che bu qi jie" 車步騎解 (2001 ed., 325ff.). See also Wang, "Qi Jiguang," 147.

62. See Hall, *Weapons*, 178–79.

63. See, e.g., Wang, "Qi Jiguang," 147, 148.

64. Qi Jiguang, *Ji xiao xin shu: shi si juan ben* (2001 edition), 135.

65. Qi Jiguang, *Ji xiao xin shu: shi si juan ben* (2001 edition), 57.

66. This system is described in fascinating detail in Qi Jiguang, *Lian bing*, esp. juan 1, "che bing" 車兵. On volley fire in this treatise, see "Za ji juan 2" 雜集卷二, "Chu lian tong lun xia" 儲練通論下, "Yuan zhan qi" 原戰器 (pp. 240–43, 2001 edition). For more on battle wagons in the Ming, see Zhou, "Ming dai zhan."

67. Qi Jiguang, *Ji xiao xin shu: shi si juan ben* (2001 edition), 49.

68. Bi, *Jun qi*, fol. 1 (346).

69. Bi, *Jun qi*, fol. 1 (346).

70. For early gunpowder weapons in Korea, see WZC3, 108–13; and Zhu Chang, "Gu Chao Xian."

71. WZC3, 109.

72. Wu Zhao, "16 zhi 17 shi ji Ri ben," 13.

73. Annals of King Sejong, juan 118 (世宗 29:11: 甲辰 [1447/11/15]), cited in and translated by Kang, Big Heads," 42–43.

74. Swope, *Dragon's Head*.

75. Yu Songnyong, cited in Palais, *Confucian*, 519.

76. In 1595, for example, the Korean king Seonjo expressed concern about the Japanese ability to "divide into three turns and fire their guns in sequence [分三運, 次次放砲]." My translation, from excerpt in Kang, "Big Heads," 17. Note that at this point, in Korean usage, the term *pao* (炮/砲), which in late Ming China was generally used to refer to cannons, referred to handheld firearms. Similarly the Ming general Song Yingchang (宋應昌, 1536–1606), who led Chinese troops against the Japanese, worried in 1593 about "the Japanese knaves [倭奴] using the method of breaking into squads and shooting in turns [用分番休迭之法]." Song, *Jing lüe*, juan 6. I learned about this quote from Kang, "Big Heads," 17, but this is my own translation and interpretation.

77. Yu Hyongwon, cited in and translated by Palais, *Confucian*, 519.

78. Kang, "Big Heads," 18.

79. Kang, "Big Heads," 18.

80. Cited in Kang, "Big Heads," 45.

81. *Pyŏnghak chinam* 兵學指南, cited in Kang, "Big Heads," 45.

82. Kang, "Big Heads," 96.

83. Kang, "Big Heads," 72.

84. Cited in Kang, "Big Heads," 64.

85. WZC3, 159; Li Yue, "Ming dai huo qi," 70; see also Feng Zhenyu, "Lun."

86. The phrase "giving up the gun" is from Perrin, *Giving*. Historians have disputed his argument, as Totman, Review, and Lorge, *Asian*, 62–64.

Chapter 13: The Seventeenth Century

1. Parker, "Limits," 331–32.

2. Parker, "Artillery Fortress."

3. Parker, "Limits," 331–32.

4. Hanson, *Carnage*, 5.

5. MS, juan 325, section on "Holland" 和蘭, "Lie zhuan 213," Wai guo 6. The text reads that the feet are one foot two inches long (尺二寸). Online at http://zh.wikisource.org/wiki/%E6%98%8E%E5%8F%B2/%E5%8D%B7325, accessed 30 May 2014.

6. Cited in Andrade, *How Taiwan*, 173.

7. Cited in Andrade, *How Taiwan*, 173.

8. The Sino-Dutch War is examined in depth in Andrade, *Lost Colony*.

9. Blussé et al., *Dagregisters*, vol. 4, E: 627.

10. See Andrade, *Lost Colony*, 316–21.

11. The book was a translation of von Wallhausen's *Kriegskunst*. Wallhausen (~1580–1627), a German who had been a soldier in the Netherlands and had served as advisor to the princes of Orange, was one of the most famous exponents of the Dutch infantry drilling methods. On the early activities of the imperial press, or, more accurately, the Moscow Printing House, see Thomas, "Slavonic Book," 486–87. On the military manual as the first secular book, see Simmons, "Printing," 48.

12. For background to this struggle and to Russo-Qing relations, see the authoritative treatment Mancall, *Russia*, esp. 1–65.

13. Andrade, Kang, and Cooper, "Korean"; Kang, "Big Heads."

14. Sin Yu 申瀏, trans. Park Taegeun 朴泰根, *Kugyok Pukchong ilgi*.

15. On the limitations of smoothbore muskets, see Hall, *Weapons*, 134–56. It is of course possible that the Koreans' barrels were rifled—more research on this topic is needed.

16. Kang, "Big Heads," 58–59.

17. Kang, "Big Heads," 101–4.

18. Cited in Kang, "Big Heads," 88.

19. See De Iongh, *Krijgswezen*.

Chapter 14: A European Naval Advantage

1. Guilmartin, *Galleons*, 16; Parker, *Military Revolution*.

2. Zou Weilian, "Feng jiao," 40.

3. Various other variants of the term appeared. In the early Qing period, for example, the gun was usually referred to without the term "barbarian" (夷), as in 紅衣炮, because the term "barbarian" was considered offensive to the Manchus. See Di Cosmo, "Did Guns," 146.

4. On the adoption of these guns, called *fa gong* (发熕), see the outstanding article by Zheng Cheng, "Fa gong kao."

5. *Ming shi*, juan 325, section on "Holland" 和蘭, "Lie zhuan 213," Online at http://zh.wikisource.org/wiki/%E6%98%8E%E5%8F%B2/%E5%8D%B7325, accessed 30 May 2014.

6. Huang Yi-long, "Ming Qing du te," 121. I follow Hucker, *Dictionary*, for the translation of the title. See Hucker, *Dictionary*, 544.

7. Deng Shiliang 鄧士亮, *Xin yue xuan gao* 心月軒稿, cited in Huang Yi-long, "Ou zhou chen chuan," 603.

8. See Andrade, *Lost Colony*, 244.

9. Shi Kang, "Ming-Qing," 145.

10. Huang Yi-long, "Ming Qing zhi ji," 770–72.

11. Sun Yuanhua, 1626, cited in Huang Yi-long, "Sun Yuanhua," 234.

12. See Hart, *Imagined*.

13. Huang Yi-long, "Sun Yuanhua," 235.

14. Wakeman, *Great Enterprise*, 59–62; Lorge, *War*, 143.

15. MSL, cited in Li Yue, "Ming dai huo qi," 70.

16. Sun Yuanhua, cited in Huang Yi-long, "Sun Yuanhua," 235. Note, by the way, the reference to telescopes. Invented less than twenty years previously in Europe (probably 1608), the telescope spread rapidly to China, evidence contrary to the argument of Huff, *Intellectual*, esp. 22–47 and 72–114.

17. Board of War Chief Secretary Liang Tingdong, cited in Dong and Huang, "Chong zhen," 68.

18. Cited in Dong and Huang, "Chong zhen," 68.

19. Huang Yi-long, "Ming Qing zhi ji."

20. Dong and Huang, "Chong zhen," 67–68.

21. Lu Zhaolong, supervising censor of the Office of Scrutiny for Rites, Chongzhen 3/5, cited in Huang Yi-long, "Sun Yuanhua," 239.

22. Lu Zhaolong, supervising censor of the Office of Scrutiny for Rites, Chongzhen 3/5, cited in cited in Huang Yi-long, "Sun Yuanhua," 239.

23. Lin Qilu 林啟陸, "Zhu yi lun lüe" 誅夷論略, cited in cited in Huang Yi-long, "Sun Yuanhua," 257.

24. See Huang Yi-long, "Wu qiao"; and Agnew, "Migrants."

25. Cooper, *Rodrigues*, 350.

26. Agnew, "Migrants," 535.

27. Huang Yi-long, "Sun Yuanhua," 255.

28. Xie Lihong, "Hong yi," 105. The best English-language account is Di Cosmo, "Did Guns."

29. See, for example, Xie Lihong, "Hong yi," 107. On the Manchu use of the cannons to defeat Li Zicheng's Shun regime, see Liu Hongliang, "Hong yi."

30. Huang Yi-long, "Ming Qing du te," 83.

31. Huang Yi-long, "Ming Qing du te," 73.

32. Boxer, "Portuguese."

33. Huang Yi-long, "Sun Yuanhua," 258.

34. Mundy, *Travels*, vol. 3, pt. 1, 203–4.

35. Zheng Dayu 鄭大鬱, *Jing guo xiong lüe* 經國雄略 (woodblock print, 1646). The quote is from the section titled *Wu bei kao* 武備考, juan no. 8, fols. 22–22v. A facsimile version is *Mei guo Ha fo*, vols. 19 and 20.

36. Section from the 中丞南公祖來視閩師, excerpted in Su, *Taiwan*, 60.

37. On the evolution of the broadside ship, see esp. Rodger, "Development"; Padfield, *Guns*, 51–56; and Parker, "*Dreadnought*."

38. Andrade, *Lost Colony*, 28.

39. *Ming shi lu Min hai guan xi shi liao*, 154.

40. Shapinsky, "Polyvocal."

41. *Zheng shi shi liao chu bian*, 1.

42. Some sources say there were only fifteen of these massive warjunks. See Chen Bisheng, "Ming dai," 88.

43. Simon de Vlieger (1601–1653), *Battle between Dutch Ships and Chinese Junks, 13 July 1633*, oil on canvas, 1650, preserved at Felbrigg Hall, Felbrigg, Norwich, Norfolk, UK, http://www.nationaltrustimages.org.uk/image/999626, retrieved 27 May 2015.

44. Letter from Governor Hans Putmans to Governor-General Hendrik Brouwer, 30 September 1633, Dutch National Archive, The Hague, VOC Collection, VOC 1113: 776–787, fols. 777v–778.

45. Cited in Andrade, *Lost Colony*, 40. What the Dutchman actually said is "more than our own *yachts*," but to avoid confusion I translated the term as "warships" because whereas today a yacht usually connotes a smaller vessel, in the seventeenth century yachts came in many sizes, and those in the East were well-armed warships, frequently the core of the Netherlanders' naval power. A Dutch war yacht often carried thirty or more large bronze and iron cannons, making it a formidable broadside ship. See Andrade, *Lost Colony*, 134 and 362–63nn27, 35.

46. See Puype, "Zeventiende," 68.

47. Cited in Kelly, *Gunpowder*, 100.

48. Rodger, "Development."

49. Parker, *Military Revolution*, 94–96. Cf. Rodger, "Development"; Guilmartin, *Galleons*, 161–63.

50. Letter from Governor Hans Putmans to Governor-General Hendrik Brouwer, 30 September 1633, Dutch National Archive, The Hague, VOC Collection, VOC 1113: 776–787, fols. 777v–778.

51. For details about the battle, see Andrade, *Lost Colony*, 41–44.

52. Cited in Andrade, *Lost Colony*, 48.

53. Cited in Andrade, *Lost Colony*, 50.

54. Cited in Andrade, *Lost Colony*, 50.

55. Andrade, *Lost Colony*, 51–53.

56. Dagregister gehouden bij den schipper Andries Pietersz, in the yacht 'Sgravenlande, 30 April 1661 to 5 July 1661, Dutch National Archive, The Hague, VOC Collection, VOC 1237: 41–56, fol. 41v.

57. See, for example, Chen Bisheng, "Zheng Chenggong," 11. Cf. Zhang Zongqia, "Zheng Chenggong," 31.

58. See Andrade, "Was the European," esp. 29–31.

59. Dagregister gehouden bij den schipper Andries Pietersz, in the yacht 'Sgravenlande, 30 April 1661 to 5 July 1661, Dutch National Archive, The Hague, VOC Collection, VOC 1237: 41–56, fols 41v–42v.

60. Cited in Andrade, "Was the European," 36.

61. Cited in Wills, *Pepper*, 73 (Wills's translation).

62. Riccio, "Hechos," 618, cited in Andrade, "Was the European," 37.

63. Cited in Andrade, "Was the European," 37.

64. Yu Yonghe, "Pi hai," 64.

65. Zheng Dayu, *Jing guo*, "Wu bei kao" 武備考, juan 8, fol. 22.

66. Intriguingly, English traveler Peter Mundy suggested that the Chinese warjunks he encountered near Guangzhou in 1637 "saile very swift and will lye Nearer the winde then wee can, turne and tacke sodainely, their sailes (whither afore or abaft the Mast) all one like hoyesailes." Mundy, *Travels*, vol. 3, pt. 1, 203. But many other sources suggest that Dutch vessels, at least, had an advantage sailing close to the wind.

67. Andrade, "Was the European," 25–26.

68. Daghregister gehouden bij den commandeur Cauw beginnende 5 Julij 1661 en eijndigende 3 Februarij 1662, Dutch National Archive, The Hague, VOC Collection, VOC 1240:1-213, 1–2.

69. See Andrade, "Was the European."

Chapter 15: The Renaissance Fortress

1. The evolution of the angled-bastion-style fortress was a long process, rather more complicated than has often been suggested. On the late medieval developments, see Richard, "Quelques idées"; DeVries, "Facing"; Contamine, *War*, 205; Mallett, "Siegecraft."

2. De León, "Spanish," 40. See esp. Parker, *Military Revolution*, esp. 1–44 and 121–27; Parker, "Artillery Fortress"; Arnold, "War"; Arnold, "Fortifications."

3. Parker, "Artillery Fortress"; Arnold, "War," 31.

4. Black, "Western Encounter," 23.

5. Sun, *Xi fa shen ji*. For a general introduction to the *Xi fa shen ji*, see Lin and Deng, "Ming mo." The section that follows is deeply indebted to Sun Laichen, who alerted me to Zheng Cheng's amazing article, "Shou yu," upon which I draw heavily.

6. Sun Yuanhua, "Chong tai tu shuo," in *Xi fa shen ji*, cited in Zheng Cheng, "Shou yu," 133.

7. Kenneth Swope suggests that Sun Yuanhua may not have constructed artillery fortresses and even questions whether Sun Yuanhua knew about artillery fortresses. See Swope, *Military Collapse*, 48.

8. Han Lin *Shou yu quan shu* 守圍全書, ca. 1638, cited in Zheng Cheng, "Shou yu," 139.

9. Zheng Cheng, "Shou yu," 141.

10. "Biography of Ma Weicheng," *Xiong County Gazeteer* 雄縣志 (Shunzhi Period, 1644–1661), cited in Zheng Cheng, "Shou yu," 142.

11. De Lucca, *Jesuits*, 175–79.

12. Von Bell, *Huo gong*.

13. Von Bell, *Huo gong*, cited in Zheng Cheng, "Shou yu," 142.

14. Cited in Zheng Cheng, "Shou yu," 142.

15. We know the religious orientation of only one of his sons, who wasn't Christian, which suggests that Ma Weicheng wasn't either. See Zheng Cheng, "Shou yu," 142.

16. "Biography of Ma Weicheng," *Xiong County Gazeteer* 雄縣志 (Shunzhi Period, 1644–1661), cited in Zheng Cheng, "Shou yu," 142.

17. Zheng Cheng adduces several sources to this effect, and the evidence, while inconclusive, is compelling. See Zheng Cheng, "Shou yu," 142.

18. "Biography of Ma Weicheng," cited in Zheng Cheng, "Shou yu," 142.

19. Zheng Cheng, "Shou yu," 142–44.

20. Zheng Cheng, "Shou yu," 144–45.

21. Zheng Cheng, "Shou yu," 145.

22. See Zheng Cheng, "Shou yu," 144.

23. Zheng Cheng, "Shou yu," 147–48.

24. Although expert besiegers could make it look easy, such as the famous Sebastien Le Prestre de Vauban (1633–1707), who codified his methods in a seminal treatise, "Mémoire pour servir d'instruction dans la conduite des sieges," written in 1669, but first published in 1740 in de Vauban, *Mémoire.*

25. I have written elsewhere about the Chinese siege of the Dutch Fort Zeelandia and here just provide an overview. Readers interested in more details can see Andrade, *Lost Colony*, and Andrade, "Artillery Fortress."

26. Koxinga to Coyet, 2 May 1661, in Blussé et al., *Dagregisters*, vol. 4, D: 528–29.

27. Koxinga to Coyet, 10 May 1661 (Yongli 15, 4th month, 12th day), Blussé et al., *Dagregisters*, vol. 4, D: 528–29.

28. Coyet to Koxinga, 10 May 1661, in Blussé et al., *Dagregisters*, vol. 4, D: 528–29.

29. Coyet, *Verwaerloosde*, 122.

30. All of these quotes are from Coyet, *Neglected*, 59–60. I've altered the translations slightly for accuracy and readability, referring to Coyet, *Verwaerloosde*, 121–23.

31. Andrade, "Did Zheng."

32. Coyet to Batavia, 25 January 1662, in Blussé et al., *Dagregisters*, vol. 4, E: 728–32, esp. fols. 728–29, quote at 734.

33. The report is included in the remarkable biography of the Qing commander Lang Tan (郎談, also known as 郎坦), compiled in the 1730s from official documents. See E Ertai, "Lang Tan." The report is at 3883–84, quote at 2883. I use the term "red barbarian cannons," but the term is in fact 紅衣炮. I retain the usage "red barbarian cannon" to avoid confusion to the reader.

34. E Ertai, "Lang Tan," 3883–84.

35. Mancall, *Russia*, 118. For more on Kangxi's meticulous planning, see Kessler, *K'ang-hsi.*

36. See Perdue, "Military."

37. Kangxi emperor, cited in Mancall, *Russia*, 132.

38. E Ertai, "Lang Tan," 3884.

39. Müller, *Sammlung*, vol. 5, 417; "Report from Voevoda of Nerchinsk, Ivan Vlasov, to Prince Konstantin Shcherbatov," after 20 June 1685, in Dmytryshyn, Crownhart-Vaughan, and Vaughan, *Russia's Conquest*, vol. 1, 469–70, 469.

40. QSL, *Sheng zu shi lu* (Kangxi reign), juan 121. E Ertai, "Lang Tan," 3884.

41. E Ertai, "Lang Tan," 3885.

42. E Ertai, "Lang Tan," 3885.

43. Witsen, *Noord*, 860.

44. Müller, *Sammlung*, vol. 5, 416.

45. "Report from the Voevoda of Nerchinsk, Ivan Vlsov, to the Voevoda of Eniseisk, Prince Konstantin Shcherbatov," after 26 August 1685, in Dmytryshyn, Crownhart-Vaughan, and Vaughan, *Russia's Conquest*, vol. 1, 471–75, 472. It's possible that some of these Qing musketeers had been trained by Russian defectors. See Ivanov, "Conflicting," 353.

46. Müller, *Sammlung*, vol. 5, 418–19.

47. E Ertai, "Lang Tan," 3885.

48. Müller, Sammlung, vol. 5, 418–19.

49. QSL, *Sheng zu shi lu* (Kangxi reign), juan 121.

50. Müller, *Sammlung*, vol. 5, 418–19.

51. "Report from the Voevoda of Nerchinsk, Ivan Vlsov, to the Voevoda of Eniseisk, Prince Konstantin Shcherbatov," after 26 August 1685, in Dmytryshyn, Crownhart-Vaughan, and Vaughan, *Russia's Conquest*, vol. 1, 471–75, 475.

52. See V. F., "Bejton," 47.

53. Golder, *Russian Expansion*, 61.

54. Müller, *Sammlung*, vol. 5, 423.

55. Witsen, *Noord*, 861; Müller, *Sammlung*, vol. 5, 423.

56. A Qing source suggests that they were around fifteen feet thick and ten feet high (寬一丈五尺高一丈). Anonymous, *Ping ding*, quote at juan 3, fols. 1v–2r.

57. Witsen, *Noord*, 769.

58. Anonymous, *Ping ding*, quote at juan 3, fols. 1v–2r.

59. Müller, *Sammlung*, vol. 5, 423.

60. Ravenstein, *Russians*, 46; Müller notes that the type of wall determined the status of Siberian settlements: Müller, *Sammlung*, vol. 5, 423.

61. The historiography is reviewed in Paul, "Military Revolution," 30.

62. Paul, "Military Revolution," esp. 35–36.

63. On Witsen and his sources, see Keuning, "Nicolaas" and Witsen's own "Voor-Reden aen den Lezer," in Witsen, *Noord*, unpaginated, 16 pages at the beginning of vol. 1.

64. To be sure, within Witsen's text itself is wording that casts some doubt. He refers to Albazin's bastions as "rondeelen," a term usually reserved for round defenses. Yet Witsen's picture of Albazin is filled with convincing details, including the placement of Chinese defenses, the locations of Russian structures, and, most notably, the design of the Chinese temporary fortress, which has the square

barbicans characteristic of Chinese defenses. It is very likely that the plate is based closely on a drawing of a participant in the siege.

65. Afanasii Ivanovich Beiton drew a map of the Amur region around 1690, and Albazin appears there as a large artillery fortress with angled bastions jutting from its walls. For a reproduction of that map, See V. F., "Bejton," 48. To be sure, there are differences between Beiton's sketch and the one in Witsen—one has only four bastions and one has eight—but the important point is that both have bastions.

66. Anonymous, *Ping ding*, quote at juan 3, fol. 1r. Cf. Witsen, *Noord*, 861.

67. Witsen, *Noord*, 862.

68. Witsen, *Noord*, 862. See also "Report to the Tsars Ivan Alekseevich and Petr Alekseevich from the Boiar Fedor Golovin," 1687, in Dmytryshyn, Crownhart-Vaughan, and Vaughan, *Russia's Conquest*, 482–83.

69. E Ertai, "Lang Tan," 3886.

70. Witsen, *Noord*, 862.

71. I provide all dates in the Gregorian calendar, which is a departure from much Western scholarship. Usually the date provided for the onset of hostilities in the Western literature is 7 July (Semenov, *Conquest*, 122; Chen, *Sino-Russian*, 82), which follows the dating of early sources, such as Witsen, *Noord*, 861; and Müller, *Sammlung*, vol. 5, 426–27. Qing sources say the siege began on Kangxi 25, 5th month, 28th day, which corresponds to 18 July 1686 in the Gregorian calendar. E Ertai, "Lang Tan," 3886. The discrepancy is resolved by recalling that the Russians were on the Julian calendar: 7 July in the Julian calendar corresponds to 17 July in the Gregorian, which closely fits the date in Qing sources.

72. Black, *War*, 72.

73. Kangxi 25, 6th month, 4th day.

74. E Ertai, "Lang Tan," 3886.

75. "Otpiski iz Udinskogo ostrozhka Andreia Iakovleva i Emel'iana Panikadil'nikova k Selengskomu prikaznomu cheloveka, s soobshcheniiem izvestiia poluchennikh im ot raznykh lits ob osade Kitaitsami Albazina i ob ubienii v vremia osada voevody Aleksei Tolbuzina," in Russia Arkheograficheskaia kommissiia, *Akty*, 264. Thanks to Matthew Payne for the translation.

76. Müller gives the date of this attempt at storming as 1 September, but he is likely wrong about that, because he is also wrong about another important event that occurred during these Russian sallies: the death of the Russian commander, Alexi Tomulsin. Whereas other Europeans had suggested that Tomulsin was killed in July 1686, Müller argued that his death occurred in September: "It was a considerable loss when in this siege the commander Tolbusin [i.e., Tomulsin] was killed. It was not, as Witsen says, the fifth day, when the enemy began shooting, that he was killed, but, as people who were there have testified, it was the beginning of September, when he was struck by an enemy cannonshot." Müller, *Sammlung*, vol. 5, 429. Yet according to Qing sources, which tend to be scrupulous in dating, Tomulsin was killed in early fighting, during July of the Julian calendar (which is the

calendar Müller and Witsen use to report their dates). E Ertai, "Lang Tan," 3886. Witsen's discussion of Tolmusin's death is at Witsen, *Noord*, 861–62.

77. Müller, *Sammlung*, vol. 5, 429.

78. Witsen, *Noord*, 861–62.

79. Witsen, *Noord*, 861–62.

80. E Ertai, "Lang Tan," 3886.

81. E Ertai, "Lang Tan," 3886.

82. E Ertai, "Lang Tan," 3886.

83. E Ertai, "Lang Tan," 3886.

84. Müller, *Sammlung*, vol. 5, 428–29.

85. Müller, *Sammlung*, vol. 5, 428.

86. E Ertai, "Lang Tan," 3886. My copy of the "Lang Tan Zhuan" is quite faded in this section.

87. E Ertai, "Lang Tan," 3886. My copy of the "Lang Tan Zhuan" is quite faded in this section.

88. Witsen, *Noord*, 861–62.

89. Müller, *Sammlung*, vol. 5, 429.

90. Witsen, *Noord*, 769.

91. Müller, *Sammlung*, vol. 5, 429.

92. Witsen, *Noord*, 862.

93. Witsen, *Noord*, 864.

94. Witsen, *Noord*, 864.

95. Witsen, *Noord*, 862.

96. Witsen, *Noord*, 862.

97. Witsen, *Noord*, 769.

98. Witsen, *Noord*, 863.

99. Müller, *Sammlung*, vol. 5, 431.

100. E Ertai, "Lang Tan," 3887. See also Mancall, *Russia*, 140–41.

101. Müller, *Sammlung*, vol. 5, 427.

102. Müller, *Sammlung*, vol. 5, 415–16. I have of course updated Müller's transliteration.

103. On the fort and its Spanish precursors, see Borao, "Fortress."

104. For more on this attempt, see Wills, "Dutch Re-occupation," and Andrade, *Lost Colony*, 317–21.

105. Joan de Meijer to Willem Volger, 11 Augustus 1666, Dutch National Archive, The Hague, VOC Collection Hague, VOC Collection, VOC 1258: 1487–1499, 1502v–1503. The phrase I translate as "used proper means of warfare" is *crijghs gebruijk int werck gestelt*.

106. Joan de Meijer to Willem Volger, 11 Augustus 1666, Dutch National Archive, The Hague, VOC Collection, VOC 1258: 1487–1499, particularly 1490–93.

107. Joan de Meijer to Willem Volger, 11 Augustus 1666, Dutch National Archive, The Hague, VOC Collection, VOC 1258: 1487–1499, 1502v–1503.

108. Balthasar Bort, "Daghregister gehouden in de oorlogs vloot bescheijden onder de vlagge van den heer admirael Balthasar Bort, op de cust van China, zedert

27en October anno 1663 tot 3en December daeraen volgende," Dutch National Archive, The Hague, VOC Collection, VOC 1244: 2546–2624, fol. 2614.

109. See Huang Yi-long, "Hong yi da pao yu Ming Qing"; and Zheng Cheng, "Shou yu," 147.

110. See Andrade, "Artillery Fortress."

111. Sun Zi, *Art of War*, "Offensive Strategy," Juan 1.

112. Deng Kongzhao, "Lun Zheng," 32.

113. For the data from these sieges, see Andrade, "Artillery Fortress."

114. Cited in Wills, *Pepper*, 46.

115. Perdue, "Military"; On military financing, see Yingcong Dai, *"Yingyun."*

116. Perdue, *China Marches*.

Chapter 16: The Opium War and the Great Divergence

1. To be sure, the Qing also acted as a "cooperative adversary," fighting in areas and in ways that favored British capacities (Sarah Paine, personal communication, June 2014), but most historians believe that the military gap was the most significant factor behind the British victory. See, for example, Garrett, "Weapons"; Lovell, *Opium*; Fay, *Opium*; Elleman, *Modern*, 13–34; Liu Hongliang, "Di yi ci"; Liu and Sun, "Ya pian"; Zhang and Liu, *Ya pian*; Liu Hongliang, *Zhong Ying*; Fan Chuannan, "Gong ma"; Richard Smith, "Reform."

2. Zhang and Liu, *Ya pian*, 2.

3. Lorge, *Chinese Martial*, 212.

4. Lorge, *Asian*, 17.

5. On the early development of steam communication in Britain and its empire, see Sarkar, "Technological."

6. See esp. Richard Smith, "Chinese Military."

7. Like the rest of the battle data in this book, the data come from Zhong guo jun shi shi bian xie zu 中國軍事史編寫組, *Zhong guo li dai*. See Appendix.

8. On this uprising, see Naquin, *Millenarian*.

9. Waley-Cohen, *Culture*, 23.

10. Wakeman, *Great Enterprise*, 1125–26; Perdue, *China Marches*, 526–27.

11. Anonymous, "Military Skill," 165–66.

12. Anonymous, "Military Skill," 167.

13. Anonymous, "Military Skill," 176.

14. Anonymous, "Military Skill," 176.

15. Anonymous, "Military Skill," 168–69.

16. Anonymous, "Military Skill," 172.

17. Anonymous, "Military Skill," 172.

18. Dickens, *Works*, 110–13.

19. Anonymous, "Military Skill," 169.

20. Anonymous, "Military Skill," 169.

21. Anonymous, "Military Skill," 177.

22. Zhang and Liu, *Ya pian*, 187.

23. Liu Hongliang, *Zhong Ying*, 8.

24. Liu and Sun, "Ya pian," esp. 565–66.

25. Zhang and Liu, *Ya pian*, 1.

26. Richard Smith, "Chinese Military," 139–40.

27. See Saidel, "Matchlocks"; and Nourbakhsh, "Iran's," 553–54.

28. Bernard and Hall, *Narrative*, vol. 1, 265.

29. Bernard and Hall, *Narrative*, vol. 1, 357.

30. Bernard and Hall, *Narrative*, vol. 1, 357.

31. Bernard and Hall, *Narrative*, vol. 1, 357.

32. Fan Chuannan, "Gong ma," esp. 102–3.

33. Richard Smith, "Chinese Military," 139–40.

34. See Fan Chuannan, "Gong ma," 105.

35. Fan Chuannan, "Gong ma," esp. 102–3.

36. Fan Chuannan, "Gong ma," 105.

37. Qianlong Emperor, cited in Fan Chuannan, "Gong ma," 105.

38. For more on the "giving up the gun" idea, see Perrin, *Giving*. Historians have persuasively argued against Perrin, as in Totman, "Review," and Lorge, *Asian*, 62–64.

39. Fan Chuannan, "Gong ma," 105.

40. Richard Smith, "Chinese Military," 140.

41. Upton, *Armies*, 20.

42. Upton, *Armies*, 20.

43. Upton, *Armies*, 21.

44. See Richard Smith, "Chinese Military," 140–44.

45. For instance, both Kenneth Pomeranz and Robert Allen—who in many ways stand on opposite sides of the revisionism debate—downplay science, arguing against scholars such as Joel Mokyr and Margaret Jacob, who claim that it was key to industrialization and modern economic growth. Pomeranz, *Great Divergence*, 46, 68; Allen, "British," 14ff. Cf. Jacob, *Scientific*; Jacob and Stewart, *Practical*; Mokyr, *Lever*; Mokyr, *Enlightened*. Allen and Pomeranz both recognize that science played some role in the divergence, but they both feel that it was not a particularly important role.

46. Rose, "Galileo's"; Drake, *Galileo*, 38–39.

47. Steele, "Military," 390; Barnett, "Mathematics," 97–98; and Steele, "Muskets," 361.

48. Robins, *New Principles*.

49. Euler, *Neue Grundsätze*.

50. Steele, "Napoleon," 456–57.

51. See Glendinning, "View."

52. Steele, "Napoleon," 457.

53. See Steele, "Rational," 291–92.

54. Steele, "Military," 368–69.

55. Aside from Brett D. Steele's work, see also W. Johnson, "Robins."

56. The development of the carronade wasn't due to Robins's ballistics alone. Practical experiments were moving gun makers in the same direction in the 1750s.

See Ffoulkes, *Gun Founders*, 83–84. On the adoption of the carronade, see Morris, *Foundations*, 206–15.

57. Morris, *Foundations*, 208.

58. *Army and Navy Chronicle* (Washington, DC), 8, no. 18 (2 May 1839): 277.

59. In fact, the mouth of the Pearl River proper was downstream, but the so-called Boca Tigris (虎門) was considered the true entrance to the river.

60. See the table in "Battles That Changed History: Second Guangzhou (Canton) 1841," in *Graphic Firing Table*, weblog, 11 May 2012, http://firedirectioncenter .blogspot.com/2012/05/battles-that-changed-history-second.html, retrieved 7 January 2014.

61. Bingham, *Narrative*, 28–29.

62. Bingham, *Narrative*, 28–29.

63. McPherson, *War*, 254–55. The Siege of Badajoz (1812) was one of the bloodiest sieges of the Napoleonic Wars, when the British lost close to five thousand men.

64. Ouchterlony, *Chinese War*, 239.

65. McPherson, *War*, 248.

66. See, for example, Belcher, *Narrative*, vol. 2, 142 and 192; Mackenzie, *Narrative*, 17.

67. Cunynghame, *Opium War*, 86.

68. Ouchterlony, *Chinese War*, 437.

69. The gun itself was carried on one horse, the carriage on another, and the ammunition on a third.

70. See, e.g., Wertime, *Coming*, 170–71.

71. Buonaparte, "Memoir," cited in Steele, "Napoleon," 459.

72. Steele and Dorland, "Introduction," 28.

73. Brett D. Steele, for example, notes that Riehn, *1812*, makes this point, and David Chandler makes a similar point in *Campaigns of Napoleon*, 135. See Steele, "Napoleon," 462.

74. Cited in Steele, "Muskets," 372.

75. Steele, "Muskets," 373.

76. Yin Xiaodong, "Ming Qing"; Yin Xiaodong, "Huo qi"; Huang Yi-long, "Hong yi da pao yu Ming Qing."

77. Cited in Andrade, *Lost Colony*, 220.

78. See Steele, "Muskets," 376–77.

79. Bernard and Hall, *Narrative*, vol. 1, 262.

80. Bernard and Hall, *Narrative*, vol. 1, 334.

81. The great reformer Li Hongzhang, for example, wrote, "The shells that explode before touching the ground are indeed a device of the gods!" Cited in Kuo and Liu, "Self," 497.

82. As Brenda Buchanan notes, "In the years before the last quarter of the eighteenth century, the 'Art and Mystery of Making Gunpowder' . . . evolved from a craft-based practice to a process based more securely on scientific methodology." Buchanan, "Art," 265.

83. Cocroft, *Dangerous*, 37. Other figures also conducted experiments into powder, such as the American adventurer Benjamin Thompson, aka Count Rumford. See Mauskopf, "Rumford."

84. Cocroft, *Dangerous*, 45.

85. WZC, 291–92.

86. Bingham, *Narrative*, 28–29.

87. Bernard and Hall, *Narrative*, vol. 1, 347.

88. Cocroft, *Dangerous*, 54–61.

89. William Congreve the younger, cited in Lloyd and Craig, "Congreve's," 427.

90. Werrett, "William," 48.

91. George Elphinstone, Viscount Keith, cited in Werrett, "William," 44.

92. See Werrett, "William," 44.

93. On a British-French high-tech engagement in the Napoleonic Wars, see Herson, "French."

94. Bernard and Hall, *Narrative*, vol. 1, 271.

95. McPherson, *War*, 68.

96. McPherson, *War*, 93.

97. Bernard and Hall, *Narrative*, 334.

98. "Amused the enemy" is from Mackenzie, *Narrative*, 110. For other rocket attacks, see Bernard and Hall, *Narrative*, vol. 1, 406; and "Report of Major General J. H. Schoedde on Attack of Chin-keang-foo, 21 July 1842, Chin-keang-foo," *Asiatic Journal and Monthly Register for British India, China, and Australasia* 39 (1842): 363. There was also a very precise but unsuccessful rocket attack during the famous San Yuan Li Incident (三元裡事件). See "Bengal Governmental Notifications, Being Extracts of Dispatches . . . from Sir Hugh Grough and Sir Le Fleming Senhouse Respecting Operation Before Canton," *Chinese Repository* 10 (1841): 541.

99. Bingham, *Narrative*, 24–25.

Chapter 17: A Modernizing Moment

1. Rawlinson, *China's*, 21.

2. Hsü, *Rise*, 193.

3. It is left out of Fairbank and Goldman, *China*; Hsu, *China*; Wright, *History of China*; Tanner, *China*; Rossabi, *A History*; and the excellent Elleman and Paine, *Modern China*. It is glossed over in Spence, *Search*; and Dillon, *China*.

4. Many scholars have looked at the question, and among the best works in English are Polachek, *Inner*; Rawlinson, *China's*; Wakeman, *Strangers*; Chen, *Lin Tse-Hsü*; Richard Smith, "Reform"; Liu, "Beginnings"; Mitchel, "Wei Yuan"; and, most recently and illuminatingly, Wang, "Transferring."

5. Mackenzie, *Narrative*, 157.

6. Mackenzie, *Narrative*, 75–76.

7. Murray, *Doings*, 20–21.

8. Anonymous, "Expedition to China," esp. 621.

9. See esp. Anonymous, "Expedition to China," esp. 621–22. Cf. W. Parker, Rear Admiral, "Report on the Capture of Amoy," 31 August 1841, in "Official Reports of the Capture of Amoy," *Chinese Repository* (Canton) 11 (January–December 1842): 148–57, Parker report at 152–55, see esp. 154.

10. Murray, *Doings*, 52–53.

11. Murray, *Doings*, 156–57.

12. Murray, *Doings*, 156–57.

13. Murray, *Doings*, 117.

14. Murray, *Doings*, 118.

15. Bernard and Hall, *Narrative*, vol. 2, 226.

16. Cunynghame, *Opium War*, 51–52.

17. Gong Zhenlin, in Wei Yuan et al., *Hai guo tu zhi*, juan 86, cited in SCC4 pt. 2, 429–30.

18. Among them were Chang Qing (長慶) and Wang Zhongyang (汪仲洋), and the latter described the paddle wheel craft he made at Zhenhai. See SCC4 pt. 2, 430.

19. Murray, *Doings*, 156–57.

20. Murray, *Doings*, 156–57.

21. The best case in English for Lin Zexu as a reformist hero is Chen, *Lin Tse-Hsü*, an old book, but rewarding. For less laudatory perspectives see Polachek, *Inner*; and Chang, *Commissioner*. See also Leonard, *Wei*.

22. See Chen, *Lin Tse-Hsü*, 7.

23. Mosca, *Frontier*, esp. 241–43.

24. On the four translators, see Wong, "Translators," esp. 42–44. For more on the Cornwall School, see Rhoads, *Stepping*; La Fargue, "Some"; Smith, *Chinese Christians*, 56–57, 212, 224n12; Sánchez-Eppler, "Copying."

25. Wong, "Translators," 43–44.

26. "Destruction of the Opium at Chunhow," *Chinese Repository* 8, no. 2 (1839): 70–77, 77.

27. Anonymous, "Third Annual," 576.

28. Anonymous, "Third Annual," 577.

29. Murray, *Encyclopedia*.

30. On Lin's geographical translations, see Leonard, *Wei*. On legal translations, see Svarerud, esp. 77–87.

31. Bernard and Hall, *Narrative*, cited in Chen, *Lin Tse-Hsü*, 13–14.

32. Bernard and Hall, *Narrative*, vol. 1, 359.

33. Bernard and Hall, *Narrative*, vol. 1, 359.

34. Bernard and Hall, *Narrative*, vol. 1, 359.

35. Lin Zexu, Memorial to the Daoguang Emperor, 24 October 1840, in Chen, *Lin Tse-Hsü*, 3.

36. Wei Yuan, *Hai guo*, juan 87, cited in Chen, *Lin Tse-Hsü*, 17.

37. Wei Yuan, *Hai guo*, juan 87, cited in Chen, *Lin Tse-Hsü*, 6.

38. See esp. Mosca, *Frontier*.

39. Rawlinson, *China's*, 19–20.

40. Rawlinson, *China's*, 21.

41. That's the judgment, in any case, of Rawlinson, *China's*, 20.

42. SCC5 pt. 7, 412.

43. Rawlinson, *China's*, 20.

44. Rawlinson, *China's*, 20.

45. Rawlinson, *China's*, 21.

46. Ding, *Yan pao*, juan 4, 16v.

47. Cited in Wang, "Discovering," 41.

48. Wang, "Discovering," 39

49. Ding, *Yan pao*, juan 4, 16v.

50. See Wang, "Transferring"; and Wang, "Discovering."

51. Church, *Dynamics*, 91–93.

52. Wang, "Discovering," 43–44.

53. Zheng Fuguang, *Huo lun*.

54. Wang, "Discovering."

55. Wang, "Discovering," 41.

56. *Calcutta Gazette*, 17 January 1828, cited in Sarkar, "Technological," 93.

57. Hsü, *Rise*, 193.

58. See Chen, *Lin Tse-Hsü*, 54.

59. Chen, *Lin Tse-Hsü*, 53–54.

60. Cited in Chen, *Lin Tse-Hsü*, 56.

61. Rawlinson, *China's*, 21.

62. Rawlinson, *China's*, 23.

63. The orthodoxy seems to have remained in force longer in China (see, for example, Fan Chuannan, "Gong ma."

64. To be sure, even experts on Lin Zexu have blamed his Confucianism for his failures. Hsin-pao Chang, for example, believed Lin was inflexible and blinded by Confucianism, which stressed morality and righteousness over technical and technological responses. Chang, *Commissioner*, 214–15.

65. See, for example, Leonard, *Wei*; Kennedy, *Arms*, esp. 18–23; Liu, "Beginnings," esp. 7–10.

66. Cited in Lovell, *Opium*, 165.

67. Lovell, *Opium*, 206–7.

68. Lovell, *Opium*, 207–8.

69. See Rawski, *Last*, 122.

70. Rawlinson, *China's*, 27.

71. Polachek, *Inner*, 273.

72. Polachek, *Inner*, 185.

73. Wang, "Discovering," 31–32.

74. See Ding, *Yan pao*, esp. juan 2.

75. Wang, "Discovering," 31–32. Many before Wang have pointed out the steepness of the technological grade, particularly in older historiography, but what is refreshing about his work is its specificity: a lack of machine tools and technical

drawing constituted an significant obstacle. But see Jing, *Barbaren*, who notes that the results of these early attempts "blieben unbefriedigend, da der Mangel an Know-how und Ressourcen ein Erreichen der westlichen Standards unmöglich machte. Über die Experimentalphase führten die Bemühungen nie hinaus" (33).

76. That's not to say that consistent insecurity is a sufficient condition. As Sally Paine points out in a recent book, although external security threats can foster state building, there is no good monocausal explanation of the process. We must take into account multiple factors. See Paine, *Nation*, esp. 299–300.

77. See Doner, Ritchie, and Slater, "Systemic." Doner et al. focus not just on geopolitical threats but also on domestic structures of power and governance, yet the necessity for significant external security threat is a key aspect of their model.

78. Woo-Cumings, "National," 319.

79. O'Meara, *Napoleon*, 472. The 1843 article is Anonymous, "Napoleon's," 33. It is quoted with approval in Cunynghame, *Opium War*, 181–83.

80. Anonymous, "Napoleon's," 33.

Chapter 18: China's Modernization and the End of the Gunpowder Age

1. On the ancient pedigree of the term "self-strengthening," see Liu, "Beginnings," 11. An excellent recent discussion in English of the historiography of self-strengthening is Wang, "Transferring," 14–51.

2. See Elman, "Naval"; Wang, "Transferring"; Meng Yue, "Hybrid"; and Fung, "Testing."

3. The literature is vast. Representative works include Wright, *Last Stand*; Hsü, *Rise*; Kuo and Liu, "Self"; Fairbank and Goldman, *China*; Chang, *Commissioner*.

4. Roger Greatrex, for example, has recently written that China was unable effectively to adopt industrial technology in the nineteenth century because of "the tenacity of the grip of Chinese tradition and the past." Greatrex, "Comparative," 101. For a more subtle recent example of this discourse, see Elleman, *Modern*, 33.

5. See, for example, Richard Smith, "Employment."

6. Meng Yue, "Hybrid," 16.

7. Among the more important works in this revisionist perspective on self-strengthening are Fung, "Testing"; Elman, "Naval"; Meng Yue, "Hybrid; and Wang, "Transferring." It's important to note, however, that these new views were not entirely unanticipated in earlier scholarship. Mary Wright, for example, treats at some length the considerable innovation that occurred during the Tongzhi Restoration. See Wright, *Last Stand.*

8. I date the beginning of the Tokugawa to 1600, when Tokugawa Ieyasu defeated his rivals to achieve centralized power at the Battle of Sekigahara; formal declaration of the shogunate didn't occur until three years later. Similarly, I date the beginning of the Qing dynasty to 1644, when the Qing established themselves in Beijing, although the Qing dynasty itself was declared in 1636 in the Manchu capital Mukden (present-day Shenyang 瀋陽). I date the end of the Qing to 1911,

year of the Xinhai Revolution, although the last emperor stepped down the following year.

9. Liu and Smith, "Military," 270.

10. For readable treatments of the Taiping Rebellion, see especially Platt, *Autumn*, and Spence, *God's*.

11. Teng, *Taiping*, 210.

12. Meadows, *Chinese*, 308.

13. Kennedy, *Arms*, 25.

14. Kennedy, *Arms*, 25.

15. For the Taiping use of Western military expertise, see esp. Lindley, *Ti-ping*. On the early roots of Qing seeking Western help, see Wang Er-minh, "China's Use," 535–54.

16. Lan Zhenlu, "Shi lun."

17. See, for example, Kuhn, *Rebellion*, 125.

18. Wang Ermin, "Qing dai," 32–33.

19. Richard Smith, "Reform," 19.

20. Spector, *Li*, 16.

21. Cited in Zheng, "Loyalty," 59.

22. Zheng, "Loyalty," 59

23. Crossley, *Orphan*, 132–33.

24. I translate Wu Xu's position as governor, but the formal title is 道臺, circuit intendant. On Yang Fang's eventful life, see Yang Xiaotong, "Ren sheng."

25. Smith, *Mercenaries*, 24–62.

26. Stevens, "American."

27. Smith, *Mercenaries*, 51–53; on the Sino-French forces, see Leibo, *Transferring*; Giquel, "La France."

28. Zhang Fuqiang, "Xiang jun."

29. Yu, "Taiping," 141–42.

30. On Zuo Zongtang and the Russians, see Hsü, *Ili*; and Chen, *Tso*; on the Sino-French conflict in Taiwan, see Gamot, *Expédition*; Thirion, *Expédition*; Ferrero, *Formose*; Rouil, *Formose*. An excellent article about Sino-French battles in Tonkin—with intriguing observations about Chinese weaknesses and strengths—is Noordam, "Technology."

31. See Spector, *Li*.

32. Teng and Fairbank, *China's*, 50–57; Kennedy, *Arms*, 29–33.

33. Wing, *My Life*, 108–12.

34. Wing, *My Life*, 151.

35. Wing, *My Life*, 162.

36. See, for example, Kuo and Liu, "Self," 522–24.

37. Meng Yue, "Hybrid," 16–17.

38. Meng Yue, "Hybrid," 21–23.

39. Meng Yue, "Hybrid," 21.

40. Giquel lived from 1835 to 1886.

41. Prosper Giquel, final report to Shen Baozhen, November 1873, in Giquel, *Foochow*, 18.

42. Cited in Kuo and Liu, "Self," 537.

43. Cited in Kuo and Liu, "Self," 534. On Shen Baozhen, see the outstanding study Pong, *Shen.*

44. Cited in Kuo and Liu, "Self," 534.

45. Wang, "Transferring," 172.

46. John George Dunn, cited in Pong, "China's," 347.

47. John George Dunn, cited in Pong, "China's," 347.

48. Cited in Pong, "China's," 348.

49. Cited in Pong, "China's," 348–49.

50. On Elder and his engines, see Thurston, *History*, 393–98. And see Knauerhase, "Compound Marine," 615–17.

51. See Knauerhase, "Compound Steam." For the broader development of maritime steam technology, see Knauerhase, "Compound Marine."

52. See Wright, *Chinese*, 77–80; and Wang, "Transferring," 190.

53. Wang, "Transferring," 186–87.

54. Clowes, *Royal*, 68.

55. Matsumoto, *Technology*, 14, and tables on 13 and 15.

56. On the development of Yokosuka, see Hashimoto, "Introducing." Even in the 1880s and 1890s, its designs and output were perhaps not as effective as once believed. See Ma, "Zhong-Ri."

57. Meng Yue, "Hybrid," 16–17; Kamiki, "Progress."

58. See, for instance, Broeze, "Transfer."

59. Broeze, "Transfer."

60. Pong, "Keeping"; Wang, "Transferring," 261.

61. Pong, "Keeping," 122.

62. Wang, "Transferring," 247.

63. Kamiki, "Progress."

64. Ma, "Zhong-Ri."

65. Many historians continue to suggest that *most* observers felt China would win, which is not true. See, for example, Elman, "Naval," 318; and Fung, "Ch'ing Policy," 137. On the other side is Hammersmith, "Sino." Sarah Paine's excellent study surveys accounts in major Western languages, and her conclusions are closer to Hammersmith's. See Paine, *Sino.*

66. This dialogue is taken from Anonymous, "Navies," 2.

67. Ballard, *Influence*, 140

68. Cited in Meng Yue, "Hybrid," 14.

69. Elman, "Naval," 314.

70. Herbert, "Military," cited in Meng Yue, "Hybrid," 14.

71. Cited in Meng Yue, "Hybrid," 14.

72. Lone, *Japan's*, 33.

73. Lone, *Japan's*, 33.

74. Lone, *Japan's*, 36.

75. Paine, *Sino*, 168.

76. Paine, *Sino*, 168.

77. Herbert, "Fight," 526.

78. Herbert, "Fight," 424–25.

79. On aiming and the power of guns, see McGiffin, "Battle," 589–93.

80. Sally Paine suggests that the poor formation emerged because of bad luck and that poor signaling and insubordination exacerbated the situation. Paine, *Sino*, 180.

81. Philo McGiffin acknowledged that the formation "has justly been criticized." McGiffin, "Battle," 594.

82. Ballard, *Influence*, 146–47.

83. Ballard, *Influence*, 147.

84. Su Xiaodong, "Bei yang."

85. Paine, *Sino*, 180.

86. McGiffin, "Battle," 596.

87. McGiffin, "Battle," 598.

88. McGiffin, "Battle," 598.

89. Fairbank and Goldman, *China*, 220.

90. McGiffin, "Battle," 601.

91. McGiffin, "Battle," 601.

92. Paine, *Sino*, 182.

93. McGiffin, "Battle," 601.

94. Hilary A. Herbert, cited in Paine, *Sino*, 184.

95. McGiffin, "Battle."

96. Letter from Richard H. Bradford to David Poyer, on David Poyer Home Page, http://www.esva.net/~davidpoyer/mcgiffhp.htm, retrieved 24 February 2014.

97. Bradford, "Prodigal."

98. Ballard, cited in Paine, *Sino*, 185.

99. Paine writes that after the Battle of the Yalu, Admiral Ding Ruchang and Li Hongzhang "made avoiding the loss of ships their top priority." Paine, *Sino*, 205.

100. *New York Times*, 23 November 1894, 1, cited in Paine, *Sino*, 204.

101. Paine, *Sino*, 204. In *her Sino-Japanese War*, Sally Paine wrote that Lin Taizeng was the grandson of Lin Zexu but has informed me in a a personal communication in August 2014 that since publishing *Sino Japanese War*, she learned that he was actually grand nephew of Lin Zexu, i.e., the grandchild of Lin Zexu's brother.

102. Foster, *Diplomatic*, vol. 2, 134.

103. Paine, *Sino*, 278.

104. Fung, "Ch'ing Policy," 133; Kong, "Jia wu"; Ma, "Zhong-Ri."

105. Paine, *Sino*, 218.

106. Paine, *Sino*, 218–19.

107. Pong, "Shen"; and Pong, "China's," esp. 357–59.

108. See Pong, "China's," esp. 357–59.

109. Paine, *Sino*, 218.

110. Elman, "Naval," 315.

111. Paine, *Sino*, 32; Elleman, *Modern*, 32–34; Ralston, *Importing*, 107–9; McCord, *Power*; Elman, "Naval"; Worthing, *Military*, 73; Richard Smith, "Employment," 132; Horowitz, "Beyond," 162.

112. Richard Smith, "Employment," 132. McCord argues similarly. McCord, *Power*, 19.

113. Richard Smith, "Reform," 32.

114. Fung, "Testing," 1028.

115. Schencking, *Making*, 5.

116. Liu, "Beginnings," 15–16.

117. Perkins, "Government"; Brandt, Ma, and Rawski, "From Divergence," 79–80 and Table 3. There is some disagreement about these figures, and recent work suggests that Qing state may have raised a higher percentage of GDP than previously believed. See Halsey, "Money," 394–95.

118. Tanzi and Schuknecht, *Public*, 25.

119. Horowitz, "Beyond," 162.

120. See He, *Paths*.

121. Wong and Rosenthal, *Before and Beyond*, 178–86; Ghosh, "Great," 37. On warfare and the European fiscal state, see Tilly, *Coercion*; Brewer, *Sinews*; and Bonney, *Rise*. On the development of fiscal state structures in the Qing, see Halsey, "Money."

122. Kuo and Liu, "Self," 503.

123. Richard Smith, "Reform," 33.

124. Richard Smith, "Reflections," 20. Although, as Sally Paine has pointed out, many the banner forces had been destroyed in previous wars by then. Personal communication, August 2014.

125. This argument has also been made in Goldstone, "Rise," 191.

126. Broadbridge, "Shipbuilding," 602.

127. Richard Smith, "Reflections," 20.

128. Kuo and Liu, "Self," 528.

129. Kuo and Liu, "Self," 529–31.

130. Kuo and Liu, "Self," 529–32.

131. Kuo and Liu, "Self," 530.

132. Morris, *Foundations*.

133. Curtis, *Yankees*.

134. On the development of smokeless powder and its implications, see Denny, *Their Arrows*, esp. 55–57.

135. Volpicelli, *China*, 312 and 316. On China's experiments with smokeless powder, see WZC, 347–51 and 373ff. See also Kennedy, *Arms*, 134. Most likely that powder was acquired from overseas, because the Chinese breakthrough in manufacturing appears to have occurred shortly thereafter, in April of 1895, the same month the Sino-Japanese treaty was signed.

376 · NOTES TO PAGES 295–301

136. Silbey, *Boxer* ("A captain Taussig wrote about the stores: . . . There were magazines containing immense stocks of both black and smokeless powder"); Preston, *Boxer*, 234–35 and 162–63.

137. One Chinese chemist was famously killed in a smokeless powder facility. See Wright, *Translating*, 63–65.

138. Gordin, "Modernization."

139. Home, "General," 267–68.

140. Waters, "General," 219.

141. Waters, "General," 220.

142. "'War' Revised at Manhattan: The Great Pyro-Spectacle Now to Be Seen in Its Best Form," *New York Tribune*, 19 July 1895, 2. The Pain Pyro-Spectacle Company even published an educational souvenir book: Pain and Neville, *Pain's*.

143. "Pain's 'China and Japan': Successful Opening of His Great Spectacle at Savin Rock," *New Haven Register*, 23 June 1896, 10.

144. "Planning to Save Pekin," *New York Times*, 11 February 1895, cited in Paine, *Sino*, 237.

Conclusions

1. Cited in Kuo and Liu, "Self," 497.

2. His words in Chinese were as follows: "中國這頭獅子已經醒了，但這是一隻和平的、可親的、文明的獅子." Video of his appearance, at *Le Figaro TV*, published 27 March 2014, http://video.lefigaro.fr/figaro/video/oui-la-chine-est-sympathique-c-est-son-president-qui-le-dit/3399781240001/, retrieved 11 December 2014.

3. On the disastrous Burma campaign and its aftermath, see Dai, "Disguised."

4. Wang et al., *Xin zhan*.

5. "Epic mistake" is from Wright, *Nonzero*, 163; same argument in Ferguson, *Civilization*, 20–33; the notion is widely shared. See, for instance, Dyson, "Case."

6. See esp. Parker, *Military Revolution*; Parker, "Artillery Fortress"; Arnold, *Renaissance*; de Léon, "Spanish."

7. Ayton and Price, *Medieval*, 17; Mortimer, "Introduction," 3.

8. This book is one example, but there are many others, including Ágoston, *Guns*; Börekçi, "Contribution"; Roy, *Military*; Rogers, "Artillery."

9. Black, *Beyond*.

10. Xu Baolin, *Zhong guo*, 19–22; Sun Laichen, "Century."

11. Arnold, "War," 40. For Chinese printing, see Brokaw, *Commerce*; Chia, *Printing*; and Chow, *Publishing*.

12. In China such developments are associated with the great military thinker Qi Jiguang, whom I have already discussed at length above. For European developments, see Roberts, "Military Revolution"; and Jones, "Military."

13. Huang Yi-long, "Sun Yuanhua," 258.

14. Bryant, "New Sociology."

15. Cook, *Hundred*; Ágoston, *Guns*.

16. Daehnhardt, *Espingarda*, esp. pp. 32–44.

17. See chapter 12. See also SCC5 pt. 7, 441–42.

18. See chapter 10.

19. See, for instance, Perdue, "Military."

20. Wakeman, *Great Enterprise*, 1125–26; Perdue, *China Marches*, 526–27.

21. Pomeranz, *Great Divergence*; Wong, *China*; Rosenthal and Wong, *Before and Beyond*; Marks, *Origins*.

22. Roy, *Military*; Ágoston, "Firearms," esp. 108; Ricklefs, "Balance."

23. See esp. Duchesne, *Uniqueness* and Bryant, "West and the Rest."

24. For a recent and compelling argument about the ways that Chinese knowledge has been discounted, see Hart, *Imagined*.

25. Elvin, "Confused," 366.

26. On the interrelation between science and economic history, see the excellent Cook, "Moving"; see also Cook, *Matters*.

27. Goldstone, "Europe's"; Goldstone, "Efflorescences."

28. Most famously Aron, *marxisme*.

29. Cited in Kuo and Liu, "Self," 534. On Shen Baozhen, see the outstanding Pong, *Shen*.

30. Cited in Kuo and Liu, "Self," 534.

31. Grueber et al., "2014."

32. See Wang, *Never Forget*.

33. Mearsheimer, *Tragedy*, esp. 400–401. For more on this "offensive neorealist" perspective, see Feng and Zhang, "Typologies," 123–25.

34. On the use of the aircraft carrier metaphor by PRC officials, see Wachman, *Why Taiwan*, 115–16 and 144–45; on "soft underbelly," see 145.

35. Major-General Peng Guangqian (彭光謙), cited in Wachman, *Why Taiwan*, 145.

36. Hu Angang, *China*, xix. David Kang refers to China's position in East Asia as a "hierarchy" instead of a "hegemony," pointing out that East Asia's geopolitical history offers a model for superpower behavior that counters standard neorealist models. See Kang, "Why China's" and Kang, *China Rising*.

Appendix 2: Datasets

1. Zhong guo jun shi shi bian xie zu 中國軍事編寫組, *Zhong guo li dai*.

2. On approaches to quantifying warfare, see Thompson, *On Global*, 5–14 and 87–111; Levy, *War*, 50–92; Singer, *Correlates*, vol. 1; Cioffi-Revilla, *Scientific*; and "Bibliographic Essay," Correlates of War Project, www.correlatesofwar.org, retrieved 19 May 2014.

3. Zhong guo jun shi shi bian xie zu, *Zhong guo li dai*.

4. David Kang, for instance, uses it to show that there was very little state-on-state warfare in East Asia in order to demonstrate that the Sinocentric hierarchical system—one great state, China, with a solar system of smaller states orbiting it in an explicit hierarchy—is more stable for international peace than the European

state system. See Kang, *East.* He leaves out rebellions and uprisings, however, and downplays the interstate wars that accompanied the rise and fall of each dynasty. He is far more concerned about currently existing (or long standing) East Asian states: Korea, Japan, China, Vietnam, etc. He averages the numbers of wars per dynasty to show that those numbers were quite low by European—or even global—standards, thus showing the stability and peacefulness of the East Asian geopolitical system. Victoria Ter-bor Hui has also used the tabulation of wars in her compelling study that compares the Warring States Period to the European state system. See Hui, *War.* She is far more sensitive than Kang to the importance of wars during dynastic transitions. (See, for example, Hui, "War"). David Zhang has used the tabulation of warfare to show the relationship between climate change and warfare in a set of seminal articles. See Zhang et al., "Global." Yuan Kang Wang has used the tabulation of wars to demonstrate the martial nature of the Song and Ming dynasties and argue against the notion that Confucian culture was somehow inimical to warfare. See Wang, *Harmony.* Similarly, Alistair Iain Johnston uses these data to argue for realism and strategic bellicosity in Chinese political decision making. See Johnston, *Cultural,* esp. 182–90. Ko, Koyama, and Sng have used warfare rates to make an intriguing and compelling argument about the deep reasons for China's unification and Europe's fragmentation, to wit, that China faced severe and persistent unidirectional external threats, which created selective pressures for imperial unification, whereas Europe faced many multidirectional threats. See Ko, Koyama, and Sng, "Unified." James Tong has used a detailed dataset of the frequency of armed revolts to seek temporal and regional patterns in Ming dynasty history (he notes, for example, that the second half of the Ming was particularly prone to such incidents), and to understand the origins of collective violence, which he suggests was generally a response to hardship. See Tong, *Disorder.* A similar motivation underlies work by C. K. Yang on the mid-Qing period. See Yang, "Some."

5. Dupuy, *Encyclopedia.*

Bibliography

Abbreviations are listed on page 317

Agnew, Christopher. "Migrants and Mutineers: The Rebellion of Kong Youde and Seventeenth-Century Northeast Asia." *Journal of the Economic and Social History of the Orient* 52, no. 3 (2009): 505–41.

Ágoston, Gábor. "Firearms and Military Adaptation: The Ottomans and the European Military Revolution, 1450–1800." *Journal of World History* 25, no. 1 (2014): 85–124.

———. *Guns for the Sultan: Military Power and the Weapons Industry in the Ottoman Empire.* Cambridge: Cambridge University Press, 2005.

———. "Military Transformation in the Ottoman Empire and Russia, 1500–1800." *Kritika: Explorations in Russian and Eurasian History* 12, no. 2 (2011): 281–319.

———. "Ottoman Artillery and European Artillery Technology in the Fifteenth, Sixteenth, and Seventeenth Centuries." *Acta Orientalia Academiae Scientiarum Hung* 47, nos. 1–2 (1994): 15–48.

Ágoston, Gábor, and Bruce Alan Masters. *Encyclopedia of the Ottoman Empire.* New York: Facts on File, 2009.

al-Hassan, Ahmad Y., and Donald R. Hill. *Islamic Technology: An Illustrated History.* Cambridge: Cambridge University Press, 1992.

Allen, Robert C. *The British Industrial Revolution in Global Perspective.* Cambridge: Cambridge University Press, 2009.

———. "The British Industrial Revolution in Global Perspective: How Commerce Created the Industrial Revolution and Modern Economic Growth." Paper presented at the annual conference of the Economic History Society, 30 March–1 April 2007. http://www.ehs.org.uk/ehs/conference2007/assets/alleniia.pdf, accessed 21 June 2013.

Allmand, Christopher. *The Hundred Years War: England and France at War, c. 1300— c. 1450.* Cambridge: Cambridge University Press, 1988.

Allsen, Thomas T. "The Circulation of Military Technology in the Mongolian Empire." In Nicola De Cosmo, ed., *Warfare in Inner Asian History (500–1800).* Leiden: Brill, 2002, 265–93.

Andrade, Tonio. "An Accelerating Divergence? The Revisionist Model of World History and the Question of Eurasian Military Parity: Data from East Asia." *Canadian Journal of Sociology* 36, no. 2 (2011): 185–208.

———. "The Artillery Fortress *Was* an Engine of European Expansion: Evidence from East Asia." In Tonio Andrade and William Reger, eds., *The Limits of Empire: European Imperial Formations in World History. Essays in Honor of Geoffrey Parker.* London: Ashgate, 2013, 155–74.

————. "The Company's Chinese Pirates: How the Dutch East India Company Tried to Lead a Coalition of Pirates to War Against China, 1621–1662." *Journal of World History* 15, no. 4 (2004): 415–44.

————. "Did Zheng Chenggong Need a Drunk German's Help to Capture Dutch Taiwan?" *Revista de Cultura* 26 (2008): 56–76.

————. *How Taiwan Became Chinese.* New York: Columbia University Press, 2008.

————. "Late Medieval Divergences: Comparative Perspectives on Early Gunpowder Warfare in Europe and China." *Journal of Medieval Military History* 13 (2015): 247–76.

————. *Lost Colony: The Untold Story of Europe's First Great Victory over the West.* Princeton: Princeton University Press, 2011.

————. "Victor Lieberman, Strange Parallels." *American Historical Review* 117, no. 4 (2012): 1173–76.

————. "Was the European Sailing Ship a Key Technology of European Expansion? Evidence from East Asia." *International Journal of Maritime History* 23, no. 2 (2011): 17–40.

Andrade, Tonio, Hyeok Hweon Kang, and Kirsten Cooper. "A Korean Military Revolution? Parallel Military Innovations in East Asia and Europe." *Journal of World History* 25, no. 1 (2014): 47–80.

Angelucci, Angelo. *Documenti inediti per la storia delle armi da fuoco Italiane.* Vol. 1, pt. 1. Turin: G. Cassone e Comp., 1869.

Anonymous. *A Description of the Chinese Junk "Keying."* London, 1848.

————. "The Expedition to China: Narrative of Events since the Battle above Canton. . . ." *Chinese Repository* 10 (January–December 1841): 618–33.

————. "Military Skill and Power of the Chinese: Actual State of the Soldiery, Forts, and Arms." *Chinese Repository* 5, no. 4 (August 1836): 165–78.

————. "Napoleon's Opinion of a War with China." *Friend of China and Hongkong Gazette* 2, no. 60 (11 May 1843): 33.

————. "The Navies of Japan and China: A Talk with Sir Edward J. Reed." *Pall Mall Gazette* (London), 1 August 1894, 1–2.

————. *Ping ding luo cha fang lüe* 平定羅刹方略, 4 juans. Circa 1689. http://archive.org/details/02080673.cn, accessed 15 August 2013.

————. "Storie pistoresi." In L. A. Muratori, ed., *Raccolta degli storici Italiani dal ciquecento al millecinquecento.* Città di Castello: S. Lapi, 1897.

————. "The Third Annual Report of the Morrison Education Society." *Chinese Repository* 10 (1841): 564–87.

Archer, Christon I., John R. Ferris, Holger H. Herwig, and Timothy H. E. Travers. *World History of Warfare.* Lincoln: University of Nebraska Press, 2002.

Arima Seiho 有馬成甫. *Kahō no kigen to sono denryū* 火砲の起原とその傳流. Tokyo: Yoshikawa Kōbunkan, 1962.

Arnold, Thomas F. "Fortifications and the Military Revolution: The Gonzaga Experience, 1530–1630." In Rogers, *Military Revolution Debate*, 201–26.

————. *The Renaissance at War.* London: Cassell, 2001.

————. "War in Sixteenth-Century Europe: Revolution and Renaissance." In Jeremy Black, ed., *European Warfare, 1453–1815.* New York: Palgrave Macmillan, 1999, 23–44.

Aron, Raymond. *Le marxisme de Marx.* Paris: Editions de Fallois, 2002.

Avery, Julie Jane. "A Record of the Defense of Xiangyang's City Wall, 1206–1207." Master's thesis, University of Massachusetts Amherst, 2009.

Ayton, Andrew, and Philip Preston, eds. *The Battle of Crécy, 1346*. Woodbridge, UK: Boydell Press, 2007.

Ayton, Andrew, and J. L. Price. *The Medieval Military Revolution: State, Society, and Military Change in Medieval and Early Modern Europe*. London: I.B. Tauris, 1995.

Balazs, Etienne, and Yves Hervouet. *A Sung Bibliography (Bibliographie des Sung)*. Hong Kong: Chinese University Press, 1978.

Balfour, S. F. "Hong Kong before the British." *Journal of the Royal Asiatic Society Hong Kong Branch* 10 (1970): 135–79.

Ballard, George Alexander. *The Influence of the Sea on the Political History of Japan*. New York: E.P. Dutton, 1921.

Barbaro, Nicolo. *Diary of the Siege of Constantinople, 1453*. Jericho, NY: Exposition Press, 1969.

Barnett, Janet Heine. "Mathematics Goes Ballistic: Benjamin Robins, Leonhard Euler, and the Mathematical Education of Military Engineers." *BSHM Bulletin* 24 (2009): 92–104.

Baron, Samuel. "A Description of the Kingdom of Tonqueen." In Dror and Taylor, *Views of Seventeenth-Century Vietnam*, 189–282.

Belcher, Edward. *Narrative of a Voyage Round the World, Performed in Her Majesty's Ship Sulphur, during the Years 1836–1842, Including Details of the Naval Operations in China, from Dec. 1840, to Nov. 1841*. Vol. 2. London: Henry Colburn, 1843.

Bernard, William Dallas, and Sir William Hutcheson Hall. *Narrative of the Voyages and Services of The Nemesis, from 1840 to 1843*. 2 vols. London: Henry Colburn, 1844.

Bi Maokang 畢懋康. *Jun qi tu shuo* 軍器圖說. Beijing: Beijing chu ban she, 2000 [originally published 1639].

Bingham, John Elliot. *Narrative of the Expedition to China: From the Commencement of the War to Its Termination in 1842; with Sketches of the Manners and Customs of the Singular and Hitherto Almost Unknown Country*. Vol. 2. London: Henry Colburn, 1843.

Biran, Michal. *Qaidu and the Rise of the Independent Mongol State in Central Asia*. New York: Routledge, 2013.

Black, Jeremy. *Beyond the Military Revolution: War in the Seventeenth Century World*. London: Palgrave Macmillan, 2011.

———. "Conclusion: Global Military History, the Chinese Dimension." In van de Ven, *Warfare in Chinese History*, 428–42.

———. *European Warfare 1494–1660*. New York: Routledge, 2002.

———. *A Military Revolution? Military Change and European Society, 1550–1800*. Atlantic Highlands, NJ: Humanities Press, 1991.

———. *War and the World: Military Power and the Fate of Continents, 1450–2000*. New Haven: Yale University Press, 1998.

———. "The Western Encounter with Islam." *Orbis* 48, no. 1 (2004): 19–28.

Blair, Claude. "The Milemete Guns." *Journal of the Ordnance Society* 16 (2004): 5–16.

Blussé, Leonard. "The V.O.C. as Sorcerer's Apprentice: Stereotypes and Social Engineering on the China Coast." In W. L. Idema, ed., *Leyden Studies in Sinology*. Leiden: Leiden University Press, 1981, 87–105.

Blussé, Leonard, et al., eds. *De Dagregisters van het Kasteel Zeelandia, Taiwan, 1629–1662 Vol. 4.* The Hague: Instituut voor Nederlandse Geschiedenis, 2001.

Bonaparte, Napoléon-Louis. *Etudes sur le passé et l'avenir de l'artillerie.* Paris: J. Dumaine, 1846.

Bonney, Richard, ed. *The Rise of the Fiscal State in Europe, c. 1200–1815.* Oxford: Oxford University Press, 1999.

Boot, Max. *War Made New: Technology, Warfare, and the Course of History, 1500 to Today.* New York: Penguin, 2006.

Borao, José Eugenio. "The Fortress of Quelang. Jilong, Taiwan: Past, Present, Future." *Revista de Cultura* 27 (2008): 60–77.

Börekçi, Günhan. "A Contribution to the Military Revolution Debate: The Janissaries' Use of Volley Fire during the Long Ottoman-Habsburg War of 1593–1606 and the Problem of Origins." *Acta Orientalia Academiae Scientiarum Hung* 59, no. 4 (2006): 407–38.

Borri, Christopher. "An Account of Cochin-China." In Dror and Taylor, *Views of Seventeenth-Century Vietnam,* 85–186.

Boulger, Demetrius Charles de Kavanagh. *The Life of Gordon.* London: T.F. Unwin, 1896.

Boxer, Charles R. "Portuguese Military Expeditions in Aid of the Mings Against the Manchus." *T'ien Hsia Monthly* 7, no. 1 (1938): 24–36.

Brace, C. Loring. "Egg on the Face, in the Mouth, and the Overbite." *American Anthropologist* 88, no. 3 (1986): 695–97.

Brackenbury, Henry. *Ancient Cannon in Europe, Part I: From Their First Employment to AD 1350.* Woolwich, UK: Royal Artillery Institution, 1865.

———. *Ancient Cannon in Europe, Part II: From AD 1351 to AD 1400.* Woolwich, UK: Royal Artillery Institution, 1866.

Bradbury, Jim. *The Medieval Siege.* Woodbridge, UK: Boydell Press, 1992.

Bradford, Richard H. "That Prodigal Son: Philo McGiffin and the Chinese Navy." *American Neptune* 38 (1978): 157–69.

Braga, J. M. *China Landfall, 1513: Jorge Alvares' Voyage to China.* Macau: Imprensa Nacional, 1955.

Brandt, Loren, Debin Ma, and Thomas G. Rawski. "From Divergence to Convergence: Reevaluating the History Behind China's Economic Boom." *Journal of Economic Literature* 52, no. 1 (2014): 45–123.

Brewer, John. *The Sinews of Power: War, Money, and the English State, 1688–1783.* Cambridge, MA: Harvard University Press, 1990.

Broadbridge, Seymour. "Shipbuilding and the State in Japan since the 1850s." *Modern Asian Studies* 11, no. 4 (1977): 601–13.

Broeze, Frank. "The Transfer of Technology and Science to Asia, 1780–1880: Shipping and Shipbuilding." In Yamada Keiji, *The Transfer of Science and Technology between Europe and Asia, 1780–1880.* Kyoto: International Research Center for Japanese Studies, 1992, 117–39.

Brokaw, Cynthia. *Commerce in Culture: The Sibao Book Trade in the Qing and Republican Periods.* Cambridge, MA: Harvard University Press, 2007.

Brook, Timothy. *Confusions of Pleasure: Commerce and Culture in Ming China.* Berkeley: University of California Press, 1998.

———. *Vermeer's Hat: The Seventeenth Century and the Dawn of the Global World.* New York: Bloomsbury Press, 2008.

Brown, Delmer M. "The Impact of Firearms on Japanese Warfare, 1543–98." *Far Eastern Quarterly* 7, no. 3 (1948): 236–53.

Bryant, Joseph M. "A New Sociology for a New History? Further Critical Thoughts on the Eurasian Similarity and Great Divergence Theses." *Canadian Journal of Sociology* 33, no. 1 (2008): 149–67.

———. "The West and the Rest Revisited: Debating Capitalist Origins, European Colonialism, and the Advent of Modernity." *Canadian Journal of Sociology* 31, no. 4 (2006): 403–44.

Buchanan, Brenda J. "'The Art and Mystery of Making Gunpowder': The English Experience in the Seventeenth and Eighteenth Centuries." In Steele and Dorland, *Heirs of Archimedes*, 233–74.

———, ed. *Gunpowder, Explosives, and the State: A Technological History.* Aldershot, UK: Ashgate, 2006.

Bulliet, Richard, Pamela Crossley, et al. *The Earth and Its Peoples: A Global History Vol. II: Since 1500.* New York: Houghton Mifflin, 2008.

Burne, Alfred H. *The Crecy War: A Military History of the Hundred Years War from 1337 to the Peace of Bretigny, 1360.* London: Eyre & Spottiswoode, 1955.

Butler, Marcia. "Reflections of a Military Medium: Ritual and Magic in Eleventh and Twelfth Century Chinese Military Manuals." PhD dissertation, Cornell University, 2007.

Cao Huabin 曹華斌. "Zhong guo gu dai nu gong de xing zhi he xun jie" 中國古代弩弓的形制和訓釋. Master's thesis, Nanchang University, 2008.

Chan, Hok-Lam. "The Compilation and Sources of the *Chin-shih*." In Hok-Lam Chan, ed., *The Historiography of the Chin Dynasty: Three Studies.* Wiesbaden: Franz Steiner Verlag GMBH, 1970, 1–42.

Chandler, David G. *The Campaigns of Napoleon.* New York: Macmillan, 1966.

Chandler, Tertius, and Gerald Fox. *3000 Years of Urban Growth.* New York: Academic Press, 1974.

Chang, Hsin Pao. *Commissioner Lin and the Opium War.* Cambridge, MA: Harvard University Press, 1964.

Chang, T'ien-tse. "Malacca and the Failure of the First Portuguese Embassy to Peking." *Journal of Southeast Asian History* 3, no. 2 (1962): 45–64.

———. *Sino-Portuguese Trade from 1514 to 1644.* Leiden: Brill, 1969.

Charney, Michael. *Southeast Asian Warfare, 1300–1900.* Leiden: Brill, 2004.

Chase, Kenneth. *Firearms: A Global History.* Cambridge: Cambridge University Press, 2003.

Chen Bingying 陳炳應. "Gan su chu tu de ji jian chong pao yan jiu" 甘肅出土的幾件銃炮研究. *Long gu wen bo* 隴古文博, no. 1 (1999): 68–72.

Chen Bisheng 陳碧笙. "Ming dai mo qi hai shang shang ye zi ben yu Zheng zhilong" 明代末期海上商業資本與鄭芝龍. In Chen Bisheng, *Zheng Chenggong lishi yanjiu* 鄭成功歷史研究, 72–98.

———. *Zheng Chenggong lishi yanjiu* 鄭成功歷史研究. Beijing: Jiuzhou chu ban she, 2000.

———. "Zheng Chenggong shou fu Taiwan zhan shi yan jiu" 鄭成功收復臺灣戰史研究. In Chen Bisheng, *Zheng Chenggong lishi yanjiu* 鄭成功歷史研究, 1–24.

Chen Botao 陳伯陶. "Wang Hong tao ping tun men." In Chen Botao, *Dong guan xian zhi* 東莞縣志, juan 31, "Qian shi lüe san" 前事略二. Reprinted in Zhang Haipeng 張海鵬, *Zhong Pu guan xi shi zi liao ji* 中葡關係史資料集. Chengdu, China: Sichuan ren min chu ban she, 1999.

Chen, Gideon. *Lin Tse-Hsü: Pioneer Promoter of the Adoption of Western Means of Maritime Defense in China.* Beijing: Yenching University Press, 1934.

———. *Tso Tsung T'ang: Pioneer Promoter of the Modern Dockyard and the Woolen Mill in China.* New York: Paragon Book Gallery, 1961.

Chen Gui 陳規 and Tang Shou 湯璹. *Shou cheng lu* 守城錄. Taipei: Taiwan shang wu yin shu guan, 1983 [originally written circa 1225]. Also available online at http://zh.wikisource.org/zh-hant/%E5%AE%88%E5%9F%8E%E9%8C%84, accessed 29 May 2014.

Chen Jiafu 陳家副. "Ming dai liang Guang zong du bing yuan yu xiang yuan zhi yan jiu" 明代兩廣總督兵源與餉源之研究. Master's thesis, National Central University, Taiwan, 2004. http://thesis.lib.ncu.edu.tw/ETD-db/ETD-search-c/view_etd?URN=90125005, accessed 4 March 2013.

Chen Lie 陳烈. "He bei sheng Kuang cheng xian chu tu de Ming tong chong" 河北省寬城縣出土的明銅銃. Kao gu 考古, no. 8 (1985): 759.

Chen Shisong 陳世松. *Song-Yuan zhan zheng shi* 宋元戰爭史. Huhehot 呼和浩特市: Inner Mongolian People's Press 內蒙古人民出版社, 2010.

Chen, Vincent. *Sino-Russian Relations in the Seventeenth Century.* The Hague: Martinus Nijhoff, 1966.

Cheng Dong 成東. "Ming dai qian qi you ming huo chong chu tan" 明代前期有銘火銃初探. Wen wu 文物, no. 5 (1988): 68–79.

———. "Zhong guo gu dai huo pao fa ming wen ti de xin tan tao" 中國古代火炮發明問題的新探討. In Zhong Shaoyi, *Zhong guo*, 23–36.

Cheng Dong 成東 and Zhong Shaoyi 鐘少異. *Zhong guo gu dai bing qi tu ji* 中國古代兵器圖集. Beijing: Jie fang jun chu ban she, 1991.

Cheng Zongyou 程宗猷. "Jue zhang xin fa" 蹶張心法. In *Jue zhang xin fa, chang qiang fa xuan, dan dao fa xuan* 蹶張心法1卷, 長槍法選1卷, 單刀法選1卷. 1843/Daoguang 22 [originally published 1621]. Copy from Japan National Diet Library, finding aid (請求記號) 859-43.

Chia, Lucille. *Printing for Profit: The Commercial Publishers of Jianyang, Fujian.* Cambridge, MA: Harvard University Press, 2002.

Chow, Kai-wing. *Publishing, Culture and Power in Early Modern China.* Stanford: Stanford University Press, 2004.

Church, Roy. *The Dynamics of Victorian Business.* London: Routledge, 2013.

Cioffi-Revilla, Claudio. *The Scientific Measurement of International Conflict: Handbook of Datasets on Crises and Wars, 1495–1988.* Boulder, CO: Lynne Rienner, 1990.

Cipolla, Carlo. *Guns, Sails and Empire: Technological Innovation and the Early Phases of European. Expansion, 1400–1700.* New York: Minerva Press, 1965.

Clausewitz, Carl von. *On War.* Translated and edited by Michael Howard and Peter Paret. Princeton: Princeton University Press, 1976.

Clephan, Robert Coltman. *An Outline of the History and Development of Hand Firearms.* London: Walter Scott, 1906.

Clowes, W. Laird. *The Royal Navy: A History from the Earliest Times to the Present.* Vol. 7. London: Sampson Low, Marston, 1903.

Clunas, Craig. *Empire of Great Brightness: Visual and Material Cultures of Ming China, 1368–1644.* Honolulu: University of Hawaii Press, 2007.

Clunas, Craig, and Zhengming Wen. *Elegant Debts: The Social Art of Wen Zhengming, 1470–1559.* Honolulu: University of Hawaii Press, 2004.

Cocroft, Wayne D. *Dangerous Energy: The Archaeology of Gunpowder and Military Explosives Manufacture.* Swindon, UK: English Heritage, 2000.

Cohen, Paul. *China Unbound: Evolving Perspectives on the Chinese Past.* London: Routledge, 2003.

Conlan, Thomas. *Weapons and Fighting Techniques of the Samurai Warrior, 1200–1877 AD.* London: Amber Books, 2008.

Contamine, Philippe. "L'artillerie royale française à la veille des guerres d'Italie." *Annales de Bretagne* 71, no. 2 (1964): 221–61.

———. *War in the Middle Ages.* New York: Basil Blackwell, 1984.

Cook, Harold. *Matters of Exchange: Commerce, Medicine, and Science in the Dutch Golden Age.* New Haven: Yale University Press, 2007.

———. "Moving About and Finding Things Out: Economies and Sciences in the Period of the Scientific Revolution." *Osiris* 27, no. 1 (2012): 101–32.

Cook, Weston F., Jr. *The Hundred Years War for Morocco: Gunpowder and the Military Revolution in the Early Modern Muslim World.* Boulder, CO: Westview, 1994.

Cooper, Michael. *Rodrigues the Interpreter: An Early Jesuit in Japan and China.* New York: Weatherhill, 1974.

Correa, Gaspar. *The Three Voyages of Vasco da Gama and His Viceroyalty.* Translated by Henry E. J. Stanley. New York: Burt Franklin, 1963 [originally published 1869].

Cosandey, David. *Le Secret de l'occident: Vers une théorie générale du progress scientifique.* Paris: Flammarion, 2008.

Costa, Paulo Oliveira e. "A Coroa Portuguesa e a China (1508–1531)—do Sonho Manuelino ao Realismo Joanino." In Antonio Vasconcelos de Saldanha and Jorge Manuel Dos Santos Alves, eds., *Estudos de História do Relacionamento Luso-Chinês, Séculos XVI–XIX.* Lisbon: Instituto Português do Oriente, 1996, 11–84.

Cowley, Robert, and Geoffrey Parker. "Editor's Note." In Cowley and Parker, *Reader's Companion to Military History*, xiii–xiv.

———, eds. *The Reader's Companion to Military History.* New York: Houghton Mifflin Harcourt, 2001.

Coyet, Frederick. *Neglected Formosa: A Translation from the Dutch of Frederic Coyett's 't Verwaerloosde Formosa.* Edited and translated by Inez de Beauclair. San Francisco: Chinese Materials Center, 1975.

———. *'t Verwaerloosde Formosa, of waerachtig verhael, hoedanigh door verwaerloosinge der Nederlanders in Oost-Indien, het Eylant Formosa, van den Chinesen Mandorijn, ende Zeeroover Coxinja, overrompelt, vermeestert, ende ontweldight is geworden.* Edited by G. C. Molewijk. Zutphen, Netherlands: Walburg Pers, 1991 [originally published 1675].

Crone, Patricia. *Pre-industrial Societies.* Oxford: Basil Blackwell, 1989.

Crossley, Pamela. *Orphan Warriors: Three Manchu Generations and the End of the Manchu World.* Princeton: Princeton University Press, 1990.

Cui Shuhua 崔樹華. "Nei Meng gu chu tu tong huo chong gai shu" 內蒙古出土銅火銃概述. *Nei Meng gu she hui ke xue* 內蒙古社會科學, no. 6 (1996): 29–32.

Cullen, Christopher. "Reflections on the Transmission and Transformation of Technologies: Agriculture, Printing, and Gunpowder between East and West." In Feza Günergun and Dhruv Raina, eds., *Science between Europe and Asia: Historical Studies on the Transmission, Adoption and Adaptation of Knowledge.* Heidelberg: Springer, 2011, 13–26.

Cunningham, Andrew, and Ole Peter Grell. *The Four Horsemen of the Apocalypse: Religion, War, Famine, and Death in Reformation Europe.* Cambridge: Cambridge University Press, 2001.

Cunynghame, Arthur. *The Opium War: Being Recollections of Service in China.* Philadelphia: G. B. Zieber, 1845.

Curry, Anne. "Guns and Goddams: Was There a Military Revolution in Lancastrian Normandy, 1415–50?" *Journal of Medieval Military History* 8 (2010): 171–88.

Curtin, Philip. *The West and the World: The European Challenge and the Overseas Response in the Age of Empire.* Cambridge: Cambridge University Press, 2000.

Curtis, William Eleroy. *The Yankees of the East: Sketches of Modern Japan.* New York: 1896.

Curzon of Kedleston, George Nathaniel Curzon, Marquess, 1859–1925. *Problems of the Far East.* London: Longmans, Green, 1894.

Daehnhardt, Rainer. *Espingarda Feiticeira: A Introdução da Arma de Fogo pelos Portugueses no Extremo-Oriente.* Oporto, Portugal: Lello & Irmão, 1994.

Dai, Yingcong. "A Disguised Defeat: The Myanmar Campaign of the Qing Dynasty." *Modern Asian Studies* 38, no. 1 (2004): 145–89.

———. "*Yingyun Shengxi:* Military Entrepreneurship in the High Qing Period, 1700–1800." *Late Imperial China* 26, no. 2 (2005): 1–67.

Daly, Jonathan. *The Rise of Western Power: A Comparative History of Western Civilization.* London: Bloomsbury, 2014.

Da Ming hui dian 大明會典. Taipei: Xin wen feng chu ban gong si 新文豐出版公司, 1976 (Minguo 65).

Dang Shoushan 黨壽山. *Wu wei wen wu kao shu* 武威文物考述. Wuwei: Guang ming yin shua wu zi you xian gong si, 2001.

Dear, Peter. "The Mechanical Philosophy and Its Appeal." In Marcus Hellyer, ed., *The Scientific Revolution.* Oxford: Blackwell, 2003, 101–29.

de Barros, João. *Da Asia de João de Barros e de Diogo do Couto: dos feitos que os portugueses fizeram no descobrimento dos mares e terras do Oriente.* 24 vols., decada tercera, parte segunda. Lisbon: Na Régia Officina Typografica, 1777.

de Equiluz, Martin. *Milicia Discurso, y Regla Militar, del Capitan Martin de Eguiluz, Bizcayno.* Antwerp: Casa Pedro Bellero, 1595 [originally written 1586].

De Iongh, D. *Het Krijgswezen onder de Oostindische Compagnie.* The Hague: Van Stockum en Zoon, 1950.

Delbruck, Hans. *The Dawn of Modern Warfare.* Lincoln: University of Nebraska Press, 1990.

de León, Fernando González. "Spanish Military Power and the Military Revolution." In Mortimer, *Early Modern Military History,* 25–42.

De Lucca, Denis. *Jesuits and Fortifications: The Contribution of the Jesuits to Military Architecture in the Baroque Age.* Leiden: Brill, 2012.

Deng, Gang. *The Premodern Chinese Economy: Structural Equilibrium and Capitalist Sterility.* London: Routledge, 1999.

Deng Kongzhao 鄧孔昭. "Lun Zheng Chenggong dui Zheng Zhilong de pi pan yu ji cheng" 論鄭成功對鄭芝龍的批判與繼承. In Deng Kongzhao, ed., *Zheng Chenggong yu Ming Zheng Taiwan shi yan jiu* 鄭成功與明鄭臺灣史研究. Beijing: Tai hai chu ban she, 2000, 19–37.

Denny, Mark. *Their Arrows Will Darken the Sun: The Evolution and Science of Ballistics.* Baltimore: Johns Hopkins University Press, 2011.

de Tousard, Louis. *American Artillerist's Companion: Or Elements of Artillery, Treating All Kinds of Firearms in Detail.* 2 vols. Philadelphia: C. and A. Conrad, 1809.

de Vauban, Sébastien Le Prestre. *Mémoire pour servir d'instruction dans la conduite des sièges et dans la défense des places.* Leiden: Jean & Herman Verbeek, 1740.

De Vos, Luc. "La bataille de Gavere le 23 juillet 1453: la victoire de l'organisation." In *XXII. Kongress der internationalen Kommission für Militärgeschichte.* Vienna: Heeresgeschichtliches Museum, 1997, 145–57.

DeVries, Kelly. "Facing the New Military Technology: Non-trace Italienne Anti-gunpowder Weaponry Defenses, 1350–1550." In Steele and Dorland, *Heirs of Archimedes,* 37–71.

———. "The Forgotten Battle of Beverhoutsveld, 3 May 1382: Technological Innovation and Military Significance." In Matthew Strickland, ed., *Armies, Chivalry, and Warfare in Medieval Britain and France.* Stamford, CT: Paul Watkins, 1998, 289–303.

———. "Gunpowder Weaponry and the Rise of the Early Modern State." *War in History* 5, no. 2 (1998): 127–145.

———. "Gunpowder Weapons at the Siege of Constantinople, 1453." In Yaacov Lev, ed., *War and Society in the Eastern Mediterranean, 7th–15th Centuries.* Leiden: Brill, 1996, 343–62.

———. *Infantry Warfare in the Early 14th Century.* Woodbridge, UK: Boydell Press, 1996.

———. "Reassessment of the Gun Illustrated in the Walter de Milemete and Pseudo-Aristotle Manuscripts." *Journal of the Ordnance Society* 15 (2003): 5–17.

———. "Sites of Military Science and Technology." In Katherine Park and Lorraine Daston, eds., *The Cambridge History of Science. Vol. 3: Early Modern Europe.* Cambridge: Cambridge University Press, 2006, 306–19.

———. "The Technology of Gunpowder Weaponry in Western Europe during the Hundred Years' War." In *XXII. Kongress der internationalen Kommission für Militärgeschichte.* Vienna: Heeresgeschichtliches Museum, 1997, 285–99.

———. "The Use of Gunpowder Weaponry By and Against Joan of Arc during the Hundred Years War." *War and Society* 15, no. 1 (1996): 1–15.

———. "A Woman as Leader of Men: Joan of Arc's Military Career." In Bonnie Wheeler and Charles T. Wood., eds., *Fresh Verdicts on Joan of Arc.* New York: Garland, 1996, 3–18.

DeVries, Kelly, and Robert D. Smith. *The Artillery of the Dukes of Burgundy, 1363–1477.* Woodbridge, UK: Boydell Press, 2005.

———. "Breech-Loading Guns with Removable Powder Chambers: A Long-Lived Military Technology." In Buchanan, *Gunpowder, Explosives, and the State,* 251–65.

———. *Medieval Military Technology.* 2nd ed. Toronto: University of Toronto Press, 2012.

Di Tema 迪特馬. "1514–1683 nian Zhong guo zai huo pao zhi zao ling yu zhong yu Ou zhou shui ping de la jin" 1514–1683 年中國在火炮製造領域中與歐洲水平的拉近. Master's thesis, Zhejiang University, 2013.

Diamond, Jared. *Guns, Germs, and Steel: The Fates of Human Societies.* New York: Norton, 2005.

Dickens, Charles. *The Works of Charles Dickens: Miscellaneous Papers Vol. 1.* London: Chapman and Hall, 1911.

Di Cosmo, Nicola. "Did Guns Matter? Firearms and the Qing Formation." In Lynn Struve, ed., *The Qing Formation in World-Historical Time.* Cambridge, MA: Harvard University Asia Center, 2004, 121–66.

———. "Introduction." In Nicola Di Cosmo, ed., *Military Culture in Imperial China*. Cambridge, MA: Harvard University Press, 2009, 1–22.

Dillon, Michael. *China: A Modern History*. London: I.B. Tauris, 2012.

Ding Gongchen 丁拱辰. *Yan pao tu shuo ji yao* 演炮圖說輯要. 4 juans. 1843. http://hdl.handle.net/2027/hvd.32044067767665, accessed 30 May 2013.

Dmytryshyn, Basil, E.A.P. Crownhart-Vaughan, and Thomas Vaughan. *Russia's Conquest of Siberia, 1558–1700*. Vol. 1. Portland: Oregon Historical Society, 1985.

Dondi, Giorgio. "Il terzo document sull'arma da fuoco in Europa." *Armi antichi: Bollettino dell'Accademia di San Marciano* (1997): 31–44.

Doner, Richard F., Bryan K. Ritchie, and Dan Slater. "Systemic Vulnerability and the Origins of Developmental States: Northeast and Southeast Asia in Comparative Perspective." *International Organization* 59 (2005): 327–61.

Dong Shaoxin 董少新 and Huang Yi-long 黃一農. "Chong zhen nian jian yuan Hua Pu bing xin kao" 崇禎年間援華葡兵新考. *Li shi yan jiu* 歷史研究 5 (2009): 65–86.

Downing, Brian. *The Military Revolution and Political Change*. Princeton: Princeton University Press, 1992.

Drake, Stillman. *Galileo at Work: His Scientific Biography*. Chicago: University of Chicago Press, 1978.

Dreyer, Edward L. "Military Origins of Ming China." In Frederick Mote and Denis Twitchett, eds., *The Cambridge History of China, Volume 7, The Ming Dynasty, 1368–1644, Part 1*. Cambridge: Cambridge University Press, 1998, 58–106.

———. "The Poyang Campaign, 1363: Inland Naval Warfare in the Founding the Ming Dynasty." In Kierman and Fairbank, *Chinese Ways in Warfare*, 202–42.

Dror, Olga, and Keith Weller Taylor, eds. *Views of Seventeenth-Century Vietnam*. Ithaca, NY: Cornell Southeast Asia Program, 2006.

Du You 杜佑. *Tong Dian* 通典. 5 vols. Edited by Wang Wenjin 王文錦. Beijing: Zhong hua shu ju, 1988 [originally written Tang dynasty]. Also available online at http://zh.wikisource.org/wiki/通典/卷149, accessed 27 March 2013.

Duchesne, Ricardo. "Reply to Mark Elvin." *Canadian Journal of Sociology* 36, no. 4 (2011): 378–87.

———. *The Uniqueness of Western Civilization*. Leiden: Brill, 2011.

Duffy, Christopher. *Siege Warfare: The Fortress in the Early Modern World, 1494–1660*. London: Routledge & Kegan Paul, 1979.

Dupuy, Trevor N. *The Encyclopedia of Military History: From 3500 B.C. to the Present*. New York: Harper & Row, 1993.

———. *The Evolution of Weapons and Warfare*. Fairfax, VA: Hero Books, 1984.

Dyson, Freeman. "The Case for Blunders." *New York Review of Books*, 6 March 2014.

Dzengseo. *The Diary of a Manchu Soldier in Seventeenth-Century China*. Translated and edited by Nicola Di Cosmo. London: Routledge, 2006.

E Ertai 鄂爾泰, compiler. "Lang Tan Zhuan" 郎談傳. In E Ertai 鄂爾泰, compiler, *Ba qi tong zhi* 八旗通志, 8 vols. Jilin Sheng Changchun shi 吉林省長春市: Dong bei shi fan da xue Press, 1985 [originally published 1739], juan 153, 3882–93.

Eaton, Richard, and Philip B. Wagoner. "Warfare on the Deccan Plateau, 1450–1600: A Military Revolution in Early Modern India?" *Journal of World History* 25, no. 1 (2014): 5–50.

Ebrey, Patricia. *The Cambridge Illustrated History of China*. Cambridge: Cambridge University Press, 1996.

Elleman, Bruce. *Modern Chinese Warfare, 1795–1989.* London: Routledge, 2001.

Elleman, Bruce, and S.C.M. Paine. *Modern China: Continuity and Change, 1644 to the Present.* Boston: Prentice Hall, 2010.

Elman, Benjamin. "Naval Warfare and the Refraction of China's Self Strengthening Reforms into Scientific and Technological Failure." *Modern Asian Studies* 38, no. 2 (2004): 283–326.

Eltis, David. *The Military Revolution in Sixteenth-Century Europe.* London: I.B. Tauris, 1998.

Elvin, Mark. "Confused Alarms: Duchesne on the Uniqueness of the West." *Canadian Journal of Sociology* 36, no. 4 (2011): 361–77.

———. "Defining the Explicanda in the 'West and the Rest' Debate: Bryant's Critique and Its Critics." *Canadian Journal of Sociology* 33, no. 1 (2008): 168–86.

———. *The Pattern of the Chinese Past.* Palo Alto, CA: Stanford University Press, 1973.

Essenwein, A. *Quellen zur Geschichte der Feueurwaffen.* Leipzig: F. A. Brockhaus, 1877.

Euler, Leonhard. *Neue Grundsätze der Artillerie: enthaltend die Bestimmung der Gewalt des Pulvers nebst einer Untersuchung über den Unterscheid des Wiederstands der Luft in schnellen und langsamen Bewegungen.* Berlin: Konigl. un der Academie der Wissenschaften, 1745.

Fa, Árpád. "The Effects of King Sigismund's Hussite Wars on the Art of War." *Academic and Applied Research in Military Science. Budapest* 9, no. 2 (2010): 285–99.

Fairbank, John King. *The United States and China.* Cambridge, MA: Harvard University Press, 2009.

Fairbank, John King, and Merle Goldman. *China: A New History.* Cambridge, MA: Belknap, 2006.

Fan Chuannan 範傳南. "'Gong ma qi she' long zhao xia de Qing dai quo qi: Qing dai huo qi fa zhan ji shi yong zhuang kuang shu lun" '弓馬騎射'籠罩下的清代火器清代火器發展及使用狀況述論. *Dong shan shi fan xue yuan xue bao* 樂山師範學院學報 23, no. 8 (2008): 100–106.

Fan Zhongyi 範中義. "*Ji xiao xin shu* shi si juan ben de cheng shu shi jian he nei rong" <<紀效新書>>十四卷本的成書時間和內容. In Yan Chongnian 閻崇年, ed., *Qi Jiguang yan jiu lun ji* 戚繼光研究論集. Beijing: Zhi shi chu ban she, 1990, 368–85.

Fan Zhongyi 範中義 and Quan Qinggang 全晰綱. *Ming dai Wo kou shi lüe* 明代倭寇史略. Beijing: Zhong hua shu ju, 2004.

Fang, Cheng-Hua. "Military Families and the Southern Song Court: The Lü Case." *Journal of Sung-Yuan Studies* 33 (2003): 49–70.

Fay, Peter Ward. *The Opium War, 1840–1842: Barbarians in the Celestial Empire in the Early Part of the Nineteenth Century and the War by Which They Forced Her Gates Ajar.* Chapel Hill: University of North Carolina Press, 1975.

Feng Jiasheng 馮家昇. *Huo yao de fa ming he xi chuan* 火藥的發明和西傳. Shanghai: Shanghai ren min chu ban she, 1978 [originally published 1954].

Feng, Liu, and Zhang Ruizhuang. "The Typologies of Realism." *Chinese Journal of International Politics* 1 (2006): 109–34.

Feng Qi 馮琦 and Chen Bangzhan 陳邦瞻. *Song shi ji shi ben mo* 宋史紀事本末, 109 juan edition. 1887 [based on sixteenth-century original version]. Also available online at http://zh.wikisource.org/wiki/%E5%AE%8B%E5%8F%B2%E7%B4%80%E4%BA%8B%E6%9C%AC%E6%9C%AB.

Feng Zhenyu 馮震宇. "Lun Fo lang ji zai Ming dai de tu hua" 論佛郎機在明代的本土化. *Zi ran bian zheng fa tong xun* 自然辯證法通訊 34, no. 3 (2012): 57–62.

Ferguson, Donald. *Letters from Portuguese Captives in Canton, Written in 1524 and 1536, with an Introduction on Portuguese intercourse with China in the First Half of the Sixteenth Century.* Bombay: Education Society's Steam Press, Byoulla, 1902.

Ferguson, Niall. *Civilization: The West and the Rest.* New York: Penguin, 2011.

Ferrero, Stéphane. *Formose vue par un marin français du XIXe siècle.* Paris: L'Harmattan, 2005.

Ffoulkes, Charles. *The Gun Founders of England: With a List of English and Continental Gun-Founders from the XIV to the XIX Centuries.* Cambridge: Cambridge University Press, 2011 [originally published 1937].

Filipiak, Kai. *Krieg, Staat und Militär in der Ming-Zeit (1368–1644): Auswirkungen militärischer und bewaffneter Konflikte auf Machtpolitik und Herrschaftsapparat der Ming-Dynastie.* Wiesbaden: Harrassowitz Verlag, 2008.

Foster, John W. *Diplomatic Memoirs.* Vol. 2. Boston: Houghton Mifflin, 1909.

Frank, André Gunder. *(Re)Orient: Global Economy in the Asian Age.* Berkeley: University of California Press, 1998.

Franke, Herbert. "The Chin Dynasty." In Denis Twitchett and John K. Fairbank, eds., *The Cambridge History of China, Volume 6, Alien Regimes and Border States, 907–1368.* Cambridge: Cambridge University Press, 1994, 215–320.

———. "Die Belagerung von Shao-hsing im Jahre 1359." In *Krieg und Krieger im Chinesischen Mittelalter (12. bis 14. Jahrhundert).* Stuttgart: Franz Steiner Verlag, 2003, 122–214.

———. "Siege and Defense of Towns in Medieval China." In Kierman and Fairbank, *Chinese Ways in Warfare,* 151–201.

———. *Studien und Texte zur Kriegsgeschichte der südlichen Sungzeit.* Wiesbaden: Otto Harrassowitz, 1987.

Froissart, Jean. *Chroniques de J. Froissart, tome huitième, 1370–1377, première partie.* Edited by Siméon Luce. Paris: Librairie Renouard, 1888.

———. *Les chroniques de Jehan Froissart, publiées avec les variants des divers manuscrits part M. le baron Kervyn de Lettenhove.* Vol. 5. Brussels: Victor Devaux, 1868.

———. *Les chroniques de Jehan Froissart, publiées avec les variants des divers manuscrits part M. le baron Kervyn de Lettenhove.* Vol. 10. Brussels: Victor Devaux, 1870.

———. *Les Chroniques de Sire Jean Froissart.* Vol. 1. Edited by J.A.C. Buchon. Paris: A Desrez, 1835.

Fukuda, Kazunori. "The Relations between China and Portugal in the Early Sixteenth Century: Some Observations on the Yue Shan Cong Tan." *Revista de Cultura* 1 (2002): 100–105.

Fung, Allen. "Testing the Self-Strengthening: The Chinese Army in the Sino-Japanese War of 1894–1895." *Modern Asian Studies* 30, no. 4 (1996): 1007–31.

Fung, Edmund S. K. "Ch'ing Policy in the Sino-Japanese War." *Journal of Asian History* 7, no. 2 (1973): 128–52.

Galambos, Imre. "Consistency in Tangut Translations of Chinese Military Texts." In Irina Popova, ed., *Tanguty v Tsentral'noj Azii: Sbornik stat'ej v chest' 80-letija prof. E. I. Kychanova.* Moscow: Oriental Literature, 2012, 84–96.

Gamot, Eugène Germain. *l'Expédition française de Formose, 1884–1885.* Paris: Librairie Ch. Delagrave, 1894.

Garrett, Richard J. *The Defences of Macau: Forts, Ships, and Weapons over 450 Years.* Hong Kong: Hong Kong University Press, 2010.

———. "Weapons of the China Wars." *Journal of the Hong Kong Branch of the Royal Asiatic Society* 38 (1998): 107–19.

Ghosh, Shami. "The 'Great Divergence,' Politics, and Capitalism." *Journal of Early Modern History* 19 (2015): 1–43.

Gibson, Walter S. *Pieter Bruegel and the Art of Laughter.* Berkeley: University of California Press, 2006.

Giquel, Prosper. *The Foochow Arsenal, and Its Results: From the Commencement in 1867, to the End of the Foreign Directorate, on the 16th February, 1874.* Translated by H. Lang. Shanghai: Shanghai Evening Courier, 1874.

———. "La France en Chine, le commerce français dans le Céleste-Empire, le Corps Franco-Chinois et les Missions en 1863." *Revue des deux mondes* 51 (May–June 1864): 962–93.

Glendinning, Paul. "View from the Pennines: Euler Goes ballistic." *Mathematics Today* 43, no. 5 (2007): 175–77. http://www.maths.manchester.ac.uk/~pag /view/gayna28.pdf, accessed 12 June 2013.

Gohlke, Wilhelm. *Geschichte der gesamten Feuerwaffen bis 1850: die Entwicklung der Feuerwaffen von ihrem ersten Auftreten bis zur Einführung der gezogenen Hinterlader, unter besonderer Berücksichtigung der Heeresbewaffnung.* Leipzig: G. J. Göschen'sche Verlagsbuchhandlung, 1911.

Golder, Frank A. *Russian Expansion on the Pacific, 1641–1850: An Account of the Earliest and Later Expeditions Made by the Russians along the Pacific Coast of Asia and North America; Including Some Related Expeditions to the Arctic Regions.* Gloucester, MA: P. Smith, 1914.

Goldstone, Jack A. "Capitalist Origins, the Advent of Modernity, and Coherent Explanation: A Response to Joseph M. Bryant." *Canadian Journal of Sociology* 33, no. 1 (2008): 119–33.

———. "Comment on Andrade." *Canadian Journal of Sociology* 36, no. 2 (2011): 209–12.

———. "Efflorescences and Economic Growth in World History: Rethinking the 'Rise of the West' and the Industrial Revolution." *Journal of World History* 13, no. 2 (2002): 323–89.

———. "Europe's Peculiar Path: Would the World Be 'Modern' if William III's Invasion of England in 1688 Had Failed?" In Philip E. Tetlock, Ned Lebow, and Geoffrey Parker, eds., *Unmaking the West: What-if? Scenarios That Rewrite World History.* Ann Arbor: University of Michigan Press, 2006, 168–96.

———. "The Rise of the West—or Not? A Revision to Socio-economic History." *Sociological Theory* 18 (2000): 157–94.

Gommans, Jos. *Mughal Warfare.* London: Routledge, 2002.

Gommans, Jos, and Dirk Kolff. *Warfare and Weaponry in South Asia, 1000–1800.* Oxford: Oxford University Press, 2001.

Gontier, Jean-Marie. *Qi Jiguang, un stratège de la dynastie Ming (1528—1587).* Paris: Institut de Stratégie Comparée, Commission Française d'Histoire Militaire, 2002. http://www.institut-strategie.fr/?p=671, accessed 11 November 2014.

Goodrich, L. Carrington. *A Short History of the Chinese People.* Mineola, NY: Dover, 2002 [originally published 1943].

Goodrich, L. Carrington, and Chaoying Fang, eds. *Dictionary of Ming Biography, 1368–1644.* 2 vols. New York: Columbia University Press, 1976.

Gordin, Michael D. "A Modernization of 'Peerless Homogeneity': The Creation of Russian Smokeless Gunpowder." *Technology and Culture* 44, no. 4 (2003): 677–702.

Gorski, Philip S. "The Little Divergence: The Protestant Ethic and Economic Hegemony in Early Modern Europe." In Lutz Kaelber and Richard Swatos, eds., *The Protestant Ethic Turns 100: Essays on the Centenary of the Weber Thesis.* Boulder, CO: Paradigm, 2005, 165–89.

Graff, David A., and Robin Higham, eds. *A Military History of China.* Boulder, CO: Westview, 2002.

Greatrex, Roger. "Comparative Perspectives upon the Introduction of Western Steamship Technology to Japan and China." *Japanese Civilization in the Modern World Part X: Technology, Senri Ethnological Studies* 46 (1998): 99–126.

Grueber, Martin, Tim Studt, et al. "2014 Global R&D Funding Forecast." *R&D Magazine,* December 2013, 13–15. http://www.rdmag.com/sites/rdmag.com/files /gff-2014-5_7%20875x10_0.pdf, accessed 3 April 2014.

Gruzinski, Serge. *The Eagle and the Dragon: Globalization and European Dreams of Conquest in China and America in the Sixteenth Century.* Cambridge: Polity, 2014.

Gu Yanwu 顧炎武 (aka Gu Tinglin 顧亭林). "Tian xia jun guo li bing shu" 天下郡國利病書. In Gu Yanwu, *Gu Yanwu quan ji* 顧炎武全集, vols. 12–17. Shanghai: Shanghai gu ji chu ban she, 2011.

Gu Yingtai 谷應泰. *Ming shi ji shi* 明史紀事. 1658. abc.lambook.com/read/2200/%E 6%98%8E%E5%8F%B2%E7%B4%80%E4%BA%8B/%E8%B0%B7%E6%87%89 %E6%B3%B0/2200/, accessed 6 October 2012.

———. *Ming shi ji shi ben mo* 明史紀事本末. Seventeenth century.

Guilmartin, John F., Jr. *Galleons and Galleys.* London: Cassell, 2002.

Haeger, John W. "1126–27: Political Crisis and the Integrity of Culture." In John W. Haeger, ed., *Crisis and Prosperity in Sung China.* Tucson: University of Arizona Press, 1975, 143–61.

Haenisch, Eric. *Zum Untergang zweier Reiche: Berichte von Augenzeugen aus den Jahren 1232–33 und 1368–70.* Wiesbaden: Franz Steiner, 1969.

Haldon, John. "'Greek Fire' Revisited: Recent and Current Research." In Elizabeth Jeffreys, ed., *Byzantine Style, Religion, and Civilization: In Honour of Sir Steven Runciman.* Cambridge: Cambridge University Press, 2006, 290–325.

Hale, J. R. *Renaissance War Studies.* London: Hambledon, 1983.

———. *War and Society in Renaissance Europe, 1450–1620.* London: Fontana, 1985.

Hall, Bert S. *Weapons and Warfare in Renaissance Europe: Gunpowder, Technology, and Tactics.* Baltimore: Johns Hopkins University Press, 1997.

Halsey, Stephen R. "Money, Power, and the State: The Origins of the Military-Fiscal State in Modern China." *Social and Economic History of the Orient* 56 (2013): 392–432.

Hammersmith, Jack. "The Sino-Japanese War, 1894–5: American Predictions Reassessed." *Asian Forum* 4, no. 1 (1972): 48–58.

Han Lin 韓霖. *Shou yu quan shu* 守圉全書. 1638.

Hana, Corinna. *Bericht über die Verteidigung der Stadt Tê-an während der Periode K'ai-hsi 1205–1208.* Wiesbaden: Franz Steiner Verlag GMBH, 1970.

Hanak, W. K. "Sultan Mehmed II Fatih and the Theodosian Walls: The Conquest of Constantinople, 1453." In Sümer Atasoy, ed., *Istanbul Üniversitesi 550. Yil Uluslararasi Bizans ve Osmanli Sempozyumu.* Istanbul: Instanbul Üniversitesi, 2004, 1–13.

Hanson, Victor Davis. *Carnage and Culture: Landmark Battles in the Rise of Western Power.* New York: Doubleday, 2001.

Hao, Zhidong. *Macau: History and Society.* Hong Kong: Hong Kong University Press, 2011.

Harari, Yuval N. *Special Operations in the Age of Chivalry, 1100–1550.* Woodbridge, UK: Boydell Press, 2007.

Hart, Roger. *Imagined Civilizations: China, the West, and Their First Encounter.* Baltimore: Johns Hopkins University Press, 2012.

Hartley, Percival Horton-Smith, and Harold Richard Aldridge, eds. *Johannes de Mirfeld of St. Bartholomew's, Smithfield: His Life and Works.* Cambridge: Cambridge University Press, 2013 [originally published 1936].

Hartman, Charles. "Chinese Historiography in the Age of Maturity, 960–1368." In Daniel Woolf, ed., *The Oxford History of Historical Writing,* vol. 2. Oxford: Oxford University Press, 2012, 37–57.

Hartwell, Robert M. "A Cycle of Economic Change in Imperial China: Coal and Iron in Northeast China, 750–1350." *Journal of the Economic and Social History of the Orient* 10, no. 1 (1967): 102–59.

———. "A Revolution in the Chinese Iron and Coal Industries during the Northern Sung, 960–1127." *Journal of Asian Studies* 21, no. 2 (1962): 153–62.

Hashimoto, Takehiko. "Introducing a French Technological System: The Origin and Early History of the Yokosuka Dockyard." *East Asian Science, Technology, and Medicine* 16 (1999): 53–72.

Haskew, Michael, Christer Jörgensen, Chris McNab, Eric Niderost, and Rob S. Rice. *Fighting Techniques of the Oriental World, AD 1200–1860.* New York: Thomas Dunne, 2008.

Haw, Stephen G. "The Mongol Empire—The First 'Gunpowder Empire'?" *Journal of the Royal Asiatic Society* 23, no. 3 (August 2013]: 1–29.

He Mengchun 何孟春. *Xu dong xu lu zhai chai wai bian* 余冬序錄摘抄外篇. Ming dynasty. http://guoxue.r12345.com/ext/xilu/wave99/msgview-950484-22847.html, accessed 7 September 2012.

He, Wenkai. *Paths toward the Modern Fiscal State: England, Japan, and China.* Cambridge, MA: Harvard University Press, 2013.

Herbert, Hilary A. "The Fight off the Yalu River." *North American Review* 159, no. 456 (1894): 513–28.

———. "Military Lessons of the Chino-Japanese War." *North American Review* 160, no. 6 (1895): 685–98.

Herson, James. "French Innovation versus British Technology at Cadiz: Missile Warfare in the Peninsular War." In *Consortium on Revolutionary Europe, Selected Papers 1995.* Tallahassee: Florida State University, Institute on Napoleon and the French Revolution, 1995, 464–75.

Higgins, Roland. "Piracy and Coastal Defense in the Ming Period: Government Response to Coastal Disturbances, 1523–1549." PhD dissertation, University of Minnesota, 1981.

Ho, Peng Yoke, and Wang Ling. "On the Karyukyo, The 'Fire-Dragon Manual.'" *Papers on Far Eastern History* 16 (September 1977): 147–59.

Hodgson, Marshall G. S. *The Venture of Islam, Volume 3: The Gunpowder Empires and Modern Times.* Chicago: University of Chicago Press, 1977.

Hoffman, Philip T. "Prices, the Military Revolution, and Western Europe's Comparative Advantage in Violence." *Economic History Review* 64 (2011): 39–59.

———. *Why Did Europe Conquer the World?* Princeton: Princeton University Press, 2015.

———. "Why Was It Europeans Who Conquered the World?" *Journal of Economic History* 72, no. 3 (2012): 601–33.

Home, Major J. M. "General Report on the Russo-Japanese War up to the 15th August 1904." In *The Russo-Japanese War: Reports from British Officers Attached to the Japanese and Russian Forces in the Field, Volume 3.* London: HMSO, 1908, 209–301.

Hong Mai 洪邁. *Rong zhai wu bi* 容齋五筆. Twelfth century.

Horowitz, Richard S. "Beyond the Marble Boat: The Transformation of the Chinese Military, 1850–1911." In Graff and Higham, *Military History of China*, 153–74.

Howard, Michael. *War in European Society.* Oxford: Oxford University Press, 1976.

Hsu, Cho-yun. *China: A New Cultural History.* New York: Columbia University Press, 2012.

Hsü, Immanuel C. Y. *The Ili Crisis: A Study of Sino-Russian Diplomacy, 1871–1881.* Oxford: Clarendon, 1965.

———. *The Rise of Modern China.* 6th ed. Oxford: Oxford University Press, 2000 [1st edition published 1970].

Hu Angang. *China in 2020: A New Type of Superpower.* Washington, DC: Brookings Institution Press, 2012.

Hu Zhenqi 胡振琪. "Ming dai tie pao" 明代鐵炮. *Shan xi wen wu* 山西文物, no. 1 (1982): 57.

Huang Kuan-Chung. "Defensive Structures and Construction Materials in Song City Walls." Translated by Wen-yi Chen, Peter Lorge, and Tracy G. Miller. *Journal of Sung-Yuan Studies* 31 (2001): 27–51.

Huang, Ray. *1587, a Year of No Significance: The Ming Dynasty in Decline.* New Haven: Yale University Press, 1981.

Huang Yi-Long 黃一農. "Hong yi da pao yu Huang Taiji chuang li de ba qi Han jun" 紅夷大砲與皇太極創立的八旗漢軍. *Li shi yan jiu* 歷史研究, no. 4 (2004): 74–105.

———. "Hong yi da pao yu Ming Qing zhan zheng—yi huo pao ce zhu ji shu zhi yan bian wei li" 紅夷大砲與明清戰爭—以火砲測準技術之演變為例. *Qing hua xue bao* 清華學報 (Taiwan) 26, no. 1 (1996): 31–70.

———. "Ming Qing du te fu he jin shu pao de xing shuai" 明清獨特複合金屬砲的興衰. *Qinghua xuebao* 清華學報 41, no. 1 (2011): 73–136.

———. "Ming Qing zhi ji hong yi da pao zai dong nan yan hai de liu bu ji qi ying xiang" 明清之際紅夷大砲在東南沿海的流布及其影響. *Zhong yang yan jiu yuan ji li shi yu yan yan jiu suo ji kan* 中央研究院歷史語言研究所集刊 81, no. 4 (2010): 769–832.

———. "Ou zhou chen chuan yu Ming mo chuan hua de xi yang da pao" 歐洲沉船與明末傳華的西洋大炮. *Zhong yang yan jiu yuan li shi hua yan yan jiu suo ji kan* 中央研究院歷史語言研究所集刊 75, no. 3 (2004): 573–634.

———. "Sun Yuanhua: A Christian Convert Who Put Xu Guangqi's Military Reform Policy into Practice." In Catherine Jami et al., eds., *Statecraft and Intellectual Renewal in Late Ming China. The Cross-Cultural Synthesis of Xu Guangqi (1562–1633)*. Leiden: Brill, 2001, 225–59.

———. "Wu qiao bing bian: Ming Qing ding ge de yi tiao zhong yao dao huo xian" 吳橋兵變：明清鼎革的一條重要導火線. *Qing hua xue bao* 清華學報 42, no. 1 (2013 民國101): 79–133.

Huber, Johannes. "Chinese Settlers Against the Dutch East India Company: The Rebellion led by Kuo Huai-I on Taiwan in 1652." In E. B. Vermeer, ed., *Development and Decline of Fukien Province in the 17th and 18th Centuries*. Leiden: Brill, 1990, 265–96.

Hucker, Charles O. *A Dictionary of Official Titles in Imperial China*. Palo Alto, CA: Stanford University Press, 1985.

Huff, Toby. *Intellectual Curiosity and the Scientific Revolution: A Global Perspective*. Cambridge: Cambridge University Press, 2011.

Hui, Victoria Tin-Bor. "War and Historical China: Problematizing 'Zhongguo.'" Paper presented at the 49th annual convention of the International Studies Association, San Francisco, 26–29 March 2008.

———. *War and State Formation in Ancient China and Early Modern Europe*. Cambridge: Cambridge University Press, 2005.

Ibn Battuta. *The Travels of Ibn Battuta*. London: Oriental Translation Committee, 1829.

Irwin, Robert. "Gunpowder and Firearms in the Mamluk Sultanate Reconsidered." In Michael Winter and Amalia Levanoni, eds., *The Mamluks in Egyptian and Syrian Politics and Society*. Leiden: Brill, 2004, 117–42.

Ivanov, Andrey V. "Conflicting Loyalties: Fugitives and 'Traitors' in the Russo-Manchurian Frontier, 1651–1689." *Journal of Early Modern History* 13 (2009): 333–58.

Jacob, Margaret C. *Scientific Culture and the Making of the Industrial West*. New York: Oxford University Press, 1997.

Jacob, Margaret, and Larry Stewart. *Practical Matter: Newton's Science in the Service of Industry and Empire: 1687–1851*. Cambridge, MA: Harvard University Press, 2004.

Jacobsen, Stefan. "Limits to Despotism: Idealizations of Chinese Governance and Legitimizations of Absolutist Europe." *Journal of Early Modern History* 17 (2013): 347–89.

Jiang Risheng 江日昇. *Taiwan wai ji* 臺灣外記. *Taiwan wen xian cong kan* 台灣文獻叢刊 no. 60. Taipei: Taiwan yin hang, 1960.

Jiang Shusheng 江樹生, ed. and trans. *Mei shi ri ji: Helan tudi celiangshi kan Zheng Chenggong* 梅氏日記荷蘭土地測量師看鄭成功. Taipei: Han sheng za zhi she gu fen you xian gong si 漢聲雜誌社股份有限公司, 2003.

Jiao Yu 焦玉. *Huo long shen qi zhen fa* 火龍神器陣法. In Liu Lumin 劉魯民, ed., *Zhong guo bing shu ji cheng* 中國兵書集成, vol. 17. Beijing: People's Liberation Army Press, 1994.

Jin Guoping 金國平. *Xi li dong jian: Zhong Pu zao qi jie chu zhui xi* 西力東漸：中葡早期接觸追昔. Macau: Ao men ji jin hui chu ban, 2000.

Jing, Chunxiao. *Mit Barbaren gegen Barbaren: die chinesische Selbstärkungsbewegung und das deutsche Rüstungsgeschäft im späten 19. Jahrhundert*. Münster: LIT Verlag, 2003.

Johnson, W. "Robins on Boring out Cannon to Accommodate Heavier Shot." *International Journal of Impact Engineering* 8, no. 3 (1989): 281–85.

Johnston, Alistair Iain. *Cultural Realism: Strategic Culture and Grand Strategy in Chinese History.* Princeton: Princeton University Press, 1995.

Jones, Colin. "The Military Revolution and the Professionalisation of the French Army under the Ancien Régime." In Rogers, *Military Revolution Debate,* 149–68.

Jones, Eric L. *The European Miracle: Environments, Economies, and Geopolitics in the History of Europe and Asia.* Cambridge: Cambridge University Press, 1981.

Joregensen, Christer, Eric Niderost, and Chris McNab. *Fighting Techniques of the Oriental World.* London: St. Martin's, 2008.

Kamiki Tetsuo. "Progress in Western Technology at the Yokosuka Shipbuilding Works, 1865–1887." *Papers on Far Eastern History* 37 (1988): 105–23.

Kang, David. *China Rising: Peace, Power, and Order in East Asia.* New York: Columbia University Press, 2013.

———. *East Asia before the West: Five Centuries of Trade and Tribute.* New York: Columbia University Press, 2010.

———. "Why China's Rise Will Be Peaceful: Hierarchy and Stability in the East Asian Region." *Perspectives on Politics* 3, no. 3 (2005): 551–53.

Kang, Hyeok Hweon. "Big Heads, Bird Guns and Gunpowder Bellicosity: Revolutionizing the Chosŏn Military in Seventeenth Century Korea." Undergraduate thesis, Emory University, 2013.

———. "Big Heads and Buddhist Demons: The Korean Musketry Revolution and the Northern Expeditions of 1654 and 1658." *Journal of Chinese Military History* 2 (2013): 127–89.

Kaufmann, J. E., H. W. Kauffman, and Robert M. Jurga. *The Medieval Fortress: Castles, Forts, and Walled Cities of the Middle Ages.* Cambridge, MA: Da Capo Press, 2004.

Keith, Matthew. "The Logistics of Power: The Tokugawa Response to the Shimabara Rebellion and Power Projection in 17th-Century Japan." PhD dissertation, Ohio State University, 2006.

Kelly, Jack. *Gunpowder: Alchemy, Bombards, and Pyrotechnics: The History of the Explosive That Changed the World.* New York: Basic Books, 2004.

Kennedy, Thomas L. *The Arms of Kiangnan: Modernization in the Chinese Ordnance Industry, 1860–1895.* New York: Columbia University Press, 1979.

Kenyon, John R. *Medieval Fortifications.* New York: St. Martin's, 1990.

Kessler, Lawrence D. *K'ang-hsi and the Consolidation of Ch'ing Rule, 1661–1684.* Chicago: University of Chicago Press, 1976.

Keuning, Johannes. "Nicolaas Witsen as a Cartographer." *Imago Mundi* 11 (1954): 95–110.

Khan, Iqtidar Alam. *Gunpowder and Firearms: Warfare in Medieval India.* New Delhi: Oxford University Press, 2004.

Kiang, Heng Chye. *Cities of Aristocrats and Bureaucrats: The Development of Medieval Chinese Cityscapes.* Honolulu: University of Hawaii Press, 1999.

Kierman, Frank A., Jr., and John K. Fairbank, eds. *Chinese Ways in Warfare.* Cambridge, MA: Harvard University Press, 1974.

Knauerhase, Ramon. "The Compound Marine Steam Engine: A Study in the Relationship between Technological Change and Economic Development." PhD dissertation, University of Pennsylvania, 1967.

————. "The Compound Steam Engine and Productivity Changes in the German Merchant Marine Fleet, 1871–1887." *Journal of Economic History* 28, no. 3 (1968): 390–403.

Ko, Chiu Yu, Mark Koyama, and Tuan-Hwee Sng. "Unified China and Divided Europe." Working paper, December 2013. http://papers.ssrn.com/sol3/papers.cfm?abstract_id=2382346, accessed 27 December 2014.

Kolb, Raimund T. "Excursions in Chinese Military History." *Monumenta Serica* 54 (2006): 435–64.

Koller, Heinrich. "Die mittelalterliche Stadmauer als Grundlage städtischen Selbstbewusstseins." In Berhnahrd Kirchgässner and Günter Scholz, eds., *Stadt und Krieg*. Sigmaringen, Germany: Jan Thorbecke Verlag, 1989, 9–25.

Kong Xiangji 孔祥吉. "Jia wu zhan zheng Zhong bei yang shui shi shang ceng ren wu de xin tai" 甲午戰爭中北洋水師上層人物的心態. *Jin dai shi yan jiu* 近代史研究, no. 6 (2000): 140–60.

Kristinsson, Axel. *Expansions: Competition and Conquest in Europe since the Bronze Age*. Reykjavik: Reykjavikur Akademian, 2010.

Kuhn, Dieter. *The Age of Confucian Rule: The Song Transformation of China*. Cambridge, MA: Belknap, 2009.

Kuhn, Philip. *Rebellion and Its Enemies in Late Imperial China: Militarization and Social Structure, 1796–1864*. Cambridge, MA: Harvard University Press, 1970.

Kuo, Ting-yee, and Kwang-Ching Liu. "Self Strengthening: The Pursuit of Western Technology." In *The Cambridge History of China, Volume 10*. Cambridge: Cambridge University Press, 1978, 491–542.

La Fargue, Thomas. "Some Early Chinese Visitors to the United States." *T'ien Hsia Monthly* 11 (1940): 136–40.

Lamers, Jeroen. *Japonius Tyrranus: The Japanese Warlord, Oda Nobunaga Reconsidered*. Leiden: Hotei, 2000.

Lan Zhenlu 藍振露. "Shi lun Tai ping Tian guo de jun huo jin kou mao yi" 試論太平天國的軍火進口貿易. *Shi xue yue kan* 史學月刊, no. 6 (June 1991): 42–47.

Landers, John. *The Field and the Forge: Population, Production, and Power in the Preindustrial West*. Oxford: Oxford University Press, 2005.

Landes, David. *The Wealth and Poverty of Nations: Why Some Are so Rich and Some so Poor*. New York: Norton, 1998.

————. "Why Europe and the West? Why Not China?" *Journal of Economic Perspectives* 20, no. 2 (2006): 3–22. http://www.jstor.org/stable/30033648, accessed 5 November 2012.

Landtsheer, Jeanine de. "Justus Lipsius's *De militia Romana:* Polybius Revived, or How an Ancient Historian Was Turned into a Manual of Early Modern Warfare." In K.A.E. Enenkel et al., eds., *Recreating Ancient History: Episodes from the Greek and Roman Past in the Arts and Literature of the Early Modern Period*. Leiden: Brill, 2002, 101–22.

Lau, D. C., and Roger T. Ames, trans. *Sun Bin: The Art of Warfare: A Translation of the Classic Chinese Work of Philosophy and Strategy*. Albany: State University of New York Press, 2003.

Leibnitz, Klaus. "Fitting Round Pegs into Square Holes? Did Balduin of Luxemburg, Archbishop of Trier Use Gunpowder Artillery in the Siege of Eltz Castle 1331/33?" N.d. http://www.vikingsword.com/library/leibnitz_round_pegs.pdf, accessed 3 January 2013.

Leibo, Steven. *Transferring Technology to China: Prosper Giquel and the Self-Strengthening Movement.* Berkeley: Institute of East Asian Studies, 1985.

Leonard, Jane Kate. *Wei Yuan and China's Rediscovery of the Maritime World.* Cambridge, MA: Harvard University Press, 1984.

Levine, Ari. "The Reigns of Hui-tsung (1100–1126) and Ch'in-tsung (1126–1127) and the Fall of the Northern Sung." In Denis Twitchett and Paul Jakov Smith, eds., *The Cambridge History of China, Volume 5, Part 1, The Sung Dynasty and Its Precursors, 907–1279.* Cambridge: Cambridge University Press, 2009, 556–643.

———. "Review of Don Wyatt, *Battlefronts.*" *American Historical Review* 114, no. 3 (2009): 733–34.

———. "Review of Yuri Pines, *Everlasting Empire.*" *Journal of the American Oriental Society* 133, no. 3 (2013): 574–77.

———. "Walls and Gates, Windows and Mirrors: Urban Defenses, Cultural Memory, and Security Theater in Song Kaifeng." *East Asian Science, Technology, and Medicine* 39 (2014): 55–118.

Lévy, André. "L'arrivée des Portugais en Chine: la perception chinoise d'après l'Histoire Officielle des Ming." *Nouvelle Revue du XVII Siècle* 16, no. 1 (1998): 7–19.

Levy, Jack. *War in the Modern Great Power System, 1495–1975.* Lexington: University Press of Kentucky, 1983.

Li Bin 李斌. "*Huo long jing* kao bian" 《火龍經》考辨. *Zhong guo li shi wen wu* 中國歷史文物, no. 1 (2002): 33–38.

———. "Ming Qing huo qi ji shu yan jiu" 明清火器技術研究. PhD dissertation, Zhong guo ke xue ji shu da xue 中國科學技術大學, 1991.

Li Dao 李燾 (1115–1184) and Huang Yizhou 黃以週 (1828–1899). *Xu Zi zhi tong jian chang bian shi bu* 續資治通鑑長編拾補.

Li Gang 李綱. *Jing kang chuan xin lu* 靖康傳信錄. 1128.

Li Huguang 李湖光. *Da Ming di guo zhan zheng shi: Da Ming long quan xia de huo qi zhan zheng* 大明帝國戰爭史：大明龍權下的火器戰爭. Beijing: Feng huang chu ban she 鳳凰出版社, 2010.

Li Quan 李筌. *Shen ji zhi di tai bai yin jing* 神機制敵太白陰經. Shanghai Shang wu yin shu guan, 1937. Also available online at http://www.cos.url.tw/book/3/O-1-023-d6.htm.

Li Wenfeng 李文鳳. *Yue shan cong tan* 月山叢談. Sixteenth century.

Li Yue 李悅. "Ming dai huo qi de pu xi" 明代火器的譜系. Master's thesis, Dong bei shi fan da xue, 2012.

Li Zengbo 李曾伯. *Ke zhai za gao,* 可齋雜稿. Song dynasty.

Liao Dake 廖大珂. "Zao qi Putaoya ren zai Fujian de tong shang yu chong tu" 早期葡萄牙人在福建的通商與衝突. *Dong nan xue bao* 東南學樹, no. 4 (2000): 71–78.

Lidin, Olof G. *Tanegashima: The Arrival of Europe in Japan.* Copenhagen: Nordic Institute of Asian Studies, 2002.

Lieberman, Victor. "Protected Rimlands and Exposed Zones: Reconfiguring Premodern Eurasia." *Comparative Studies in Society and History* 50 (2008): 692–723.

———. *Strange Parallels: Southeast Asia in Global Context, c. 800–1830, Volume 1: Integration on the Mainland.* New York: Cambridge University Press, 2007.

———. *Strange Parallels: Southeast Asia in Global Context, c. 800–1830, Volume 2: Mainland Mirrors: Europe, Japan, China, South Asia, and the Islands.* New York: Cambridge University Press, 2009.

———. "Transcending East-West Dichotomies: State and Culture Formation in Six Ostensibly Disparate Areas." In Victor Lieberman, ed., *Beyond Binary Histories: Re-imagining Eurasia to c.1830*. Ann Arbor: University of Michigan Press, 1999, 19–102.

Liew, Foon Ming. *The Treatises on Military Affairs of the Ming Dynastic History (1368–1644), Part I*. Hamburg: Gesellschaft für Natur- und Völkerkunde ostasiens e. V., 1998.

Lin Jinshui 林金水 and Zou Ping 鄒萍. *Zhongguo gu dai guan zhi yi ming jian ming shou ce* 中國古代官制譯名簡明手冊. Shanghai: Shi ji chu ban ji tuan, 2004.

Lin Jun 林俊. *Jian su ji* 見素集. Taipei: Taiwan shang wu yin shu guan, 1983 [originally written 1585].

Lin, Justin Yifu. *Demystifying the Chinese Economy*. Cambridge: Cambridge University Press, 2012.

Lin Wenzhao 林文照 and Deng Yongfang 郭永芳. "Ming mo yi bu zhong yao de huo qi zhua zhu: Xi fa shen ji" 明末一部重要的火器專著: 西法神機. *Zi ran ke xue shi yan jiu* 自然科學史研究 6, no. 3 (1987): 251–59.

Lin Wenzhao 林文照 and Guo Yongfang 郭永芳. "Ming Qing jian Xi fang huo pao huo qiang chuan ru Zhong guo li shi kao" 明清間西方火炮火槍傳入中國歷史考. In Huang Shengzhang 黃盛璋, ed., *Ya zhou wen ming* 亞洲文明, collection 1 (第一集). Hefei: Anhui jiao yu chu ban she, 1992, 165–78.

Lindley, Augustus. *Ti-ping Tien-Kwoh: The History of The Ti-ping Revolution, Including a Narrative of the Author's Personal Adventures*. 2 vols. London: Day & Son, 1866.

Lipsius, Justus. *De militia romana*. Antwerp: Ex officina Plantiniana, apud viduam & filios Ioannis Moreti, 1614.

Liu, Ganglin William 劉光臨. "Song China's Water Transport Revisited: A Study of the 1077 Commercial Tax Data." *Pacific Economic Review* 17, no. 1 (2012): 57–85.

Liu Hongcai 羅宏才. "Ding bian xian fa xian de yi jian Ming dai tie chong" 定邊縣發現的一件明代鐵銃. *Wen bo* 文博, no. 4 (1988): 92–93.

Liu Hongliang 劉鴻亮. "Di yi ci ya pian zhan zheng shi qi Zhong Ying shuang fang huo pao de ji shu bi jiao" 第一次鴉片戰爭時期中英雙方火炮的技術比較. *Qing shi yan jiu* 清史研究, no. 3 (2006): 31–42.

———. "Hong yi da pao yu Qing shun zhan zheng" 紅夷大炮與清順戰爭. *He nan ke shu da xue xue bao, she hui ke xue ban* 河南科技大學學報, 社會科學版 23, no. 1 (2005): 14–19.

———. *Zhong Ying huo pao yu ya pian zhan zheng* 中英火炮與鴉片戰爭. Beijing: Ke xue chu ban she, 2011.

Liu Hongliang 劉鴻亮 and Sun Shuyun 孫淑雲. "Ya pian zhan zheng shi qi Zhong Ying tie pao cai zhi de you lie bi jiao yan jiu" 鴉片戰爭時期中英鐵砲材質的優劣比較研究. *Qing hua xue bao* 清華學報 38, no. 4 (2008 [民國九十七年]): 563–98.

Liu, Kwang-ching. "The Beginnings of China's Modernization." *Chinese Studies in History* 24 (1990): 7–23.

Liu, Kwang-ching, and Richard J. Smith. "The Military Challenge: The North-West and the Coast." In John K. Fairbank and Kwang-Ching Liu, eds., *The Cambridge History of China, Volume 11, Late Ch'ing, 1800–1911, Part 2*. Cambridge: Cambridge University Press, 1980, 202–73.

Liu Lumin 劉魯民, ed. *Zhong guo bing shu ji cheng* 中國兵書集成. Vol. 17. Beijing: People's Liberation Army Press, 1994.

Liu Qi 劉祁. *Gui qian zhi* 歸潛志. 1235. http://wenxian.fanren8.com/06/15/355/12. htm, accessed 21 March 2014.

Liu Qing 劉慶 and Mao Yuanyou 毛元佑. "Zhongguo Song Liao Jin Xia jun shi shi" 中國宋遼金軍事史. In Shi Zhongwen 史仲文 and Hu Xiaolin 胡曉林, eds., *Bai juan ben Zhong guo quan shi* 百卷本中國全史, vol. 11. Beijing: Ren min chu ban she, 1994.

Liu Shanyi 劉善沂. "Shan dong guan xian fa xian Ming chu tong chong" 山東冠縣發現明初銅銃. *Kao gu* 考古, no. 10 (1985): 914.

Liu Xianting and Zhu Shida, trans. *Tai bai yin jing*. Library of Chinese Classics Series. Beijing: Military Science Publishing House, 2007.

Liu Xiaolei 劉小雷. "Wuwei tong huo pao: shi jie shang zui gu lao de jin shu guan xing huo qi" 武威銅火炮：世界上最古老的金屬管形火器. *Gansu Daily* 每日甘肅, 17 October 2012. http://gansu.gansudaily.com.cn/system/2012/02/17/012373433.shtml, accessed 21 September 2012.

Liu Xu 劉旭. *Zhong guo gu dai huo yao huo qi shi* 中國古代火藥火器史. Zhengzhou 鄭州: Da xiang chu ban she, 2004.

Lloyd, Christopher, and Hardin Craig Jr. "Congreve's Rockets, 1805–1806." In Christopher Lloyd, ed. *The Naval Miscellany Vol. IV. Publications of the Navy Records Society, Vol. XCII.* London: Navy Records Society, 1952, 423–93.

Lo, Jung-Pang. "The Emergence of China as a Sea Power during the Late Sung and Early Yuan Periods." *Far Eastern Quarterly* 14, no. 4 (1955): 489–503.

Lone, Stewart. *Japan's First Modern War: Army and Society in the Conflict with China, 1894–5.* London: St. Martin's, 1994.

Lorge, Peter. *The Asian Military Revolution: From Gunpowder to the Bomb.* Cambridge: Cambridge University Press, 2008.

———. *Chinese Martial Arts: From Antiquity to the Twenty-First Century.* Cambridge: Cambridge University Press, 2011.

———. "Development and Spread of Firearms in Medieval and Early Modern Eurasia." *History Compass* 9, no. 10 (2011): 818–26.

———. *War, Politics, and Society in Early Modern China, 900–1795.* London: Routledge, 2005.

Lovell, Julia. *The Opium War: Drugs, Dreams and the Making of China.* London: Picador, 2011.

Lu Xun 魯迅. "Dian de li bi" 電的利弊. In Lu Xun, *Lu Xun quan ji* 魯迅全集, vol. 5. Beijing: Ren min wen xue chu ban she, 1981 [originally published 1933], 14–15.

Lu Wenbao 陸文寶. "Xin fa xian Zhang Shicheng 'Tianyou' nian ming tong chong xiao kao" 新發現張士誠'天祐'年銘銅銃小考. In Zhong Shaoyi, *Zhong guo*, 143–46.

Lu Yidong 魯亦冬. *Zhongguo Song Liao Jin Xia jing ji shi* 中國宋遼金夏經濟史. In Shi Zhongwen 史仲文 and Hu Xiaolin 胡曉林, eds., *Bai juan ben Zhong guo quan shi* 百卷本中國全史, vol. 11. Beijing: Ren min chu ban she, 1994.

Luh, Jürgen. *Ancien Régime Warfare and the Military Revolution: A Study.* Groningen: Instituut voor Noord- en Oost-Europese Studies, 2000.

Ma Youyuan 馬幼桓. "Zhong-Ri jia wu zhan zheng Huang hai hai zhan xin tan yi li" 中日甲午戰爭黃海海戰新探一例. *Qing hua xue bao* 清華學報 24, no. 3 (1994): 297–318.

Mackenzie, Keith Stewart. *Narrative of the Second Campaign in China.* London: Richard Bentley, 1842.

Malanima, Paolo. *Pre-modern European Economy: One Thousand Years (10th–19th Centuries)*. Leiden: Brill, 2009.

Mallett, Michael. "Siegecraft in Late Fifteenth-Century Italy." In Ivy A. Corfis and Michael Wolfe, eds., *The Medieval City under Siege*. Woodbridge, UK: Boydell Press, 1995, 245–56.

Mancall, Mark. *Russia and China: Their Diplomatic Relations to 1728*. Cambridge, MA: Harvard University Press, 1971.

Marks, Robert B. *The Origins of the Modern World: A Global and Ecological Narrative*. Oxford: Rowman & Littlefield, 2002.

———. *Tigers, Rice, Silk, and Silt: Environment and Economy in Late Imperial South China*. Cambridge: Cambridge University Press, 1998.

Marx, Karl. "Division of Labour and Mechanical Workshop. Tool and Machinery." In *Economic Manuscripts of 1861–63*. http://www.marxists.org/archive/marx/works/1861/economic/ch35.htm, accessed 23 February 2013.

Matsumoto, Miwao. *Technology Gatekeepers for War and Peace: The British Ship Revolution and Japanese Industrialization*. New York: Palgrave Macmillan, 2006.

Mauskopf, Seymour. "From Rumford to Rodman: The Scientific Study of the Physical Characteristics of Gunpowder in the First Part of the Nineteenth Century." In Brenda Buchanan, ed., *Gunpowder: The History of an International Technology*. Bath, UK: Bath University Press, 1996, 277–93.

May, Timothy. *The Mongol Conquests in World History*. London: Reaktion Books, 2012.

McClellan, James E., III, and Howard Dorn. *Science and Technology in World History: An Introduction*. Baltimore: Johns Hopkins University Press, 2006.

McCord, Edward. *The Power of the Gun: The Emergence of Modern Chinese Warlordism*. Berkeley: University of California Press, 1993.

McFarlene, Bruce, Steve Cooper, and Miomir Jaksic. "The Asiatic Mode of Production: A New Phoenix? (Part 1)." *Journal of Contemporary Asia* 35, no. 3 (2005): 283–318.

McGiffin, Philo. "The Battle of the Yalu: Personal Recollections by the Commander of the Chinese Ironclad Chen Yuen." *Century Illustrated Monthly Magazine* 50 (1895): 585–604.

McJoynt, Albert. "An Appreciation of the War for Granada (1481–92): A Critical Link in Western Military History." In Donald Kagay and L. J. Andrew Villalon, eds., *Crusaders, Condottieri, and Cannon: Medieval Warfare in Societies around the Mediterranean*. Leiden: Brill, 2003, 239–52.

McNeill, William H. "Drill/Marching." In Cowley and Parker, *Reader's Companion to Military History*, 141–42.

———. "The Gunpowder Revolution." *MHQ* 3, no. 1 (1990): 8–17.

———. "Men, Machines, and War." In Ronald Haycock and Keith Neilson, eds., *Men, Machines, and War*. Waterloo, Canada: Wilfrid Laurier University Press, 1988, 1–20.

———. *The Pursuit of Power: Technology, Armed Force, and Society since A.D. 1000*. Chicago: University of Chicago Press, 1982.

McPherson, Duncan. *The War in China. Narrative of the Chinese Expedition from Its Formation in April, 1840, to the Treaty of Peace in August, 1842*. 3rd ed. London: Saunders and Otley, 1843.

Meadows, Thomas. *The Chinese and Their Rebellions: Viewed in Connection with Their National Philosophy, Ethics, Legislation, and Administration.* London: Smith, Elder, 1856.

Mearsheimer, John J. *The Tragedy of Great Power Politics.* New York: Norton, 2002.

Mei guo Ha fo Da xue Ha fo Yan jing Tu shu guan cang Zhong we shan ben cong kan 美國哈佛大學哈佛燕京圖書館藏中文善本叢刊. Vols. 19–20. Guangxi: Guangxi Normal University Press, 2009.

Meng Yue. "Hybrid Science versus Modernity: The Practice of the Jiangnan Arsenal, 1864–1897." *East Asian Science, Technology and Medicine* 16 (1999): 13–52.

Mielants, Eric. "Europe and China Compared." *Review* (Fernand Braudel Center) 25, no. 4 (2002): 401–49.

Ming shi lu 明實錄. 133 vols. Nangang: Academia Sinica History and Literature Research Center 中央研究院歷史語言研究所, 1962–1968 [Ming dynasty].

Ming shilu Minhai guanxi shiliao 明實錄閩海關係史料. *Taiwan wen xian cong kan* 台灣文獻叢刊. No. 296. Taipei: Taiwan yin hang, 1971.

Mitchel, Peter MacVicar. "Wei Yuan and the Early Modernization Movement in China and Japan." PhD dissertation, Indiana University, 1970.

Mo, Pak Hung. "Effective Competition and Economic Development of Imperial China." *Kyklos* 48 (1995): 87–103.

Mokyr, Joel. *The Enlightened Economy: An Economic History of Britain 1700–1850.* London: Penguin, 2011.

———. *The Lever of Riches: Technological Creativity and Economic Progress.* New York: Oxford University Press, 2002.

Montesquieu. *The Spirit of the Laws.* Vol. 1. Translated by Thomas Nugent. London: Colonial Press, 1900.

Morillo, Stephen. "The Age of Cavalry Revisited." In Donald J. Kagay and L. J. Andrew Villalon, eds., *The Circle of War in the Middle Ages.* Woodbridge, UK: Boydell Press, 1999, 45–58.

Morillo, Stephen, Jeremy Black, and Paul Lococo. *War in World History: Society, Technology, and War from Ancient Times to the Present.* Vol. 1. New York: McGraw-Hill, 2009.

Morris, Ian. *The Measure of Civilization: How Social Development Decides the Fate of Nations.* Princeton: Princeton University Press, 2013.

Morris, Roger. *The Foundations of British Maritime Ascendancy: Resources, Logistics, and the State, 1755–1815.* Cambridge: Cambridge University Press, 2011.

Mortimer, Geoff, ed. *Early Modern Military History, 1450–1815.* New York: Palgrave Macmillan, 2004

———. "Introduction: Was There a Military Revolution?" In Mortimer, *Early Modern Military History*, 1–5.

Mosca, Matthew. *From Frontier Policy to Foreign Policy: The Question of India and the Transformation of Geopolitics in Qing China.* Palo Alto, CA: Stanford University Press, 2013.

Mote, Frederick W. "A Millennium of Chinese Urban History: Form, Time, and Space Concepts in Soochow." *Rice University Studies* 59, no. 4 (1973): 35–65.

———. *Imperial China, 900–1800.* Cambridge, MA: Harvard University Press, 1999.

Mundy, Peter. *The Travels of Peter Mundy in Europe and Asia, 1608–1667.* Vol. 3, pt. 1. London: Hakluyt Society, 1919.

Murai Shosuke. "A Reconsideration of the Introduction of Firearms to Japan." *Memoirs of the Research Department of the Toyo Bunko* 60 (2002): 19–38.

Murray, Alexander. *Doings in China, Being the Personal Narrative of an Officer Engaged in the Late Chinese Expedition, from the Recapture of Chusan in 1841, to the Peace of Nankin in 1842*. London: Richard Bentley, 1843.

Murray, Hugh. *An Encyclopedia of Geography*. London: Longman, 1834.

Myers, Norman, and Jennifer Kent. *The New Consumers: The Influence of Affluence on the Environment*. Washington, DC: Island Press, 2004.

Nakajima Gakusho 中島樂章. "16 shi ji 40 nian dai de Shuang dao zou si mao yi yu Ou shi huo qi" 16 世紀40 年代的雙嶼走私貿易貿易與歐式火器. In Zheng Fangping 郭萬平 and Zhang Jie 張捷, eds., *Zhou shan Pu luo yu dong ya hai yu wen hua jiao liu* 舟山普陀與東亞海域文化交流. Zhejiang: Zhejiang University Press, 2009, 34–43.

Nan Bingwen 南炳文. "Zhong guo gu dai de niao chong yu Ri ben" 中國古代的鳥槍 與日本. *Shi xue ji kan* 史學集刊, no. 2 (1994): 60–66.

Naquin, Susan. *Millenarian Rebellion in China: The Eight Trigrams Uprising of 1813*. New Haven: Yale University Press, 1976.

Navarro, Peter. *The Coming China Wars: Where They Will Be Fought and How They Can Be Won*. Upper Saddle River, NJ: Pearson, 2008.

Needham, Joseph. *The Grand Titration: Science and Society in East and West*. London: George Allen & Unwin, 1969.

———. *Science and Civilisation in China, Vol. 5, Part 7, Military Technology: The Gunpowder Epic*. Cambridge: Cambridge University Press, 1986.

Needham, Joseph, et al. *Science and Civilisation in China, Vol. 4, Physics and Physical Technology, Part 2: Mechanical Engineering*. Cambridge: Cambridge University Press, 1965.

———. *Science and Civilisation in China, Vol. 5, Chemistry and Chemical Technology, Part 6, Military Technology: Missiles and Sieges*. Cambridge: Cambridge University Press, 1994.

———. *Science and Civilisation in China, Vol. 7, Part 2: General Conclusions and Reflections*. Cambridge: Cambridge University Press, 2004.

Neiberg, Michael S. *Warfare in World History*. London: Routledge, 2001.

Newitt, Malyn. *A History of Portuguese Overseas Expansion, 1400–1668*. London: Routledge, 2004.

Ng, Chin Keong. "Trade, the Sea Prohibition, and the Fo-lang-chi." In Francis Dutra and Joao Camilo dos Santos, eds., *Proceedings of the International Colloquium on the Portuguese and the Pacific*. Santa Barbara: Center for Portuguese Studies, University of California, 1995, 381–424.

Niu Dasheng 牛達生 and Niu Zhiwen 牛志文. "Xi Xia tong huo chong: wo guo zui zao de jin shu guan xing huo qi" 西夏銅火銃：我國最早的金屬管形火器. *Dao gen* 尋根, no. 6 (2004): 51–57.

Noordam, Barend. "Technology, Tactics, and Military Transfer in the Nineteenth Century: Qing Armies in Tonkin, 1884–1885." In A. Füchter and S. Richter, eds., *Structures on the Move: Technologies of Governance in Transcultural Encounter*. Berlin: Springer Verlag, 2012, 169–88.

Nourbakhsh, Mohammad Reza (Farhad). "Iran's Early Encounter with Three Medieval European Inventions (875–1153 AH/1470–1740 CE)." *Iranian Studies* 41, no. 4 (2008): 549–58.

O'Connell, Robert L. *Of Arms and Men: A History of War, Weapons, and Aggression.* New York: Oxford University Press, 1989.

———. *Soul of the Sword: An Illustrated History of Weaponry and Warfare from Prehistory to the Present.* New York: Free Press, 2002.

Ollé, Manel. *La invención de China: Percepciones y estrategias Filipinas respect a China durante el siglo XVI.* Wiesbaden: Harrassowitz Verlag, 2000.

Oman, Charles. *A History of the Art of War in the Sixteenth Century.* New York: E.P. Dutton, 1937.

O'Meara, Barry Edward. *Napoleon in Exile; or, A Voice from St. Helena. The Opinions and Reflections of Napoleon on the Most Important Events of His Life and Government in His Own Words.* 2 vols.. London: W. Simpkin and R. Marshall, 1822.

Ostwald, Jamel. *Vauban under Siege: Engineering Efficiency and Martial Vigor in the War of the Spanish Succession.* Leiden: Brill, 2007.

Ōta, Gyūichi, J.S.A. Elisonas, and Jeroen Pieter Lamers. *The Chronicle of Lord Nobunaga.* Leiden: Brill, 2011.

Ouchterlony, John. *The Chinese War: An Account of All the Operations of the British Forces from the Commencement to the Treaty of Nanking.* London: Saunders and Otley, 1844.

Padfield, Peter. *Guns at Sea.* New York: St. Martin's, 1974.

Pain, Henry J., and Richard Neville. *Pain's New Pyro Spectacle, War between Japan: Pain's Amphitheatre, Manhattan Beach.* New York: Pain's Pyro-Technical Company, 1895.

Paine, S.C.M., ed. *Nation Building, State Building, and Economic Development: Case Studies and Comparisons.* Armonk, NY: M.E. Sharpe, 2010.

———. *The Sino-Japanese War of 1894–1895: Perceptions, Power, and Primacy.* Cambridge: Cambridge University Press 2003.

Palais, James B. *Confucian Statecraft and Korean Institutions: Yu Hyongwon and the Late Choson Dynasty.* Seattle: University of Washington Press, 1996.

Park Taegeun 朴泰根. *Kugyok Pukchong ilgi* 國譯北征日記. Kyŏnggi-do, Sŏngnam-si: Han'guk Chŏngsin Munhwa Yŏn'guwŏn, 1980.

Parker, Geoffrey. "The Artillery Fortress as an Engine of European Overseas Expansion, 1480–1750." In Tracy, *City Walls,* 386–416.

———, ed. *The Cambridge Illustrated History of Warfare.* Cambridge: Cambridge University Press, 2008.

———. "Crisis and Catastrophe: The Global Crisis of the Seventeenth Century Reconsidered." *American Historical Review* 113, no. 4 (2008): 1053–79.

———. "The *Dreadnought* Revolution of Tudor England." *Mariners Mirror* 82, no. 3 (1996): 269–300.

———. "The Limits to Revolutions in Military Affairs: Maurice of Nassau, the Battle of Nieuwpoort (1600), and the Legacy." *Journal of Military History* 71, no. 2 (April 2007): 331–72.

———. *The Military Revolution: Military Innovation and the Rise of the West.* Cambridge: Cambridge University Press, 1996.

Parrott, David. *The Business of War: Military Enterprise and Military Revolution in Early Modern Europe.* Cambridge: Cambridge University Press, 2012.

———. "Had a Distinct Template for a 'Western Way of War' Been Established before 1800?" In Hew Strachan and Sibylle Scheipers, eds., *The Changing Character of War.* Oxford: Oxford University Press, 2011, 48–63.

Partington, J. R. *A History of Greek Fire and Gunpowder*. Baltimore: Johns Hopkins University Press, 1999 (1960).

Paschalidou, Efpraxia. "The Walls of Constantinople: An Obstacle to the New Power of Artillery." In *XXII. Kongress der internationalen Kommission für Militärgeschichte*. Vienna: Heeresgeschichtliches Museum, 1997, 172–78.

Paul, Michael C. "The Military Revolution in Russia, 1550–1682." *Journal of Military History* 68, no. 1 (2004): 9–45.

Pelliot, Paul. "Le Hoja et le Sayyid Husain de l'Histoire des Ming." *T'oung Pao*, second series, 38 (1948): 81–292.

Peng Quanmin 彭全民. "Ming kang Pu ming chen Wang Hong mu zhi kao shi" 明抗葡名臣汪鋐墓志考釋. *Nan fang wen wu* 南方文物, no. 3 (2000): 114–20.

———. "Wang Hong yu Folangji zhi yuan" 汪鋐與佛朗機之緣. In *Shenzhen bo wu guan kai guan shi zhou nian ji nian wen ji* 深圳博物館開館十周年紀念文集. Beijing: Zhong hua shu ju, 1998, 191–205.

———. "Wo guo zui zao xiang xi fang 'fo lang ji' xue xi de ren: Wang Hong lüe kao" 我國最早向西方"佛郎機"學習的人——汪鋐傳略考. *Dong nan wen hua* 東南文化, no. 9 (September 2000): 66–69.

Perdue, Peter C. *China Marches West: The Qing Conquest of Central Eurasia*. Cambridge, MA: Belknap, 2005.

———. "Military Mobilization in Seventeenth and Eighteenth-Century China, Russia, and Mongolia." *Modern Asian Studies* 30, no. 4 (1996): 757–93.

Perkins, Dwight H. "Government as an Obstacle to Industrialization: The Case of Nineteenth-Century China." *Journal of Economic History* 27, no. 4 (1967): 478–92.

Perrin, Noel. *Giving up the Gun: Japan's Reversion to the Sword, 1543–1879*. Boston: D.R. Godine, 1979.

Petrucci, Maria Grazia. "Pirates, Gunpowder, and Christianity in Late Sixteenth-Century Japan." In Robert Antony, ed., *Elusive Pirates, Pervasive Smugglers: Violence and Clandestine Trade in the Greater China Seas*. Hong Kong: Hong Kong University Press, 2010, 59–71.

Philippides, Mario, and Walter K. Hanak. *The Siege and the Fall of Constantinople in 1453: Historiography, Topography, and Military Studies*. Farnham Surrey, UK: Ashgate, 2011.

Pines, Yuri. *The Everlasting Empire: The Political Culture of Ancient China*. Princeton: Princeton University Press, 2012.

Pinto, Fernão Mendes. *Peregrinação*. Vol. 2. Lisbon: Livraria Ferreira, 1908.

———. *The Voyages and Adventures of Ferdinand Mendez Pinto, the Portuguese*. Translated by Henry Cogan. London: T. Fisher Unwin, 1891.

Planitz, Hans. *Die deutsche Stadt im Mittelalter: von der Römerzeit bis zu den Zunftkämpfen*. Graz-Köln: Bölau-Verlag, 1965.

Platt, Stephen. *Autumn in the Heavenly Kingdom: China, the West, and the Epic Story of the Taiping Civil War*. New York: Knopf, 2012.

Polachek, James. *The Inner Opium War*. Cambridge, MA: Council on East Asian Studies, 1992.

Pomeranz, Kenneth. *The Great Divergence: China, Europe, and the Making of the Modern World Economy*. Princeton: Princeton University Press, 2000.

Pong, David. "China's Modern Navy and Changing Concepts of Naval Warfare up to the Time of the Sino-French War." In Lee Kam-keung, Lau Yee-cheung, and Mak

King-sang, eds., *Coastal Defense and Maritime Economy of Modern China,* Hong Kong: Modern Chinese History Society of Hong Kong, 1999, 341–66.

———. "Keeping the Foochow Navy Yard Afloat: Government Finance and China's Early Modern Defence Industry, 1866–75." *Modern Asian Studies* 21, no. 1 (1987): 121–52.

———. *Shen Pao-chen and China's Modernization in the Nineteenth Century.* Cambridge: Cambridge University Press, 1994.

———. "Shen Pao-chen and the Great Policy Debate of 1874–1875." In *Proceedings of the Conference on the Self-Strengthening Movement in Late Ch'ing China, 1860–1894.* Taipei: Institute of Modern History, Academia Sinica, 1988, 189–225.

Preston, Diana. *The Boxer Rebellion: The Dramatic Story of China's War on Foreigners That Shook the World in the Summer of 1900.* New York: Bloomsbury, 2000.

Prestwich, Michael. "The Battle of Crécy." In Ayton and Preston, *Battle of Crécy,* 159–252.

———. "Training." In Clifford Rogers, ed., *The Oxford Encyclopedia of Medieval Warfare and Military Technology,* vol. 1. Oxford: Oxford University Press, 2010, 370–72.

Prouteau, Nicolas, Emmanuel de Crouy-Chanel, and Nicolas Facherre, eds. *Artillerie et fortification: 1200–1600.* Rennes: Presses Universitaires de Rennes, 2011

Ptak, Roderich. "Early Portuguese Relations up to the Foundation of Macao." *Mare Liberum: Revista de Historia dos Mares* 4 (1992): 289–97.

———. "Macau and Sino-Portuguese Relations, ca 1513/1514 to ca 1900." *Monumenta Serica* 46 (1998): 343–96.

———. "The *Wugongchuan* (Centipede Ships) and the Portuguese." *Revista de Cultura* 5 (2003): 73–83.

Puype, J. P. "Victory at Niewupoort, 2 July 1600." In Marco van der Hoeven, ed., *Exercise of Arms: Warfare in the Netherlands, 1568–1648.* Leiden: Brill, 1997, 69–112.

———. "Zeventiende-eeuwse termen met betrekking tot wapens, toebehoren en aanverwante onderwerpen." In Jan Piet Puype and Marco van der Hoeven, eds., *Het Arsenaal van de wereld: De Nederlandse wapenhandel in de Gouden Eeuw.* Amsterdam: De Bataafsche Leeiuw, 1993, 64–70.

Qi Jiguang 戚繼光. *Ji xiao xin shu* 紀效新書. 18 juan version. Beijing: Zhong hua shu ju, 1999.

———. *Ji xiao xin shu: shi si juan ben* 紀效新書:十四卷本. Beijing: Zhong hua shu ju, 2001.

———. *Lian bing shi ji* 練兵實紀. Edited and annotated by Qiu Xintian 邱心田. Beijing: Zhong hua shu ju, 2001.

Qi Zhouren 齊周仁. "Zhao Yurong and the Xin si qi qi lu" 趙與褣與<<辛巳泣蘄錄>>. *Qichun wen hua yan jiu* 蘄春文化研究 10 (February 2010). http://www.hbqc.com /article-90-1.html, accessed 6 September 2012.

Qian Qianyi 錢謙益. "Han Chen Youliang" 漢陳友諒. In *Guo chu qun xiong shi lüe* 國初群雄事略. Beijing: Zhong hua shu ju, 1982, juan 4, 87–111.

———. "Zhou Zhang Shicheng" 周張士誠. In *Guo chu qun xiong shi lüe* 國初群雄事略. Beijing: Zhong hua shu ju, 1982, juan 8.

Qing shi lu 清實錄. 60 vols. Beijing: Zhong hua shu ju chu ban, 1986–1987 [Qing dynasty].

Ralston, David. *Importing the European Army: The Introduction of European Military Techniques and Institutions in the Extra-European World, 1600–1914.* Chicago: University of Chicago Press, 1996.

Raphael, Kate. "Mongol Siege Warfare on the Banks of the Euphrates and the Question of Gunpowder (1260–1312)." *Journal of the Royal Asiatic Society of Great Britain and Ireland* 19, no. 3 (2009): 355–70.

Rathgen, Bernhard. *Das Geschütz im Mittelalter.* Düsseldorf: VDI Verlag, 1987 [originally published 1928].

Ravenstein, Ernst G. *The Russians on the Amur; Its Discovery, Conquest, and Colonisation, with a Description of the Country, Its Inhabitants, Productions, and Commercial Capabilities.* London: Trübner, 1861.

Rawlinson, John L. *China's Struggle for Naval Development, 1839–1895.* Cambridge, MA: Harvard University Press, 1967.

Rawski, Evelyn. *The Last Emperors: A Social History of Qing Imperial Institutions.* Berkeley: University of California Press, 1998.

Reinaud, M., and M. Favé. *Histoire de l'artillerie, 1re partie: du feu grégeois des feux de guerre et des origins de la poudre a canon.* Paris: J. Dumaine, 1845.

"Report of Major General J. H. Schoedde on Attack of Chin-keang-foo, 21 July 1842, Chin-keang-foo." *Asiatic Journal and Monthly Register for British India, China, and Australasia* 39 (1842): 363.

Rhoads, Edward J. M. *Stepping Forth into the World: The Chinese Educational Mission to the United States, 1872–81.* Hong Kong: Hong Kong University Press, 2011.

Riccio, Victorio. "Hechos de la Orden de Predicadores en el Imperio de China." In José Eugenio Borao, ed. and trans., *Spaniards in Taiwan,* vol. 2. Taipei: SMC, 2002, 586–627.

Richard, Jean. "Quelques idées de François de Surienne sur la défense des villes à propos de la fortification de Dijon (1461)." *Annales de Bourgogne* 16 (1944): 36–43.

Ricklefs, Merle. "Balance and Military Innovation in Seventeenth-Century Java." In Douglas Peers, ed., *Warfare and Empires: Contact and Conflict between European and Non-European Military and Maritime Forces and Cultures.* Aldershot, UK: Ashgate, 1997, 101–10.

———. *War, Culture and Economy in Java, 1677–1726: Asian and European Imperialism in the Early Kartasura Period.* Sydney: Allen and Unwin, 1993.

Riehn, Richard. *1812: Napoleon's Russian Campaign.* New York: John Wiley, 1991.

Roberts, Michael. "The Military Revolution, 1560–1660." In Rogers, *Military Revolution Debate,* 13–35.

———. *The Military Revolution, 1560–1660: An Inaugural Lecture Delivered before the Queen's University of Belfast.* Belfast: M. Boyd, 1956.

Robins, Benjamin. *New Principles of Gunnery: Containing the Determination of the Force of Gun-Powder and an Investigation of the Difference in the Resisting Power of the Air to Swift and Slow Motions.* London: J. Nourse, 1742.

Robinson, David. *Martial Spectacles of the Ming Court.* Cambridge, MA: Harvard-Yenching Institute, 2013.

Rodger, N.A.M. "The Development of Broadside Gunnery." *Mariners Mirror* 82, no. 3 (1996): 301–24.

Rogers, Clifford J. "The Artillery and Artillery Fortress Revolutions Revisited." In Prouteau, Crouy-Chanel, and Facherre, *Artillerie et fortification,* 75–80.

———. "The Idea of Military Revolutions in Eighteenth and Nineteenth Century Texts." *Revista de Historia das Ideias* 30 (2009): 395–415.

———, ed. *The Military Revolution Debate: Readings on the Military Transformation of Early Modern Europe.* Boulder, CO: Westview, 1995.

———. "The Military Revolutions of the Hundred Years War." *Journal of Military History* 57, no. 2 (1993): 241–78.

———. "'Military Revolutions' and 'Revolutions in Military Affairs': A Historian's Perspective." In T. Gongora and H. von Riekhoff, eds., *Toward a Revolution in Military Affairs? Defense and Security at the Dawn of the Twenty-First Century.* Westport, CT: Greenwood, 2000, 21–35.

———. *Soldiers' Lives through History: The Middle Ages.* Westport, CT: Greenwood, 2007, 68–69.

———. *War Cruel and Sharp: English Strategy under Edward III, 1327–1360.* Woodbridge, UK: Boydell Press, 2000.

Rong Yingtai 谷應泰. *Ming shi ji shi ben mo* 明史紀事本末. Seventeenth century.

Rose, Paul-Lawrence. "Galileo's Theory of Ballistics." *British Journal for the History of Science* 4, no. 2 (1968): 156–59.

Rosenthal, Jean-Laurent, and R. Bin Wong. *Before and Beyond Divergence: The Politics of Economic Change in China and Europe.* Cambridge, MA: Harvard University Press, 2011.

Rossabi, Morris. *A History of China.* Chichester: Wiley Blackwell, 2014.

———. "The Reign of Khubilai Khan." In Denis Twitchett and John K. Fairbank, eds., *The Cambridge History of China, Volume 6, Alien Regimes and Border States, 907–1368.* Cambridge: Cambridge University Press, 1994, 414–89.

Rouil, Christophe. *Formose, des batailles presque oubliées.* Taipei: Xin ge Fa guo shu dian, 2001.

Roy, Kaushik. "Military Synthesis in South Asia: Armies, Warfare, and Indian Society, c. 1740–1849." *Journal of Military History* 69, no. 3 (2005): 651–90.

———. *Military Transition in Early Modern Asia, 1400–1750: Cavalry, Guns, Governments, and Ships.* London: Bloomsbury, 2014.

Russia Arkheograficheskaia kommissiia. *Akty istoricheskie. Dopolneniia, Vol. 10, 1682–1700.* Saint Petersburg, Russia: 1867.

Saidel, Benjamin Adam. "Matchlocks, Flintlocks, and Saltpetre: The Chronological Implications for the Use of Matchlock Muskets among Ottoman-Period Bedouin in the Southern Levant." *International Journal of Historical Archaeology* 4, no. 3 (2000): 191–216.

Salamagne, Alain. "L'attaque des places-fortes au XV e siècle à travers l'exemple des guerres anglo et franco-bourguignonnes." *Revue Historique* 289, no. 1 (1993): 65–113.

Sánchez-Eppler, Karen. "Copying and Conversion: An 1824 Friendship Album 'from a Chinese Youth.'" In Monica Chiu, ed., *Asian Americans in New England: Culture and Community.* Durham: University of New Hampshire Press, 2009, 1–41.

Sarkar, Suvobrata. "Technological Momentum: Bengal in the Nineteenth Century." *Indian Historical Review* 37 (2010): 89–109.

Sawyer, Ralph D. *Fire and Water: The Art of Incendiary and Aquatic Warfare in China.* Boulder, CO: Westview, 2004, 3–237.

———, trans. *Strategies for the Human Realm: Crux of the T'ai-pai Yin-ching.* Lexington, KY, 2012.

Sawyer, Ralph D., and Mei-chün Sawyer. *Ancient Chinese Warfare*. New York: Basic Books, 2011, 125.

Schencking, J. Charles. *Making Waves: Politics, Propaganda, and the Emergence of the Imperial Japanese Navy, 1868–1922*. Stanford, CA: Stanford University Press, 2005.

Schmidtchen, Volker. "Riesengeschütze des 15. Jahrhunderts." Part 1. *Technikgeschichte* 44, no. 2 (1977): 153–73.

———. "Riesengeschütze des 15. Jahrhunderts." Part 2. *Technikgeschichte* 44, no. 3 (1977): 213–37.

Scott, Melissa. "The Victory of the Ancients: Tactics, Technology, and the Use of Classical Precedent." PhD dissertation, Brandeis University, 1992.

Semenov, Iurii Nikolaevich. *The Conquest of Siberia: An Epic of Human Passions*. London: Routledge, 1944.

Serdon-Provost, Valérie. "Les débuts de l'artillerie a poudre d'après l'iconographie médiévale." In Prouteau, Crouy-Chanel, and Facherre, *Artillerie et fortification*, 61–74.

Shapinsky, Peter D. "Polyvocal Portolans: Nautical Charts and Hybrid Maritime Cultures in Early Modern East Asia." *Early Modern Japan* 14 (2006): 4–26.

Shi Baozhen 史寶珍. "Zhen jiang chu tu de Ming dai huo qi" 鎮江出土的明代火器. *Wen wu* 文物, no. 7 (1986): 91–94.

Shi Jungui 石俊貴 and Li Hong 李鴻. "Nei Meng gu chu tu de Ming chao chu nian tie ke di lei ji shi" 內蒙古出土的明朝初年鐵殼地雷紀實. *Qing bing qi* 輕兵器, no. 4 (2002): 36.

Shi Kang 石康 (Kenneth Swope). "Ming-Qing zhan zheng zhong da pao de shi yong" 明清戰爭中大炮的使用. *Qing shi yan jiu* 清史研究, no. 3 (2011): 143–49.

Shi Wanlin 師萬林. "Gan su Zhang ye fa xian Ming dai tong chong" 甘肅張掖發現明代銅銃. *Kao gu yu wen wu* 考古與文物, no. 4 (1986).

Silbey, David J. *The Boxer Rebellion and the Great Game in China*. New York: Macmillan, 2012.

Simmons, J.S.G. "Printing." In Robert Auty and Dimitri Obolensky, eds., *Companion to Russian Studies: Volume 2, An Introduction to Russian Language and Literature*. Cambridge: Cambridge University Press, 1977, 47–53.

Singer, Joel D. *The Correlates of War*. Vol. 1. New York: Free Press 1979.

Sit, Victor F. S. *Chinese City and Urbanism: Evolution and Development*. Singapore: World Scientific Press, 2010.

Smith, Adam. *An Inquiry into the Nature and Causes of the Wealth of Nations*. Vol. 2. Oxford: Clarendon, 1869.

Smith, Carl T. *Chinese Christians: Elites, Middlemen, and the Church in Hong Kong*. Hong Kong: Hong Kong University Press, 2005.

Smith, David. *The Dragon and the Elephant: China, India, and the New World Order*. London: Profile Books, 2008.

Smith, Kay (formerly Robert Smith). "All Manner of Peeces: Artillery in the Late Medieval Period." *Royal Armouries Yearbook* 7 (2002): 130–38.

———. "Artillery and the Hundred Years War: Myth and Interpretation." In Anne Curry and Michael Hughes, eds., *Arms, Armies and Fortification in the Hundred Years War*. Woodbridge, UK: Boydell Press, 1994, 151–60.

———. *Rewriting the History of Gunpowder*. Sundby Lolland, Denmark: Middelaldercentret, 2010.

Smith, Paul Jakov. "Eurasian Transformations of the Tenth to Thirteenth Centuries: The View from Song China, 960–1279." *Medieval Encounters* 10, nos. 1–3 (2004): 281–308.

———. "Introduction: The Sung Dynasty and Its Precursors, 907–1279." In Denis Twitchett and Paul Jakov Smith, eds., *The Cambridge History of China, Volume 5, Part 1, The Sung Dynasty and Its Precursors, 907–1279*. Cambridge: Cambridge University Press, 2009, 1–37.

Smith, Philip. "Meaning and Military Power: Moving on from Foucault." *Journal of Power* 1, no. 3 (2008): 275–93.

Smith, Richard. "Chinese Military Institutions in the Mid-Nineteenth Century, 1850–1860." *Journal of Asian History* 8, no. 2 (1974): 122–61.

———. "The Employment of Foreign Military Talent: Chinese Tradition and Late Ch'ing Practice." *Journal of the Royal Asiatic Society Hong Kong Branch,* 15 (1975): 113–36.

———. *Mercenaries and Mandarins: The Ever-Victorious Army in Nineteenth Century China.* Millwood, NY: KTO Press, 1978.

———. "Reflections on the Comparative Study of Modernization in China and Japan: Military Aspects." *Journal of the Royal Asiatic Society Hong Kong Branch* 16 (1976): 14–24.

———. "The Reform of Military Education in Late Ch'ing China, 1842–1895." *Journal of the Royal Asiatic Society Hong Kong Branch* 18 (1978): 15–40.

Smith, Robert. See Smith, Kay.

Smith, Ronald Bishop. *Martim Afonso de Mello: Captain-Major of the Portuguese Fleet Which Sailed to China in 1522, Being the Portuguese Text of Two Unpublished Letters of the National Archives of Portugal.* Bethesda, MD: Decatur Press, 1972.

———. *A Projected Portuguese Voyage to China in 1512.* Bethesda, MD: Decatur Press, 1972.

Snooks, Graeme. *The Dynamic Society: Exploring the Sources of Global Change.* New York: Routledge, 1996.

So, Kwan-wai. *Japanese Piracy in Ming China during the 16th Century.* East Lansing: Michigan State University Press, 1975.

Song Lian 宋濂, et al. *Yuan shi* 元史. Vol. 18 of the series *Er shi si shi* 二十四史 (20 vols.). Beijing: Zhong hua shu ju, 1997 [Ming dynasty].

Song Yingchang 宋應唱. *Jing lüe fu guo yao bian* 經略復國要編. Wanli Period [1572–1620, probably circa 1595].

Spector, Stanley. *Li Hung-chang and the Huai Army: A Study in Nineteenth-Century Chinese Regionalism.* Seattle: University of Washington Press, 1964.

Spence, Jonathan. *God's Chinese Son: The Taiping Heavenly Kingdom of Hong Xiuquan.* New York: Norton, 1996.

———. *The Search for Modern China.* New York: Norton, 1990.

Stavros, Matthew. "Military Revolution in Early Modern Japan." *Japanese Studies* 33, no. 3 (2013): 243–61.

Steele, Brett D. "Military 'Progress' and Newtonian Science in the Age of Enlightenment." In Steele and Dorland, *Heirs of Archimedes*, 361–90.

———. "Muskets and Pendulums: Benjamin Robins, Leonhard Euler, and the Ballistics Revolution." *Technology and Culture* 35, no. 2 (1994): 348–82.

———. "Napoleon and the Ballistics Revolution." In *Consortium on Revolutionary Europe, Selected Papers 1995*. Tallahassee: Florida State University, Institute on Napoleon and the French Revolution, 1995, 455–63.

———. "Rational Mechanics as Enlightenment Engineering: Leonhard Euler and Interior Ballistics." In Buchanan, *Gunpowder, Explosives, and the State*, 281–302.

Steele, Brett D., and Tamera Dorland, eds. *The Heirs of Archimedes: Science and the Art of War through the Age of Enlightenment*. Cambridge, MA: MIT Press, 2005.

———. "Introduction." In Steele and Dorland, *Heirs of Archimedes*, 1–33.

Stevens, Keith. "The American Soldier of Fortune Frederick Townsend Ward Honoured and Revered by the Chinese with a Memorial Temple." *Journal of the Royal Asiatic Society Hong Kong Branch* 38 (1998): 285–91.

Stone, John. "Technology, Society, and the Infantry Revolution of the Fourteenth Century." *Journal of Military History* 68 (2004): 361–80.

Streusand, Douglas E. *Islamic Gunpowder Empires: Ottomans, Safavids, and Mughals*. Boulder, CO: Westview, 2011.

Strickhausen, Gerd. "Bemerkungen zu frühen Feuerwaffen im 14. Jahrhundert." In Olaf Wagener and Heiko Laß, eds., *Würfen hin in Steine / gröze und niht kleine: Belagerungen und Belagerungsanlagen im Mittelalter*. Frankfurt: Peter Lang, 2006, 47–57.

Su Pinxiao 粟品孝. *Nan Song jun shi shi* 南宋軍事史. Shanghai: Shanghai gu ji chu ban she 上海古籍出版社, 2008.

Su Tongbing 穌同炳. *Taiwan shi yan jiu ji* 臺灣史研究集. Taipei: Guo li bian yi guan Zhong hua cong shu bian shen wei yuan hui 國立編譯館中華叢書編審委員會, 1980.

Su Xiaodong 蘇小東. "Bei yang hai jun guan dai qun ti yu jia wu hai zhan" 北洋海軍管帶群體與甲午海戰. *Jin dai shi yan jiu* 近代史研究, no. 2 (1999): 151–72.

Sun Laichen. "The Century of Warfare in Eastern Eurasia, 1550–1683: Repositioning Asian Military Technology in the 'Great Divergence' Debate." Paper presented at the Emory University Seminar in World History, 18 March 2014.

———. "Chinese Military Technology and Dai Viet: c. 1390–1497." Asia Research Institute Working Paper Series no. 11, September 2003.

———. "Military Technology Transfers from Ming China and the Emergence of Northern Mainland Southeast Asia (c. 1390–1527)." *Journal of Southeast Asian Studies* 34, no. 3 (2003): 495–517.

———. "Ming-Southeast Asian Overland Interactions, 1368–1644." PhD dissertation, University of Michigan, 2000.

Sun Yuanhua 孫元化. *Xi fa shen ji* 西法神機, edited by Wang Zhaochun 王兆春. Zhengzhou: He nan jiao yu chu ban she, 1994 [circa 1632]. Woodblock edition available online at http://echo.mpiwg-berlin.mpg.de/MPIWG:3YN478NP, retreived 24 May 2015.

Svarerud, Rune. *International Law as a World Order in Late Imperial China: Translation, Reception, and Discourse, 1847–1911*. Leiden: Brill, 2007.

Swope, Kenneth. "Crouching Tigers, Secret Weapons: Military Technology Employed during the Sino-Japanese-Korean War, 1592–1598." *Journal of Military History* 69, no. 1 (2005): 11–41.

———. *A Dragon's Head and a Serpent's Tail: Ming China and the First Great East Asian War, 1592–1598*. Norman: University of Oklahoma Press, 2009.

———. *The Military Collapse of China's Ming Dynasty, 1618–1644*. London: Routledge, 2014.

Tallett, Frank. *War and Society in Early Modern Europe, 1495–1715*. London: Routledge, 1997.

Tang Shou 湯璹. "De' an shou yu lu" 德安守禦錄. In Chen and Tang, *Shou cheng lu*, juans 3 and 4.

Tanner, Harold Miles. *China: A History*. Indianapolis: Hackett, 2009.

Tanzi, Vito, and Ludger Schuknecht. *Public Spending in the 20th Century: A Global Perspective*. Cambridge: Cambridge University Press, 2000.

Tao, Jinsheng. *Two Sons of Heaven: Studies in Sung-Liao Relations*. Tucson: University of Arizona Press, 1988.

Teng, Ssü-yü. *The Taiping Rebellion and the Western Powers*. Oxford: Clarendon, 1971.

Teng, Ssu-yü, and John K. Fairbank. *China's Response to the West: A Documentary Survey, 1839–1923*. Cambridge, MA: Harvard University Press, 1954.

Thiele, Dagmar. *Der Abschluss eines Vertrages: Diplomatie zwischen Sung- und Chin-Dynastie 1117–1123*. Wiesbaden: Franz Steiner Verlag GMBH, 1971.

Thirion, P. *L'expédition de Formose: souvenirs d'un soldat*. Paris: Lavauzelle, 1898.

Thomas, Christine. "The Slavonic Book in Russia, Ukraine, and Belarus." In Michael F. Suarez and H. R. Voudhuysen, eds., *The Book: A Global History*. Oxford: Oxford University Press, 2013, 485–501.

Thompson, William R. *On Global War: Historical-Structural Approaches to World Politics*. Columbia: University of South Carolina Press, 1988.

Thornton, John K. *Warfare in Atlantic Africa, 1500–1800*. London: University College London Press, 1999.

Thurston, Robert Henry. *A History of the Growth of the Steam-Engine, Parts 1–2*. New York: Appleton, 1878.

Tilly, Charles. *Coercion, Capital, and European States, AD 990–1992*. Cambridge, MA: Blackwell, 1992.

Tittmann, Wilfried. "Die Eltzer Büchsenpfeile von 1331/3." *Waffen- und Kostümkunde* 36 (1994): 117–28.

———. "The Guns of Archbishop Baldwin of Trier and the Guns in the Milemete Manuscripts of 1326/7: Some Critical Comments." *Journal of the Ordnance Society* 17 (2005): 5–23.

Tomlinson, Richard. *From Mycenae to Constantinople: The Evolution of the Ancient City*. London 1992.

Tong, James. *Disorder under Heaven: Collective Violence in the Ming Dynasty*. Palo Alto, CA: Stanford University Press, 1991.

Totman, Conrad. "Review of Perrin, *Giving up the Gun*." *Journal of Asian Studies* 39, no. 3 (1980): 599–600.

Tout, T. F. "Firearms in England in the Fourteenth Century." *English Historical Review* 26, no. 104 (1911): 666–702.

Toy, Sidney. *A History of Fortification: From 3000 BC to AD 1700*. London: William Heinemann, 1955.

Tuo Tuo 脫脫, et al. *Jin shi* 金史. Vol. 17 of the series *Er shi si shi* 二十四史 (20 vols.). Beijing: Zhong hua shu ju, 1997 [Yuan dynasty].

———. *Song shi* 宋史. Vols. 14–16 of the series *Er shi si shi* 二十四史 (20 vols.). Beijing: Zhong hua shu ju, 1997 [Yuan dynasty].

Tracy, James D., ed. *City Walls: The Urban Enceinte in Global Perspective*. Cambridge: Cambridge University Press, 2000.

Tracy, James D. "Introduction." In Tracy, *City Walls*, 1–18.

Truxillo, Charles. *Crusaders in the Far East: The Moro Wars in the Philippines*. Fremont, CA: Jain, 2012.

Turchin, Peter, Thomas Currie, Edward Turner, and Sergey Gavrilets. "War, Space, and the Evolution of Old World Complex Societies." *Proceedings of the National Academy of Sciences* 110, no. 41 (2013): 16384–89.

Turnbull, Stephen. *The Hussite Wars, 1419–36*. Wellingboorough, UK: Osprey, 2004.

———. *Pirates of the Far East, 811–1639*. Oxford: Osprey, 2012.

———. *Siege Weapons of the Far East (2): AD 960–1644*. Oxford: Osprey, 2012.

Udagawa Takehisa 宇田川武久. *Teppo denrai: heiki ga kataru kinsei no tanjo* 鉄砲伝来: 兵器が語る近世の誕生. Tokyo: Chuo Koronsha, 1990.

Ulsch, MacDonnell. *Cyber Threat! How to Manage the Growing Risk of Cyber Attacks*. Hoboken, NJ: John Wiley, 2014.

Upton, Emory. *The Armies of Asia and Europe: Embracing Official Reports on the Armies of Japan, China, India, Persia, etc.* New York: Appleton, 1878.

V. F. "A Bejton und seine Karte von Amur." *Imago Mundi* 1 (1935): 47–48.

van de Ven, Hans, ed. *Warfare in Chinese History*. Leiden: Brill, 2000.

van Nimwegen, Olaf. *The Dutch Army and the Military Revolutions, 1588–1688*. Translated by Andrew May. Woodbridge, UK: Boydell Press, 2010.

van Reyd, Everhard. *Histoire der Nederlantscher Oorlogen begin ende Voortganck tot den Jaere 1601*. Leeuwarden: Gilbert Sybes, 1650.

van Zanden, Jan L. *The Long Road to the Industrial Revolution: The European Economy in a Global Perspective, 1000–1800*. Leiden: Brill, 2009.

Vaughan, Richard. *Philip the Bold: The Formation of the Burgundian State*. Cambridge, MA: Harvard University Press, 1962.

Villani, Giovanni. *La Seconda parte delle historie universali de suoi tempi, di Guouan Villani, cittadino Fiorentino*. Venice, 1559.

Volpicelli, Zenone (aka Vladimir). *The China-Japan War Compiled from Japanese, Chinese, and Foreign Sources*. New York: Charles Scribner's Sons, 1896.

von Bell, Adam Schall 湯若望, and Jiao Xu 焦勗. *Huo gong qie yao* 火攻挈要. 1643.

———. *Huo gong qie yao* 火攻挈要. Shanghai: Shang hai gu ji chu ban she, 2002.

von Müller, Gerhard Friederich, ed. *Sammlung russischer Geschichte des Herrn Collegienraths Müllers in Moscow*. Vol. 5. Offenbach am Main: Ulrich Weiss, 1779.

von Wallhausen, Johann Jacob. *Kriegskunst zu Fuß*. Oppenheim: Hieronymo Gallero, 1614.

Vries, Peer. "Challenges, (Non-)responses, and Politics: A Review of Prasannan Parthasarathi, *Why Europe Grew Rich and Asia Did Not*." *Journal of World History* 23, no. 3 (2012): 639–64.

———. "Governing Growth: A Comparative Analysis of the Role of the State in the Rise of the West." *Journal of World History* 13, no. 1 (2002): 67–138.

Wachman, Alan. *Why Taiwan? Geostrategic Rationales for China's Territorial Integrity*. Singapore: NUS Press, 2008.

Wade, Geoff. "The Portuguese as Represented in some Chinese Sources of the Ming Dynasty." In Jorge M. dos Santos Alves, Portugal e a China, ed., *Conferencias nos encontros de historia luso chinesa*. Lisbon: Fundacao Oriente, 2000, 263–316.

———. *Southeast Asia in the Ming Shi-lu: An Open Access Resource*. Singapore: Asia Research Institute and the Singapore E-Press, National University of Singapore. http://epress.nus.edu.sg/msl, accessed 26 October 2012.

Wakeman, Frederic. *The Great Enterprise: The Manchu Reconstruction of the Imperial Order in Seventeenth-Century China.* Berkeley: University of California Press, 1986.

———. *Strangers at the Gate: Social Disorder in South China, 1839–1861.* Berkeley: University of California Press, 1966.

Waley-Cohen, Joanna. *The Culture of War in China: Empire and the Military under the Qing Dynasty.* London: I.B. Tauris, 2006.

Wallerstein, Immanuel. "The Rise of the States-System: Sovereign Nation-States, Colonies, and the Interstate System." In *World Systems Analysis: An Introduction.* Durham, NC: Duke University Press, 2004, 42–59.

Wang Chong 王崇. "A cheng ban la cheng tong huo chong de lai li" 阿城半拉城銅火銃的來歷. *Heilongjiang shi zhi* 黑龍江史志 268, no. 3 (2012): 33–34.

Wang Dongqing 王冬青 and Pan Rudan 潘如丹. "Ming chao hai jin zheng ce yu jin dai xi fang guo jia de di yi ci dui Hua jun shi chong tu" 明朝海禁政策與近代西方國家的第一次對華軍事衝突. *Jun shi li shi yan jiu* 軍事歷史研究, no. 2 (2004): 138–47.

Wang Er-minh 王爾敏. "China's Use of Foreign Military Assistance in the Lower Yangtze Valley, 1860–1864." *Jin dai shi yan jiu suo ji kan* 近代史研究所集刊, 2 (1971): 535–83.

———. "Qing dai yong ying zhi du" 清代勇營制度. *Jin dai shi yan jiu suo ji kan* 近代史研究所集刊, 4 (上) (1973): 1–52.

Wang Fuzhun 王福諄. "Gu dai da tie pao" 古代大鐵炮. *Zhu zao she bei yan jiu* 鑄造設備研究, no. 3 (2008): 46–56.

Wang Hsien-chun. "Discovering Steam Power in China, 1840s–1860s." *Technology and Culture* 51, no. 1 (2010): 31–54.

———. "Transferring Western Technology into China, 1840s–1880s." PhD dissertation, University of Oxford, 2007.

Wang Jian 王建, Li Xiaoyu 李曉寧, Qiao Liang 喬良, and Wang Xiangsui 王湘穗. *Xin zhan guo shi dai* 新戰國時代. Beijing: Xin Hua, 2004.

Wang Rong 王榮. "Yuan dai huo chong de zhuang zhi fu yuan" 元代火銃的裝置復原. *Wen wu* 文物, no. 3 (1962): 41–45.

Wang Shilin 汪仕林. "5 ceng wei jian ru qin Shen zhen wen wu bao hu dan wei xi ri hui huang ru jin po luo bu kan" 5層違建"入侵"深圳文物保護單位 昔日輝煌如今破落不堪. *Sou fang zi xun zhong xin* 搜房資訊中心, 18 March 2012. http://news.sz.soufun.com/2012-03-18/7281816_all.html, accessed 29 March 2014.

Wang Yangming 王陽明. "Shu Fo lang ji yi shi" 書佛郎機遺事. In *Wang Yangming quan ji* 王陽明全集, vol. 3, "Wu zhen lu zhi wu" 悟真錄之五, "wai ji liu" 外集六.

Wang, Yuan-kang. *Harmony and War: Confucian Culture and Chinese Power Politics.* New York: Columbia University Press, 2011.

Wang Zhaochun 王兆春. "Hong wu shi nian da tie pao." In Men Kui 門巋 and Zhang Xijin 張燕瑾, eds., *Zhong hua guo cui ci dian* 中華國粹大辭典. Beijing: Guo ji wen hua chu ban gong si, 1997.

———. "Qi Jiguang dui huo qi yan zhi he shi yong de gong xian" 戚繼光對火器研製和使用貢獻. In Yan Chongnian 閻崇年, ed., *Qi Jiguang yan jiu lun ji* 戚繼光研究論集. Beijing: Zhi shi chu ban she, 1990, 136–56.

———. *Shi jie huo qi shi* 世界火器史. Beijing: Jun shi ke xue chu ban she, 2007.

———. *Zhong guo gu dai bing qi* 中國古代兵器. Beijing: Shang wu yin shu guan, 1994.

———. *Zhong guo huo qi shi* 中國火器史. Beijing: Jun shi ke xue chu ban she 軍事科學出版社, 1991.

———. *Zhong guo ke xue ji shu shi: jun shi ji shu juan* 中共科學技術史：軍事技術卷. Beijing: Ke xue chu ban she, 1998.

Wang Zhen 王禎. *Nong shu* 農書. Yuan dynasty.

Wang, Zheng. *Never Forget National Humiliation: Historical Memory in Chinese Politics and Foreign Relations*. New York: Columbia University Press, 2012.

Waters, Colonel W. H.-H. "General Report on the Experiences of the Russo-Japanese War, March 1905." In *The Russo-Japanese War: Reports from British Officers Attached to the Japanese and Russian Forces in the Field, Volume 3*. London: HMSO, 1908, 106–209.

Watson, Henry Charles. *Eight Lectures Delivered at the School of Musketry, Hythe*. London: W. S. Paine, 1862.

Weber, Max. *General Economic History*. Translated by Frank H. Knight. New York: Greenberg, 1927.

Wei Yuan 魏源, et al. *Hai guo tu zhi* 海國圖志. 1852 [original 50-juan version published 1843].

Welsch, Christina. "Forging the Conqueror's Sword: How Two Indias Created One Empire." Undergraduate thesis, Emory University, 2010. http://pid.emory.edu /ark:/25593/7t96n, accessed 30 April 2014.

Weng Wanda 翁萬達. *Weng Wanda ji* 翁萬達集. Shanghai: Shanghai gu ji chu ban she, 1992.

Werhahn-Mees, Kai. "Neue Abhandlung über den disziplinierten Dienst von Ch'I Chi-kuang." PhD dissertation. Ludwig-Maximillians-Universität, Munich, 1977.

Werner, Sabine. *Die Belagerung von K'ai-feng im Winter 1126/27*. Stuttgart: Franz Steiner Verlag, 1992.

Werrett, Simon. "William Congreve's Rational Rockets." *Notes and Records of the Royal Society of London* 63, no. 1 (2009): 35–56.

Wertime, Theodore A. *The Coming of the Age of Steel*. Chicago: University of Chicago Press, 1962.

Whiting, Marvin C. *Imperial Chinese Military History: 8000 BC–1912 AD*. Lincoln: iUniverse, 2002.

Wills, John E., Jr. "The Dutch Re-occupation of Chi-lung, 1664–1668." In Leonard Blussé, ed., *Around and About Formosa: Essays in Honor of Professor Ts'ao Yung-ho*. Taipei: Ts'ao Yung-ho Foundation for Culture and Education, 2003, 272–90.

———. *Pepper, Guns, and Parleys: The Dutch East India Company and China, 1622–1681*. Cambridge, MA: Harvard University Press, 1974.

———. "Relations with Maritime Europeans." In Denis Twitchett and Frederick W. Mote, eds., *The Cambridge History of China, Volume 8, The Ming Dynasty, 1368–1644, Part 2*. Cambridge: Cambridge University Press, 1998, 333–75.

Wilson, Andrew R. "The Maritime Transformation of Ming China." In Andrew Erickson et al., eds., *China Goes to Sea: Maritime Transformation in Comparative Historical Perspective*. Annapolis: Naval Institute Press, 2009, 238–88.

Wing, Yung 容閎. *My Life in China and America*. New York: Henry Holt, 1909.

Witchard, Anne V. *Thomas Burke's Dark Chinoiserie.* Farnham, UK: Ashgate, 2009.

Witsen, Nicolaas. *Noord en Oost Tartarye, ofte bondig ontwerp van eenige dier landen en volken.* Vol. 2. Göttingen: François Halma, 1705.

Wong, Lawrence Wang-chi. "Translators and Interpreters during the Opium War between Britain and China." In Myriam Salama-Carr, ed., *Translating and Interpreting Conflict.* Amsterdam: Editions Rodopi, 2007, 41–60.

Wong, R. Bin. *China Transformed: Historical Change and the Limits of European Experience.* Ithaca, NY: Cornell University Press, 2000.

Wong, Young-tsu. "Security and Warfare on the China Coast: The Taiwan Question in the Seventeenth Century." *Monumenta Serica* 35 (1981–1983): 111–96.

Woo-Cumings, Meredith Jung-En. "National Security and the Rise of the Developmental State in South Korea and Japan." In Henry S. Rowen, ed., *Behind East Asian Growth: The Political and Social Foundations of Prosperity.* New York: Routledge, 1998, 319–40.

Worthing, Peter. *A Military History of Modern China: From the Manchu Conquest to Tian'anmen Square.* Westport, CT: Praeger, 2007.

Wright, David. *Translating Science: The Transmission of Western Chemistry into Late Imperial China, 1840–1900.* Leiden: Brill, 2000.

Wright, David C. "The Mongol General Bayan and the Massacre of Changzhou, 1275." *Altaica* 7 (2002): 108–21.

———. *The History of China.* 2nd ed. Santa Barbara, CA: Greenwood, 2011.

Wright, Mary. *The Last Stand of Chinese Conservatism: The T'ung-Chih Restoration, 1862–1874.* Stanford, CA: Stanford University Press, 1957.

Wright, Richard N. J. *The Chinese Steam Navy.* London: Chatham, 2000.

Wright, Robert. *Nonzero: The Logic of Human Destiny.* New York: Pantheon, 2000.

Wright, Tim. "An Economic Cycle in Imperial China? Revisiting Robert Hartwell on Iron and Coal." *Journal of the Economic and Social History of the Orient* 50, no. 4 (2007): 398–423.

Wu Changgeng 吳長庚 and Li Shicai 李世財. "Lun Wang Hong yu Jia jing guan chang zhi liu bi" 論汪鋐與嘉靖官場之流弊. *Jiangxi she hui ke xue* 江西社會科學, no. 12 (2005): 239–44.

Wu Guifang 吳桂芳. "Yi zu Ao yi jin gong shu" 議阻奧夷進貢硫, 1565. In Zhang Haipeng 張海鵬, ed., *Zhong Pu guan xi shi zi liao ji* 中葡關係史資料集. Chengdu, China: Sichuan ren min chu ban she, 1999, 204–5.

Wu Kuan 吳寬. *Huang chao ping Wu lu* 皇朝平吳錄. Ming dynasty.

———. *Ping wu lu* 平吳錄. Ming dynasty. http://www.guoxue123.com/other/gcdg/gcdg/010.htm, accessed 15 November 2012.

Wu Zhao 吳超. "16 zhi 17 shi ji Ri ben huo qi zai Dong ya qu yu de liu bu yu ying xiang kao shu" 16至17世紀日本火器在東亞區域的流布與影響考述. *Dong fang lun tan* 東方論壇, no. 2 (2013): 12–16.

Wyatt, Don J., ed. *Battlefronts Real and Imagined: War, Border, and Identity in the Chinese Middle Period.* New York: Palgrave Macmillan, 2008.

Xie Lihong 解立紅. "Hong yi da pao yu Man zhou xing shuai" 紅衣大炮與滿洲興衰. *Man xue yan jiu* 滿學研究, no. 2 (1994): 102–18.

Xu Baolin 許保林. *Zhong guo bing shu tong lan* 中國兵書通覽. Beijing: Jie fang jun chu ban she, 1990.

Xu Dong 許洞. *Hu Qianjing* 虎鈐徑. Circa 1004.

Xu Mianzhi 徐勉之. *Bao yue lu* 保越錄. 1359.

Xu, Yinong. *The Chinese City in Space and Time: The Development of Urban Form in Suzhou.* Honolulu: University of Hawaii Press, 2000.

Yan Congjian 嚴從簡. *Shu yu zhou zi lu* 殊域周咨錄. Beijing: Zhong hua shu ju, 2000.

Yan Su'e 閆素娥. "Guan yu Ming dai niao chong lai yuan wen ti" 關於明代鳥銃的來源問題. *Shi xue yue kan* 史學月刊, no. 2 (1997): 103–5.

Yang, C. K. "Some Preliminary Statistical Patterns of Mass Actions in Nineteenth-Century China." In Frederic Wakeman and Carolyn Grant, eds., *Conflict and Control in Late Imperial China.* Berkeley: University of California Press, 1975, 174–210.

Yang Hong 楊泓. "Xiang mo bian juan hua zhong de pen huo bing qi: tan xun gu dai guan xing she ji huo qi fa ming shi jian de xin xian suo wu ku he lan qi" 降魔變絹畫中的噴火兵器—探尋古代管形射擊火器發明時間的新線索武庫和蘭錡. In Zhong Shaoyi, *Zhong guo,* 95–99.

Yang Qianmiao 楊倩描 and Wang Zengyu 王曾瑜. *Nan Song shi* 南宋史. In Zhou Baozhu 周寶珠, Yang Qianmiao, and Wang Zengyu, eds., *Er shi wu shi xin gao* 二十五史新編, vol. 10 *Bei Song shi* and *Nan Song shi* 北宋史, 南宋史. Shanghai: Shanghai gu ji chu ban she, 1997.

Yang Weizhen 楊維楨. "Tong jiang jun" 銅將軍. Circa 1367. Full text on Sou yun wang 搜韻網, http://sou-yun.com/PoemIndex.aspx?dynasty = Ming&author = %E6%9D%A8%E7%BB%B4%E6%A1%A2&type = GuFeng&page = 9&lang = t, accessed 22 May 2015.

Yang Xiaotong 楊曉童. "Ren sheng gui ji yu huan hai chen fu: Yang Fang chu bu yan jiu" 人生軌跡與宦海沉浮：楊坊初步研究. Master's thesis, Ningbo University, 2010.

Yang Xunji 楊循吉. "Tai fu shou cheng" 太傅收城. In *Wu zhong gu yu* 吳中故語. Ming dynasty. http://www.hudong.com/wiki/%E3%80%8A%E5%90%B4%E4%B8%AD%E6%95%85%E8%AF%AD%E3%80%8B, accessed 20 November 2012.

Yao Jiarong 姚家榮. "Xi pao de ying yong yu Ming dai de guo fang" 西砲的應用與明代的國防. Master's thesis, Hong Kong Lingnan University, 2004.

Yin Qichang 殷其昌. "He zhang chu tu de Ming dai tong chong" 赫章出土的明代銅銃. *Gui zhou she hui ke xue* 貴州社會科學, no. 5 (1982): 71–90.

Yin Xiaodong 尹曉冬. "Huo qi lu zhu Bing lu de xi fang zhi shi lai yuan chu tan" 火器論說《兵錄》的西方知識來源初探. *Zi ran ke xue shi yan jiu* 自然科學史研究, no. 2 (2005): 144–55.

———. "Ming Qing zhi ji bing shu wen xian zhong dan dao zhi shi miao shu de bian xi" 明清之際兵書文獻中彈道知識描述的辨析. *Zi ran ke xue shi yan jiu* 自然科學史研究, no. 4 (2009): 465–75.

Yin Xiaodong 尹曉冬 and Yi Degang 儀德剛. "Ming mo Qing chu Xi fang huo qi chuan hua de liang ge jie duan" 明末清初西方火器傳華的兩個階段. *Nei Meng gu shi fan da xue xue bao (Zi ran ke xue Han wen ban)* 內蒙古師範大學學報（自然科學漢文版) 36, no. 4 (2007): 504–8.

Yongjin Zhang. "Curious and Exotic Encounters: Europeans as Supplicants in the Chinese Imperium, 1513–1793." In Shogo Suzuki, Yongjin Zhang, and Joel Quirk, eds., *International Orders in the Early Modern World: Before the Rise of the West.* New York: Routledge, 2013, 55–75.

Yu Ben 俞本. *Ji shi lu* 紀事錄. In Qian Qianyi 錢謙益, "Zhou Zhang Shicheng" 周張士誠. In Qian Qianyi, *Guo chu qun xiong shi lüe* 國初群雄事略. Beijing: Zhong hua shu ju, 1982, juan 8.

Yu, Maochun. "The Taiping Rebellion: A Military Assessment of Revolution and Counterrevolution." In Graff and Higham, *Military History of China*, 135–52.

Yu Yonghe 鬱永河. "Pi hai ji you" 裨海紀遊. *Taiwan wen xian cong kan* 臺灣文獻叢刊, no. 44. Taipei: Taiwan yin hang, 1959.

Yuan Xiaochun 袁曉春. "Shan dong Peng lai chu tu de Ming wan kou pao" 山東蓬萊出土的明碗口炮. *Wen wu* 文物, no. 1 (1991): 91–92.

Zeng Gongliang 曾公亮. *Wu jing zong yao* 武經總要. In *Zhong guo bing shu ji cheng* 中國兵書集成, vol. 3. Beijing: Jiefangjun Chubanshe, 1988 [originally written 1044].

———. *Wu jing zong yao qian ji* 武經總要前集. Beijing: Zhong hua shu ju, 1959 [facsimile of 1506–1521 edition].

Zhang, David D., Peter Brecke, Harry F. Lee, Yuan-Qing He, and Jane Zhang. "Global Climate Change, War, and Population Decline in Recent Human History." *Proceedings of the National Academy of Sciences of the United States of America* 104, no. 49 (2007). http://www.pnas.org/content/104/49/19214.full.pdf+html?sid=37f39b72-e0b7-4df8-91c1-4212ab9f6c78, accessed 16 April 2014.

Zhang Fuqiang 張富強. "Xiang jun ji tuan yu jie bing zhu jiao" 湘軍集團與借師助剿. *Fu yin zi liao: Zhong guo jin dai shi* 復印資料: 中國近代史, no. 1 (January 1989): 87–93.

Zhang Haipeng 張海鵬. *Zhong Pu guan xi shi zi liao ji* 中葡關係史資料集. Chengdu, China: Sichuan ren min chu ban she, 1999.

Zhang Jianxiong 張建雄 and Liu Hongliang 劉鴻亮. *Ya pian zhan zheng zhong de Zhong Ying chuan pai bi jiao yan jiu* 鴉片戰爭中的中英船炮比較研究. Beijing: Ren min chu ban he, 2011.

Zhang Tingyu 張廷玉, et al. *Ming shi* 明史. Vols. 19–20 of the series *Er shi si shi* 二十四史 (20 vols.). Beijing: Zhong hua shu ju, 1997 [Qing dynasty].

Zhang Wen 張文. "Huo qi ying yong yu Ming Qing shi qi Xi nan di qu de gai tu gui liu" 火器應用與明清時期西南地區的改土歸流. *Min zu yan jiu* 民族研究, no. 1 (2008): 85–94.

Zhang, Yimin. "The Role of Literati in Military Action during the Ming-Qing Transition Period." PhD dissertation, McGill University, 2006.

Zhang Zongqia 張宗洽. "Zheng Chenggong shou fu Taiwan ji." 鄭成功收復臺灣記. In *Zheng Chenggong cong tan* 鄭成功叢談. Xiamen: Xiamen da xue chu ban she, 1993, 15–42.

Zhao Shizhen 趙士禎. *Shen ji pu* 神器譜. Shanghai: Xuan lan ju shi 玄覽居士, 1941 [1598].

Zhao Wannian 趙萬年. *Xiangyang shou cheng lu* 襄陽守城錄. 1207. http://zh.wikisource.org/wiki/%E8%A5%84%E9%99%BD%E5%AE%88%E5%9F%8E%E9%8C%84, accessed 15 August 2012.

Zhao, Yong. *Who's Afraid of the Big Bad Dragon: Why China Has the Best (and Worst) Education System in the World.* San Francisco: Jossey-Bass, 2014.

Zhao Yu[rong] 趙與[褣]. *Xin si qi qi lu* 辛巳泣蘄錄. Beijing: Zhong hua shu ju, 1985 [Song dynasty].

Zheng Cheng 鄭誠. "Fa gong kao: 16 shi ji chuan Hua de Ou shi qian zhuang huo pao ji qi yan bian" 發熕考—16 世紀傳華的歐式前裝火炮及其演變. *Zi ran ke xue shi yan jiu* 自然科學史研究 32, no. 4 (2013): 504–22.

———. "Shou yu zeng zhuang: Ming mo Xi yang zhu cheng shu zhi yin jin" 守圍增壯: 明末西洋築城術之引進. *Zi ran ke xue shi yan jiu* 自然科學史研究 30, no. 2 (2011): 129–50.

Zheng Dayu 鄭大鬱. *Jing guo xiong lüe* 經國雄略. 1646.

Zheng Fuguang 鄭復光. *Huo lun chuan tu shuo* 火輪船圖說. 1846.

Zheng Ruozeng 鄭若曾. *Chou hai tu bian* 籌海圖編. Beijing: Zhong hua shu ju, 2007.

———. Chou hai tu bian 籌海圖編. In Zhong guo bing shu ji cheng bian wei hui 中國兵書集成編委會, ed., *Zhongguo bing shu ji cheng* 中國兵書集成, vols. 15–16. Beijing: Jie fang jun chu ban she, 1990.

Zheng shi shi liao chu bian 鄭氏史料初編. *Taiwan wen xian cong kan* 台灣文獻叢刊, no. 157. Taipei: Taiwan yin yang, 1962.

Zheng, Xiaowei. "Loyalty, Anxiety, and Opportunism: Local Elite Activism during the Taiping Rebellion in Eastern Zhejiang, 1851–1864." *Late Imperial China* 30, no. 2 (2009): 39–83.

Zhong guo bing shi shi bian xie zu 中國軍事史編寫組, ed. *Zhong guo jun shi shu fu juan: li dai zhan zheng nian biao* 中國軍事史附卷: 歷代戰爭年表. 2 vols. Beijing: People's Liberation Army Press, 1985.

Zhong guo jun shi shi bian xie zu 中國軍事編寫組. *Zhong guo li dai zhan zheng nian biao* 中國歷代戰爭年表, 2 vols. Beijing: People's Liberation Army Press, 2003.

Zhong Shaoyi 鐘少異, ed. *Zhong guo gu dai huo yao huo qi shi yan jiu* 中國古代火藥火器史研究. Beijing: Zhong guo she hui ke xue chu ban she, 1995.

———. "Zhong guo qing tong chong pao zong xu" 中國青銅銃炮總敘. *Zhong guo li shi wen wu* 中國歷史文物, no. 2 (2002): 18–25.

Zhong Shaoyi 鐘少異, Qi Mude 齊木德, Wang Zhaochun 王兆春, et al. "Nei Meng gu xin fa xian Yuan dai tong huo chong ji qi yi yi" 內蒙古新發現元代銅火銃及其意義. *Wen wu* 文物, no. 11 (2004): 65–68.

Zhou Weiqiang 周維強. "Fo lang ji chong yu Chen Hao zhi pan" 佛郎機銃與宸濠之叛. *Dong Wu li shi xue bao* 東吳歷史學報, no. 8 (March 2002): 95–125.

———. "Ming dai zhan che yan jiu" 明代戰車研究. PhD dissertation, Tsing-hua University, Taiwan, 2008.

Zhou Zheng 周錚 and Xu Qingsong 許青松. "Fo lang ji chong qian tan" 佛郎機銃淺探. *Zhong guo li shi bo wu guan guan kan* 中國歷史博物館館刊, nos. 15 and 16 (1991): 50–56.

Zhu Chang 朱唱. "Gu Chao xian yin ru yu gai jin huo yao he huo qi de li shi yan jiu" 古朝鮮引入與改進火藥和火器的歷史研究. *Dong jiang xue kan* 東疆學刊 25, no. 1 (2008): 35–42.

Zhuge Liang 諸葛亮. *Bing yao* 兵要. In Zhuge Liang 諸葛亮, Zhuge Liang Ji 諸葛亮集. Compiled by Zhang Shu 張澍 (1781–1847). Edited by Duan Xizhong 段熙仲 and Wen Xuchu 聞旭初. Beijing: Zhong hua shu ju, 1960, juan 2, 40–43.

Zou Shouyi 鄒守益. *Wang Yangming xian sheng tu pu* 王陽明先生圖譜. Shanghai: Cheng Shouzhong 程守中, 1941 [facsimile of 1557 edition].

Zou Weilian 鄒維璉. "Feng jiao Hong yi jie shu" 奉剿紅夷捷疏. In *Guan lou ji* 觀樓集, juan 18. Reprinted in Su Tongbing 穌同炳, *Taiwan shi yanjiu ji* 臺灣史研

究集. Taipei: Guo li bian yi guan Zhong hua cong shu bian shen wei yuan hui, 1980, 17–64.

Zurndorfer, Harriet. "What Is the Meaning of 'War' in an Age of Cultural Efflorescence? Another Look at the Role of War in Song Dynasty China (960–1279)." In Marco Formisano and Hartmut Böhme, eds., *War in Words: Transformations of War from Antiquity to Clausewitz*. Berlin: Gruyter Verlag, 2010, 89–113.

Index

Page numbers in *italics* refer to figures, graphs, maps, and tables

Nagashino, battle of (1575), 170
Napoleon I, 1, 4, 250–51, 272, 319n1
Napoleonic Wars, 8, 244, 252–53
naval warfare: Battle of Poyang Lake,
58–64, *59*, 331n15; broadside ships,
204–5, 299; and Calvo's plan to conquer
China, 120–21; and carronade, 247, 249;
and Chinese military weaknesses prior to
Opium War, 240, 255–56; and Chinese
modernization attempts following Opium
War, 258, 260, 262–67; Chinese ships
of the 17th century, 202–10, 360n66;
Dutch advantages, 206–10, 360n66; and
funding issues, 283, 292; and "No Alternative" weapon, 61, 62; and Opium War,
247, 249, 254–56; Portuguese advantages, 121; and rockets, 254; shipyards,
schools, and factories, 279–81; and
Sino-Dutch conflicts of the 17th century,
196–210; and Sino-Japanese War,
284–94, *288–89*; and Sino-Portuguese
War, 126–31; and Song-Jin Wars, 39–40;
steamships, 238, 255–56, 263–66, 271,
273, 275, 278–94, *288–89*, 304; Zheng
Zhilong's fleet, 203–6
Needham, Joseph, 10, 51, 53, 75–76,
326n35, 329n32
Neiberg, M. S., 322n35
Nemesis (British warship), 252, 255–56,
258, 260
Neuchâtel guns, 104, *105*
New Principles of Gunnery (Robins), 246,
251
Newton, Isaac, 245
Nian Rebellion (1851–1869), 273, 277
Ningbo, battle of (1842), 249
Ningyuan, battle of (1626), 199
"No Alternative" weapon, 61, 62
Nobunaga, Oda, 170
nomads, 111–12
Nurhaci, 199

Oman, Sir Charles, 175
Opium War (1839–1842), 5, 237–56, *248*,
303–4, 365n1; Battle of Ningbo, 249;
and Chinese modernization attempts,
257–72; Second Battle of Chuanbi, 252,
254–56

Ordruik, siege of (1377), 90
Orléans, siege of (1429), 92
Ottoman Empire, 92–95, 164, 298, 301,
338n49, 340nn4,6,91
Ouchterlony, John, 250

Paine, Sally, 371n76, 374nn80,99,101
Pan Ding-gou, 129
Pan Shirong, 265
Parker, Geoffrey, 3, 28, 117–18, 122,
145, 148–49, 154, 159, 163, 170, 188,
342n6
Perdue, Peter, 239, 302, 321n26
Peregrinations (Mendes Pinto), 167–69
Petrarch, 78–79
Petrucci, Maria, 354n22
Philip the Bold, 88, 90
piracy, 169–72, 184, 203–4
Polachek, James, 270
Pomeranz, Kenneth, 302, 320n8, 366n45
Portugal, 5, 114; Chinese adoption of
Portuguese "Frankish" cannons, 10,
135–43, 299, 348n23, 349nn33,38,45;
and introduction of matchlock ar-
quebus (*espingarda*) into East Asia,
167–69; Portuguese advisors to the
Ming, 199–201; Sino-Portuguese War,
124–31, 135–37, 346n27; Vasco Calvo's
plan to conquer China, 119–23
Poyang Lake, battle of (1363), 58–64, *59*,
331n15
Prince of Ning, 137–38
Ptak, Roderich, 349n38
punctuated equilibrium, 118
Pyongyang, battle of (1894), 286

Qian Qianyi, 69
Qi Jiguang, 163, 172–86, 194, 276
Qin dynasty (221–206 BCE), 26
Qing dynasty (1644–1911), 3; and centralized rule/hegemony, 117, 297–98;
and Confucianism, 294; dynastic transitions, 4, 187, 188, 198, 371n8; and end
of the Gunpowder Age, 294–95; failure
of early military reforms, 257–72,
274–75; fortifications and walled cities,
98; and funding issues, 292–93; Great
Qing Peace (mid-18th century to 1839),